FORMULA ONE AND BEYOND

THE AUTOBIOGRAPHY

Max Mosley

**SIMON &
SCHUSTER**

London · New York · Sydney · Toronto · New Delhi

A CBS COMPANY

First published in Great Britain by Simon & Schuster UK Ltd, 2015
A CBS COMPANY

1 3 5 7 9 10 8 6 4 2

Simon & Schuster UK Ltd
1st Floor
222 Gray's Inn Road
London WC1X 8HB

www.simonandschuster.co.uk

Simon & Schuster Australia, Sydney
Simon & Schuster India, New Delhi

A CIP catalogue record for this book
is available from the British Library.

Hardback: 978-1-47115-019-7
Ebook ISBN: 978-1-47115-021-0

Typeset by M Rules
Printed and bound by CPI Group (UK) Ltd, Croydon, CR0 4YY

Simon & Schuster UK Ltd are committed to sourcing paper
that is made from wood grown in sustainable forests and supports the Forest
Stewardship Council, the leading international forest certification organisation.
Our books displaying the FSC logo are printed on FSC certified paper.

To Jean, Alexander and Patrick

CONTENTS

PREFACE   ix

ACRONYMS   xiii

1   Growing up   1

2   Oxford and after   12

3   The Bar and racing   25

4   International Formula Two   32

5   The first year of March   48

6   A difficult business   63

7   Some progress   72

8   A last year with March   83

9   FOCA: the early days   94

10 FOCA versus the CSI   117

11 Balestre takes over   128

12 The FOCA–FISA war   134

13 The Concorde Agreement   155

14 Bernie builds his business   163

15 A peace of sorts   174

16 An attempt at UK politics   183

17 Back to motor sport and FIA elections   187

18 Bernie's £1 million donation and more politics 197

19	The commercial rights to Formula One	208
20	The car manufacturers get involved	216
21	The sport: far more than Formula One	226
22	Mainly work – but not entirely	237
23	Imola 1994: Senna's death and its effect	248
24	Conflict in Formula One	261
25	More trouble in Formula One	272
26	A breakaway?	280
27	Resignation	297
28	Money and the Formula One teams	309
29	Cheating	333
30	Crashing the car industry	355
31	Global road safety	366
32	Trouble with the EU Commission	375
33	The *News of the World*	390
34	Mosley v News Group Newspapers	414
35	Strasbourg	428
36	Exposing a criminal enterprise	435
37	Leveson and after	450
	APPENDIX: How the FIA works	473
	INDEX	483

PREFACE

When in 1969 I decided to abandon a promising career as a lawyer and go into motor racing, my father said I'd probably go bankrupt but it would be 'good training for something serious later on'. Bankruptcy was narrowly avoided, and the motor racing did ultimately evolve into something very serious. Controversy was inevitable and a great deal of misinformation has appeared on the web and in print. I believe the time has come to tell what really happened, hence this book.

Primarily it's the inside story of Formula One and its evolution since the 1960s. Much of it is not generally known and some not known at all. Part describes some of the many business and political conflicts along the way; part is how we reduced the risks for motor sport participants (and later for all road users); and part sets out to explain how Formula One made Bernie Ecclestone very rich (or perhaps it was the other way round).

Although mainly about motor sport, particularly Formula One, it is also an account of serious political work in the EU on passenger car safety and the environment, as well as a major conflict with the EU Commission's Competition Directorate. It describes how we used Brussels politics and lobbying to bring about important changes to road cars and road safety generally, and how it all started with Formula One.

Motor sport is not for everyone so I have tried to explain what happened and why in a way the non-enthusiast will readily understand and I hope find interesting. Also included is an outline of my life before starting in Formula One, including an attempt to explain why, together with many friends who I think were otherwise sane individuals, I was prepared to accept the appalling risks of driving racing cars in the 1960s.

Many different activities took place simultaneously; for example, the Formula One controversies that happened at the same time as Brussels politics. I thought it best to split the topics broadly into separate chapters without worrying too much about overall chronology. I hope this approach will be useful for those who may be interested in some parts of the story but perhaps not all of it.

The final chapters contain an account of an unprovoked attack by Rupert Murdoch's *News of the World*. It felt like being mugged on the street and I decided to hit back, hoping at the very least to make it more difficult for his newspapers to do anything similar to others in the future. Apart from defeating them in the courts, I explain how I was later able to help uncover serious criminality at the newspaper.

Inevitably, I've had to leave a lot out. It would be possible to write several books on the material. If I went into all the detail, the result would be longer still. Nevertheless, the salient information, at least most of what I have been able to remember or find in contemporaneous documents, notes and writings, is here. I hope and think I have covered all the questions that matter.

It may seem strange that there is no account of my family life. My wife and family are mentioned when directly relevant to the story but not otherwise. The reason is we have always been very private and want to keep it that way. Both my wife Jean and my surviving son Patrick have said they would prefer our family life to be left out. I agree with them and have respected their wishes.

A number of people have helped me by looking at my account of events they were involved in and adding to, and in some cases correcting, my memories. I am very grateful to Pierre de Coninck, Dominic Crossley, Ken Daly, Alan Donnelly, Robin Herd, Mike Kingston, Stephen Kinsella, Jean Mosley, Patrick Mosley, Adam Parr, Marco Piccinini, Tony Purnell, David Reeves, David Ward, Charlie Whiting, Richard Woods and Peter Wright for taking so much trouble. I am particularly grateful to Maurice Hamilton for checking the motor racing facts and giving me valuable advice on the overall structure; to Robert Skidelsky, who very kindly looked at the manuscript as someone not involved with motor sport and helped me greatly in my attempts to make the motor sport sections comprehensible; and to my PA, Pat Tozer, who took on the task of sorting out the huge quantity of disordered files, photographs and press cuttings I had accumulated. Finally, Ian Marshall at Simon & Schuster recognised the need for some work on my English and the overall structure, and I am very grateful to him as well as to Rob Bagchi, Lorraine Jerram and Katie Thraxton who between them greatly improved it. After all that, the mistakes that remain are mine alone.

ACRONYMS

AA	Automobile Association
AAA	American Automobile Association
ACCUS	Automobile Competitions Committee for the United States
ACEA	Association des Constructeurs Européens d'Automobiles
ACN	Automobile Club Nationale: motoring club also holding the sporting power
ACO	Automobile Club de l'Ouest
AIT	Alliance Internationale de Tourisme
ANWB	Royal Dutch Touring Club
ASN	Association Sportive Nationale: club with sporting power only
BBM	A UK political lobbying company
BPICA	Bureau Permanent International des Constructeurs d'Automobiles
CanAm	North American race series 1966–87
CATARC	China Automotive Technology & Research Centre
CEO	Chief Executive Officer
CFO	Chief Financial Officer
CSI	Commission Sportive Internationale (later FISA)
DFT	Department for Transport (UK)
DFV	Double four valve (Cosworth F1 engine)
ECU	Electronic control unit

ERTICO	Intelligent Transport Systems Europe
ESC	Electronic stability control
F1	Formula One
F2	Formula Two: single-seat racing cars under F1
F3	Formula Three: single-seat racing cars under F2
FFSA	Fédération Française du Sport Automobile
FIA	Fédération Internationale de l'Automobile
F1CA	F1 Constructors' Association (early name of FOCA)
FIFA	Fédération Internationale de Football Association
FIM	Fédération Internationale de Motocyclisme
FISA	Fédération Internationale du Sport Automobile
FOCA	Formula One Constructors' Association
FOTA	Formula One Teams' Association
FVA	Four valve A series (1960s Cosworth F2 engine)
GP	Grand Prix
GP2	Single-seat racing series just below F1
GPDA	Grand Prix Drivers' Association
GPWC	Grand Prix World Championship
Group A	Road cars modified for competition
Group B	Road-going cars built for competition
Group C	Two-seat racing cars
IOC	International Olympic Committee
IP	Intellectual Property
IPCC	Intergovernmental Panel on Climate Change
IPO	Initial Public Offering
IRAP	International Road Assessment Programme
IT	Information Technology
Kart	Miniature racing car with no bodywork
Karting	Kart racing
KERS	Kinetic Energy Recovery System
MEP	Member of the European Parliament

MOT   Ministry of Transport test (UK)

NASCAR   National Association for Stock Car Auto Racing (American)

NCAP   New Car Assessment Programme

NHRA   National Hot Rod Association (American)

NHTSA   National Highway Traffic Safety Administration (USA)

OAS   Organisation de l'armée secrete

RAC   Royal Automobile Club

SMMT   Society of Motor Manufacturers and Traders

SO   Statement of Objections (EU)

Sports Prototype   Modern version of Group C

STP   An oil and fuel additive for cars

TRL   Transport Research Laboratory (UK)

WADA   World Anti-Doping Agency

WCR   World Championship Racing: an association of race organisers

WMSC   World Motor Sport Council

WRC   World Rally Championship

1

GROWING UP

My parents, Oswald and Diana Mosley, were imprisoned shortly after my birth in 1940 under a wartime regulation that allowed the government to lock anyone up without the need for a trial. After serving as a minister in the 1929 Labour government during his relatively brief career in conventional politics, my father had led the British Union of Fascists and campaigned strongly against the Second World War. I believe this campaign was the main reason the government wanted him out of the way. My mother had supported him, and (unlike my father) she and her sister Unity were also friendly with Adolf Hitler.

About a year after they were first interned my parents were moved into accommodation together in a wing of Holloway Prison along with other interned couples. The then prime minister, Winston Churchill, was a close friend of my mother's family, and he and his wife had known her since childhood. He also knew my father well from his days in mainstream politics and would have appreciated that neither of them would ever have acted against their country's interests, despite their strong opposition to the war. Party politics prevailed and some of his coalition partners had scores to settle, but Churchill did what he could to make their lives less disagreeable.

My parents' imprisonment made very little difference to me. Our family was one of those where children were handed over to a nanny and saw their parents once a day at most. Nanny Higgs looked after my older brother Alexander and me and had already been with my mother's first two children, Jonathan and Desmond Guinness, in the 1930s. The only unusual feature in my case was visiting my parents in Holloway Prison rather than in the drawing room at teatime. While my parents were interned we stayed with my aunt, Pamela Jackson, my mother's sister and the most conventional of the six Mitford sisters.

I sometimes stayed overnight at the prison with my parents and can remember the high walls and ash pathways, and hearing bombs falling on London. Being a small child it never occurred to me there was anything odd about all this. In November 1943 they were released and bought a house at Crux Easton in Hampshire. The war was still on and the house was under some sort of flight path. A plane crashed near the house one night, so close my father went round checking that everyone was all right. Later, we would go and play with remnants of the plane in the crater. On another occasion, out for a walk with Nanny Higgs, two planes collided overhead, one crashing in a field nearby, the other some distance away. My father and some men armed with fire extinguishers raced off on a lorry, but came back to report the pilot had been killed. It affected him greatly because he himself had flown during the First World War.

Quite soon my parents found Crowood, a much larger house with 1100 acres near Ramsbury in Wiltshire. One of the conditions imposed on my father on release from prison was a restriction on buying a large tract of land. I'm not sure why. Someone said perhaps they feared he would build an aerodrome for the Germans. In practice, though, it was difficult to stop him buying a large estate because there was no legal basis for such a spurious stipulation. As a result, we arrived there in 1944, not long after my fourth birthday.

It was a big house about a mile from the village, set back from the road and surrounded by its own fields. Behind it was a small wood that led to another wood of about 100 acres which were wonderful places for a child to explore and get lost in.

Both my parents had been married before, my mother to Bryan Guinness, my father to Cynthia Curzon. My mother had two sons, my father two sons and a daughter from their first marriages. The four boys all went to Eton with varying success. Of the four, only Nicholas was old enough to fight in the war, which he did with great distinction, winning the MC. The two Guinness boys and the younger Mosley were all at Eton during and after the war. Michael Mosley became captain of the Oppidans, apparently an important position in the Eton schoolboy hierarchy. Aged five or six, I was taken to Eton to visit my half-brothers. At that early age it struck me as a very sinister place for some reason and I asked my parents never to send me there. They didn't, and in retrospect perhaps that was a mistake on my part. I shall never know.

Summer holidays were spent on Inch Kenneth, a small island off the Isle of Mull that belonged to the Mitford grandmother, Sydney Redesdale. My first visit was in the summer of 1945, just after the war had ended. Unity Mitford, my aunt, was staying there. She had been in Munich on the morning of 3 September 1939 when Britain declared war on Germany and, being friendly with Hitler, was very distressed. She shot herself in the head but surprisingly did not die and was eventually repatriated via Switzerland. The bullet wound left her with brain damage from which she died in 1948.

When we arrived on the island, a German warship was moored nearby, presumably waiting for orders as the war was over. One day my aunt Unity set out in a rowing boat with just me as passenger, drew alongside the warship and started talking to the sailors in German. I don't know what was said but she may well have been expressing support for Hitler. The sailors seemed relaxed and amused but very surprised at this strange visit.

To begin with, we weren't sent to school but were taught by an elderly man my parents found living on the Crowood estate. His house was two miles away across the fields, and I would spend the time walking there dreaming of perpetual-motion machines (sadly, when I modified one of my toys, my concept proved flawed). When my brother was eight, he was sent to a prep school near Faringdon in Oxfordshire. He hated it so much that my parents took him away and hired a tutor at home, which benefited me, allowing me, too, to escape the horrors of an English boarding school in the 1940s. Living on the estate, I was given my first shotgun at the age of nine and allowed to go shooting with the gamekeeper; and every other Saturday I would head by bus to the County Ground to watch Swindon Town's home games in the Third Division.

After the war, the authorities had rather pettily refused to allow my parents passports. However, they could not lawfully stop a British subject leaving or returning if he could find a country that would let him in without a passport. Spain was prepared to admit my father, so all he needed was a yacht to get there. In 1949 we were all about to set sail when the authorities gave in and issued passports for the entire family rather than look foolish. We set off for Spain and the South of France via the Bay of Biscay and inevitable seasickness.

The dying wish of Katherine Maud, my Mosley grandmother, was that my brother and I should be christened. Aged nine, I was not in favour but was told it wouldn't really change anything. A bigger problem was finding someone religious to be a godparent. Happily, John Betjeman, a close friend of my parents who lived nearby, was glad to be asked.

Apart from the passport problem, the authorities in the UK made other difficulties for my father. He kept pigs at Crux Easton and when they mysteriously started to lose weight and the local vet could do nothing, someone decided to prosecute him for starving them. Using his resources to get expert help, the source, an obscure bug, was discovered. Having studied all available literature on the subject, he defended himself in the local magistrates' court and had a most enjoyable time cross-examining the government vet about the bug and his failure to identify, or even suspect, it. My father followed this with some heavy comments to the court about the decision to prosecute rather than investigate properly. The local magistrates appeared to agree with him.

The case was thrown out but it should never have been brought. On top of this, he had a dispute with the Inland Revenue, which leading counsel told him he would have won for any other person in England. No doubt irritated by all this, my father sold everything in 1950 and moved with all his financial assets to Ireland, which back then was still in the sterling area.

It was a big step. The family had always lived in England and part of its fortune had been the chief or ground rents for large parts of Manchester (hence Mosley Street, one of the main Manchester thoroughfares). My brother and I were very sad to leave Crowood.

The Irish government was much better disposed towards my father. His opposition as a young MP in the early 1920s to the excesses of the Black and Tans during the Irish War of Independence was well known there and by no means forgotten. For me, too, this was the start of a whole new life because the tutor who accompanied us stayed only for a short time. When my brother turned 13, he was sent to school in France by my parents, who wanted us to learn the two main languages of continental Europe.

It was thought extravagant to keep the tutor on just for me, so I was left to my own devices, with no school or lessons at our house in Clonfert, County Galway. I had learned to ride properly at a Dublin riding school when we first arrived in Ireland and became completely obsessed with horses. For nearly two years, my life was riding, hunting, snipe shooting on the bogs and playing hurling with the local lads.

That corner of Galway had some inspirational hurling players at the time. The sport is a sort of aerial hockey in which there's no restriction on hitting the ball in the air and you are allowed to catch it. It's extraordinarily fast and, since there was no head protection in those days, quite dangerous. I've always thought it the best ball game ever invented, and never understood why it did not achieve the international recognition of soccer, rugby or cricket.

When I too reached 13, I had to join my parents in a house they had bought near Paris, shortly after leaving England. It was Palladian in style and rather embarrassingly called the *Temple de la Gloire*. I was supposed to learn French but made little progress and took lessons in other subjects given by a friend of my parents. There was much discussion of Nietzsche, Spengler and the like between my brother, father and the teacher in Paris. It all seemed rather pointless to me. Likewise when my parents' friends came for dinner parties, I would sit in silence, noticing how everyone became less and less coherent as the evening wore on. I always thought these political and philosophical discussions were a waste of time. No one was actually going to do anything.

As we were growing up, my father did try to point my brother and me in what he saw as the right direction. When I was 13 and Alexander nearly 15, he took us both to a sort of music-hall show featuring naked ladies near the Place Pigalle in Paris. My mother (very surprisingly) came too, but (very unsurprisingly) didn't like it, saying it smelt like a stable. Much later, when I was in my early twenties, he took my wife Jean and me to Madame Arthur's, a famous transvestite nightclub in the same neighbourhood. Presumably by then he thought my tastes were settled. There was even a political element to his approach – when, as teenagers, my brother and I complained that we had sometimes to wait outside a luxury restaurant while he and my mother were having dinner, he would say (only half-jokingly) this was to make us more politically aware.

In September 1953 I was sent to school in Germany to learn the language. The school belonged to an acquaintance of my mother's friend Frau Wagner, the composer's daughter-in-law. She had been more or less the queen of Bayreuth before the war and was close to Hitler, who adored Wagner. I was put alone on a train to Munich, with a vocabulary taught by my mother comprised solely of *ja, nein* and *wo ist mein Gepäck?* She presumably thought that would be useful should I lose my luggage. With some difficulty, I found the connecting train to Traunstein.

It was the wrong kind of school, a *humanistisches Gymnasium*, meaning it specialised in Latin and Greek. I found these difficult to learn in a language I didn't understand and, anyway, such modest ability as I had was in maths and science. I should have gone to a different type of school entirely, but at least I was ahead of the class they put me in at maths despite my long fallow period in Ireland.

In the autumn of 1954, my parents' house in Ireland burnt down. My parents were already spending much more time in France than in Ireland. As far as Ireland went, they decided to buy a house jointly with my mother's eldest son, Jonathan Guinness, and his then wife, Ingrid. It became a sort of holiday home for both couples, but my parents' base was now their house at Orsay, near Paris. France was their permanent home and the Irish house was later sold.

I was expelled from the German school after about 18 months when I was caught climbing across the roof into the girls' part of the building. Alexander, who had joined me there after his two years in France, also had to leave after going to the local *Gasthaus* with some friends and urinating drunkenly outside the school's main entrance. My father was annoyed. I don't think he objected to me trying to get into the girls' part of the school – he had, after all, encouraged an interest in girls – nor did he see much wrong with what my brother did, but he didn't like the disturbance our expulsions caused to his way of life.

We were sent to stay with his eldest son, who is a sort of saint and put up with what must have been an extraordinary inconvenience for him and his wife. Nick started trying to find a school for us in England. There were lots of brochures, some of them from establishments that sounded very sinister indeed, particularly in light of what we now know about what went on in those days. This was the 1950s, after all, and most people did not suspect the motivation of some in the teaching profession. In the end, supported by Nick, Alexander and I settled on Millfield in

Somerset. It seemed the most civilised and my parents did not object. Being expelled in Germany and sent to an English school turned out to be a stroke of luck, as without some sort of basic English education I would never have got into Oxford.

Millfield was a strange school. It gave sports scholarships and had some exceptional athletes, but in those days it was mainly somewhere for people like me who had experienced difficulties at other schools. But it did have some outstanding teachers, including a lady who got me interested in physics and an English teacher, Robert Bolt, who went on to write *A Man for All Seasons* and the screenplays for *Lawrence of Arabia* and *Doctor Zhivago* among others, and win two Oscars.

After two terms there, I set out to persuade my father to let me leave, live on my own in London and go to a crammer. I waited until he was in a benign mood and broached the subject. To my delight, he agreed and a few months later, in 1956, I was free. I think he agreed because his own parents had turned down a similar request. He was an outstanding fencer and won the public schools championships in all three weapons aged only 15, but his parents refused to let him leave Winchester and pursue his fencing in Budapest. As an adult he was nevertheless on the British national fencing team for several years, despite having a permanently injured leg as a result of a flying accident in the First World War.

I was 16 years old and alone in London, living in Bloomsbury and spending most evenings in Soho at the 2i's Coffee Bar, supposedly the birthplace of British rock'n'roll. Certainly, several of the regular performers became famous later. Being in London, I had some contact with my father's political associates and was taken round the East End. I supported my father generally but had other interests, preferring to spend my time in the 2i's.

My father owned an empty flat near Victoria station and for a brief period in late 1957 he let me hold parties there. It was cold and squalid but no one interfered with us. One of my acquaintances went to a school in south London with connections to nearby St Martin-in-the-Fields High School for Girls. Some of the more adventurous pupils came to our parties, and I started going out with one of them, Jean Taylor, whose father had been in the Coldstream Guards and was now in the City of London police. Just over two years later she became my wife.

In March 1958 I took the entrance exam for Christ Church, Oxford, hoping to read physics. Although by then I had some relevant A-levels, I was still very weak academically, speaking excellent German but never recovering much of the ground I had lost in the years missing from my education. At the time there was pressure on places at Oxford because of the abolition of national service. Applicants who had done their two years in the armed forces were still taking some of the available places. I think Roy Harrod, a major Christ Church figure and friend of my parents, must have put in a word for me, or perhaps they didn't have that many people wanting to read physics. For whatever reason, they accepted me, but the senior physics tutor did once tell me, 'We were scraping the bottom of the barrel, Mosley, when we took you.'

He was right because, when I arrived there, I had done very little physics. I should have spent at least another year at school, but my parents had not been to university so had no idea of what was involved. One of their great friends was Derek Jackson, who had been married to my aunt Pamela for several years. He was a world-class physicist and had been professor of spectroscopy at Oxford. He was an eccentric figure, a leading amateur steeple-chase jockey as well as a very serious scientist, and was now their neighbour in France. I think he made them think physics was easy and that an undergraduate probably just read a book or two with a little guidance from a tutor. As for me, I was in too much of a hurry and did not stop to think about my academic shortcomings.

2

OXFORD AND AFTER

Oxford was in a state of transition when I arrived in 1958. Some of the undergraduates had done two years' national service and were relatively grown-up, but most had arrived straight from school. Everyone wore jackets and ties. I didn't fit in with either group after my two years in London, and wore jeans, which was almost unheard of then. I couldn't wait to get back to London whenever I had the chance.

I was struggling academically, being nowhere near the necessary standard in physics and maths, and was a trial for my tutor. We spent our weekly hour with me thinking about another week of relative freedom before the next tutorial, while he was no doubt dying to get back to his research. I somehow survived the exam at the end of the first academic year and was off to London with a long summer vacation in prospect.

Jean and I moved into a flat together, which was very unusual for teenagers in those days. We realised that her father would be wondering where she was, so when we heard he had asked my father if he knew anything, we decided it was time to leave. I spent my entire savings on a motor scooter. We set off with minimal luggage, found a boat to France and watched the scooter being loaded by a crane.

We eventually reached my parents' house near Paris and spent a few days there before heading to Spain. Jean and I both disliked my red hair, so during our stay with my parents we tried to dye it brown. The result was awful, but my parents were tolerant and didn't seem to mind being seen out and about with a sort of freak. 'The devil makes work for idle hands,' said my father quietly when he first saw the results. His soft, half-joking tone made Jean laugh so much she felt she had to leave the room.

My mother insisted on buying us both crash helmets although they were not compulsory in those days. It took us three days to reach Valencia, where we abandoned the helmets. The local couples all rode scooters like the Spanish traditionally ride horses, with the girl sitting side-saddle on the back. This meant they could wear any kind of dress and Jean was soon doing the same. Society was quite nanny-free in those days, but the combination of no helmets and riding side-saddle was of course very unsafe.

Back in London, my father had decided to stand for parliament in North Kensington at the 1959 general election. Until then, his politics had been largely peripheral to my life. I knew some of his followers and I supported him, but one of the reasons I wanted to be a scientist was because scientific ideas could be tested by experiment, whereas in politics it seemed there was no proof, merely opinion; proof, if it came at all, was after the event, often in the form of some catastrophe. My brother and I both tried to help, but members of his party conducted the campaign. The result was very poor, a pity in a way because he would have livened up the House of Commons.

I can only describe my father as I saw him. He was an excellent if rather distant parent who was always interesting, as well as interested, and I enjoyed his company. My political instincts from an early age can crudely be described as liberal and slightly left. To me, freedom and liberty of the individual have always been paramount. The imprisonment of my parents without charge or trial certainly had an influence on my thinking. When I first heard about the rule of law and discovered John Stuart Mill and his writings, I found some sort of intellectual basis for my instincts. But in my youth I nevertheless agreed with my father's ideas. If this appears contradictory it might perhaps seem less so to anyone who reads his books.

My father's campaign in North Kensington had effects within the family. His eldest son, Nick, was horrified by what was going on. He was an associate of Father Trevor Huddleston, a well-known anti-apartheid campaigner in South Africa as well as in England. The rift with my father became more serious when Nick encouraged my brother Alexander to get away from what was happening, and provided the money for him to go and live in Chile.

Nick had been close to my father in the years after the war and used to come to Crowood with his friends to shoot. They were natural allies. My father liked Nick and was very pleased about his excellent war record, but politics divided them. They were two very clever people, but it always seemed to me that they overreacted to their differences, Nick perhaps more than my father who was well used to being friends with people who disagreed with him politically.

There may have been factors I was unaware of. I knew little of their quarrel at the time. Nick later wrote about his parents and I was very much against when he did it back in the 1980s. I felt he was raking up things that were largely forgotten and this would be to the detriment of his children and mine. I felt there was no need for it, nothing to be gained, and we should all be getting on with our lives, not worrying about our parents. But Nick's efforts will be important to historians who want a complete picture of my father and what motivated him.

Back in Oxford, I went to great lengths to avoid moving into college as one was supposed to in the second year. I thought it too much like going back to school. I liked to spend the weekends in London with Jean, and in lodgings I could come and go as I pleased.

Towards the end of my second year someone told me I would never survive in the Oxford Union because of my father. They would all take me to pieces in argument. I found the challenge intriguing and started going to debates. Until then, insofar as I had any Oxford life, I had mixed only with scientists. As I started to get to know non-science contemporaries, a new world opened up. They were mainly slightly older than me and clever, among them Peter Jay, Phillip Whitehead, Paul Foot and Robert Skidelsky. I was invited to join the supposedly secret 'P' dining club in Christ Church, whose members were a mixture of dons and undergraduates. They were all clever, but at that time not one of them was a scientist. I began to think I should perhaps have read a different subject, but in fact some knowledge of physics proved invaluable later in life.

In the 1960 summer vacation, Jean and I got married. We spent all our wedding presents on a car and moved into a flat in Oxford. We had very little money, just subsistence from my father, but Jean got a job and we managed. Because we had a flat, almost a home, it became a magnet for friends. Paul Foot and Robert Skidelsky were regular visitors, and Jean used to make them egg and chips in the evenings. Now that I was spending all my time in Oxford, I was able to participate in university life, including the Oxford Union. At the end of that Michaelmas term, I decided to stand for election in the Union.

I thought I had absolutely no chance of winning office but might just get on the committee. They used to announce the election results in reverse order and I was very relieved with the confirmation that I hadn't come last when the first name read out was not mine. When they got to the pre-election favourite for secretary and still hadn't mentioned me, I was completely astonished. I never thought I could win because of my family name, although I had never experienced any sort of discrimination at Oxford.

Following the election, we had an interesting term in the Union. Phillip Whitehead, then chairman of the Oxford University Conservative Association but later a Labour MP and MEP, was the president. We secured an outstanding selection of speakers, including Jawaharlal Nehru and Jim Callaghan.

Would-be physicists had to spend three days each week in the Clarendon Laboratory doing experiments. It wasn't conducive to learning much about physics, but one did learn about experiments. Apart from the large room where we worked, the laboratory was full of rather eccentric-seeming scientists doing research. Later in life, I again met some of the people from the university's physics department and remembered why I had chosen the subject. The ideas are utterly fascinating and, in the end, *everything* is physics. Had I been better prepared when I went to Oxford I might have gone into the world of research and spent my professional life in happy obscurity doing something really interesting. Instead, my life took a dramatic turn in an unexpected direction.

My first encounter with motor racing came in May 1961, during the Easter vacation. Jean's employer was a volunteer flag marshal at nearby Silverstone and received a couple of free tickets for big events. He very kindly offered her his two for the International Trophy, a major Formula One race held at Silverstone (though run for the previous year's cars as the engine formula had just changed). Neither of us had ever been to a motor race. There was the usual traffic jam on the approach to the circuit so we were delayed getting in. After parking the car, I heard an unfamiliar sound and got to the fence just in time to see the Formula Junior race come under the Daily Express Bridge and around Woodcote, then a long, sweeping corner. It was an extraordinary moment. I knew instantly this was something I absolutely had to do.

Stirling Moss won the main race in the wet, driving a Cooper and lapping the entire field. Bruce McLaren spun off without damage right below where we were sitting, and the conditions were so bad that many leading drivers of the day, including Graham Hill, Jim Clark and John Surtees, followed McLaren off the track. Little did I realise that, seven years later, I would know Bruce well or that he would found a company that would feature prominently in my life for over 40 years. After that first experience, I managed to persuade Jean to come with me to Formula One races in France, including one at Reims when we had to sleep in our car because all the hotels were full.

After taking my finals in 1961, I went to a rather rudimentary racing drivers' school at Finmere, near Silverstone. A few laps round an old airfield in an ancient Cooper Formula Junior and an old Lotus 11 convinced me that I had somehow to get hold of a car and start racing. I had no money so I would have to wait, but

I was determined that it would only be a matter of time before I found a way.

I never caught up academically and it became clear I was not going to be a scientist. But I enjoyed debate and I decided to read for the Bar. On graduation, I joined Gray's Inn, but it was going to be another three years before I could be called and the Bar exams would not be a full-time job.

Immediately after finishing at Oxford, I decided to have another attempt at the Union. At the end of my term as secretary I had stood for the presidency, but by then it seemed the name had become a problem. There were tiresomely hostile articles in some of the undergraduate press, so I thought why not try again but without the name? With the connivance of a close friend, John McDonnell (today an eminent QC), who later became president, I decided to reappear as an Indian and visited a theatrical costumier to acquire the disguise. They told me to go out and about wearing it, accustom myself to the role and practise the accent. There had been the occasional racist attack in the area where we lived, so I felt slightly uneasy, but went ahead anyway and was immediately fascinated by how differently people treated me in my Indian persona.

The ultimate test was putting on the disguise, but wearing my normal clothes, and waiting to greet Jean when she got back from work. We only had gas lighting so the room was not brightly lit. She was very surprised and startled to find an Indian stranger sitting in her armchair. 'Where's Max?' she asked. In my Indian accent I said I didn't know but found her very attractive. I got out of the armchair and advanced towards her. She gave a little cry and rushed out of the room. The landlady heard the commotion and appeared. She had great difficulty understanding what was going on. Jean was tired after her day at work and not very pleased, but at least it proved the disguise worked.

Next, I went to the Union in my new guise and sat through a debate. Afterwards, in the Randolph Hotel, where all the main participants used to congregate after the debates, John McDonnell introduced me to all sorts of people who, although they did not realise it, knew me quite well. No one seemed to twig and I ended up on a sofa next to Robert Skidelsky. He was very polite and asked what I was doing in the university. I said I was reading for a pass degree in politics, philosophy and economics. He looked slightly surprised – people didn't usually set out to get a pass degree. I feared he would soon become bored with his new acquaintance, although be too polite to let this show, so I leant towards him and said quietly in my normal voice: 'You know who it is really, don't you?' He jumped. In the end, funny though it would have been, I decided that driving down to Oxford each week to pursue my Union career would be too much like hard work.

After leaving Oxford, the first opportunity that came along was political – a by-election in Moss Side, Manchester, that my father's party decided to contest. He asked me to be the agent, so Jean and I moved up to Manchester for a short but interesting new diversion. Fortunately, the candidate was Walter Hesketh, a former policeman and an entirely reasonable person, who had been a national cross-country champion in his youth and once ran the 373 miles from Edinburgh to London in record time.

My main job was dealing with the press. At first they were quite hostile but by the end of the campaign relations were good. When the time came to hand in the nomination papers, I checked the Representation of the People Act and set off for the town hall, accompanied by a group of reporters. The returning officer was the lord mayor, who wasn't there, so I was told to come back the next day at a time he had decreed. No one had told me about this and the act quite clearly said I could hand the papers in there and then, but the officials would not budge. It seemed to me the mayor's decision to ignore the act without bothering to inform everyone affected was high-handed. I spent a few minutes looking at penalties under the Representation of the People Act and set out for the magistrates' court with the press still in tow.

Outside the office of the magistrate there was a small queue of ladies seeking maintenance summonses against husbands who had abandoned them. When it came to my turn to go in, the elderly JP and her clerk were quite startled by my request for a summons against the lord mayor for a breach of the act. After a brief discussion, with me citing the relevant passages in the act, it was obvious the summons had to be granted. Understandably, though, the JP and her clerk felt this was outside their territory and told me to ask the stipendiary magistrate. This I was happy to do, but of course it was in open court. I stood up when invited to speak and made my request. After some discussion and another look at the act, the stipendiary granted the summons, to the delight of the journalists. Traipsing around after me had yielded a story that made headlines in the local evening press. Telephoned at home in France and asked for a comment, my father simply said: 'Boys will be boys.'

A few weeks later at the hearing, the lord mayor, a rather grand local solicitor who was dressed very formally in a lawyer's black jacket and pinstripes with his gold chain of office around his neck, stood in the dock. The stipendiary invited me to open my case from the witness box. I couldn't resist referring to the mayor as 'the prisoner in the dock'. As I had expected, this provoked a furious response: 'I am not a prisoner!' he said in a very posh voice. (You have to imagine something like, 'Ay em nut ah prizner!')

I affected to look puzzled and the stipendiary explained gently that the mayor, although in the dock, was not really a prisoner. He was eventually acquitted, having claimed he had delegated his responsibilities to his deputy, which led the stipendiary to note his regret at refusing my request to issue an additional summons against the deputy. Although he never for one moment betrayed what he thought, I suspect the stipendiary found the whole thing very entertaining. The local press certainly did and the candidate eventually got a respectable four-figure vote.

When the campaign was over Jean and I moved back to London with rather more than a souvenir from our stay in Manchester. There was a garage near the constituency owned by Rodney Bloor, a well-known racing driver who competed in Formula Junior. I went out of my way to get to know him and he sold me a Lotus Elite (one of the original ones, not the later model of the same name). It was way beyond my means but was such a beautiful car I couldn't resist and persuaded Jean to agree.

Having been a child during the war I had always felt that some basic military training was important. I didn't like the feeling that I would have to start from scratch should war break out again. As I now had some spare time but couldn't afford to start racing, I joined the Territorial Army Parachute Regiment.

The headquarters of 44 Independent Parachute Brigade Group was at the Duke of York's Barracks on the Kings Road, near to where Jean and I were living in World's End, Chelsea. After a fairly tough selection course, I was sent to the Parachute Training School in Abingdon. In those days your first jump was from a balloon, which felt like standing on top of the Eiffel

Tower wearing a rucksack and leaping off. It's much easier from a plane.

In London, my father suddenly became the target of violence. He had been holding regular meetings all over the place for years with no significant problems, but out of the blue those who disliked him decided to attack. I went with him to a meeting in the East End where we were rushed by a group of people. I reacted as one would and a police superintendent arrested me. Next day in court, I applied to have my case heard immediately on the grounds that my arrest had been widely reported and the facts should come out. The magistrate agreed and I cross-examined the superintendent with some success along the most obvious lines: My elderly father is attacked; the police, though present, do not protect him. Do you say I should stand idly by? Should my reaction have been: well, that's all right? No? So why did you arrest me? I was acquitted.

By now, I was working on Part 1 of the Bar exams, which weren't difficult but meant I had to spend my days in an armchair reading the necessary books. So when the TA Paras were sent to Cyprus for a big exercise, I was completely unfit. The climax was a 48-hour mock battle in the Troodos Mountains against an excellent regular army regiment.

We were flown around for most of the night, before parachuting with our equipment on to the beach at dawn, a long way from the mountains. As we advanced on foot and the sun got up, I began thinking I'm exhausted, I can't go any further. I'll go as far as that next tree and give up. I can't do that, I'd then think – people would say: 'Oh yes, I remember Max Mosley, he's the one who sat down.' More than 24 hours later I was still going. It was nothing compared to real war but nevertheless a valuable experience for me.

Back in London, I met some of my father's supporters, who wanted to know why I looked so fit. Despite the fact that my father had disapproved of me joining the TA, thinking it a waste of time, several of them applied, which inevitably alerted the newspapers. In those days the paras had right-wing connotations, notably in France with Algeria and the OAS. As a result of press stories, the applicants withdrew but the army authorities quite rightly ignored all attempts to undermine my position and I remained in the TA until just after I started at the Bar.

There were frequent exercises, mainly on Salisbury Plain, including the odd night drop. We enjoyed it when, as sometimes happened, the opposition was trainee police. However, my most enduring memory is stepping across an electric fence, getting stuck and ending up straddling it, a leg each side. I think it gave unusually powerful shocks.

In the first year or two after Oxford, I often received invitations to debate in various universities, which were sometimes about my father and his ideas, sometimes the usual undergraduate issues of the day. But my interest gradually declined. I wanted above all to go motor racing, my spare time was taken up with the TA and, though still sympathetic to my father's ideas, they seemed to me increasingly unlikely ever to be relevant in the real world. I remained on excellent terms with him, but by late 1963 I was working for my Bar finals and destined to take no further part in his politics. My father decided to stand for parliament one last time at the 1966 general election but I did not get involved or visit the constituency. He realised I had moved on and never held it against me.

Our holidays were usually spent with my parents, sometimes in Ireland, more often at their house in France. Very many of their friends lived in Paris or nearby; others would visit them when passing through. My mother's sister, Nancy Mitford, was almost a neighbour and they were very close despite Nancy's denunciation of my mother early in the war. When skirts suddenly became very short and they were both about 60, they had a discussion and agreed the choice was dowdy or ridiculous. Both unhesitatingly opted for ridiculous. Towards the end of the 1960s Nancy was diagnosed with cancer. My mother used to visit her every day at her house in Versailles. She died in 1973.

Other frequent visitors were the Duke and Duchess of Windsor, who lived further down the Vallée de Chevreuse. She and my mother got on well, while he and my father liked to discuss how things would have been had they been respectively king and prime minister. One Christmas we were all in the Paris house of one of my parents' friends and the Duke announced he wanted to dance 'the twist'. Except for Jean and me, everyone there was elderly and, apart from the Duke, none of them had ever heard of the twist. Jean bravely volunteered and they were off. He didn't want to stop. The Duchess became more and more anxious because he had a detached retina that she feared he was about to lose altogether. But it was a success and the 'Dook', as he was known (because of his acquired semi-American accent), certainly enjoyed himself. It was a long way from World's End and Salisbury Plain.

3

THE BAR AND RACING

After my Bar finals, Jean and I went on holiday in the Lotus. We got back to London in time for me to be called to the Bar in June 1964, and in the autumn that year I started a pupillage in Lord Hailsham's chambers with Maurice Drake, who later became a High Court judge. It was excellent experience because he had a very diverse practice – divorce, crime, defamation, planning, just about everything – very different from the modern Bar which increasingly tends to be specialised.

Apart from my work as a pupil, the chambers used to get briefs from the RAC to defend motorists, some of which came to me. They paid a mere two guineas but were a good way to learn what to do in court. The cases were always difficult to defend, but sometimes one could secure an acquittal. My strategy was to try to make the police witness say something improbable or, ideally, if there were two, say different things. They all gave evidence in the same formulaic way and had clearly been taught to do so as part of their training. In local magistrates' courts there was usually an older police sergeant in charge, who would think it all quite funny, saying things like, 'The lads didn't do so well today, did they?' when my tactics worked.

But in talking to traffic police while waiting for cases to come on I learned a lot about their work and the horrific effects of some road accidents. In my later professional life, police in all countries were always supportive of our safety work. They are the ones who have to deal with the aftermath of accidents that most people never see. It is grim and unpleasant work; often very sad, too.

Shortly after I started, the Tories lost the general election and Lord Hailsham returned from his cabinet position as Secretary of State for Education to practise law again. He was an eccentric figure and used to bicycle to chambers with clips on his trouser legs. He had known my mother in the 1930s and I had met him when he came to the Oxford Union. He was very kind and friendly and delighted me one day when I heard him through the wall shouting into the phone: 'I'll give you until I count to three to come to the point: one, two, goodbye!' I think he was talking to a solicitor. He used to write his opinions by hand so his clients would know it really was his opinion and not something drafted for him by someone more junior.

Once qualified, I was able to start teaching law in the evenings to earn money to go racing. Jean was still working so we didn't see much of each other during term time, except at weekends. I also began to get more serious cases, including some jury trials, which I found fascinating. Had I started off in common law chambers where there was a big criminal practice, I might have stayed there, but in the end I joined patent chambers. This was partly because I had an introduction to R.G. Lloyd QC, a trademark expert and head of a well-known set, and partly because I knew it would give me the flexibility to go racing. In common law chambers you could never get the clerk to postpone a hearing if you had a race somewhere on the Continent.

By early 1966, I had earned enough money from teaching to buy a racing car and started looking at ads in *Autosport*. I went to see someone near Birmingham who was selling a racing version of the Lotus 7 that had a 1.0 litre engine and was (he claimed) road legal. He took me for a ride in it on local roads and it seemed very fast but, he explained, it was far from the quickest in an actual race.

In the end, I decided on a U2, which was very similar to the racing version of the Lotus 7 and competed in the same category, known as Clubmans Sports Cars. I bought a second-hand rolling chassis (a complete car but with no engine). I had decided to race in the 1.5 litre class, so now had to source an engine. A cousin had an interest in a garage run by a former Team Lotus mechanic, Len Street, and I persuaded Len to build and install one for me. I took it for a test at Silverstone and the experience was amazing – so much faster and more sensitive than any road car I had driven, even the 1961 Lotus Elite bought from Rodney Bloor.

My first race was at Snetterton. I knew no one in the motor racing world and couldn't afford to take anyone with me from Len Street's garage, so I set off on my own. I managed to persuade the scrutineers (the officials who check cars to make sure they are not dangerous or outside the regulations) to start the engine when I was unable to get it going myself.

After a push-start at the beginning of the race, I was going round thinking I might at least set fastest lap. Then the race leaders came round to lap me. I was astonished how much faster than me they were. They were driving flat out through a corner where I was braking and changing down. It was a learning year of beginning to understand the difference between being quick on the roads and racing, even at club level.

Later that season, standing among the other drivers at Goodwood looking at the list of practice times, I heard one say, 'Max Mosley, he must be a relation of . . .' and I waited for the inevitable, only to hear him continue '. . . Alf Moseley, the coach builder from Leicester.' I realised here was a whole new world. No one knew about my background and, if anyone did, they wouldn't care. It was the first time I felt that whatever interest there might be was about me rather than my family. If I could do something in motor racing my antecedents would probably not come into it.

As I got to know other competitors in the Clubmans Sports Car category, my understanding of what was required for success grew. One of the leading drivers introduced me to David Reeves, who ran Meadspeed Racing from a small lock-up in Walthamstow, preparing cars for club racing. He was virtually a one-man band but had two part-time employees who started to accompany me to the races. One of them, Colin Gardner, now runs a successful chauffeur-driven car business in Farnham. The other, Bob Hornegold, went on to build golf courses all over the world and has since become one of the UK's leading anglers. A third helper was Gordon Anstey, who could not hear or speak but had an uncanny understanding of racing car suspension.

David realised very quickly that my car needed to be properly set up if it was to perform at its best. Setting up a car was a new concept for me, but I was happy to follow his advice. We took the U2 to Major Arthur Mallock's workshop near Northampton to be adjusted. He was the originator and designer of the U2 make, a great figure in club racing and a very talented engineer. For reasons of cost, the major components of the U2 came mainly from scrap road cars which were attached to a space frame of Mallock's design. As part of the setting-up process, it was important to get the corner weights right and Mallock would do this wheel by wheel using bathroom scales, with blocks of wood under the other three wheels to keep the car level. If the scales gave an unwanted reading he would kick them until it was correct. If this failed, more basic adjustments were made either to the scales or to the car. Of course today this is all done with rather more sophisticated instruments.

I ran out of money during the 1966 season and had to borrow to keep going. The winter was spent getting ready for 1967 and again teaching in the evenings to earn money for racing. Every Saturday I went over to Walthamstow to work on a new car in the Meadspeed workshop. I was not much use but could make small metal components on the lathe.

We went to John Young for the engine. He had a very successful business, preparing racing Ford Anglias with his brother Mike from a garage behind the Ford dealership in Ilford, east London. John could tune Weber carburettors by ear without any instrument, and like aerospace engineers of the period he always wore a white boiler suit with a brass buckle. This he would unconsciously polish with his sleeve while explaining how to support the floats in a Weber carburettor during transit. I could not afford an engine with a steel (as opposed to production) crankshaft, but John's talent went a long way to making up for this.

I went back to Snetterton for my first race in 1967 and won, albeit narrowly, with two cars close behind. It was a great feeling after all the work we had put in. It began a season of victories and class lap records, with Colin Gardner and Bob Hornegold assisting at the races. Although the U2 was basically a two-seater, I was able to make it comply with the letter of the then International Formula Two (single seat) rules, so I entered it in a major Formula Two race at Crystal Palace. I had to overcome objections from the officials, who took one look at it and said: 'You can't bring that thing in here.' But here again my work at the Bar proved useful: armed with the rule book, I was able to convince them they had to accept it. Even so, the *Autosport* report, written by Simon Taylor, said: 'Max Mosley was in a Meadspeed-entered U2 which had a pushrod 1500cc Ford engine – hardly the car to be found on an International F2 grid!'

One of the great attractions of Formula Two in those days was the presence of Formula One drivers, who would take part if there was no Grand Prix that weekend. Several I had seen racing in Formula One, including my first race as a spectator in 1961, were at the Crystal Palace event. Driving on the circuit with several Formula One stars in a wholly inappropriate car was another significant learning curve. Mine was much slower than the proper Formula Two cars, quite apart from my lack of experience and skill. I had asked Bruce McLaren, who was driving one of his own cars, for some advice on keeping out of the way. 'Always stay where you are and let them go round you,' he said. 'Don't try to move out of the way at the last moment because of the risk of a misunderstanding.'

The most intriguing lesson came from observing the big names doing most of their braking in the entrance to the corner, putting the brakes on at the point where I was thinking about taking them off. We practised on the Saturday at Crystal Palace for the race on the Monday, which gave me the chance to put the mudguards back on my U2 and compete at Brands Hatch in an ordinary club race on the Sunday. Applying what I had learned the previous day, I took 1.6 seconds off the class lap record.

This made me realise I really wanted to have a go at the big time. Jean's employer had a friend who knew Ken Tyrrell and kindly invited us to his house to meet the great man. Ken gave me a lot of good advice, including a warning about how fast Formula Two was – even Jacky Ickx, who had just started driving for him, had been surprised. Neither of us had a clue that our paths would cross again in a big way in just over two years. Even when I had disagreements with him later on, I never forgot how generous he had been to take time and trouble when I had been a small-time club driver and a complete nonentity.

Graham Hill did something similar when I sought his advice before going out on the Nürburgring in my Formula Two car a year or so later. Like Ken, he had no idea that I might one day become significant in motor racing, but nevertheless took a great deal of trouble to prepare me for the notorious 'Ring. Like Ken, he did it as a pure act of kindness and I tried always to follow their example when people sought my advice.

Being the only one in chambers that August, I was briefed in a major trademark case. My application in the High Court was successful and I was kept on in what became a very big case, which allowed me to begin to earn reasonable money at the Bar. At last I was able to give up teaching in the evenings, Jean could stop work and I could devote even more time to racing. Fortunately, a discerning Inland Revenue official allowed me to set my racing costs against my Bar earnings, ruling that my participation in the sport was 'an adventure in the nature of a trade'. Without his far-sighted judgment, the cost of competing would almost certainly have ended my involvement in motor sport before it really began.

4

INTERNATIONAL
FORMULA TWO

After the Crystal Palace experience, I decided I absolutely had to try to get a real Formula Two car for 1968 and go racing internationally. By autumn 1967, I was earning enough to buy a new Brabham BT23C from Frank Williams, then already established as a top racing car dealer. I got further backing from a cousin, Henrietta Guinness, supervised by her trustees. She had come with Jean and me to a club race at Mallory Park (which I won) and thought it all brilliant. 'Wow! I'm going to enter a Lamborghini at Indianapolis!' she said. I suggested we go for something slightly more modest to begin with.

Early in 1968, I collected the car from the Brabham factory. Ron Tauranac, the designer responsible for the Brabham cars, came out of his office to say hello and for me it was like meeting the Pope. I asked him about the rollover bar, which didn't look strong enough to protect the driver if the car turned over. He explained it wasn't meant to – it was simply to pass the pre-race inspection. I was delighted with the car and managed to engage an outstanding professional racing mechanic, Jon Redgrave. He reinforced the rollover bar (adding undesirable weight) and off we went testing at Brands Hatch.

The Brabham was a huge step up from the U2, cornering as if on rails and with astonishing acceleration. Coming out on to the main straight at Brands, I made to overtake another car but moved the steering wheel too quickly and lost control. Fortunately it spun up the straight and came to rest in clouds of tyre smoke without hitting anything. It taught me straightaway that a real racing car was very sensitive and you couldn't take liberties. The next test was at Thruxton and this time Jean came with me, saw the car run and thought it alarmingly fast. I knew it would take me some time to get used to the speed, and the almost violent way it changed direction and reacted to any bumps on the circuit.

I also went testing at Snetterton and came up behind a Formula Ford being driven surprisingly, even irritatingly, fast. Back in the paddock the driver got out dressed in scruffy jeans rather than overalls and also wearing plimsoles, something we were always told never to do. Rubber-soled shoes were supposed to be dangerous because they slipped if the pedals were oily. That was my first encounter with James Hunt.

It is difficult to describe the delight of driving a proper single-seat racing car once you get used to it. If you imagine the best road car you have ever driven, the difference between a real racing car and the best road car is far greater than the difference between the best road car and an old banger. The response, the feeling of being part of the car, the way it seems to have unlimited grip until you reach the limit are extraordinary. Anyone who has driven even the very best road cars would be astonished if they tried a real racing car. It's another world.

Of course, I was very aware that the cars were mobile bombs with no protection for the driver, not even seatbelts – just a frame of light, mild steel tubing covered with thin fibreglass as bodywork. Inside the frame were two long petrol tanks, one each side, with the driver lying between them. They were made of very thin aluminium and held in place with tie-wraps. It was obvious that they would fracture in any heavy impact but if you wanted the thrill, you had to accept the risks. A Formula Two car was a smaller version of Formula One. Indeed, Formula Two in 1968, with a 1.6 litre engine, was virtually identical to the 1.5 litre Formula One up to and including 1965. Both had just over 200 bhp. Formula Two lap times at circuits like Monza and Zandvoort were faster than Formula One three years earlier. Even my times would have been fully competitive in the Formula One events up to 1965.

I fitted seatbelts but only one other Formula Two car had them. When I first asked the racing authorities about seatbelts I was told not to fit them because, they said to my amazement, it was better to be thrown clear in an accident. Then, at the end of the 1960s, Dr Michael Henderson, a safety expert who was a racing driver himself, wrote a seminal book on motor racing safety. In it, he showed that many injuries could be prevented by seatbelts, which would keep the driver away from the steering wheel and sharp parts of the car in an accident. He also pointed out that if the car caught fire (as often happened back then) it was better to be conscious after impact to give you some chance of getting out. Seatbelts were made compulsory in racing cars shortly after Dr Henderson's book appeared. He went on to have a very distinguished career in road traffic as well as racing safety, and is today a Fellow of the FIA Institute for Motor Sport Safety and chairman of the Australian Institute for Motor Sport Safety.

The first Formula Two race was at Hockenheim in Germany, where I felt well out of my depth. Several Formula One drivers were there, plus works teams from Ferrari, Lotus and Matra. It was an amazing feeling sitting on the grid with Graham Hill just in front and Jim Clark a bit further up. Both were world champions and both had been in that first race I saw at Silverstone in 1961. I had woken up that morning to hear rain falling. This was not good – 1967 had been a dry summer so I had no experience of racing in the wet. The rain kept falling until just before the start and the track was still wet for the race.

Immediately after the start, I found myself blinded by thick spray. The circuit headed into a forest with trees either side and nothing but a narrow grass verge between the trees and the track. I tried to keep on the road by looking for the tree tops above the spray, but when I got to fifth gear and about 140 mph I thought: This is madness, like driving in dense fog. I backed off, feeling rather cowardly and expecting everyone behind me to come past. But they didn't and, when we got back to the stadium where the track twists and turns and the spray was less of a problem, I could see what was going on.

In front of me was Graham Hill in the works Lotus. He had won the Formula One World Championship in 1962 and, although no one knew at the time, was destined to win a second world title that year. Our cars were similar and both had the same Cosworth FVA engine. I decided if I never did anything else, I had to overtake him. After all, he was a world champion. I managed this a few laps later by going into the blinding spray in his slipstream on the very fast back straight and pulling out into clear air when his car suddenly loomed out of the fog. I crept slowly past. We were both travelling at about 170 mph. I caught his eye as I got alongside. I could imagine what he was thinking.

I finished 11th, with Graham just behind in 12th place, in the first heat of this two-part race.

Back in the paddock after that first heat, someone came up as I got out of my car and asked me in German if Jim Clark was dead. I had been aware something had happened. An ambulance had been parked on the verge by a very fast part of the track, which at that point was a gentle curve. It was flat out in the dry but seemed (to me at least) marginal in the wet. Someone had obviously had an accident. I had no idea it was Jim Clark but I knew the likelihood of the driver surviving after going off the track into a thick forest at 170 mph would be minimal.

Jim Clark's death made it impossible to maintain the pretence to Jean that Formula Two was safe. If Jim Clark, a double world champion and probably then the world's best driver, can get killed, why not you? she asked. Another top British driver, Mike Spence, was killed a few weeks later at Indianapolis and two more drivers at that first Hockenheim race were dead by July – one in Formula Two, the other in Formula One. When I suggested to any of the officials I encountered that the racing was unnecessarily dangerous, the response was always: 'You don't have to do it if you don't want to, it's entirely voluntary. And if you think a corner is dangerous, slow down.' I resolved that should I one day be in a position to do something about the entirely unnecessary risks, I would.

After a race at Thruxton in the UK, the next Formula Two Championship event was at Jarama, near Madrid. At the start of the sixth lap I felt a bump when braking for the corner at the end of the start-finish straight and in my mirrors saw one of the Ecurie Intersport McLarens going off the road. At the end of the race, Jon Redgrave said: 'The driver of that McLaren is looking for you. Says you had him off . . . by the way, he used to play rugby for France.' It was Guy Ligier. We had what turned out to be an amicable discussion and have been friends ever since – a friendship that became significant later on in Formula One when he had his own team. But even years later, he never failed to mention the Jarama incident whenever we met, particularly if there were strangers present. After I became president of the FIA, it was his favourite joke.

I also became friendly with those Formula One drivers who also raced Formula Two, people like Jochen Rindt, Graham Hill and Piers Courage. Piers's car and mine were entered by Frank Williams. At the second Hockenheim race in June my car touched Jo Schlesser's in a slipstreaming bunch at nearly 170 mph and became airborne. When it landed with a violent bang, I managed to keep it on the circuit and out of the trees, but it was too damaged to continue. My future business partner, Alan Rees, told me later he'd found himself underneath it, looking up at the engine's sump. Because the car had been in the air for some distance in the braking zone it hadn't slowed and there was no way to stop or even slow significantly before reaching the corner. A group of photographers and others were standing on the part of the infield I was approaching, watching Rindt and the leaders who had just rounded the corner into the stadium. Fortunately, one of them saw me coming and they scattered just in time.

A picture of my car apparently standing on its back wheels among a bunch of other cars found its way into one of the magazines and I was relieved that Jean never saw it. After the race, realising I had very nearly gone into the trees at 170 mph, I had a long talk to Piers over dinner. He wondered why I was racing. He said it was different for him: if he weren't a racing driver he'd have to be an accountant, which he would hate. By contrast, he said, I had an interesting and successful career at the Bar and didn't need to race. He had a point, but he also well understood that once you have driven a full-on racing car, the temptation to carry on doing it becomes irresistible. Like others, I wanted to do it so badly I was prepared to risk everything.

Because it was my front wheel touching his back wheel, the bump had no effect on Schlesser and he was able to continue without difficulty. But tragically he died three weeks later driving a Honda in the French Grand Prix at Rouen. His car crashed on the second lap and caught fire. When the local fire brigade tried to extinguish it with water, it burned even more fiercely because the chassis was made of magnesium sheet.

With some difficulty, my car was repaired for the next race at Monza. The chassis had been bent by the impact when it landed and, although Kurt Ahrens's very big mechanic helped Jon Redgrave try to straighten it, a three-degree twist remained. That weekend, Piers was racing Formula One, so Jonathan Williams (no relation) drove Frank Williams's other car. There were more than 40 cars for the 22 places on the grid. I just managed to qualify last on the grid, with several professional drivers failing – but only by gritting my teeth, getting a tow in someone's slipstream and taking the *Curva Grande* flat with a very slight lift at close to 170 mph. When I later discussed with Rindt the consequences of going off there, saying it would mean a grizzly end in the trees, he said: 'If you think like that, you shouldn't be racing.'

There was a major accident during the race involving the entire Ferrari works team and a number of other cars. One car was upside down and on fire, and its driver, Jean-Pierre Jaussaud (who later twice won the Le Mans 24-hour race), was prone on the track with a broken leg. In those days there was no thought of stopping the race, so the car burned for lap after lap until the fire engine arrived. I could feel the heat each time I drove past. An Italian newspaper had a whole page on the story, including a picture that happened to include my car going past the burning wreck. Again, thankfully, Jean never saw it. I finished eighth but was intrigued that some drivers slowed after the incident while others didn't. I was one of those who didn't – the danger had not increased just because there had been an accident.

A few weeks earlier I had tried to follow Rindt in a Formula Two race at Zolder in Belgium. I was astonished to see him behind me after only a few laps because I knew he was quicker than me but couldn't possibly be lapping me that soon. There had been an incident on the start line that I had luckily avoided. I was told later that someone hit Rindt from behind (he was on pole) and he'd ended up facing the wrong way. He had to wait until the entire field had gone past before he could start so, when he caught me, he wasn't lapping me but coming up through the field.

Two years later he told me that that was one of only two occasions in his career when he had driven at his absolute limit. The other, he said, was during the last laps of the 1970 Monaco Grand Prix, when he realised he was catching Jack Brabham and could win the race (which he did). In that Zolder race he overtook me round the outside on the first of the (then) very fast corners at the back of the circuit. Watching him do this from close up, it was clear there was a big gap between my driving and his. I began to suspect I didn't have the talent to get to the very top.

In September and back in the UK, I had one more outing in a club race. Jim Moore, a well-known club racer, was winning Formula Libre races all over the country, races in which you could compete with any kind of car. Moore had a very powerful single-seater with a 5.0 litre engine called a Kincraft, which was the forerunner of the Formula 5000 that emerged in the 1970s. A journalist friend suggested I take him on in my 1.6 litre Formula Two, so I did. The race was on the (then) Silverstone club circuit with two long straights plus shorter straights to Maggotts and then to Becketts, very suited to a car like the Kincraft which had much more power than mine with its smaller engine. But my car was more agile than his and I was confident I could get under the outright lap record for the club circuit. I felt I had a good chance of winning yet it turned out to be more difficult than I had imagined, and had been hyped up a bit like a Wild West gunfight. It was a close-run thing with positions being swapped, but in the end, to my relief, he spun. We shared a new outright lap record for the club circuit, a full two seconds under the old one, which lasted for some years.

Meanwhile, the Bar was going well. The work was coming in and I was making the odd trip abroad. My clerk could always arrange things so I could be away on the Friday of a big race weekend. I had lunch each day in Gray's Inn with the same small group of contemporaries, who were a bit mystified by the racing but always seemed intrigued. They were probably too polite to say what they really thought. They all ended up on the bench, including three in the Court of Appeal and one in the House of Lords (now the Supreme Court). I met most of them again recently after a gap of more than 40 years and, after talking to them, I sometimes feel slightly envious, thinking of the life I might have had at the Bar surrounded by clever people.

But I didn't really fit. I once spent ages on an opinion thinking that, as it was going to be read by top management, I should distil it carefully and not produce page upon page of important-sounding waffle. When it had been typed, the clerk appeared, pretending to weigh the few sheets in his hand and saying, 'I can't charge 200 guineas for this, Mr Mosley.' Also around that time in 1968 I was walking up Middle Temple Lane one day when I saw a senior Queen's Counsel coming the other way. If all goes well, that's me in 30 years' time, I thought. I didn't like the idea and began to realise I was getting near the end.

My Formula Two car was kept at Frank Williams's garage in Slough. That team was the forerunner of his immensely successful Formula One team and nominally consisted of Piers Courage and me, but Frank was also preparing a car for Piers to drive in the winter Tasman Series in Australia and New Zealand. Doing a bit of moonlighting for Frank on the Tasman car was an Oxford contemporary, Robin Herd, who had been in the same first year as me, also doing physics. After that year (and a first in Mods) Robin changed to engineering and went on to get the top first in his year, one of the best ever.

After Oxford, he had worked on Concorde at Farnborough as one of the youngest ever principal scientific officers. From there he went to McLaren and designed a succession of outstandingly successful cars, including the one Bruce drove in that Crystal Palace race back in 1967. Robin's CanAm cars were hugely successful, with Bruce McLaren and Denny Hulme winning everything in North America, and he was now working at Cosworth on a revolutionary four-wheel drive Formula One car. When we met again by chance in Frank's workshop, we hadn't seen each other for nearly ten years but immediately hit it off. We had dinner in London and agreed we ought to get together and do something in motor sport.

Apart from the Tasman Series, Frank wanted to enter Formula One with Piers. He was close to getting sponsorship from Reynolds Metals, a huge American aluminium company, who had invited him to visit their headquarters in Richmond, Virginia, with his designer. Frank asked Robin to go with him but he couldn't because of his job at Cosworth. So Frank called me up in chambers and asked if I would pretend to be his designer. 'After all,' he said, 'you've got a physics degree so you can do the technical talk. You won't have to design anything.' I couldn't resist the temptation. I had never been to America and thought it would give me an insight into how motor racing finance worked at the top level. I said OK, if we can fly first class, I'm on. I took a few days off and travelled with Frank to Virginia.

The meetings were interesting. Reynolds had a new technology for aluminium engine blocks that allowed the piston to run directly against the aluminium without the need for the usual steel liner. There was much talk of crystalline molecular structures and viewing different aspects through an electron microscope. They thought racing might usefully demonstrate this technology to the car industry. Frank had also invited Bruce McLaren to the meeting (unwisely as it turned out) and Bruce joined in the technical discussions, looking through the microscope and nodding knowingly about the crystalline structure. I was pretty sure he had no more idea than I did what this was really about, but he made a great impression. As the supposed designer I tried to do the same and it was all going rather well.

The Reynolds bosses were clearly impressed but there was an awkward moment at a reception they gave for us. Mr Reynolds introduced me to the company's chief stress analyst and invited him to 'ask Mr Mosley a few questions about stress analysis to test him out'. That was quite shrewd. Unlike a real racing car designer, I knew virtually nothing about stress analysis. I managed to distract the expert by asking him about his current work and he told me they were offering aluminium products to replace steel for oil drilling in Alaska. This was to save weight when transporting the equipment by air.

He then launched into a long and interesting explanation about the stresses involved in drilling for oil and the problems with aluminium in this application. When Mr Reynolds joined us again, he hadn't finished. He didn't want to admit he'd done all the talking and hadn't asked me anything, so he gave me an excellent report. Yet, unsurprisingly, it was Bruce who won the Reynolds sponsorship. His great CanAm reputation, gained with Robin's cars, far outgunned the story Frank and I could tell.

Back in the UK, Robin and I had a number of meetings and decided we could probably match the current Formula One establishment. That season some Formula One races had attracted only 13 cars, of which just eight or so were serious contenders. At some races, the back markers came solely to collect the start money. They would sit on the grid dripping oil, do a couple of laps and then stop or suffer an engine blow-up. It seemed ripe for a new team and we were full of confidence. Robin was genuinely successful and did not want to go on working for others, while I wanted more from life than the Bar, which for me was about being paid very well to fix other people's problems but never ending up in charge.

We decided to form a company to make racing cars. Robin recruited Alan Rees, a school friend of his and someone I knew as a successful Formula Two driver (the one who had passed underneath my airborne car at Hockenheim the previous year). He was also Jochen Rindt's team manager in Formula Two. Alan in turn recruited Graham Coaker, a production engineer. At Robin's suggestion, we decided to call the company March. The 'a' was because with the initials of our four surnames we needed a vowel to make it into a word.

While all this was going on, I had bought a Lotus Formula Two car and intended to continue racing in 1969. It turned out to be a major mistake – it would have been much wiser to keep the Brabham that had been properly set up from the beginning and always worked well. But over the winter, I started thinking about how I could make up the difference between the top drivers and me. I discussed this with Robin and we hit on something novel: a vertical wing. Lots of racing car designers were beginning to fit wings but they were all horizontal, intended to push the car downwards towards the ground to make it grip better.

This new idea was to use a wing with a symmetrical profile mounted vertically on the car, so sticking straight up and generating side force to help the car round corners. On the straight it would have no angle of attack and thus minimal drag, but as soon as you entered a corner, the slip angle of the tyres would mean the wing had an angle of attack and would generate lift. But because the wing was vertical, the lift would be a sideways force pointing inwards, so helping you get round the corner.

Because the wing was symmetrical, the effect would be the same in both left- and right-handed corners, at least in still air. Another advantage was that up to a certain limit, and with the right profile, the force would increase if the car became more sideways, so it would help you if you made a mistake. With the wing producing a force inwards it would be like leaning on something in the corner. The maximum possible cornering speed would increase, possibly substantially. Better still, it would tend to unload the outer tyres, thus increasing their performance. Robin had a book from which we were able to select a suitable symmetrical profile.

David Reeves fabricated a pair of wings that were very sophisticated and made of magnesium sheet with countersunk rivets.

We also fitted a standard horizontal wing supported by the two vertical wings, so that no one would suspect the vertical ones were anything more than aerodynamically shaped supports for a normal wing. We hoped no one would understand how the system really worked. David fitted the whole thing to the Lotus and we went to Silverstone to try it. There were several top teams testing there that day, including a number with Formula One cars. I went out on the track and as soon as I entered a corner at a reasonable speed, I could feel the effect. It was startling. I went into the next corner faster and felt it even more strongly, but then the entire structure collapsed. David and I had underestimated the forces.

Improbably (if you didn't know how it worked), it had collapsed inwards, but among all the experts at Silverstone that day, the only one who seemed to notice the anomaly was John Surtees. He came up as we were packing it all away and asked why the structure had collapsed inwards. Why not outwards in the direction of the cornering force on the car, as you would expect? I think he'd got it. But no sooner had we made a much stronger version than there was a major accident at the 1969 Spanish Grand Prix when the wings on both Lotus Formula One cars collapsed. Graham Hill and Jochen Rindt were lucky to escape serious injury. The FIA immediately introduced a maximum wing height and other restrictions with which the vertical wing could never comply. It was the end of my hoped-for unfair advantage.

The first big event was a Formula Two race at the Nürburgring on 27 April. The car was hopeless. It had the wrong springs and was bottoming. I could smell the fibreglass. Then came a suspension failure. It was a very high-speed accident and the car came to rest next to a camping ground, seriously damaged. I was surprised to be unhurt. As I was getting out of the car, a track marshal came up and offered me a small self-locking nut of a particular kind, asking if it was mine. I recognised it as coming from the suspension of my car. I suspected no one had tightened it at the factory before delivery and I no longer had Jon Redgrave as my mechanic (although he was with me again when we started the March Formula One team). Unusually, Jean was present in the pits for this race and had a long wait wondering what had happened. I think that finally did it for her with racing.

Lotus repaired the car. I collected it from the factory and took it to test at nearby Snetterton, where I had another major component failure. This time, one of the front disc brakes sheared round the hub so the car veered suddenly to one side under braking. As I tried to get it under control I could see out of the corner of my eye people jumping off the bank they had been watching from, to get out of the way. That's always a bad sign. By luck it ended without a crash.

In those days Lotus had a poor reputation for reliability and were attempting to counter it with advertisements in motoring magazines showing five serious-looking men in white coats. The caption said they were the five inspectors who checked every Lotus component before it was fitted. I took the car back to the factory and, rather unkindly, asked if I could meet the five inspectors who had checked the failed component. At least they didn't try to charge me for the repairs after the Nürburgring crash.

By now I was beginning to focus on March. Alan Rees was running the same Lotus 59 model for Rindt and Hill, both of whom had been at the Nürburgring. I think these two and mine were the only Lotus 59s ever built. At Alan's suggestion, I lent mine to his team for Ronnie Peterson, then a name in Formula Three, to drive at Albi, in France. On a wet track during practice he caused a sensation by keeping up with Jackie Stewart. Here was a real talent. The car still exists and is owned by someone in Germany. The Brabham ended up in Zimbabwe, I was told, and was destroyed in an accident. Only the battery survived and apparently still had my name on it.

Having taken the big decision, I had lunch with my father and took the opportunity to tell him I had decided to give up the Bar and go into motor racing full time. I said I had so far achieved very little, yet by the time he was my age he had fought in the First World War, qualified as a pilot in the Royal Flying Corps, been in parliament nearly eight years, was nationally known for having strongly opposed the government's use of the Black and Tans in Ireland, resigned from the Conservatives and stood again successfully in his Conservative seat, this time as an independent, then crossed the floor to become a major figure in the Parliamentary Labour Party and, soon after, a minister in the 1929 Labour government. His response after I had been through that catalogue was: 'Well, that just shows what a mistake it is to start too soon.' I could see his point. He was by then 73 and had played no significant role in British politics since he was 34.

5

THE FIRST YEAR OF MARCH

The original March was a Formula Three car designed by Robin Herd using components originally intended for other racing cars because there was no time to get long-lead items made. It was built in the summer of 1969, in Graham Coaker's garden shed, by Bill Stone, an extraordinary New Zealand racing driver and engineer. He had been racing one of Robin's McLaren Formula Two cars but had run out of money, so Robin offered him a job. He was our first employee and played a fundamental role in the early days of March. When Bill left us he went on to have an outstanding motor sport career, mainly with his own engineering business, and continued to compete, winning his last race – according to *Autosport*, a wet Formula Ford event in New Zealand in 2011 – at the age of 70.

The March car's first race was in September 1969 at Cadwell Park, a small English circuit, with Ronnie Peterson driving. He ran near the front, finishing third, but in the next race at Mont-lhéry near Paris he crashed and was injured. Bill Stone repaired the car but we had to find another driver. Our two leading contenders were Ian Ashley and James Hunt, a choice between 'Crashley and Shunt' as I (perhaps mischievously) described it to a journalist. James got the drive and the name stuck, but he didn't seem to mind.

Alan Rees was an outstandingly good judge of drivers, picking both Ronnie and James. Alan and Robin wanted Jochen Rindt to drive for us in Formula One for 1970 and, having seen him in action from close up, I could only agree. But we knew he would probably not accept. Nonetheless, I drove to Geneva to try to persuade him, and he and his wife, Nina, put me up for the night and were very hospitable. However, he was dismissive of the new project and didn't believe in our plans – to him it was all just 'schoolboy dreams', with a Formula Three car being built in Graham's 'shack' mainly from other people's components.

Jochen's manager at the time was a certain Bernie Ecclestone. I didn't know him back then although, of course, I knew of him. I never imagined that we would meet up a couple of years later and begin a significant working relationship. Bernie had been urging Jochen to drive for Brabham in 1970 rather than for Lotus, whose cars Bernie thought dangerous. When my attempt to recruit Jochen reached Bernie's ears, he realised that Robin was planning to leave Cosworth to be the designer and a partner in a new Formula One team. He immediately tried to persuade Robin to go in with him and Jochen. This would be a much better way, he said, to start a new team.

Bernie had some good arguments: he had money, we didn't; and in Jochen he also had the driver everyone thought was the quickest around, with the possible exception of Jackie Stewart. Fortunately for the March project, Robin's response was that he had agreed a deal and was not prepared to go back on it. In the end, Bernie also failed to convince Jochen to go to Brabham. Had he succeeded, Jochen might not have died at Monza in September 1970.

By now, I had given up the Bar. My clerk thought it was a temporary aberration and I would be back once I had got motor racing out of my system, but I was fully engaged on March. My first priority was finding a factory, somewhere convenient for Robin, who lived near Northampton, as well as for Alan Rees and Graham Coaker, who were both based in Slough. I went looking one weekend with Jean and found a small unit on an industrial estate in Bicester, one of a group of four across two buildings. Each was 3000 square feet, including a small office. We took one unit and found ourselves sharing the building with a dairy in the other part. Sometime later we took the remaining two in the other half of the development. It was a reasonable journey for the other three and I was quite happy to drive down from London each day.

We opened the factory in September 1969 with no significant capital to speak of but hoped we could manage without. We each put in £2500. I borrowed mine from my mother; Robin and Alan both won theirs by betting on the 1969 World Championship; while Graham Coaker, who at 37 was more grown-up than us 30-year-olds, actually had some savings. We announced we would design and build Formula One cars and compete in the Formula One World Championship with our own team in 1970. Given the cost and complexity of modern Formula One, it would cost hundreds of millions to mount an equivalent operation today if, indeed, it could be done at all.

Our business model was based on us also building Formula Two, Formula Three, Formula Ford and CanAm cars for sale. These were for international racing series and championships through which a driver could eventually reach Formula One. The entry level for a driver was national club racing of the kind I had competed in with my U2. Next came Formula Ford, which was sometimes international, then Formula Three, a fully international FIA formula from which a very successful driver could go straight into Formula One. Formula Two was just below Formula One, with very similar cars.

CanAm was a North American series for powerful open sports cars. Apart from these there were races such as the 24 Hours of Le Mans for sports and GT (closed) cars as well as touring cars. The top drivers back then would take part in all sorts of races, sometimes even in a support race at a Formula One event. All you needed to compete, even in Formula One, was an international licence issued by your national sporting authority.

Our announcement caused a sensation in British motor sport because something so ambitious had never been attempted before. There was much speculation about who was behind it, and *The Times* ran a long piece explaining that no one would try such a thing with less than half a million (about £16 million in today's money). I never suggested we had the money but did not feel it was my job to deny the rumours. We came close to attracting a major sponsor from the outset. Bayer AG, the German industrial giant whose trademark case I became involved with, had developed a self-skinning plastic foam that we thought might be suitable for a chassis. It would have been like Frank Williams's proposed Reynolds Metals deal only bigger and more spectacular, but sadly the technical complications were too great and the deal never materialised.

Having failed to secure Jochen, we hoped to run Chris Amon, a friend of Robin then driving for Ferrari. The second driver would be Ronnie Peterson, with whom we now had a three-year contract. Robin managed to persuade Chris to join us, which was quite a coup because he was an absolutely top driver whose presence in the team gave us credibility. He was having a difficult time at Ferrari, who were going through a very bad patch, finishing the 1969 season joint last of the six teams competing in what was then the International Cup for Formula One Manufacturers, the forerunner of the modern Constructors' World Championship.

Sports car racing was much bigger than Formula One when March opened for business. Events such as Le Mans, Sebring and the ADAC 1000-kilometre race attracted huge crowds and large fields of cars, including Ferraris, Porsches and Ford GT40s. For the 1970 season, Porsche needed a Formula One seat for Jo Siffert, their top driver, to stop him going to Ferrari where he would have been able to drive in Formula One as well as the all-important sports cars. With all the publicity about the new March Formula One team, Porsche thought this might be a solution for Siffert. Their racing manager arranged to visit us in Bicester, which was a nerve-racking experience. Porsche were then, as now, a formidable company with immensely high standards and we had almost nothing in the factory, even in the way of basic machine tools.

So less than six months before our first Grand Prix I had to show Porsche's racing boss round a small, almost empty unit next to a dairy. Somehow we convinced them we were serious and a deal was done. Siffert was a top driver so this gave us added credibility and Porsche's contribution covered almost 30 per cent of our Formula One budget. From a historical perspective, that is a measure of how much more important sports car racing once was compared with Formula One. That the position today is reversed may have something to do with how the two series have been managed for the past 40 or so years. Long-distance races for sports cars, or so-called sports prototypes, continued to be organised in the traditional fashion but, as we shall see, Formula One was about to enter a new era.

Then we had another stroke of luck. Ken Tyrrell had just won the 1969 Formula One World Championship with Jackie Stewart driving a French Matra with a Cosworth engine. This was known as a Ford Cosworth because, thanks to Walter Hayes, a senior Ford executive, Ford had put up the money for Keith Duckworth to develop it. The Cosworth DFV eventually became the most successful Grand Prix engine of all time. For 1970, Matra wanted their car to run with their own newly developed V12 engine, but Jackie and Ken trusted the Cosworth. They also had a relationship with the Ford Motor Company they were not prepared to break.

Matra refused to let Tyrrell run a Matra chassis with a Ford engine and none of the established Formula One constructors would sell them a chassis, so they came to us. We sold them three rolling chassis – i.e. cars with no engines or gearboxes – for £6000 each. ('What good is a car with no engine?' asked one of my aunts when I tried to explain what we were doing.) This was the supposedly profitable price we had worked out from our budget. Walter Hayes, who had arranged for Ford to pay for Tyrrell's chassis, called Robin and me to his Regent Street office and told us the price was £9000, not £6000. I said: 'We can't possibly do that – we've agreed £6000 with Tyrrell.' His reply was, 'Leave Ken to me. It's £9000.' If he had not done that, March would have folded within the year.

To much scepticism and disbelief, we announced we would run the new March Formula One car at Silverstone on 6 February 1970, less than five months after we had opened the factory. Someone said 'March' stood for Much Advertised Racing Car

Hoax, but we had some amazing individuals working with us, all of whom Alan, Robin and I had come across in our previous racing activities. All were attracted by the prospect of a new and very different venture. They included David Reeves from the Meadspeed days; Jon Redgrave, my former Formula Two mechanic; Pete Kerr and Pete Briggs from Alan Rees's Formula Two team at Winkelmann Racing; Bill Stone, the New Zealand racing driver who had built the original March Formula Three car; and Ray Wardell and John Muller, who were known in the sport as being at the very top of their fields, and others.

John Thompson, a sheet metal expert who had worked with Robin at McLaren and then Cosworth, was a key figure because of his expertise in monocoque construction. A monocoque is a structure in which the loads are supported by an external skin, like an eggshell, rather than the classic framework of steel tubing. Intuitively, you would expect it to be less crash-resistant than the steel tubing, and Colin Chapman was criticised on safety grounds when he produced the first monocoque Formula One car, the Lotus 25, in 1962. In practice, though, monocoque structures are much stronger and safer than the earlier space frames and eventually became ubiquitous. Among his other achievements, John Thompson was very involved with the first Ferrari monocoque.

Quite early on, Robin discovered that the petrol tanks on our Formula One car would not hold enough fuel to finish some of the longer races and he came up with aerodynamic-looking side pods to house additional tanks. We didn't want anyone to think there had been a mistake, so I put out a press release saying these were 'low aspect-ratio wings, specially designed to work in the turbulent conditions between the wheels'. That sort of hyperbole amused the technical experts, but Robin was tolerant and it kept the press happy. There was also a degree of truth in it. The original plan was to fit them for the 20 per cent or so of races that needed additional fuel, but we all liked the look and kept them on even when not strictly necessary.

The side pods were styled like aerofoils by Peter Wright, then with Specialised Mouldings, the leading supplier of fibreglass components to the racing car industry. He had tried the idea on a BRM in 1969 hoping to find some downforce, but decided they had no real effect. However, they were just what Robin needed to contain the extra fuel tanks. Peter was later to develop the idea further at Lotus, where he eventually designed the first ground-effect car. Once the gap to the side was closed, there was a massive increase in downforce with little increase in drag. In a way, the March 701 was ahead of its time. More recently, Peter has been head of the FIA GT Commission and a key member of the FIA groups dealing with safety and technical matters, both track and road.

We hired Silverstone to showcase the car and the international motor racing press, together with the entire British Formula One establishment, turned up on the day. Some of the other teams had probably come to watch us fail. In a quiet moment, I went to one end of the paddock and surveyed the scene. It was an extraordinary sensation seeing the area full with almost everyone who was anyone in British motor racing and realising our small group had achieved this – and in such an astonishingly short time. To everyone's surprise, two Formula One cars actually ran: one in Tyrrell's colours for Jackie Stewart; the other, our own factory car, for Chris Amon. I think there was a suspicion that we would mock up a Formula One car and run the old Formula Three car from the previous autumn.

It is difficult to exaggerate the impact we made by producing two functioning Formula One cars. Now we had real credibility for the first time. Stewart and Amon both went out, as did the other team drivers, Johnny Servoz-Gavin for Tyrrell and Jo Siffert in ours. Ronnie Peterson did a few laps, his first in a Formula One car. He spun the wheels in top gear on the Hangar Straight, no doubt due to the low temperature and cold tyres, loved it and clearly could not wait to have another go.

To all this we added a sensational and unexpected announcement: we had sold a car to Andy Granatelli, the American boss of STP (a well-known fuel additive), who were going to compete in the 1970 Formula One World Championship with Mario Andretti driving. Granatelli was more or less the king of American racing and Mario was the number one US driver, having just won the 1969 Indianapolis 500 in an STP car. To back all this up, Granatelli was at Silverstone in person, accompanied by Mario and a large entourage. And, to top it all off, we were able to announce that our own team was going to be sponsored by STP. It was one of those days you never forget and I had to keep reminding myself it was real. But the first round of the 1970 championship was only four weeks away. We still had a great deal of work to finish and, despite all the publicity, there was very little hard cash coming from STP.

The first race was the South African Grand Prix on 7 March 1970, not quite six months after we opened the factory. The cars were flown out almost immediately after our Silverstone debut and Robin went on ahead to do some testing with Chris Amon, who was an outstanding test driver. Jackie Stewart was there, doing the same for Tyrrell. Both covered several hundred laps using Firestone and Dunlop tyres respectively.

Firestone were paying the cost of our testing, as well as helping greatly with the process of setting up the cars. Their money was keeping us going. At one point Robin, who was anxiously waiting for some parts, sent me a telex saying their failure to arrive was 'screwing the whole issue'. I sent him one back saying if we didn't get the miles done for Firestone, there wouldn't be an issue left to screw. Fortunately, Robin had a sense of humour even at that difficult time.

Come the race, to everyone's surprise Amon and Stewart recorded identical fastest times in practice, Jackie taking pole because he had set his time first. A hitherto sleepy Formula One (as already noted, there had been only 13 cars at some races in 1969) suddenly woke up. As we walked down the track to the grid before the start feeling very pleased that everything we had set out to accomplish had been achieved, I cannot deny that a touch of hubris infected Robin and me. But the hostility of the other teams was palpable: not only did we have the two fastest cars on the grid at our very first race, we had upset the established order. We had five cars at Kyalami because Mario Andretti was there in the STP in addition to two each for us and Tyrrell. This meant there would now be too many entries at some races and not all would make it on to the grid at races where only 16 starters were allowed. This did indeed cause problems later in the season, particularly at Monaco and the Spanish Grand Prix. It took the other teams a long time to forgive us.

Some of our cars lacked reliability in that first race, but Stewart left everyone behind and would have won easily had his tyres not given him problems. He still finished third but Amon had a collision on the run into the first corner. Then came two races which didn't count for the championship (as was usual back then), with Stewart winning the Race of Champions at Brands Hatch and Amon the International Trophy at Silverstone, while at the next round of the World Championship, the Spanish Grand Prix, Stewart not only won but lapped the entire field.

So within seven months of opening our factory in a small building shared with a dairy we had won three of the first four Formula One races of 1970 and had led the fourth. To complete the picture, one of our cars had lapped all the other competitors in only its second World Championship race. No wonder the Formula One establishment was unhappy.

This was all achieved despite time being a massive limitation on the design of Robin's March 701. Apart from the difficulty of setting up a factory and building a Formula One and other cars from scratch, Robin had to settle for components that were readily available, such as a heavy front radiator. He also had to use an external oil tank because there was no time to obtain a fuel tank that included space for an oil tank. This meant, among other problems, a very high moment of inertia, making the car reluctant to turn into corners and bad over bumps. Robin knew this would happen, but there was nothing to be done if we wanted to get to the first race. At least he knew the car would be fine on smooth tracks with fast corners.

The arrival of Jo Siffert meant that there was no car for Ronnie Peterson in the works team. Since we had promised him Formula One in 1970, we made an arrangement with Colin Crabbe, an enthusiast who had a successful business restoring and dealing in historic cars. He had run Vic Elford, a top race and rally driver, as a private entrant in Formula One and was, we thought, just the right person to run Ronnie. Colin did an excellent job and was rewarded when Ronnie finished seventh in his very first race, the 1970 Monaco Grand Prix.

Immediately after doing the deal with Colin, we were off with the other teams to the Spanish Grand Prix at Jarama, near Madrid. Arriving in a group at the airport we were accosted by an English solicitor, who told the other team principals, much to their amusement, that I had recently secured his acquittal on a dangerous driving charge in front of a jury. I don't think they really believed until then that I'd ever been a serious lawyer.

At the Belgian Grand Prix at Spa, the race after Monaco, Chris Amon missed winning by a hair's breadth, finishing only 1.1 seconds behind Pedro Rodriguez in the BRM. All through that race, with Amon just behind Rodriguez, Robin kept saying: 'Don't worry, the BRM will break – they always do.' Just that once it didn't, but it was an outstandingly brilliant drive on the old Spa circuit by Amon, who also set fastest lap.

Our early elation vanished when the season began to take on a grim aspect. In June, Bruce McLaren was killed testing at Goodwood, then Piers Courage was killed in the Dutch GP at Zandvoort and later Jochen Rindt died during practice for the Italian GP at Monza in September. These were all people I knew, and in the case of Jochen and Piers knew really well. Combined with the earlier deaths of three of the 21 drivers on the grid at my first Formula Two race (all in that first summer) it was an awful toll of young lives. I resolved once again that if I ever had anything to do with it, motor racing would become much safer. That feeling became even stronger over the next few years as more drivers died, some of them, like Roger Williamson, in horrific circumstances. We did what we could as constructors, but I had to wait 20 years before I could mobilise the governing body to bring about real change.

Money was increasingly a problem but one of the ways we kept afloat was selling Formula One cars. Thanks to Walter Hayes's price increase (which we retained for all subsequent sales) this was a profitable part of our business. One of our customers was Hubert Hahne, a German driver to whom we delivered a car just in time for his home Grand Prix, painted silver in the German tradition. Although a competent driver, he was out of his depth in Formula One and, along with other professional racing drivers, failed to make the grid. He sued us, claiming we had sold him a dud, and his lawyers managed to get a court order to seize our transporter and cars in Germany on the way back from the next Grand Prix.

From my days at the Bar I had some legal contacts in Germany and managed to secure the release of our cars, but it was a major inconvenience at the height of the season and an expense we couldn't afford. To settle the issue, we agreed with Hahne and his lawyers that he would bring the car to Silverstone and Ronnie Peterson would drive it. If he got under an agreed time that would be the end of the matter. In those days Woodcote was a fast continuous corner and on his third lap Ronnie came through it flat out and on slight opposite lock. He was under the agreed time. I think Hahne realised then just how much ability it took to be competitive in Formula One. No one could blame him for not matching Ronnie.

Despite repeatedly denying rumours, Ken Tyrrell abandoned his March cars after Monza and raced with his own Tyrrells.

The final race of that first 1970 season was in Mexico City. Spectators climbed over the fences and lined the sides of the track with nothing between them and the cars. The risks were obvious and none of the teams wanted to start the race. The FIA officials agreed, saying it was impossibly dangerous for the public. Pedro Rodriguez, as the top Mexican driver and a national hero, went round the circuit pleading with the crowd to get back behind the fences, but to no avail. In the end the police asked us to race despite the obvious danger, arguing that the crowd would riot if the race was cancelled and that would be even more perilous.

The race took place between walls of humanity and Chris finished a creditable fourth in what was his last appearance for March in Formula One. He continued to drive our CanAm car in America and, when Robin was present to set the car up, he was able to run comfortably with the all-conquering McLarens. March came third in the 1970 Constructors' Championship, partly thanks to Stewart and Tyrrell's successes in the early part of the season.

Late in 1970, Graham Coaker left the company. Things hadn't really worked out and he was not able to contribute as much as he and we had all hoped. Part of our settlement with him was a Formula Three car, which he took testing at Silverstone, had an accident and broke his leg. Graham was taken to the local hospital in Northampton and all seemed well, but then complications set in and tragically he died. I couldn't help feeling it would have been better if we'd left him alone and not involved him in March at all.

At the end of the season we still owed Chris most of his retainer, which was a problem because we had no money left. We gave him the two CanAm cars in lieu but I've always felt bad about that. His fee was originally agreed by Robin and Alan, who overruled me when I said we couldn't afford him and should make do with Siffert and Peterson as our works team. Chris nevertheless made a great contribution in testing and set-up. He was a major talent, one of the greatest of his generation, but, extraordinarily, he never won a World Championship Formula One race although he came very close indeed at the 1970 Belgian Grand Prix.

The following season, driving for Matra, Chris had pole at the Italian Grand Prix and looked certain to win. Bernie Ecclestone bet me a pound he wouldn't. Handing over the pound after the race, I asked how he could be so sure. He said Chris's luck was so bad, something would happen even if he were leading on the last lap. Perhaps a cow would walk across the track and stop him, but he wouldn't win. In fact, it wasn't a cow: Chris went to remove a tear-off from his helmet visor when leading the race with nine laps to go and the entire visor came off, leaving him blinded by the airflow at 200 mph. He eventually finished sixth. But Chris was lucky in the most important way of all – unlike so many of his contemporaries he survived. He became a successful farmer and is a well-known figure in his native New Zealand and still active in the local motoring community.

6

A DIFFICULT BUSINESS

With Jo Siffert joining BRM and Chris leaving for Matra, we decided we would just run Ronnie Peterson in 1971, backed up by drivers who brought money. Robin Herd designed a revolutionary new Formula One car with an unusual front wing. It also had side radiators like Colin Chapman's Lotus 72, a layout for Formula One that continues to this day. The first iteration had inboard front brakes like the Lotus 72, the main purpose of which was to reduce unsprung weight, but we had two successive shaft failures of the kind that were believed to have caused Jochen Rindt's fatal accident. No one could explain the failures because the calculated stresses in the shafts at maximum braking were way below the point at which they would be expected to fail, so Robin went back to the classic outboard configuration.

We used copper brake discs in return for money from the American Copper Industry Association, who hoped copper discs would be adopted by the car industry. Unfortunately, they never worked properly – they seemed to have a variable coefficient of friction, which was disconcerting for the driver. Even so, we persisted with different variants because we needed the funds. We also fitted an Alfa Romeo engine in one of the cars, again for money. Andrea de Adamich, an Italian lawyer who had won the European Touring Car Championship for Alfa Romeo in 1966, usually drove that car. Andrea was a delightful person and he and I got on well, both being lawyers.

Peterson surprised everyone at the Monaco Grand Prix, including Robin, Alan and me. He overtook several top drivers to finish second, a particularly difficult feat on the Monaco circuit. He later told me that this had given him real confidence for the first time because he now realised he could match the top drivers of the day. We were already convinced, but it is surprising how many outstanding drivers doubt their own ability at first. Peterson eventually finished second in the World Championship that year despite all the troubles with the copper discs, and March finished joint third with Ferrari in the Constructors' Championship. Robin also designed very successful monocoque Formula Two and Formula Three cars that year.

At the last race of the season, a non-championship event at Brands Hatch, all the Formula One team principals were invited to race each other in Ford Mexico saloon cars. All had raced professionally and two were former world champions, so what had been intended as a bit of fun got very competitive – and so much damage was done to the cars that we were never invited to do it again. It was my last ever race, albeit not a serious one, and I had a start-to-finish battle with Frank Williams. I was ahead of him in practice but he just beat me in the race. Only Jack Brabham and John Surtees, the two ex-world champions, plus Colin Chapman (a brilliant driver whose bankers would never let him race seriously) ended in front of Frank and me.

It was the only time my parents ever came to a race. There was a disaster in the main event later that day, when Jo Siffert, our driver from the previous year who was then driving for BRM, died trapped in his burning car. My parents never wanted to come again. I think the black smoke and knowledge that someone had just died on a beautiful autumn day reminded my father of his time in the Royal Flying Corps in the First World War.

Earlier in 1971, Niki Lauda had turned up at the factory with some money. He was by no means a typical racing driver, but was obviously intelligent and had great charm. Jean and I took him to our favourite Indian restaurant in Bute Street and we both liked him. Robin and Alan were very happy to run him in Formula Two. He was competent but there was little sign yet of just how good he would become. Niki was determined to do both Formula One and Formula Two the following year and we did a deal with him for a big proportion of our budget, but the money failed to arrive. He explained that he had a bank that was going to support him but his grandfather, a major Austrian business figure, had persuaded the bank to cancel the deal. Understandably, he didn't want Niki to be a racing driver with a high chance of dying when it was already clear he was someone who would be a success in the business world.

Niki told me not to worry – he'd find another bank. In the meantime, he gave me a suspicious-looking letter that he said was from his father, confirming we would get our money and, amazingly, we did. Our own bank manager in Oxford could hardly believe it when the payment arrived, saying it was like someone getting the Trustee Savings Bank to pay for Formula One. It showed what an extraordinary character Niki was, even in his early twenties. His grandfather died not long after and never saw Niki become one of the most successful Austrians of his generation, not only a three-time world champion but also the founder and owner of a successful airline.

Despite Niki's contribution, we were still desperately short of money. We were trying to run a capital-intensive business with virtually no capital. Robin and I raised some money from our families, but my contribution was minimal because my father would not get involved and all I could raise was a modest sum from my mother and my half-brother, Jonathan Guinness. The total was a long way short of what was needed to capitalise the business properly. We drew very small salaries, a lot less than we would have earned had Robin worked for a team and I stayed at the Bar.

We lost another of the four founders when Alan Rees decided to leave the company, but we all remained on good terms and Alan later enjoyed success with the Shadow Formula One team. Some of our competitors tried to recruit Ronnie Peterson, but he had one more year on his contract and stayed completely loyal despite our financial weakness.

Robin designed another revolutionary Formula One car for 1972 but this one didn't work. Because of his extraordinary talent, Ronnie managed to extract a reasonable performance from it, but Niki, in the second car, deemed it undrivable. Niki was right, but because he was a relatively inexperienced paying driver and Ronnie had just finished second in the World Championship, we listened more to Ronnie. It did not take long for Robin to recognise Niki's talent as a test driver. He was getting quicker and quicker, combining his rapid progress with great analytic ability. When driving for us he was hardly ever as fast as Ronnie, but he was the one who went on to win three World Championships. In a way, that may be a measure of Ronnie's outright speed.

We had a serious dilemma – it was mid-season, the car wasn't working as we'd hoped and our resources were very limited indeed. Earlier in the year we had supplied a Formula One version of our very successful Formula Two car to a group of City financiers who were sponsoring Mike Beuttler, and it was obvious that this car was better than ours. Halfway through the season we gambled on abandoning the revolutionary car and adopted the same solution as Beuttler for our works team. However, we never recovered that season and Ronnie's abilities were largely wasted in the final year of his first contract with us.

With hindsight, had Robin developed the 1971 car over the winter we would have been contenders the following season. It was already a very good car and, given time and our 1971 experience, it would almost certainly have been a race winner in Ronnie's hands and might have persuaded him to stay at March. Things would have been very different for us in Formula One. But racing has always been full of 'ifs'. After that, we used modified Formula Two cars for the remaining years of our involvement in Formula One.

Robin had been doing all the development work with Niki from mid-season and, with Ronnie unhappy and about to leave us for Lotus, the obvious move was to run him as the lead driver in 1973. But the problem was that we could only compete in Formula One if we had a driver with sponsorship and Niki had already spent all his money. He and Robin had assumed that one way or another we would be able to run him, so it fell to me to tell him we couldn't give him a drive for 1973. It was a terrible moment for him (and for me), which I later learned had even led him to consider suicide.

Earlier in the 1972 season, the head of Ford Competitions in Germany, former top sports car driver Jochen Neerpasch, asked us to run a car in a Formula Two race at the Nürburgring for Jochen Mass, a promising young German driver. Neerpasch was already running him in touring car racing. We couldn't afford to but we did it anyway. Mass won the race and Neerpasch was delighted. A few weeks later we met at the Monaco Grand Prix, where he revealed that BMW were coming back to racing in 1973 and that he was going to join them and be in charge of the programme. He also told us that BMW already had a Formula Two engine that had been developed by Paul Rosche 'in the cellar' – i.e. without management's official sanction. Neerpasch said we could have the engine exclusively for 1973 if we bought the entire production of 50 units. Robin and I both took a very deep breath and agreed. As part of the deal we agreed Robin would concentrate on our BMW Formula Two cars – all the more reason for the later decision to run a modified version in Formula One.

Our 1972 Formula Three team was not a success, and during the Monaco race weekend our works driver, James Hunt, told the press (possibly truthfully) that the car was no good. I sacked him, telling him that a works driver should never say such things even though I understood his frustration. He had a wonderfully laid-back attitude and was great company, at the track and off it. James took the sacking in his stride and we remained friends, even laughing about it later. He needed to keep racing for his career, so we lent him a 1971 Formula Two chassis which was still a very competitive car but needed an engine. He told me some time after that he'd found himself standing next to Lord Hesketh in a gentlemen's loo and got talking to him. It was an auspicious meeting because Hesketh ended up buying James an engine, making him a serious rival to our works Formula Two team of Peterson and Lauda, but, more importantly from James's point of view, it was the start of a relationship with Hesketh that would take them both into Formula One.

When the first BMW engine was delivered, their mechanics came from Munich to help with the installation. They removed the cylinder head to reveal cans of beer hidden inside. They were sure we would open it up as soon as it arrived to look at its secrets and were surprised we hadn't. It was the start of a great collaboration between the two companies and we sold a lot of Formula Two cars for the 1973 season on the strength of the BMW engine. By then we had a fully professional manufacturing operation with David Reeves in charge of the factory. Cars were delivered on time and were very well finished. It was a proper business, hampered only by the Formula One team.

It only became apparent how much of the factory's resources were being consumed when we eventually stopped competing in Formula One. In those days a leading independent Formula One team might have 20 employees. Ours had about half that but the team personnel used constantly to go to the production side for 'just' jobs – as in, 'could you just do this please?' – to the detriment of the commercial side of the business. By contrast, a top modern Formula One team has upwards of 700 employees plus significant outside contractors, but one questions whether there has been a corresponding increase in its appeal to spectators.

Jean-Pierre Beltoise and Jean-Pierre Jarier drove for our STP-sponsored Formula Two team in 1973, and Jarier won the first race at Mallory Park in Leicestershire. We would have been delighted but for several of the BMW engines blowing up, including Beltoise's. A lump of his engine came bouncing down the track and finished almost where I was standing with Paul Rosche, BMW's race engine expert and the man who had kept the engine programme alive when officially it had been terminated. He turned to me and said in his strong Bavarian accent: 'I think we have a problem ...' We did, but at least it meant we didn't have to take delivery and pay for the remaining engines until we could afford to.

We won the 1973 European Formula Two Championship with Jarier but our 1973 Formula One team was not a contender. With Peterson having gone to Lotus, we gave Jarier the Formula One drive, but when his modest French sponsorship money did not come through, we put Roger Williamson in the car for the British Grand Prix. He was a very talented British Formula Three driver and had backing from Tom Wheatcroft, the owner of the Donington Park circuit. Unfortunately, there was a multiple collision at the end of the first lap that eliminated Roger and eight other drivers. A fortnight later, Roger died in a horrific crash during the next race, the Dutch Grand Prix at Zandvoort. The car was upside down and on fire. David Purley was the only Formula One driver who stopped to help. Despite his desperate attempts to wave down the other drivers none of them stopped; the race continued and was won by Jackie Stewart in a Tyrrell. The marshals were afraid of the fire and stayed back. Despite being uninjured, Roger was unable to get out from under the car and could only shout for help. By the time a fire engine arrived, it was all over.

Had any of the other drivers stopped they could have helped Purley but, despite his desperate attempts, he could not lift the car on his own. A former captain in the Parachute Regiment, he was a tough individual, but I don't think he ever really recovered from the terrible experience of hearing Roger shouting for help in the fire yet being unable to reach him. Roger's father was with me in the pits, asking if his son was all right. Having watched the terrible scene unfold on a television monitor in a broadcast van behind our pit, I had the awful job of saying I didn't think he was.

The authorities asked for one of the team to assist getting the body out of the car and our chief mechanic, Pete Kerr, undertook the dreadful task. And that was the extent of any official involvement: the authorities did not appear to be interested in asking why the race was not stopped, why no one went to Purley's aid or why it took so long to put out the fire. When I learned the full horror of what had happened, I was once again seriously tempted to walk away from motor racing. I went home asking myself yet again if this was really where I wanted to be – and more determined than ever to change the sport's attitude to safety should I ever have the opportunity.

7

SOME PROGRESS

In 1973, we sold a Formula One car to Hesketh for Hunt to drive and his first race in the March was the Monaco Grand Prix. Hesketh was building his own car, but Hunt completed the season in the March (finishing second in the United States Grand Prix at Watkins Glen) and used it for the first two races of 1974 before the Hesketh car's debut in South Africa.

The Hesketh team was a strange set-up. When they first started, I came round a corner in the Brands Hatch paddock at the non-championship Race of Champions to find Hesketh and his entourage sitting in a circle. This was before they bought a March and when they were running a Surtees. They said their only engine had blown up and they were asking 'the great chicken in the sky' to send them another. I told them the great chicken of Bicester could probably help and we lent them an engine. That was why, from then on, Hunt always called me *Grand Poulet*, a name that always puzzled the journalists. Hunt went very well during the season and the press fell in love with

Hesketh. To them he was a fun-loving gentleman among all those hard-nosed Formula One professionals.

Our successful Formula Two season in 1973 earned us excellent sponsorship for the 1974 European Championship and we won it again. We had two top drivers: Hans-Joachim Stuck, backed by Jägermeister, and Patrick Depailler, who was supported by Elf. Hans was the son of the prewar driver Hans Stuck, a German hero. Jochen Neerpasch took me to see Stuck senior to help convince him that Hans-Joachim should drive for BMW in touring cars and for us in Formula Two and Formula One. It was a fascinating visit, and he still had his trophies from the great days of the prewar Auto Union team for which he drove so successfully.

We put Hans alongside Howden Ganley and Vittorio Brambilla in our Formula One team for 1974. The cars turned a wheel for the very first time at the start of practice at the Argentine Grand Prix, which is never the best way to begin a season. With Robin contractually bound to concentrate on our Formula Two cars for BMW, I had to become the race engineer. Fortunately, as well as being our driver, Howden was an experienced race car engineer and knew what to do at that first race in Buenos Aires to get an entirely new and untested car to work. For me it was an interesting new experience, and I soon discovered that Robin was right when he told me the problems of adjusting a car to a circuit would usually succumb to rational analysis, except when caused by some fundamental characteristic of the car. I was given the job because of Robin's absence in Formula Two, but the knowledge I acquired was very useful in later life. I often looked back and thought: if only I had known all that when I was driving myself.

Roy James, the getaway driver in the Great Train Robbery, came to see me one day. He had just been released from prison and had been a very promising Formula Junior driver before he was locked up. He was doing the rounds of the teams, hoping to get back into the sport, but more than a decade in jail had taken its toll and we couldn't help. He was a silversmith by trade, however, and Bernie Ecclestone commissioned one of the major Formula One trophies from him, which is still handed out at the FIA prize-giving each year.

Vittorio Brambilla drove for us again in 1975 and, with Robin back in Formula One, he started to be competitive. Lella Lombardi drove our second car. She was a well-known sports car driver and had backing from Count Zanon, a wealthy Italian enthusiast. The Spanish Grand Prix was at Montjuïc, a circuit in Barcelona that was spectacular but dangerous, made worse by the organisers' failure to tighten the bolts on the Armco barriers lining the track. Understandably, the drivers were unhappy and went on strike, locking themselves in a large motor home belonging to Texaco. Brambilla did not join them, as he spoke almost no English. While the drivers were talking, the Formula One mechanics went round the circuit tightening the bolts. Practice started with only Brambilla and the Lotus of Jacky Ickx, but the sound of their engines eventually brought the other drivers out and a full practice session began.

In the race the two Ferraris took each other off, fortunately without injury. However, another car, driven by Rolf Stommelen, lost its rear wing and crashed, killing four spectators and seriously injuring Stommelen. The race was stopped. Lella was sixth in our car and became the first, and so far only, woman to score a point – strictly half a point, as the race was stopped early – in a World Championship race. Stommelen died in 1983 when another rear-wing failure caused him to crash at 190 mph at Riverside in California.

Later in 1975, we were economising and Robin, although back in Formula One, didn't come to the Austrian Grand Prix, leaving me once again in charge of car set-up as the so-called performance engineer. Apart from our own car, Roger Penske's team was there with Mark Donohue driving. They had just bought a March 751 from us because the Penske Formula One car had problems. Mark went off during practice and sustained a blow on the head. He did not appear to be seriously hurt, although a marshal was killed during the incident. However, he developed a headache and was flown to a hospital in Graz. He had suffered a cerebral haemorrhage and died the following day. Mark was an outstanding engineer and great company. He used to joke that the reason successful drivers at Indianapolis were much older than in Formula One was you needed to be old and react slowly if the car got out of shape. A quick correction, he said, would put you in the wall.

The race was in the wet and, although the rain was supposed to stop, I decided to gamble on full wet settings. We had little to lose if it dried up, but with such extreme settings I knew we might do exceptionally well if by any chance it didn't. We were eighth on the grid and everyone else was on dry settings. The weather forecast turned out to be wrong, the rain got steadily worse and Brambilla took the lead. Denny Hulme (1967 world champion) was there as an adviser to the officials and effectively in charge. Encouraged by Bernie, he came down the pit lane to ask if he should stop the race for safety reasons. I said yes, anxious to quit while ahead. It had indeed become very dangerous and I knew Brambilla might go off the road at any moment. Vittorio saw the chequered flag and put both arms in the air in delight at winning. Having let go of the steering wheel in appalling conditions he crashed just after the finish line. Luckily he didn't hurt himself and the damage to the car was slight. We had won our first Grand Prix since 1970.

At the first race the following season, Peterson came up in the paddock and told me he was not happy at Lotus. We had remained good friends and started discussing the possibility of him coming back to March. Lella's backer, Count Zanon, was a Peterson fan, so over dinner I told him Ronnie would like to leave Lotus and drive for us. Provided Colin Chapman agreed to let him go, the only problem was his retainer. Zanon immediately offered to pay it.

With Ronnie keen to join us, the next task was to negotiate a deal with Lotus. Colin Chapman agreed to swap Ronnie for Gunnar Nilsson, a very promising Formula Three driver who was under contract to March. Gunnar was the 1975 British Formula Three champion and clearly destined to be a top Formula One driver (sadly, he died of cancer before his career really got going). Chapman was very unhappy when he found we had got Ronnie, now released from his Lotus contract, but he hadn't actually got Nilsson. He did not give the negotiation his full attention and left most of it to an underling. In his mind, it was a straight swap: Ronnie for Gunnar. Once Ronnie had signed, I explained that we could only *release* Gunnar; we couldn't actually force him to drive for Lotus. Colin ended up having to pay him more than he had planned and it took him a good two years to forgive me.

Robin stayed in touch with Gunnar, who told him that Lotus seemed to have made some sort of technical breakthrough and that his car felt really good. Gunnar had been told that this was due to a special kind of bearing they were now using. Then everyone in the paddock started to wonder about the Lotus and a rumour spread that it had a revolutionary new differential.

This gained further credence when Bob Dance, a senior Lotus mechanic, was seen in the paddock with something carefully wrapped in a cloth that looked as though it might well be a differential – it was the right size and shape and clearly very secret. Apparently, it was really a teapot but the ruse worked. Everyone had been thrown off the scent.

The reason for the performance gain was something quite different. A year later at Zolder, the Lotus was exceptionally fast in the wet, which made us think they must have found a way to generate more downforce. Then, on our way out of the paddock, we saw a Lotus being brought back to the garages after stopping out on the circuit. The underneath of the car was very shaped and smooth. It was the first real ground-effect car designed by Peter Wright, the ultimate version of the trend he had started with the March side pods back in 1970. Robin realised immediately what they had done, but there was no way we could attempt to replicate it at that point in the season. It would have meant a completely new car, something for which we had neither the time nor the money.

Peterson took pole at the 1976 Dutch Grand Prix but our car had a problem. Robin's unconventional nose worked well and the car was fast in qualifying, but its shape reduced the airflow to the front tyres and they tended to overheat in the race. At the Italian Grand Prix, however, there was a slight rain shower during the race which gave the tyres a rest and Ronnie won, with Regazzoni's Ferrari close behind. Winning the Italian Grand Prix made Count Zanon feel that everything he had done had been worthwhile. For us, a clear win, with none of the special circumstances of the previous year's Austrian Grand Prix, was a triumph.

Robin and I divided the work of setting up the cars, with him looking after Brambilla, who was not as quick as Ronnie but gave excellent feedback, and me looking after Ronnie but with the advantage of the set-up worked out by Robin and Vittorio. We would get to a point in practice where there was nothing more we could do to solve whatever problems Ronnie was having. Then he would go out, drive round them and invariably put the car somewhere near the front of the grid. What an absolutely extraordinary talent he was.

Niki Lauda had a very serious accident at the Nürburgring in his Ferrari and, as is well known, was given the last rites. He came back too soon and was still bleeding from the burns to his head at that Italian Grand Prix, but nevertheless finished fourth. By the last race of the season, the Japanese Grand Prix, Niki was leading the World Championship by three points from James Hunt. On race day, heavy rain and minimal visibility caused the start to be repeatedly delayed in the hope that the rain would ease. There was a huge television audience waiting to see whether Niki or James would win the title and the light was beginning to fade. Although it was undoubtedly extremely dangerous, the majority of the drivers agreed to start. On the second lap Niki pulled into the pits and stopped.

By the time the race had finished it was almost dark and there was real confusion in the pit lane. Hunt was third, which made him world champion, one point ahead of Niki, but neither James nor his team could quite believe it was true. Although the rain had stopped, everything was wet. Hunt walked down the road behind the garages, stopping everyone he knew and asking them to confirm the result to him.

Amid the puddles by the Fuji garages with nothing more to do, the full gloom of my situation descended on me. It was the end of the season, all three of our cars had retired in the race for very minor and unnecessary reasons, March had no sponsors yet for 1977 and, with the possible exception of Stuck, no drivers. The depressing effect of a disastrous race is always increased by the celebrations of the successful teams and here Lotus were the delighted party after an unexpected win for Mario Andretti. By contrast, McLaren, strangely enough, were muted – they still did not quite believe what they had done and that their man James really was world champion.

I needed a lift back to the hotel but couldn't face going with one of the joyful teams, so I wandered down to the Ferrari garage. They were in an even worse state than me, having just watched their driver lose the World Championship – stopping because of the conditions, only to see the track dry, the sun come out and the race develop in a way that would have enabled Lauda to retain the title. Daniele Audetto, the Ferrari team manager, and I squeezed into the front seat of a Rolls-Royce that the Japanese Ferrari importer had provided. Daniele's wife was in the back with Clay Regazzoni and another of their team personnel. Niki had long gone by helicopter to the airport.

We drove back to the hotel in almost complete silence, with me suffering cramp as Daniele is very tall and the seat was not big enough for two. Every now and then Daniele would say: 'I cannot understand – I cannot understand.' Clay said nothing and I muttered something about not knowing what it was like unless one was actually in one of the cars. When the Ferrari team is unhappy, the pall is so great that it affects anyone in contact with them. I felt very sorry for Daniele, especially as he was rumoured to be leaving the team. I had the consolation that our disastrous race was the fault of the team and thus ultimately my fault and Robin's. Daniele, however, had contributed nothing to his misfortune.

The restaurant at the hotel was ugly and brightly lit with neon lights. The entire McLaren team, including Teddy Mayer and Alastair Caldwell, were sitting at a table with James Hunt, all looking slightly shell-shocked. At the same time, they all appeared to be concentrating hard on not doing or saying something silly, despite the fact that they had already had plenty of champagne and felt so happy they could hardly contain themselves. I sat down at another table with Ronnie and Barbro Peterson, Carlos Pace and his wife. Carlos also had his mother-in-law there, who seemed very nice but her presence was quite incongruous. Towards the end of dinner, James came over, by this time in very good form on the champagne that Teddy was buying for all of us.

'I've got this fantastic new trick with the telephone,' he said. 'You know how they say *"mushi mushi"* for "hello" – and they keep saying *"hai hai"*? Well, if you get a call, you pick the phone up and say *"mushi mushi"*. You then get a lot of Japanese and when it stops you simply say *"hai hai"*. Then more Japanese and you say *"mushi mushi"* again. You can keep them talking for ever like this.'

Through the champagne and the wine this struck everyone on our table as incredibly funny. We all went off to the telephone on the pay desk and took it in turns. Fortunately, the Japanese are far too polite to get as cross as one might have expected.

This was typical of James, who was always up for some fun and would liven up even the most boring sponsor's party. On the way to one in Brazil we were sharing a car and he asked if I'd mind if we dropped in on a friend of his on the way. We arrived at a very grand modern apartment block and took the lift to the top floor. The flat had wonderful views over Rio. James's friend produced a piece of polished stone and laid out three lines of white powder.

Knowing I was a bit of a prude about such things, James turned to me and said: 'You don't want yours, do you, Max?' I confirmed I didn't and he had mine as well as his. It certainly put him in a good mood for the party. James was also said to be president of the São Paulo Divers' Club. That kind of diving (as opposed to driving) was apparently one of his specialities, but is beyond the scope of this book.

On the plane home I decided to have my talk with Vittorio. He had asked in Canada whether we could offer him a drive in 1977 and I had said we were unsure. Prior to Japan, Robin and I had decided we could not go on with him because he had too many accidents, but we did not want to leave him in a difficult position. I asked him what his plans were and he said he had had an offer from Surtees and two other teams, one of which was Brabham. I knew there was no chance that Bernie would take him, and I suspected that the other team he had in mind was Ferrari. I was sure he had no chance there, either. But Surtees was certainly a possibility and I had already been told that John was interested, so at least he had somewhere to go. Then he said that despite these offers he would be interested in staying at March under certain conditions, which were that he was to be clear number one – he thought that the pressure of Ronnie's presence had contributed to his accident record – and that we put more effort into his car than we had in 1976. I did not really accept the first point – Grand Prix drivers are always under extreme pressure and their ability to cope with it is part of their basic mental equipment. And the second point I knew to be untrue – Vittorio had benefited from Robin's full attention all season, while Ronnie had only had me.

His complaints gave me the opening to say that our ideas on the problems and their solutions were so far apart that I saw no possibility of reconciling them. It seemed best that we should simply part friends. We shook hands and wandered back to our seats from where we had been standing by the lavatories at the back of the plane.

We had been unable to persuade Ronnie to stay with us for another season and he went to Tyrrell for 1977. He had a very poor season with Tyrrell and in hindsight he should have stayed with us. Having lost both Brambilla (to Surtees) and Ronnie, we took on two paying drivers. One of them was Alex Ribeiro, a Brazilian who liked to have a 'Jesus Saves' sticker on his car. The mechanics put them all over the factory, each time with a Green Shield Stamps sticker underneath. While Alex was discussing a deal with me, my phone rang. It was Bernie, who asked if Ribeiro had told me he could have a deal with Brabham. 'Yes,' I replied. 'Well,' said Bernie, 'he can't. He's got nowhere to go except you.' That was helpful to me if a bit unfair on Alex.

Our other driver was Ian Scheckter, older brother of Jody who was to become world champion two years later. He had a potential sponsor in Rothmans and initial contacts with the tobacco company were promising. It was a good moment because I was able to tell them that we had a revolutionary car we were about to reveal and eventually the deal was done. Scheckter was our man and we had our two drivers for 1977. The only snag, and not an unimportant one, was that neither of them had ever raced in Formula One.

8

A LAST YEAR WITH MARCH

Back from Japan, I found Robin Herd and our other Formula One engineer, Martin Walters, busy planning the technical evolution of our cars in 1977 and trying to restructure our team. In the latter part of 1976 our cars had become very fast, thanks to a lot of testing with Peterson and a massive technical programme involving the engineering and aerodynamic departments in several different universities, as well as the wind tunnel at MIRA (Motor Industry Research Association) and our own computer resources. Robin and I had an understanding that he would not take any major technical or managerial decisions without first consulting me, and I would not make any deal or involve us in anything of consequence without discussing it with him beforehand. As a result, I was involved in all the major technical decisions between Robin and Martin.

During 1976 we had managed to find the necessary speed – all three of our cars were in the first six on the grid in Watkins Glen – but we lacked reliability. This was partly due to basic design – for example, the front tyre overheating problem – and partly due to poor detail design and preparation. Our programme for 1977 had, as its first priority, the elimination of this unreliability without losing sight of the need for an improvement in performance. Robin and Martin devised a very detailed schedule of modifications for reliability, a plan to eliminate the fundamental design faults in the chassis and a host of technical improvements geared towards better lap times.

The most spectacular aspect of our performance programme was the six-wheel car. We had been planning this for some time and quietly getting it built. Then we heard a rumour that another team was also developing a six-wheel car with four-wheel drive like ours – a rumour that was substantiated when *Autosport* actually broke the story. The big difference between ours and the Tyrrell six-wheeler was that our tandem wheels were at the rear, which eliminated the huge rear tyres and their immense aerodynamic drag. So we quickly threw the car together and unveiled it in mid-November to a slightly disbelieving press. Some of them actually suspected it was a joke or a device to snare a sponsor, which shows how naive even people in the business can be about the problems of racing car building, getting special castings made and so on. In fact, Robin and I secretly believed the new device would be spectacularly successful, but we did not want to admit this to anyone in case it was not. Motor racing is littered with revolutionary innovations for which great success was promised but never realised.

A few days later there was the press day at March to show the new six-wheeler for the first time. We still had not finalised the deal with Rothmans so it carried no advertising – a pity because the pictures appeared in newspapers all over the world. The press reaction was good and most of the other constructors were pleased. It helps Formula One generally to have new and innovative machinery. We spent most of the day pushing the car about and standing beside it, having our pictures taken. All very fine, I thought, as long as there are some races to take it to. I was very conscious of the coming problems between FOCA and the race organisers' WCR group.

The following Monday I flew to Marseille for a quick visit to the Ricard circuit, where many of the teams were testing. Partly I wanted to see the new cars, and partly to have another talk with Count Zanon. James and Niki turned up, James arriving by helicopter while Teddy Mayer waited for him at Marseille. James looked a bit run-down from all the celebrating and Niki looked worse than I had seen him since the accident. He had undergone surgery to fix his right eye, which he had not been able to shut, and looked really unwell. Despite this he got straight on to me to find out who the sponsor was that would have paid for him to drive for us if he had left Ferrari. He obviously wanted a personal deal. When he got back from Japan, Ferrari asked what he would do next time it rained during a race. Being Niki, he replied: 'The same thing as in Japan if I think it's dangerous.' His answer provoked a summons to Maranello to discuss his future, but before setting off he made quite certain of alternative accommodation for 1977 should he have needed it by calling some English teams including ours. By then, with his 1975 championship win and the sensational events of 1976, we were assured of finance should he have joined our team.

However often I made the journey to South America for the first race of the new season, there was always an enormous sense of elation stepping from an icy European winter into the damp heat of Rio de Janeiro, our first stop in Latin America. It is instant summer and the relief is so intense after the European cold you wonder why everyone there seems to be suffering from the heat.

Robin arrived in Buenos Aires with our bags very late and rather the worse for wear after coming via Caracas following problems with the flights. We got back to the hotel in the early hours after an interesting drive through army roadblocks. In 1977, Buenos Aires was like Belfast, only with the added excitement of the South American temperament. There were odd bursts of gunfire and an incident seemed possible at any moment.

Our six-wheeler was not ready and we arrived in Argentina with only slightly modified versions of the 1976 cars. Getting the six-wheeler to work with the complexities of four driven wheels and two differentials proved difficult. With two inexperienced drivers, we recruited Howden Ganley to do the testing and he demonstrated that the gain in straight-line speed over a conventional car was spectacular. Traction was also extremely good and the rear wing worked much better without the large rear wheels because there was a smoother airflow. However, more work was required to ensure complete reliability.

Unhappily, before it could be completed the FIA brought in a rule that Formula One cars could have only four wheels, a major disappointment. Howden still enthuses about the car today and I have no doubt it would have given us a significant performance advantage. Other teams would have been able to copy it but it would have taken them several months. The only consolation was the success of a version of the six-wheeler in hill climb and historic events. Together with the loss of my vertical wing (chapter 4) this was the second really annoying FIA rule change at short notice that cost us time, money and a potential winning edge.

During the first official practice there was an explosion in one of the cars just after it passed the pits. Bits of car were flying through the air and spooked all the soldiers guarding the race into throwing themselves to the ground and adopting firing positions. It also caused a stampede in the pits, but in the middle of the confusion Ian recorded a decent time despite braking hard to avoid the debris. The organisers stopped practice and would not restart it for the last five minutes. Juan Manuel Fangio, who was in charge, blithely said there was more practice tomorrow, which was perfectly true but showed how little he knew of the minute-by-minute planning of a modern Grand Prix practice period.

The fire extinguisher in Mario Andretti's Lotus had been the source of the explosion: as pressure built up due to the heat, a safety valve had apparently not functioned and it had detonated with such force that the whole front of the car back to and including the pedals had been destroyed. Mario had managed to slow the car from 160 mph with no brakes, his visor covered in oil and peering through a small hole in the bodywork that had peeled back over his head. I met him later in the hotel waiting for the lift. He said the worst part was that he'd had a severe blow to his feet, which were numb, and as he slowed the car he suspected his toes had been blown off. His anxiety had been to get out and see if they were still there. We talked about how most cars had the extinguisher under the seat. 'Yeah ... a thing like that could de-nut you,' he said. We agreed that would be even worse than the toes.

The next day at breakfast I bumped into Niki and congratulated him on being faster than Reutemann in practice. 'I was really trying, I tell you,' he said. 'And I am really happy to be in front of him. He is the big hero now with the Old Man and I am the big wanker. Oh, I say, let Mr Reutemann do the testing. I will go to Argentina and do my best but if the car is shit it's his car not mine. Now the car is really bad and I am trying like hell to be quicker than him.' I said if he could go quicker in

Argentina, he would be quicker everywhere and his position then would be very strong. Reutemann would be discredited as a test driver by the poor performance of the car and, worse still, demonstrably slower than Niki. 'This is what I am trying. You know, in Ricard I was not even allowed in the pit – in case I disturb Mr Reutemann,' he said contemptuously. 'You really looked ill that time in Ricard,' I said. 'I know, I was, but now I am a hundred per cent,' he replied. Despite the scars he looked as fit and alert as ever.

'Did you feel depressed after Japan?' I asked. 'No, I never regretted it. You know how tired we are at the end of the season – you, us, the mechanics, everyone. Well, after what happened to me I was nearly dead, I had no reserves left. So when the race started, I couldn't see and I was aquaplaning everywhere – it was obvious madness. I had nothing left to make myself put the foot down and go. So I stopped.' I knew exactly what he meant. 'You know what I don't like is the sneaky way Reutemann got into Ferrari when things were bad for me – this is what I am really angry about.'

'Oh, come on, Niki – you would have done exactly the same,' I said. 'You of all people.' He smiled. 'OK, but then he is stupid because if he can do this to me, he should realise I will do it ten times worse to him.' It struck me just how much Niki had developed since his early days with us and that I should really like to have him back at March. Reutemann only ever had one chance and that was that Niki had lost his speed. It was now clear that he had not and I thought Reutemann would be about ready to give up by Spain. Niki, of course, went on to win the 1977 World Championship and, having thus conclusively won the contest with Ferrari that started at the Ricard test session, departed to join Bernie's team for the 1978 season.

By the end of the second day's practice our two drivers were, as predicted, at the back and proving better at damaging their engines than giving us the information on the cars' handling, which is essential for good performance. However, we had anticipated this – we knew it would be a struggle for the first few races. As Niki had said during breakfast: 'I don't know how you do it – every year you start again with new drivers. Do you give them a form to fill: name, address, telephone number ...?' I thought to myself, you're right – next year it might be an idea to start with you.

After the race, which was won by Wolf's Jody Scheckter, Derek Gardner (Tyrrell's designer) and I went together to the airport. We discussed car technicalities over dinner in that vaguely defensive manner of bluff and counter-bluff we all used, ever fearful of giving something away. Then Niki appeared, followed by Bernie and Gordon Murray, with Teddy Mayer. Teddy was blaming himself for a suspension failure on James's car – he thought he had put too many spacers in the suspension and it had gone solid. Bernie was pleased with his second place but justifiably disappointed he had not won. Niki was in a determined mood, having run well ahead of Reutemann until his engine had failed and now he was going back to confront the Old Man. 'The car has never been so bad. It understeers into the corner then oversteers at the exit and no way to get rid of it. So I am going to tell them, OK – I am ready to work – let's do some proper testing. So either we work and do it properly or I have the biggest wank you ever see while they pay me a fortune.' The Ferrari technicians in Argentina wanted to get Forghieri, their chief engineer, out to Brazil for the next race, thinking he might cure the problem. But Niki was in no doubt – the problem was fundamental and needed a major development programme.

Then Niki raised the question of why the McLaren was so fast – it was clearly superior in both practice and the race. We agreed it was not particularly good aerodynamically, wasn't light, probably had an above average engine and a six-speed gearbox (compared with five in all the other cars except the Brabhams), but none of these things could really explain its performance. 'Ah,' I said, 'now we are getting into the area which cannot be discussed. Robin and I are certain we know and I daresay Derek is' – he nodded – 'and this is the area where all the work will take place.' I wondered if Derek really thought he knew and, if so, whether his theory was the same as ours. Niki did not pretend to know but I could see he was intensely curious. As the discussion developed I became more and more convinced that he was the most intelligent driver by far – and that it would be an immense advantage to have him in the team.

Six weeks after that discussion in the Buenos Aires airport, I was in South Africa for the Grand Prix and standing on the pit wall exactly opposite the spot where a marshal ran across the track with a fire extinguisher and was hit by Tom Pryce in his Shadow, killing both. It was a horrific thing to witness from a few feet away and desperately sad to see Tom's young wife utterly distraught on the flight back to London. Yet again I asked myself why I was involved in this and, to make matters worse, Robin had to leave Formula One to me in order to concentrate once again on Formula Two. Neither Ian nor Alex lived up to our hopes, or would have been able to help us develop a revolutionary six-wheel car. After all the initial promise, it turned out to be a very uninspiring season.

I was spending an increasing amount of time on FOCA business with Bernie and, at the same time, both Robin and I had just about exhausted our enthusiasm for carrying on competing in

Formula One. When we received an offer to sell March's Formula One assets to the ATS team, we took it; and by late autumn 1977, at the end of our eighth season, we got out of Formula One. March was now solely a commercial racing car builder and no longer needed me. We had very competent people to sell the cars and Robin was able to take overall charge both technically and commercially. I remained a director of the company, but sold my shares to Robin and had no further direct involvement in the company we had built.

Our cars had been immensely successful. During the 1970s March won a large number of Japanese and European championships, as well as innumerable American championships and racing series. We became the world's biggest and most successful commercial racing car constructors and, at that time, the European Formula Two Championship was not far behind Formula One. Its prestige only started to decline when the established Formula One drivers stopped taking part but, even then, each race was a major event in its own right and attracted large crowds.

With such clear superiority in all the main racing categories you would have expected March to be a leading Formula One team. That we were not was almost certainly because we never found a major sponsor. Had I found the money, I think we would have established ourselves consistently among the elite teams. Then we might even have given up the commercial racing car business or hived it off as a separate company. When Bernie took over Brabham at the end of 1971, it had a thriving business building cars for Formula Two, Three and similar categories, just like March. But he found it very difficult and soon gave up to concentrate on Formula One. I am sure we would have been frontrunners in Formula One had we been able to do the same.

The point was proved after we stopped Formula One and I left. Robin went on to great success in American oval racing, which takes place on oval-shaped circuits usually with banked corners (unlike almost all race circuits in Europe and around the world – including America – which have corners like ordinary roads) and in those days was every bit as competitive and technically sophisticated as Formula One. He started by selling an adapted Formula One car to an American team. It worked really well and other sales followed. The same technical and production team that had been so successful in European Formula Two then began producing cars for the top American single-seat championship and March became the leading producer of these cars. At one point, of 33 cars starting the Indianapolis 500, no fewer than 31 were built by March in Bicester. In this period, March came through the elaborate Indianapolis qualifying procedures to gain pole position five times and record five victories in succession from 1983.

Understandably, Robin became a sort of icon at Indianapolis. He would go to a car, listen to the driver's comments on how the car was handling and advise the team on adjustments to improve the set-up. Because he was always able to make the car perform better, his skill would motivate the driver to improve his lap time. Inevitably, there was a certain amount of jealousy among the old Indianapolis hands and there was a story (apocryphal, I'm sure) that it sometimes amused him to make meaningless changes to the set-up, whereupon the driver would nevertheless immediately improve his lap time. 'Two clicks on rebound on the left rear damper' was said to be one of his favourites, something even the most expert driver would find difficult to detect. But they couldn't argue with the results. Robin called it blessing the car and his services were much in demand.

March went on to become a public company traded on the stock exchange but, in the end, even Robin had had enough. The moment came on a flight to Miami. He sealed his decision with a quantity of brandy large enough to prompt a humorous customs official in the arrival hall to suggest he should perhaps pay alcohol duty on himself.

There is much more to tell about Robin, including his adventures in rallying, but that must be left for him. He made a great contribution to British motor sport. As for me, giving up running a team was far from the end of my immersion in Formula One. I was about to become ever more entangled in the sport, its politics and the battle to transform and control it.

9

FOCA: THE EARLY DAYS

In parallel with my work for March, I had also been heavily involved with the Formula One teams' association. Starting in 1969, I attended the meetings on behalf of March and played an increasingly prominent role in the association's affairs. Then, at the end of 1971, Bernie Ecclestone bought the Brabham team and appeared at his first meeting. I had known him slightly before then as he had been around Formula One since the 1950s, but we'd never had any meaningful contact. During that first meeting it quickly became clear that here was someone who understood business as well as motor racing, a very different character from the other team principals who made up what was then called the Formula One Constructors' and Entrants' Association. They were all enthusiasts and ex-racers, good at motor racing but not really connected to the world outside.

Those like Colin Chapman who had serious outside businesses tended to send their team managers to the meetings rather than come themselves. Bernie, too, had a number of business interests beyond Brabham but plainly intended to be hands-on. Pretty soon we formed an alliance and, before long, he and I were negotiating on behalf of all the teams.

Back then I was a very straightforward barrister while Bernie was renowned as the country's top used car dealer. Because of his reputation, other dealers would come from all over the UK to try to get the better of him. Some of them ended up phoning him from a motorway service area on their way home to clarify exactly what deal they had done. It was said that he could value an entire showroom of cars at a glance. At dealers' meetings where batches of cars were swapped, he was reputed to introduce two or three fictitious cars into negotiations and, at the end of an evening of swapping, end up with his fictitious cars back plus two or three real ones. This was said to have stopped when, to liven things up (a Bernie trait – he was easily bored without a challenge), he introduced an imaginary articulated lorry into the swaps one day and had to pay a lot to purchase it later from a Manchester dealer who had realised what was going on.

I really liked the idea of working with someone whose brain was that fast. Working with him was also fun, because the jokes came thick and fast. One was a competition between us to see who could be first to get a particular team principal to do or say something we had agreed on beforehand. Another typical Bernie joke was sprung when I had arranged to join him for coffee in the workingmen's cafe where he met his cronies every Saturday morning. After I ordered my coffee, the waitress appeared with a huge English breakfast, put it in front of me and took no notice when I said I just wanted a coffee. It turned out he'd told her his friend had just been released from prison that morning and would be very hungry, but too proud to accept food he couldn't pay for. She was to put a big breakfast in front of him as soon as he sat down, and not take no for an answer.

But Bernie's speed of thought was also a weakness. He was so good at tactics and opportunism that he had no need to worry about strategy. Each situation was turned to his advantage. His old solicitor from his car-dealing days once said to me he had 'a great talent for getting himself out of trouble – that he got himself into in the first place'. This did not always work, especially in the plodding and meticulous world of lawyers and High Court judges. His relative inability to think strategically led (at least in my view) to him making errors when Formula One finances entered the big league and he had to deal with the City. But as a master tactician he has been immensely and deservedly successful.

In the early days, one of Bernie's sayings was that the only place he wanted respect was in his bank manager's office. I found this attitude very appealing, contrasting markedly with the vanity and needless self-promotion of many in Formula One. Some might say that principle slipped somewhat in his later years, but even now you seldom see him profiling despite all the opportunities a Formula One race provides. For instance, he has never been on the podium with the drivers.

At that stage of FOCA's development a division of labour between Bernie and me was beginning to emerge: he was interested in the business while I was fascinated by the politics. We spent a long time on the phone almost every evening. He wanted to make the teams, but above all himself, prosperous while my goal was to stop what I saw as elderly and incompetent people interfering in 'our' sport.

As the governing body, the FIA united all the motoring clubs that organised the races (see appendix) and had complete control over every aspect of Formula One, including the rules. The competing teams had no say other than through two national clubs, the UK's RAC and Italy's ACI. But these were just two of the 15 members of the Commission Sportive Internationale, or CSI, the FIA's sporting committee. The commercial interests of the race organisers, who wanted to minimise their costs, were in direct conflict with those of the teams, who wanted to be paid as much as possible to participate. Eight of the 15 CSI member countries were race organisers but had no team, while Italy and the UK were potentially conflicted, being race organisers as well as representing their country's teams. In addition to the CSI rules, each organiser decided his own race and practice schedules and the date of his event; all he needed was CSI approval. The teams' position was, to say the least, weak.

This would have been bad enough if the CSI members had been experienced motor racing professionals, but they were mainly former wealthy gentlemen drivers plus a few club officials. The FIA president was Prince Paul Alfons von Metternich-Winneburg, a former racer, soldier and great-grandson of Klemens von Metternich, the Habsburg Empire politician who established the Congress of Vienna in 1815. His successor, Jean-Marie Balestre (see below), was always proud of the fact that, with one brief exception, he was the first FIA president without a grand European title.

This was what Bernie and I were up against when we started in 1972. One of our first deals centred on a non-championship race in Brazil and was made with the agreement of the Brazilian club. The teams all wanted to go but TV Rede Globo, who were promoting and paying for the race, couldn't send the money in advance because of exchange control regulations. Without the certainty of payment the teams were unwilling to travel, but it was agreed that I should fly to São Paulo, collect the money in cash and call Bernie once it was in the hotel safe. Only then would the teams load the cars.

When I arrived, it was obvious Rede Globo was a huge company and entirely serious, but its CEO explained it was going to be absurdly expensive for them to buy that many dollars on the black market and give me the whole sum in cash. Once the race was run, they said, the central bank would permit them to export the agreed fee, so I decided to take the risk and gave the green light. The teams arrived and raced, the money was all paid, and a Brazilian World Championship race followed a year later. It has been a fixture ever since. During the 1970s it was always difficult to get permission to export the money. To make things easier for the promoter, we would be given a certain amount of cash in local currency on arrival and hand enough to the teams to pay their hotel bills and expenses, which would then be deducted from their prize money.

In Rio, I collected the money from a nondescript office that looked like a travel agency where, once identified, I was led to a back room with security cameras everywhere. Then a man would enter with a large quantity of cash and count it out on the table. On my first visit I simply packed it into in my briefcase and made to go. Everyone was horrified. Where were my armed guards? No one knew what was in the case, I thought, and walking down the street with armed heavies seemed to advertise that you had something valuable. I didn't fancy a gunfight with me in the middle. But they also pointed out that the Grand Prix was at Interlagos and I had to take the plane down to São Paulo – what if the airport security look in your briefcase? Fortunately they didn't.

Soon after the Brazil race, Argentina decided it, too, wanted a Grand Prix. There was a great tradition of Argentinian drivers including Juan Manuel Fangio and Carlos Reutemann, who had begun to make a real impression. Bernie and I met some generals from the Argentinian military junta near Heathrow. The atmosphere was stiff, since they were clearly more used to giving orders than negotiating. They had brought a rather bulky old-fashioned tape recorder to record the proceedings, but when they weren't looking Bernie interfered with it and the tape started to spool on to the floor. Nevertheless, we did a deal.

Marco Piccinini, Enzo Ferrari's choice to succeed Luca di Montezemolo as team manager, appeared for the first time at an early Argentinian race. We decided the newcomer was a natural target for a joke. Bernie sent a journalist to the Ferrari pit to ask Marco why Ferrari had not objected to the race being shortened, explaining that, with their Alfa Romeo 12-cylinder engines, Bernie's Brabhams could not hold enough fuel to complete the distance so he had managed to persuade the officials to truncate it. All the other teams were peering through small gaps in the garage doors as Marco stomped off to the control tower to confront the officials, knowing it was completely forbidden to make a change of that kind without the agreement of all the competitors.

Sure enough, there was a call over the PA summoning 'Mr Ecclestone' to the tower. Once there, Bernie listened to the arguments then asked Marco in front of the officials why Ferrari wanted the race shortened. The officials were, of course, completely bemused – no one had said anything to them about shortening the race and Marco was the one complaining about it being shortened, not demanding that it happen. You can imagine how much worse the language barrier must have made the resulting confusion.

I bumped into Marco in the car park a short time later, as I was about to leave for the hotel. Although in his early twenties he was already a serious and intelligent man, and couldn't understand the trick or our motives for playing it. I tried to explain how in

England on a building site, they would send the new employee to fetch some rubber nails, tartan paint and such like, but I didn't get the impression he thought it at all funny.

In 1971 there had been a problem at the Monaco Grand Prix when only 18 starters were allowed from the 23 cars present, among them Mario Andretti, now driving for Ferrari. He had mechanical problems in the only dry practice session. As a result, he didn't qualify for the grid and could not start despite having won the South African Grand Prix two months earlier and lying second in the World Championship.

There was no real reason for 18 starters. The number was derived from a complicated FIA formula dreamt up by one of the old boys running the sport. It included the length of the circuit and the maximum speed reached by the cars but, when questioned, they could provide no rational basis for their formula. The teams agreed to ask for a sensible number of starters at Monaco and elsewhere for the 1972 season.

After the arguments in 1971, the Monaco club had a new, much younger president, Michel Boeri. Bernie and I had met him in Madrid at the previous race and we thought the problem was fixed. We had agreed there would be 25 starters at Monaco but when I arrived in Monte Carlo in the early hours of the first day of practice, I found a note waiting for me from Andrew Ferguson, the secretary of the teams' association, saying the organisers had decreed there would not be 25 starters after all.

That year, the teams were all sharing an underground garage more or less where the Grimaldi Forum is now. Bernie and I called a meeting and it was agreed that no one would practise until the organisers confirmed that 25 cars would start the race. Shortly after the start of the scheduled session, the French Matra was at the top of the ramp ready to go out. Then it was wheeled back into the garage, which sent a very clear message: if even the French, who were practically on home territory, were with us, it was serious.

The spectators were looking at an empty circuit, wondering what was going on. Suddenly, a number of police appeared, taking up positions at the garage exits, implying that if we didn't run, they would impound the cars and sue us for damages in the Monaco courts. To test the situation (but also for his amusement) Bernie got in one of his Brabhams and had his mechanics push it to the entrance where a policeman was blocking the way. The car went over the policeman's foot. Much whistle blowing and shouting resulted, but it became obvious this was a genuine threat. Given the sort of people running the teams in those days (and it would probably be the same today), this simply made us more determined than ever.

Shortly after the appearance of the police, a deputation from the organisers turned up, headed by Boeri. Having (as they thought) put on the squeeze, they were ready to negotiate. In fact, they were under more pressure than we were because the public were getting restive, whistling and catcalling round the empty circuit. I was deputed to walk up the ramp and talk to them because I spoke French. We had a deal, I said. Twenty-five cars would start the race – and we wouldn't go out to practise until our agreement was confirmed in writing.

They explained the impasse was not the Automobile Club de Monaco's fault but the FIA's insistence that we adhere to their formula restricting the number of cars; they were confident they could persuade the FIA to concede once its representative turned up, but we must start practice immediately to appease the public.

In those early days they probably thought we were naive. Of course we knew that once the teams had practised and one had an advantage, our unity would break down. I said no: first sign the agreement, then we practise. But, they told me, only the FIA representative could sign and he was nowhere to be found. 'Well, you'd better find him,' I replied, knowing we had to be completely intransigent. 'We are not going to practise until he has signed.' A short time later an old boy with white hair appeared and signed the document we had prepared on the roof of a car parked nearby. We had won and practice began.

Another problem back then was passes, which were issued at the organiser's discretion. We never knew how many we were going to receive and some races insisted on a paradoxical system where passes were available only from the circuit office – which could not be reached without a pass. At a FOCA meeting before the 1974 Monza race, Bernie and I suggested we issue our own passes. Peter Warr, the Team Lotus manager, explained patiently that we would be refused entry with homemade passes. But if we all have our own passes and refuse to use theirs, we said, they will realise pretty soon that they will have to let us in if they want a motor race.

On our charter flight to Milan for the Italian Grand Prix, everyone was given one of our new passes, a simple piece of yellow cardboard with 'Monza' and 'Box' printed on it because we thought 'Box' was the Italian for 'pits'. When we got to the circuit the next day, the Monza gatekeepers, ever pragmatic motor sport aficionados, let us in without difficulty. They had been surprised when the first mechanics arrived early with our passes, but quickly got the message. This was an important victory in the battle to control Formula One and led us to make our own permanent FOCA passes valid for the entire season. The only place we had trouble when the new system really got going the following year was Circuit Paul Ricard for the French Grand Prix, where I remember driving into the paddock with a number of gatekeepers hanging on the car like ripe fruit.

In 1975 Bernie and I went to Brussels to negotiate the teams' European prize fund. This was our first encounter with Jean-Marie Balestre, then head of the French Federation, later to become president of the FIA's CSI, motor sport division, and eventually president of the FIA itself. His background was in newspapers; he had worked closely with Robert Hersant, the French newspaper magnate and politician. Both had controversial careers during the Second World War: Hersant was later penalised for collaboration and photographs even exist of Balestre in SS uniform. His enemies used to produce them at every opportunity. On the Continent, membership of the SS was more or less OK for a German, but definitely not considered appropriate for a Frenchman.

However, Balestre said he was at all times working undercover for the French Resistance. Although he spent some time in prison after the war, he eventually received the Légion d'honneur for his services to France, as well as a Resistance pension. Late one night over a second bottle of wine, he told me how difficult it had been at the beginning of the war. He had been only 18 when the war started. More recently, reading Philip Short's biography of François Mitterrand, I began to understand how nuanced and ambiguous things were in France at that time and feel more sympathetic towards Balestre than we did back in the 1980s.

At that first meeting we had no idea that he was soon to play such a major role in our lives. He already had a reputation for being tough and was sitting at the table with other FIA notables, including Metternich. Apart from the odd local rally or hill climb, Balestre had never competed but had been a successful journalist and editor of the French magazine *L'Auto-Journal* before engaging in motor sport politics at national level. It was obvious he was out to make an impression, and I think he wanted to sort us out to show his fellow FIA bosses how tough he was. It was certainly true that by then we were already seen in FIA circles as far too big for our boots.

Bernie loved occasions like this. He got up from the table as Balestre began to speak and started to walk around the room adjusting the pictures. Balestre was trying to explain on behalf of the race promoters that there was no more money, they could not afford the prize fund we wanted, but Bernie appeared to be wholly preoccupied with the art and not listening. Balestre became so tense he snapped the pencil he was holding and then we cranked up the pressure by employing our dependable tactic: we said we had to leave to catch our plane (in fact, we were booked on a much later flight).

Faced with the talks breaking down and having to explain to the other organisers that there was no agreement, which would mean that none of them could prepare a budget, they pleaded with us to stay longer. I finally relented and agreed to see if we could catch a later flight, and came back in to say I had succeeded but the airline couldn't hold the seats for long. On our way out, Bernie slipped in an extra $5000 per race for our prize fund, but by then they were too tired and bemused to resist.

The next skirmish arose during the 1975 German Grand Prix when we had a difficult negotiation with the organisers of the Canadian Grand Prix, who refused to meet our asking price. Eventually, we set a deadline of midnight and Bernie told them if they hadn't agreed by then, we would not race in Canada that year. The race was less than two months away and transport arrangements were already pressing. They ignored him, so the following morning we announced the cancellation of the Canadian race. Immediately the organisers contacted us to say they would pay after all.

I arrived late to the meeting of the teams in the Nürburgring paddock to find all except Bernie wanting to go. It's OK, they said, the organisers have agreed the money so we can go – Canada is an important race and the sponsors want us there. I joined in, arguing that, if we went, every negotiation would end in cancellation before a deal could be done. Once you threaten, you must carry out the threat even if you don't want to, otherwise you lose all your credibility. After a long discussion the majority eventually agreed. We maintained our stance and the race was cancelled.

The organisers were furious and sued everyone including the FIA but ultimately lost. Although it would have been much easier to go, sticking to our guns made all the race promoters take us more seriously. From then on they knew that deadlines mattered and a threat to cancel would be carried out.

From 1972 to 1978 we endured a seemingly never-ending succession of confrontations with the FIA's CSI, both in its guise as rule-maker and when it was acting (or trying to act) as a cartel of race organisers. While the last thing we wanted was the organisers acting in concert, the FIA's aim was to unite them. The first serious attempt to counter us was run by Henri Treu, a Dutchman with a family yacht business, who set up a race promoters' association. When that didn't work the CSI deployed its secretary-general, Claude Le Guezec, who was in charge at the time of our 1975 confrontation in Brussels. Claude, a former racer, was more formidable than Treu, but a bit of research in the Gray's Inn library had given us a new weapon in the shape of (then) Articles 85 (no price fixing) and 86 (no abuse of a dominant position) of the Treaty of Rome. However, we never had to deploy EU competition law against Le Guezec because he was soon pretty much on our side.

In the paddock immediately after the very wet 1976 Japanese Grand Prix I bumped into Huschke von Hanstein, a leading figure in German motor sport and the CSI. By then the constructors as a whole faced a major battle with World Championship Racing, a grouping of race organisers backed by the CSI and led by Pat Duffeler, who had been in charge of the Marlboro Formula One sponsorship programme. Duffeler was well known to all the race organisers and to the CSI. As early as 1972 he had organised dinner parties for senior CSI members where they had found themselves sitting next to very attractive young hostesses hired by the tobacco company. As men do, the poor old boys fancied their chances but the ladies always disappeared on the stroke of midnight when their contractual time was up. WCR planned to unite the organisers and finally defeat us.

If they succeeded, all the hard-won improvements in Formula One that Bernie and I had introduced in the four years since we started working together would be lost and it would be back to the old ways: race schedules to suit each individual organiser rather than our mechanics, minimal prize money and no say for the British teams on the technical rules. Inevitably, the brunt of this contest would fall on Bernie and me – as if we had not got enough to do – and there would be reprisals against both of us as the architects of change should WCR win.

Von Hanstein was WCR's leading CSI supporter and was able to commit the German and Austrian races. I knew we faced a protracted and arduous battle with WCR. We also faced the prospect of Duffeler becoming a major figure in racing and interfering with all our plans to expand the sport and increase its importance. Worse, he would inevitably come under the influence of his backers, the militant old guard among the race organisers who wanted to keep the sport just as it had been in the days of Fangio. They did not understand that it needed to evolve and change, become more professional and modern, or face the prospect of declining to the point where there was not enough money to maintain it.

'Huschke, why don't you support us instead of Duffeler? Why do we have to have these internal fights instead of working together to promote the sport?' I asked.

'It's your friend, the little guy,' he replied. 'Each year he wants more and more money and the organisers can't afford it – now he wants $350,000. Obviously we have to do something.'

'Come on, Huschke,' I said, 'you know that's not the issue. Bernie and I have always said FOCA will share the profit or loss with any organiser, but they always refuse. I've never known people so anxious to keep their losses to themselves. You know you should come in with us – it's more fun on the winning side.'

I felt less confident than I sounded – and Huschke wandered off into the gloom and puddles looking quite happy and laughing quietly to himself. One could not help rather liking him despite him being one of our more dangerous opponents. It was interesting that he was, in effect, blaming the foundation of WCR on Bernie's latest prize-money scheme.

Shortly after my return from Japan I flew to Nice, which I have always preferred in the winter because there are no crowds, the weather is usually beautiful and one feels a sense of instant relaxation. I found Count Zanon in a restaurant with his wife and we started lunch. Ronnie and Barbro joined us a little later, having come from their flat in Monaco. Ronnie had just had his first drive in the six-wheel Tyrrell and I was curious to hear what he thought of it. His impression was that it had much better brakes than the March, as we had expected, but that otherwise it was difficult to distinguish from an ordinary car. The only effect of the four small front wheels was to make the bumps in the track more noticeable.

But I was even more curious about the Monaco race. I knew WCR was a Monaco company and Michel Boeri, the president of the Monaco club, was a leading WCR supporter on the CSI. His race was one of those that would not agree our terms, so I asked Ronnie what he had heard. He said the Monaco organisers were not in the least worried because they would simply run a Formula Two race if FOCA would not go and were confident they would get all the top drivers. They don't seem to realise, said Ronnie, that the drivers are all under contract and are anyway on the side of the constructors. I told him that Monaco did not seem to understand that they had upset so many people – including sponsors – at one time or another; that there was a formidable group of people who would take some pleasure in putting an end to that race. This was partly true and I knew it would make them worry a bit when it got back. It does no harm to make an opponent feel uneasy and I felt there was room for a little worry in the Principality.

A few days later, Bernie and I met the Austrian organisers at Bernie's flat in London. They obviously wanted to do a deal, but were prevented by a board who felt they ought to follow Germany. We could be reasonably sure that Brazil, South Africa, Long Beach, Japan, Belgium, Sweden, Britain, Watkins Glen and Canada were on our side, while WCR were backed by Argentina, Spain, Monaco, France, Germany and Italy. Austria and Holland were in the balance, so it was important to win over Austria to break up their stranglehold on that solid group of races in August.

We worked out a contract with the two Austrians, making a concession about practice times, and they left with the draft to seek board approval. Bernie spent the next week trying to consolidate our position with the friendly races and make inroads among the unfriendly ones. The Germans would probably have come over if we had agreed to race on the Nürburgring, but this would have involved breaking faith with the drivers and was out of the question following our agreement with them that the 'Ring was quite simply too dangerous for modern Formula One cars. We had all agreed 1976 would be the last race on the circuit even before Niki Lauda's accident.

While all this was going on, Duffeler was constantly trying to fix a meeting with Bernie and even waited for him when he went to collect Niki to take him to Brands Hatch for James Hunt's victory celebration. I advised strongly against meeting him on two grounds. First, it would give him status – he would find it difficult to take the constructors on if we ignored him. Secondly, there was a possibility that we might have to attack the CSI in the courts for backing WCR, and negotiating with it might prejudice our position. The basis of a legal attack would have been to restrain the CSI from using its monopoly position to influence commercial matters in the sport, using the Treaty of Rome again. We might claim the CSI was doing this by backing WCR, so it was important that Bernie should reject Duffeler's advances.

First, however, there was a constructors' meeting, held as usual at a hotel near Heathrow. Bernie and I recounted the latest news from the WCR battle amid much hilarity, but we warned the members that it was not going to be easy. Someone suggested that, as there was no Ferrari representative at the meeting

(Daniele Audetto having already left), Bernie should go and see Enzo Ferrari to keep him informed, a proposal that was expanded to include me. Bernie and I did not tell the meeting that we had already made arrangements for a visit the following Thursday because we knew that Ferrari's support in the crisis was essential. We believed he would back us if he were fully briefed, and it was crucial that we dispel the assumption that the argument was principally about money, despite all reports to the contrary.

We wanted to make clear to him that the whole contest was one for control of Formula One; whether we could continue to have practice times to suit the teams or whether they should be scheduled to suit the lunch hour of the local dignitaries; whether we could continue to have our own pit passes or whether we would have to beg for them (perhaps to Mr Duffeler) then spend the night locating personnel, sponsors, drivers and so forth to give them their passes; plus a number of similar issues which were trivial to anyone except those who earned their living in motor racing.

That night, Bernie and I had dinner with the RAC chairman, Sir Clive Bossom (whose father's name, Winston Churchill famously said, 'means neither one thing nor the other'). Also there were Dean Delamont, head of the RAC's motor sport division and a powerful figure in the CSI, and Jack Sears, once an outstanding driver and at that point chairman of the RAC Competitions Committee. We had an extremely good dinner and Sir Clive told me at one point that the RAC had some 80,000 bottles of claret in the cellar. I made a mental note that I ought to try to become a member.

We explained our fears about the WCR situation; that we had heard rumours (and read in the *Sunday Times*) of financial links

between WCR and members of the CSI and FIA; how concerned we were that the CSI might use its power to revoke
licences in order to back a commercial body like WCR; and that
we felt it was wrong that the FIA should have a secret Swiss company.

They seemed genuinely shocked at the suggestion that there
might be some impropriety and Sir Clive decided to use his position as a vice-president of the FIA to get sight of the FIA
accounts. Dean confirmed our view that, having published the
calendar, the CSI could not cancel races or revoke circuit
licences, and certainly not in order to force WCR on an unwilling organiser. We discussed the *Sunday Times* story and the
possibility of further revelations (which came about ten days
later), and decided that we should all do what we could to calm
the situation while Sir Clive discovered what the true facts were.
We left the dinner feeling that the RAC were genuine in their
concern and would be formidable allies if, as seemed very probable, the CSI overstepped the bounds of their remit as the
governing body of a sport.

Having travelled to Italy the previous day, we set out in thick
fog at 7.30am from our Milan hotel for our Thursday meeting in
Maranello. When we got there we were ushered straight into
Enzo Ferrari's presence. He was then 80 years old and enormously impressive, an example of someone who had stayed at
work despite his age. He still had all his faculties, reinforced by
the authority of his vast experience. We were aware, as Bernie
had said on the way down, that the 'old boy has forgotten more
strokes than you and I could think up in a month. He could
destroy Duffeler and that mob, no trouble at all.' Bernie used to
say he had met only two people he would really want to be like,
and one of them was Ferrari. I always suspected the second one

didn't exist, but Bernie intended each of his friends to think they were the one and be suitably pleased.

'Now we can do something useful,' Ferrari said as we sat down, making it clear he shared our view that the occasional constructors' gatherings in Maranello were not very helpful (although enjoyable) but a meeting of this kind could be. He spoke no English but he had a way of speaking which was so clear that even with my limited knowledge of Italian, picked up from Brambilla, I managed to communicate with him quite well.

We quickly found we were at one on objectives and tactics. He was strongly of the view that we should steer the row with the CSI and WCR away from money, which was in any event not the main issue, and on to the real questions of where the sport was going and how it should be run. He told Bernie to talk less about money, more about the sport. 'You should never let people know you're running a brothel,' he said. 'You have to pretend it's a hotel and keep the brothel in the basement.' Bernie saw the wisdom of this and started talking about safety and the sport in public, saving the finance for his dealings with promoters.

Ferrari also felt we should prepare and publish formal statutes for the constructors' association instead of keeping them secret. He pointed out that the power base of WCR was Monaco, where the company was registered, and the Monaco club's president, Michel Boeri, was their main CSI supporter. 'That is easily dealt with,' he said. 'We anyway don't want to race at Monaco, that race is a farce – the road is too narrow, no one overtakes and it discredits motor racing by presenting a false image of the sport to the public.'

Bernie and I agreed with all this and the more we talked, the clearer it became that his approach and ours were the same. This was a considerable relief because he was a formidable, if not essential, ally in the fight to repel WCR and was obviously going to make a big contribution to the actual planning of the battle. With Ferrari on our side, we were 100 per cent stronger.

We crossed the road to their private restaurant, by now getting rather tight for time as our flight to London was at 5.15pm. However, someone had mentioned I was a wine enthusiast, so Piero Ferrari immediately brought out some remarkable bottles from his father's private store. The lunch had started in a good atmosphere after the successful meeting and got more and more jolly as the excellent wine went round. As I was the driver, I could see Bernie (who hardly drinks at all) getting a bit nervous at the thought of me driving 150 miles back to Milan in the fog. We made it to Linate airport but the fog was dreadful and the plane sat at the end of the runway for nearly 30 minutes, hoping the fog would lift. It did and we got off, but not before I resolved I would not leave England again until I was on the plane to Argentina at the start of the 1977 season.

Yet two days later, we were in the air again – this time heading for Brussels. In 1975 we had signed a three-year agreement with Zolder for the Belgian Grand Prix, an agreement that had become very expensive for the organisers due to currency fluctuations. Bernie had offered them a new, cheaper deal, more in line with what other countries were paying, provided they could get the Belgian club (the RACB), in the shape of Count de Liedekerke, its vice-president and chairman of its motor sport committee, to countersign the contract. If we could win over Belgium conclusively by securing the club as well as the organiser, it would be a major blow to WCR, all the more effective because Pierre Ugeux, the president of the CSI, was Belgian and, we thought, in WCR's camp.

The Zolder organisers met us at the airport and had a typist to prepare the new contract, but there was no Count de Liede-kerke. He was shooting, we were told, but would countersign the next day. We demanded they telephone him, and it became clear as they talked to him that it was not going to be so straightfor-ward. We had only agreed to go because they had promised us the count, and we informed them that we would not sign unless he did. So we agreed the contract, got it typed up and set off to find the count's shooting party.

After a lot of searching we found his rather nice chateau, spir-ited him away from his guests and listened while he said he thought the contract fine but it needed his committee's approval.

'OK, forget it,' we said, playing hardball again. 'No, no, we must agree,' they insisted. So in the end the count signed – sub-ject only to repudiation by the RACB motor sport committee. We thought it would be harder for the committee to repudiate its chairman's signature than refuse to ratify an agreement. We returned home in good humour – now we could claim Belgium was with us, and various legal measures were open to us under Common Market law if the club repudiated our agreement and tried to cancel the race.

Next day there was another constructors' meeting about the rules. Mauro Forghieri was there for Ferrari and fortunately agreed with me that we should not rewrite them but simply rearrange them in a sensible order. Rewriting them would leave us, not the CSI, responsible for the next row about the rules.

While we had been on the count's trail the previous day, there had been a major meeting of WCR in Monaco, attended by the Argentinians – represented by Eduardo Bordeo, president of the sporting committee – and Fangio, the former five-time world cham-pion driver (and reputedly Bordeo's father). After the meeting,

Duffeler had issued a press statement saying he was meeting Bernie in Paris on Friday to negotiate. We immediately told the press that we had no intention whatsoever of meeting Duffeler in Paris, and that any problems in Formula One could wait until the next CSI Formula One Working Group meeting in December.

One English motor racing journalist thought our refusal to meet was wrong because it was disrespectful of Fangio. That was a view I could not understand – just because he was a great driver didn't mean that all normal business dealing had to stop if he became involved, or that his view in a negotiation was of more value than anyone else's. On the contrary, what was he likely to know about it all? Better he should keep out of the dust and dirt of the conflict so we could go on regarding him as a great driver rather than a mediocre organiser.

Having been rebuffed by us, Duffeler decided to visit Ferrari with Fangio and Bordeo. Mauro Forghieri contacted Enzo Ferrari on the phone from the constructors' meeting so that we could agree a plan. Ferrari said: 'Leave it to me – I will tell them that questions to do with money and the Argentine Grand Prix must be dealt with by Ecclestone.' Bernie and I were delighted. We could picture him letting them talk on and on about the good old days and then, when they eventually got round to money and Argentina, making a characteristic little gesture of dismissal and indicating that such details must be discussed with Ecclestone and Mosley – that he did not concern himself with such things. There was also a good chance that he would not what he called 'receive' Duffeler at all.

Meanwhile, everyone at the Ricard winter testing had backed our confrontation with the CSI. Emerson Fittipaldi felt strongly about the way the CSI was behaving and said it was time to follow the lead of golf and tennis and bring in the new order.

Walter Wolf, a self-made millionaire who was young and aggressive, was even more explicit. He had been on Austrian television and sorted out Huschke as well as the presenter, who told him that the Formula One teams were all in it for the money. He replied he had been in Formula One just over a year (having bought the Frank Williams team) and so far spent nearly a million dollars – he could only hope his other money-making enterprises did rather better. So far, the war with WCR was going quite well but, worryingly, it was increasingly a contest with the CSI itself.

10

FOCA VERSUS THE CSI

By the end of 1976, our policy of refusing to meet Duffeler had brought the CSI decisively into the battle. With ten of the 15 CSI members also race organisers, they couldn't just abandon Duffeler. At the same time we had proved back in 1975 with the Canadian Grand Prix that we could cancel a race provided the teams stuck together. We were much stronger than when we started in 1972 but not yet in control. We needed Ferrari for political reasons, but we also needed the sponsors because they paid most of the bills.

Pierre Ugeux, the CSI president, called a meeting of his Formula One Working Group for the following Friday (3 December). It was to be preceded by a lunch for the sponsors, to which we were not invited although Duffeler and his WCR cronies were. We thought this difficult to reconcile with the CSI's protestations of impartiality, as was the fact that a circular that Bernie had been advised was actionable had been sent out by Duffeler in FIA envelopes from the FIA offices, stamped 'Urgent'. We knew that the meeting would be full of WCR members, either in that guise or wearing their CSI hats. We discussed not going but decided we could do more damage if we were there than if we were absent. We imagined that the CSI–WCR plan was to win the support of the sponsors over lunch and then present us with a united CSI–WCR front backed up by team sponsors, and thus force a settlement on their terms. Our meeting was arranged for 3.30pm, allowing them time for a good lunch.

Our first move was to send a telex asking for an earlier meeting, saying we had to catch a plane at 6pm which, predictably, was refused. From the airport we went straight to the Martini Terrace in the Champs-Élysées. It was an extraordinary place, literally a terrace at roof level overlooking the Champs-Élysées. There were fountains, glass doors, a bar and various working rooms, exactly in keeping with the image Martini promoted in their advertising at the time.

There we occupied ourselves talking to Claude Le Guezec, the former CSI secretary who had worked against us in that capacity but was now a valuable ally, and giving interviews to French press and TV in an attempt to redress some of the pro-WCR propaganda which had come out in France. We also began to prepare a major press conference immediately preceding the CSI's annual press conference on 16 December, timed to cause them maximum embarrassment, and briefed some of the sponsors on the points of dispute so that we could count on some friends at the lunch.

The Automobile Club de France occupies a historic building on the Place de la Concorde next to the Hôtel de Crillon, the part on the left as one looks up the Rue Royale towards La Madeleine. The FIA is housed there, too, courtesy of the French club. Up the back stairs and through some narrow old corridors that had creaking floorboards and a slight smell of Gauloises and garlic were the CSI's offices. It was the sort of place that would be frightening in a fire, as most of the stairs and corridors were like secret passages known only to the initiated.

Bernie and I knew our way round the place quite well, so we went in the back way and appeared as if by magic in the room where the meeting was to be held. This was one of the main rooms in the front part of the building which are everything one would expect from a historic French institution. Like the RAC, with its stock of claret, there are many powerful reasons for wanting to become a member of the Automobile Club de France.

When we arrived for the meeting, we found a man from *Sports Illustrated* in the room, who told us in all seriousness that he had been sent to cover the end of Grand Prix racing. That seemed a bad start – they obviously intended a major row – but it was not unexpected. Bernie was amusing himself by giving the reporter some involved rigmarole about racing coming to an end because the cars were getting too many wheels, when a CSI official came in and announced a delay. Bernie said: 'Go back and tell them it's 3.30pm now, we are leaving at 4.30pm no matter what and as it's their meeting we don't care how short it is.'

Two minutes later Ugeux appeared and the others came in one by one. Boeri from Monaco, Chambelland from Ricard, Balestre, president of the French Federation, Prince Metternich, president of the FIA, which was a surprise, and the two sponsors' representatives, François Guiter of Elf and David Zelkowitz from Philip Morris. Everyone except Metternich, the two sponsors and possibly Ugeux, was a WCR man, but there was no Duffeler. We had made his absence a condition of our presence. He and the two Argentinians, Fangio and Bordeo, plus our old friend Huschke, were all waiting outside with the press.

For 50 minutes we debated whether or not the Brussels agreement amounted to a three-year contract in terms finally settled in April 1976. We were better prepared than Ugeux and company and had numerous supporting documents. We clearly had the best of this and felt the opposition weakening, and Metternich and the sponsors beginning to lean our way. At one stage Balestre seemed to fall asleep.

It was obvious that the sponsors' lunch had not gone according to the WCR script because there was a certain lack of confidence right from the start. At 4.20pm Bernie whispered to me: 'Right, start winding them up.' I got out the Argentina file and began getting really heavy about interference with contractual relations, abuse of the licensing power, formal protests and so forth. We had strong evidence in support and one or two devastating letters, so it was a difficult position for them to defend. Just at the worst moment Bernie stood up, looked at his watch, started hurriedly packing away his papers saying: 'Christ! We're going to miss that bleeding plane – come on, Max.'

As one, the opposition said: 'No – you can't leave now.' 'Why not?' I said. 'It was you who insisted the meeting start at 3.30pm.' 'Yes, but we had an important working lunch,' Ugeux replied. 'That's true enough – you worked so hard that you exhausted Mr Balestre and he just fell asleep,' I said. The barb did not escape Balestre, who went purple with anger and shouted: 'I'm asleep because you make me tired with your endless talk about the sport when what we should discuss is the money. I have a business with a hundred-million-pound turnover and I have to sit here and listen to this rubbish.'

'Then why don't you sod off back to your office,' said Bernie as I too stood up.

At that moment François Guiter intervened to ask us to take a later flight as the meeting was so important. This was the cue for Bernie and me to go into our usual, carefully engineered, routine of changing plane tickets. During the interlude involving Bernie (this time) going in and out of the room to see about a later flight (on which, of course, we were already booked), the meeting inevitably calmed down again and relations became quite friendly. This was the ideal moment to try to make progress. In the atmosphere of relief after a row, people are amenable – like troops who have been stood down, they find it very hard to start fighting again.

Sure enough, we soon agreed that the important thing was to present a picture of unity, pledging that we would undoubtedly resolve all our differences, and that we should put out a release to this effect without delay. Boeri said it must state that WCR was not represented at the meeting. We seized on this as something we would not have dared to demand but very helpful because it signalled to the press that Duffeler had not been there, and it fitted with our strategy of ignoring him. Everyone signed the release and Bernie and I caught the later plane, feeling pleased with the day's work. We had conceded nothing and had per-suaded the CSI to support our thesis – that there were no real problems and all the races would take place. The survival of WCR depended on there being a conflict between teams and race organisers. Without this, it had no raison d'être.

Later that evening, probably at Duffeler and Von Hanstein's suggestion, Ugeux sent us a letter saying that the release was only to calm the press and that nothing had really been agreed, but for us this changed nothing – the release had gone out and they had signed it.

The following Friday, the UK's Guild of Motoring Writers had arranged a debate between Bernie and Ugeux. Sir Clive Bossom and Dean Delamont were there as pseudo referees and the *Daily Express*'s David Benson, chairman of the journalists' guild, acted as moderator. Bernie and I both anticipated that Ugeux would contrive to bail out and we would be greeted by Duffeler in his place. Sure enough, that's precisely what happened. In order to preserve our record of not meeting Duffeler (but also for the fun of annoying him) we insisted that he sit at a separate table. Three tables faced the assembled press and questions began.

Duffeler was an American who was born in Belgium and spoke with a vaguely French accent. He had a habit of smiling all the time, especially when in difficulty, as a result of which Bernie always referred to him as 'Laughing Boy'. He was very unimpressive that day – his answers were rambling and vague – and the press began to see through him. Duffeler could have handled the situation better if he had been brief and to the point – at least giving the impression of openness and candour. Bernie is not at his best in front of a large audience, but our formidable array of telexes and letters gave him the best of the debate and I felt we had come out of it well. The press was beginning to grasp our central argument: that there was no real issue between the organisers and us, and all that it really amounted to was a land grab to keep us constructors in our place. Although his long, evasive answers had succeeded in blocking hostile questions, the press's frustration was taken out on him in his absence. Our claim that WCR fomented trouble in order to exist had a ready audience. It was an interesting lesson.

In the middle of that week we heard that the Belgian club had repudiated Count de Liedekerke's signature, but the organisers said they would stick by the contract no matter what. We knew we had a secret weapon in the shape of an unpleasant lawsuit that we could use against the club if necessary, so we were not unduly worried. A major step forward, however, came on the Saturday when Bernie managed finally to sign Austria.

At that moment I was in Munich to meet BMW and attend their 1976 end-of-season party. When I got back to my hotel after the meeting I got a message to ring Bernie in London and he told me his news. After a quick shower, I set out for the BMW party in good spirits and, sure enough, there was Huschke. I could not resist going straight up to him and saying: 'You people were right about Austria in the old days – now they are independent and look what they've done: just signed a deal with Bernie and dropped WCR.'

The news obviously worried him and we discussed the whole issue all over again. He wanted to know why we wouldn't talk to Duffeler, so I pretended it was because we didn't like him. I could not admit that the real reason was that if we negotiated with him, his standing and authority among the organisers would increase. I was surprised Huschke hadn't worked that out.

The following week was taken up with CSI meetings, most importantly another Formula One Working Group scheduled for Thursday afternoon. Ugeux had made it clear he wanted 'Laughing Boy' there but we still decided to go, having first asked that one or two neutrals, such as Dean Delamont and Mal Currie, the Watkins Glen organiser, should come as well as the WCR supporters.

When we arrived in Paris we went straight to our French lawyer because we suspected that the fact that the FIA, as a non-profit-making body under French law, had made substantial profits and also set up a Swiss company, apparently without official permission, might make them vulnerable to attack in the French courts. It was important to have a secret weapon with which to cause alarm and confusion in the CSI, in case we had a head-on collision with them over WCR. The lawyer confirmed our view and said that, provided we had proof, our case would be formidable. As most of the evidence was contained in official CSI minutes, we emerged feeling quietly pleased.

We then had lunch with Claude Le Guezec and deliberately selected a cafe near the FIA headquarters in the hope that some of the CSI delegates would see us and be alarmed because of Claude's former position as head of the CSI secretariat. Sure enough, we were spotted and one of our opponents, Ottorino Maffezzoli from the Automobile Club of Milan and race director at Monza, actually joined us for a while. As he was one of the original directors of the WCR company in Monaco, we thought it right to give him a big injection of despair. At this stage of the negotiations morale and fortitude were everything, and all anxiety among the enemy was useful. We dropped hints about secret deals with other WCR organisers and tried to make him feel isolated and in danger. There was some basis for our claims, as Claude was busily trying to seduce Spain on our behalf, but it was all done in a friendly atmosphere with plenty of jokes.

After lunch we set off to the meeting at the Hotel Inter-Continental, where we found Michel Boeri waiting in the corridor and making a point of saying how stupid the present row was and how pointless that races should be endangered. I got the strong impression that he was at last beginning to worry about his own race in Monaco, which was no bad thing.

The talks were long and inconsequential, with Duffeler issuing periodic ultimatums that no one took much notice of. Bernie and I were unhelpful, particularly when he was speaking. We did everything we could to avoid discussing the one issue Duffeler wanted to bring up – namely, money. WCR's objective, after all, was to stop Bernie increasing the prize fund. In the end, we were able to avoid the subject altogether by pointing out that the working group chairman had ruled at the first meeting that it could not discuss money. All this wasted time and served the purpose of avoiding any sort of negotiation with Duffeler. At one stage, François Guiter of Elf said he thought the version of the original Brussels agreement that gave us the film and television rights in lieu of an increase in prize money should be avoided at all costs. We must, he said, cosset the television and make things easy and cheap for them or they would not come.

I thought it was an extraordinary mistake to make by someone whose company was so dependent on television for returns on sponsorship. The only way to get good television coverage was to see that the show was so good they had to broadcast it and then charge them heavily for the privilege. That way they would take trouble and do it properly: no one takes trouble over a free show – they just use it to fill airtime. If we had the rights, we would build them into something spectacular over a few years (as, indeed, Bernie eventually did), probably with cameras on the cars. It had the potential to be the first sport in which you could actually see things as a participant rather than a spectator, and it could easily become the number one sport on television – what was needed was drive and imagination, not a few feet of free film and the odd air ticket. But there was no point in saying any of this at this meeting. Half the room would not have understood and the other half would not have listened.

Eventually, we got the meeting on to the usual minutiae of Formula One race organisation and you could feel the frustration, particularly Duffeler's. He issued yet another ultimatum: if there was no financial agreement within 24 hours he would do 'something terrible', but he did not state what that would be. As his deadline fell after the end of the CSI Bureau meeting, which would have had to take any relevant decisions, this seemed melodramatic and pointless, but there the meeting ended.

Next day, at the CSI press conference after their Bureau meeting, Ugeux and the rest seemed to be avoiding our eyes as they went in. Bernie thought it meant trouble – big trouble – which was disquieting. No one readily faces a world war even if they have major secret weapons stashed up their sleeves, like our French lawsuit. You never quite know what to expect.

We bumped into the RAC's Dean Delamont, who had been at the meeting, and asked him what had happened. He was obviously confused because there had been the usual row and it had ended inconclusively, but he said Ugeux was hoping to impose a solution.

In the event we were delighted. Ugeux's solution was the original Brussels deal almost to the letter. What is more, it was a profit-sharing scheme where we received half of any increase in race receipts. This was an open-ended bargaining weapon for us, as many of the WCR organisers (the ones affected because they had not yet made a deal with us) would rather make a new deal on our terms than accept the auditing of their books that profit-sharing would imply.

Bernie quickly presented our trophy for the best organiser to Chris Pook of Long Beach at the FIA prize-giving and we rushed off to catch our plane, letting the press think we thought we would accept but playing up our lack of enthusiasm. We spent the plane journey debating whether Ugeux, who had prefaced his statement by saying that the time for playing poker had run out, had deliberately slipped us four aces under the table or genuinely thought it a bona fide solution. Either way, we were delighted. All we had to do now was wait.

Except, that is, for the first race which was in Argentina and still not resolved. Bernie had done a deal on the telephone with César Carmen, president of the Argentinian club, which was intended to replace our original agreement with the organisers' representative that the club had vetoed, with the result that the organisers quit in disgust. Bernie's deal naturally upset Bordeo who, as president of their sporting committee, was still in Paris holding hands with Duffeler. There was a major row in the club that ended with the president Carmen saying to Bordeo: 'All right, you get on with it!' As a result, Bordeo was telling the press in Paris that there was no race, at least until 6 February, and no deal had been done. Bernie and I were saying all was well – the race would take place on 9 January as scheduled – and Duffeler was telling his loyal band of WCR supporters that the race would be postponed until 23 October to allow time to sort out the constructors.

In the end, faced with our ultimatum of 9 January or no race, they all agreed: Bordeo, Carmen and who knows who else. Even the Argentinian ambassador appeared at one stage of the Paris meetings, and agreement was finally struck in the week before Christmas, with the first instalment of money following punctually on 24 December. But as we got ready to leave for Argentina, worrying news began to arrive of awkward practice times, agreed by the CSI and apparently designed with the sole purpose of annoying us. It looked as if we were in for trouble and I told Bernie we could expect to find Laughing Boy installed in Buenos Aires and ready for us. Bernie doubted this. 'But if we do,' he said, 'We'll let him do his worst in Argentina. Then we'll put him in a radcon [the metal trunks in which we carried spare parts for the cars] and speak to him through the lid and explain things to him.' At least that was something to look forward to.

11

BALESTRE TAKES OVER

Apart from his work for the constructors as a whole, Bernie was still running his own team. At Brabham he had an outstanding designer in Gordon Murray, who came up with the idea of building a car that was sucked down by an enormous fan, creating a partial vacuum under it. This gave it vastly increased grip and when it appeared at the 1978 Swedish Grand Prix it literally ran rings round the opposition. It could easily overtake round the outside of Anderstorp's long and relatively slow corners. Bernie's team kept the fuel tanks full in qualifying to slow the car down and conceal the full extent of its advantage. But was it legal? Aerodynamic devices had to be fixed and immovable while the car was running.

Bernie and Gordon claimed the fan was nothing to do with the car's aerodynamics, but was just a more efficient way to cool the engine. After all, all road cars used fans and radiators. When we were alone, I asked Bernie about this. He said: 'Yes, it's just for cooling.' Then he added conspiratorially, making a show of looking around to make sure he couldn't be overheard: 'Mind you, it does go down a few inches on its springs whenever you blip the throttle.' Sailing close to the wind with the rules has always been part of Formula One and, after winning the Swedish Grand Prix with Niki Lauda at the wheel, Bernie voluntarily withdrew the car. Fighting the issue with the other teams would have weakened or even destroyed his position in FOCA.

There was a multiple accident just after the start of the 1978 Italian Grand Prix. Bernie went to the scene, aided by police bodyguards who had been provided by the Italian authorities because of threats from the Red Brigades. Ronnie Peterson's car had been damaged and caught fire. The marshals did an excellent job and he was not significantly burned, though he had other injuries including a broken leg, but they were not thought life-threatening. Early the next morning, however, Ronnie died in hospital from an embolism resulting from the leg fracture. It was so unnecessary and, for me, deeply depressing – he had been a real friend, who became yet another example of the tragic waste of young lives. Ronnie was extraordinarily talented and universally liked. In one of today's cars, he would have been unhurt.

Monza was always complicated and the following year Bernie and I had an incident with a policeman who stopped our car and had an argument with the driver. It seemed to me he was drunk and we could not work out what he was complaining about. We had almost arrived at the restaurant, so I said in my limited Italian I would go there on foot and ask them to send for a proper policeman. He took umbrage at this and wanted an argument, but nevertheless Bernie and I set out for the place 100 metres or so away. We ignored his demand to stop, whereupon he drew his gun and repeated his order, which we ignored again. He then cocked and fired his pistol. Bernie always says he heard the bullet whiz by, but I think the policeman fired in the air.

Anyway, we still ignored him and continued into the restaurant where we asked the proprietor to call some more responsible police, who duly appeared. Among them was one of the police bodyguards from the year before, who dismissed his trigger-happy colleague.

Once FOCA became properly established as the constructors' association in the mid-1970s, Enzo Ferrari began taking an interest and started to invite all the teams regularly to his head-quarters in Maranello, near Modena. Originally, we had called the association F1CA (F1 Constructors' Association), but Ferrari told us that '*fica*' was not a polite word in Italian. He suggested we make the simple change to FOCA, as in Formula One Con-structors' Association.

Sometimes all the team principals went to Maranello; some-times, as already mentioned, it was just Bernie and me. Ferrari really enjoyed holding court with the teams; he loved the racing gossip and always gave us an excellent lunch in the building by the test track. He believed Parmesan cheese was an aphrodisiac and liked to put a big lump of it in front of Bernie when he wasn't looking, saying in Italian: 'This will get him going!' After a lunch that always included plenty of Lambrusco, we would be let loose on the Ferrari test track.

On another occasion, after meeting Ferrari with all the teams, we arrived back at Bologna airport after dark and in freezing fog to find the pilot of the plane we had hired saying the airport was closed but he'd managed to book hotel rooms for us all in the town. None of us wanted to spend Saturday night in Bologna, so we asked Colin Chapman, an experienced pilot, to go with him out to the runway and explain that it was all right to take off, but even Chapman came back shaking his head. Undeterred, Bernie suggested we all go out and sit in the plane; then we persuaded the pilot to start an engine to keep us warm; then we said we might as well go to the end of the runway in case the fog lifts for a few minutes.

At that point, Bernie nearly ruined everything because, when the plane started to move, people in the terminal building who were resigned to spending the night there started to crowd into the windows, curious to see what was happening. Bernie pointed this out and then, loud enough for the pilot to hear, joked: 'They've come to watch the shunt.' The fog stubbornly didn't lift but after a while we persuaded the pilot to make a run despite the icy surface. Chapman sat in the co-pilot seat reading off the speeds so that the pilot could concentrate on looking for the runway lights through the fog. Once we were a few feet above the ground it was a beautiful clear night.

Although there were no jets except for the occasional hired one, private flying in turbo-prop and piston aircraft was becoming more common in Formula One. But, like the racing, it was by no means safe. Taking off from a field behind Brands Hatch with Colin Chapman at the controls of his own plane, we were all in a hurry to get to Gatwick, but Bernie and his driver Nelson Piquet had to stand as the plane was too full. With a very heavy load, Chapman was only just able to clear the telephone wires at the end of the field, but explained they weren't a problem – he'd often had telephone wire wrapped round the wheels of his plane. Electricity cables, however, were a far more serious issue.

By the late 1970s, we had pushed the money paid by the race promoters to the point where some were complaining they couldn't pay. We knew that this was not really true – just a bargaining position – so we countered each time by offering to take over the financial risk of the event while they continued to run all the sporting and regulatory elements. We first used this ploy in 1974, but no one took us up on our offer until 1977 when the Automobilclub von Deutschland, the traditional promoter of the German Grand Prix, unexpectedly accepted and wanted us to start the following year. Suddenly, the teams were responsible for the finances of the 1978 German Grand Prix at Hockenheim.

By then, backed by the teams, Bernie and I were effectively running Formula One. The president of the CSI, Pierre Ugeux, was a mild-mannered man whose day job was running one of the Belgian national utilities. We got on well with him and, after the confrontation with WCR, he pretty much let us run things as we pleased. During that year, though, Jean-Marie Balestre, the president of the French national sporting authority whom we had encountered during our Paris stand-off over WCR, was elected to succeed Ugeux as head of the governing body.

With a successful publishing business, quite why Balestre was so ambitious to succeed in motor sport politics was not clear. He certainly liked the limelight and loved going on the podium at the end of the race to be pictured with the drivers. Yes, he had an interest in safety, but I always suspected this was primarily because it made relations with the drivers easier. Balestre understood very little of the technicalities of the sport, but he did understand the really big political issues. He was one of the first to recognise that the commercial management of Formula One had to be kept separate from sporting control, although, as we shall see, when first elected he tried to seize all the money and power for the FIA. It would be unfair to criticise him for his vanity and self-promotion, even though this verged on the eccentric towards the end, because many people who put themselves forward for prominent public roles have the same motivation. In the end, what matters is achievement and he was undoubtedly a person of genuine ability.

Relations with Balestre were good immediately after his election and he said he wanted to work with us. But, perhaps understandably, it became clear that as the new president of the FIA's sporting commission, the CSI, and thus head of motor sport's world governing body, he was not prepared to accept that we, not the FIA, ran Formula One.

Although it didn't seem like it at the time, Balestre's presidency was just what motor sport needed. He was a catalyst for change and, without him, things might well have continued as before and resulted in the fragmentation of international motor racing and rallying into a number of governing bodies, as happened with boxing and other sports. The same forces that led tennis, cricket and even chess to splinter away from their established structures were certainly pressing in motor sport and, as we shall see, we ourselves even set up a rival body, the World Federation of Motor Sport, in case we were unable to persuade Balestre to back off. But multiple governing bodies would have hindered development and greatly delayed improvements to safety, as we were to explain to the European Commission when they suggested just such a framework a few years later. Taking his presidency as a whole, Balestre unquestionably did more good than harm, but only after his major dispute with FOCA which very nearly put an end to our attempts to improve and modernise Formula One.

12

THE FOCA–FISA WAR

Following his 1978 election as head of international motor sport, Jean-Marie Balestre had made it clear that he wanted the FIA to have control over all technical, sporting and commercial aspects of Formula One. To the teams, this was anathema. The immediate problem was money – if Balestre had control of the FIA, which included almost all the promoters of Formula One events, it would be able to impose lower rewards for the teams and simultaneously demand higher entry fees. We knew that such abuse of monopoly might well be illegal, at least in Europe, but we also knew Brussels was very political. Securing a decision against the FIA, whose member organisations had close relations with several European governments, would be difficult.

Even more worrying in the medium and longer term was our certainty that Balestre would follow the interests of the car industry rather than those of the independent and predominantly British teams. The FIA had a long tradition of backing the car industry despite the fact that the industry's interests by no means always coincided with those of the ordinary motorists who made up the membership of the FIA clubs.

Major car manufacturers had a history of coming and going in Formula One, and their participation from one year to the next depended on the whim of the main board. For the industry, Formula One was essentially a marketing tool like any other. If they came in, they needed to win and winning was much easier if a compliant governing body was prepared to manipulate the technical rules to help them. The British FOCA membership, by contrast, consisted of teams whose sole business was Formula One. We had nowhere else to go without enormous, and possibly fatal, disruption to our businesses. The danger of total control falling into the hands of an FIA that would not worry about the British teams but do the bidding of the car industry seemed obvious and potentially ruinous.

As a result, a power struggle for the control of Formula One became inevitable. Our main weapon was the backing of a large majority of the teams ranged against the FIA with its support from the three manufacturers' teams: Alfa Romeo, Renault and traditionally Ferrari. The FIA also had control of the technical regulations and the right to change them at short notice if it could claim this was being done for reasons of safety. Short-notice changes caused major difficulties for UK teams because we lacked the resources to redesign and build new cars quickly. And safety was a very subjective concept in those unscientific days. Public opinion made it extremely difficult for our side to resist a change labelled 'safety'. As a former journalist, Balestre fully understood this and also knew that if he could get the drivers on his side, our position would be untenable.

Hostilities began with a collision at the start of the 1979 Argentine Grand Prix between John Watson, a FOCA (McLaren) driver, and Jody Scheckter in his Ferrari. Balestre decided to set up an ad hoc commission which fined Watson without hearing him. The fine was not paid and Watson was left facing exclusion from the Brazilian Grand Prix two weeks later.

In Brazil, Bernie and I had a stormy meeting with Balestre: we said it was outrageous to impose a fine without a hearing and, if Watson were excluded, the teams would not race. After a lot of argument, Balestre agreed that all future Formula One decisions would be taken by the official F1 Working Group, on which we were all represented. He promised to announce this at a press conference but went back on his word and spoke ambiguously, so we got him in a room on his own and insisted he write out the agreement by hand. Watson's team sponsors, Marlboro, then paid the fine.

A few days later, on 16 February, the teams all met with Enzo Ferrari at Maranello and agreed to ask the FIA for autonomy in running Formula One. The FIA Committee was meeting the next day and predictably refused. At that committee meeting, Balestre proposed that the FIA change the name of motor sport's international governing body, from Commission Sportive Internationale (CSI) to 'Fédération Mondiale du Sport Automobile'. He had already had an armband made with this name and had worn it at the Argentine Grand Prix. However, '*mondiale*' (world) was a bit too grand for the committee, who turned it down, and his armband was never seen again.

Balestre was really keen on the '*mondiale*' aspect. Soon after becoming president of the CSI, he changed the name of its executive committee to 'World Council' and, on one occasion much later, shortly after my election, he and I were delayed momentarily by security as we entered the Crillon hotel (which is next door to the FIA headquarters in Paris). Balestre asked what the security was for and was told the president of a particular country was there on an official visit. 'But that's just one country,' he told the security man. 'We are both *world* presidents!' I caught the man's eye and could see he understood why I was struggling to keep a straight face.

After his minor renaming setback, Balestre settled for the more modest Fédération Internationale du Sport Automobile (FISA). Once this was agreed he could say he was president of an international sports federation rather than merely the president of the FIA's sporting commission, the CSI. The main reason he gave the committee for needing a more prestigious name was the growing threat of FOCA. Legally, however, the FISA was still only a commission of the FIA and Balestre merely a vice-president of the FIA itself. He eventually became president in 1985.

The unity of the teams did not last – several issues divided us. Fundamentally, the UK teams were better at chassis design and using aerodynamics to increase speeds, particularly cornering speeds, while the continental teams, mainly big car companies plus Ferrari, led the way in engines and using power output for speed. We all had to rely on the same engine, built by Cosworth in Northampton, whose sole business, unlike the multinational car manufacturers, was making racing engines. It had to make a profit and could spend only very limited amounts on development. The sport was essentially a contest between two engineering superiorities: the more powerful cars of Alfa Romeo, Ferrari and Renault versus the less powerful but more agile chassis of the British teams.

One side or the other could gain an advantage, depending on how the rules were framed. As already noted, our problem was that because of the close relationship between the car industry and the FIA, the big car companies had much more influence over the governing body than we did.

However, Ferrari – although (then) 50 per cent owned by Fiat – was in many ways more akin to a FOCA team than, for example, Renault. They had enormous prestige in Formula One, being the only team to have participated in the World Championship continuously from its start in 1950, and the company was also world famous as the builder of outstandingly desirable road cars. Enzo Ferrari himself was politically astute, siding with FISA or FOCA according to his interests at any given moment. He was essentially the fulcrum between us and FISA and, by a small movement towards one or the other, could produce an effect out of all proportion to the size of his team. Yet, although Ferrari would often disagree with FOCA about technical matters (where his interests were usually closer to those of the big car companies), he did not want Balestre in charge of Formula One's finances.

The political situation was further complicated by the emergence of a new engine technology. Until the late 1970s, everyone, including the car manufacturers, used a 3.0 litre engine without supercharging. The car manufacturers' engines usually had 12 cylinders, while the UK teams' Cosworth DFV engine had eight. The 12s were more powerful but were also heavier and used more fuel, and there was a sort of balance provided the rules were not changed to favour one type of engine over the other.

The rules also allowed a Formula One car to use a 1.5 litre supercharged engine as an alternative to the 3.0 litre naturally aspirated engine. However, in the 1970s a new form of supercharging was emerging using waste energy from the exhaust. It was known as 'turbocharging' and promised much greater efficiency plus, at least in theory, a lot more power. In 1977, Renault appeared in Formula One with the first 1.5 litre turbocharged engine. Initially, the UK teams did not take the new technology seriously, and there was much amusement at the British Grand Prix when Renault were seen using a broom to put out small fires in their exhaust system. But it gradually became clear that further development would result in the 1.5 litre turbocharged engine outclassing the current naturally aspirated engines and taking over Formula One.

The debate about engines continued throughout 1979. Apart from the danger of all naturally aspirated engines becoming obsolete, we stood against an equivalence formula as a matter of principle, saying that one type of engine was bound eventually to prove the best. Once that happened, one of the technologies would be obsolete and a lot of money would have been wasted. But, more fundamentally, the UK teams and Cosworth lacked the resources to develop turbocharging.

On 7 September 1979 at Monza, FISA and FOCA jointly announced that the conflicts of the previous eight months were over. Peace had broken out and there would be a major technical meeting the following month to discuss engine rules. We were arguing for naturally aspirated engines only; the manufacturers wanted rule stability – in other words, to continue to allow both types of engine. For FOCA, this was life-threatening. In those days, most of the capital of a UK Formula One team was tied up in its engines. If these were rendered obsolete by new technology, many FOCA teams would be in financial difficulty and without the money to pay for entirely new engines.

While all this was going on, it was generally acknowledged that cornering speeds were dangerously high. Everyone wanted to slow the cars, but British teams wanted to do this by limiting engine power and tyres, the continental teams by banning the

UK teams' aerodynamic devices. According to FIA regulations, rule changes in Formula One needed two years' notice but this could be bypassed if change was necessary on safety grounds. FISA claimed that slowing the cars was a safety measure and rule changes to achieve this could be brought in at short notice. We pointed out that, on this basis, virtually all rule changes could be said to be for safety because their purpose was almost invariably to limit performance in order to keep speeds under control. However, early in 1980 FISA announced summarily that it was going to ban skirts, a key aerodynamic device for the FOCA teams, from 1981, citing safety reasons.

By now it was becoming clear to every British team that the combination of FISA and the big continental car companies was a threat to their survival. Like Cosworth, all were independent businesses that had to make a profit to survive. They did not have the resources to deal with rapid changes, in particular those that might result in obsolete equipment and capital written off. It seemed to me that the best way to counter this potentially fatal risk would be to challenge Balestre's personal authority and thus reduce FISA's influence. Bernie agreed and we began.

Balestre's fondness for the limelight provided our first avenue of attack in March 1980 at the South African Grand Prix. He always liked to go on the podium with the winning drivers after the race, which we saw as profiling and an infringement of the rights of the race sponsor who had paid the organiser to use the podium for promotion. The marshal in charge of the podium was a large South African working for the race sponsor and I explained our problem to him: Balestre always insists on taking part despite the drivers' annoyance and distracts attention from the sponsor's promotional girls.

'Don't worry, we'll stop him,' said the marshal. 'You won't be able to, he's a very determined man,' I said. The marshal swelled visibly. 'Leave it to me,' he replied. Having lit the fuse, I went back to the nearby Kyalami Ranch hotel to enjoy a cup of tea in the garden and await the results of my mischief-making. Sure enough, Balestre appeared, red in the face with fury. 'You won't believe what happened,' he said (not for one moment suspecting me). 'They stopped me going on the podium by force!'

'How awful – that's outrageous,' I replied, very sympathetically.

Shortly after this, the FISA and FIA meetings were due to be held in Rio de Janeiro. We decided that the time had come for a full-on confrontation with Balestre. I travelled to Rio without Bernie, who was getting on with Formula One business back home. The night before the FISA Executive Committee (soon to be renamed World Motor Sport Council), I got hold of a list of all the committee members' rooms and slid an eight-page attack on Balestre, and the way he was running the sport, under each door.

It had the expected effect. He was livid. Next day he opened the meeting by saying there had been an affront to the dignity of the FISA, to which I responded that it would not have been necessary had he conducted himself properly. It was a very stormy meeting and for the first time he couldn't keep control. We had a clear case that the proposed ban on skirts was illegal and, as Balestre realised he was in difficulty, his arguments became increasingly bizarre. He said all members of FOCA had their personal private jet aircraft; he revealed that he had persuaded Mercedes to enter Formula One (both claims were completely untrue); and that his conscience forced him to ban the skirts. He finished by saying my drivers' letters against a ban were all extracted under duress.

Balestre lost two of the votes in the Executive Committee but, with a Plenary Conference of the FISA the next day, he was able to get the decisions reversed, saying he would resign if he failed. I did not have the right to speak there so was at a disadvantage, but the chairman of the RAC, Sir Clive Bossom, spoke up against Balestre. He was very effective and loyal in defending what he rightly saw as British interests.

For the first time, Balestre's authority was seriously under threat, but he nevertheless got his way by playing the system against us. They passed a ban on skirts for 1981, the introduction of a fuel-flow formula (later rescinded) and, surprisingly, a 30 kg increase in the minimum weight, something that would be very helpful to the manufacturers' teams with their heavier engines but bad for our side. The Italian delegate, Stefano Marsaglia, who also represented the car industry in FISA, had unexpectedly proposed this. I later learned it was Marco Piccinini, the Ferrari team manager, who called him from Italy the night before and persuaded him to give it a try without really expecting it to pass. An inquiry into the South African podium incident was also established, demonstrating that even quite childish (if entertaining) provocations were taken very seriously by Balestre and could have a significant effect.

The Rio measures abolished FOCA's seat on the FISA Executive Committee, as well as seats as of right for the major sporting countries. I pointed out that this would give Balestre absolute power because he could circulate a list of candidates among his allies at the next election and co-ordinate the vote to guarantee victory for himself and his cronies. Conversely, anyone who annoyed him and was left off the list would not be elected. Combining this with the threat of taking away an important international race or rally would be enough to keep all countries in line.

We launched our second offensive at the 1980 Belgian Grand Prix with FOCA's announcement that, in future, cars and paperwork must be checked in the garages and our mechanics would no longer push the cars to the organiser's bay. Ferrari, who were always a '*légaliste*' team, did not join us and pushed their cars as required but all FOCA teams stayed put. Also, several of our teams told their drivers not to go to the compulsory drivers' briefing immediately before the race, and the stewards duly fined them for non-attendance.

We told the drivers not to pay on the grounds that making them attend a briefing just before the race was distracting and unsafe. The dispute went through appeal, but this was really a dispute about who ran Formula One and Balestre was not ready to back down. The end result was that the drivers' licences were suspended for non-payment of fines, which meant they were barred from the next race, the 1980 Spanish Grand Prix. We arrived in Madrid knowing there was going to be a confrontation and it began with negotiations behind the scenes.

In the early morning of the first day of practice, Balestre came to my room in his pyjamas saying we needed to talk. We agreed to meet shortly downstairs and I said I would alert Bernie. Balestre arrived in the hotel lobby for our meeting, to which he had also invited Marco Piccinini. Ferrari were traditionally FIA loyalists and Marco was greatly respected as a politician and strategist upon whose wisdom Balestre leaned heavily.

By now it was about 7am and there was pressure to find a solution before practice, which was due to start shortly at the circuit. Our objective was to engineer a split in the governing body and we knew this would become more probable if the race were threatened. A cancellation would cause internal and external problems for the FIA but would not be without cost to our side.

Balestre indicated that he had a core group of supporters in the FIA on whom he could rely absolutely, and backed this up by producing a handwritten list.

We were all sitting at a small table in the hotel lobby and Balestre put his list on the table with all his other papers. Bernie and I knew the list was an invaluable weapon, identifying potential dissidents within the FIA and which ones we might usefully approach and those best to leave alone. When talking in front of people whose English was not perfect, we often used cockney rhyming slang. 'You do the Cain and Abel,' said Bernie, 'and I'll hoist it' – meaning, you tip over the table and I'll get the list, which, of course, Balestre did not understand.

I stood up, 'accidentally' upending the table, and while I stood there apologising profusely, Bernie joined Balestre on hands and knees solicitously helping him gather his papers. When the papers were finally back on the table the list had vanished. Balestre was in despair. He kept repeating: *'Ma liste, ma liste, merde! Où est ma liste?'* We helped him hunt for it but without success. It was safely in Bernie's pocket.

There was no agreement and Balestre remained in the hotel while Bernie and I went to the circuit. We arrived to find the media in a state of agitation and the teams wanting to know what was going on. The Jarama circuit belonged to the main Spanish motoring club, the Real Automóvil Club de España, whose chairman was the Marqués de Cubas. RACE had been one of the FIA's founding clubs in 1904 and was still very important internationally, but had delegated the power to run motor sport in Spain to another organisation, the Federación Española de Automovilismo (FEA).

The Marqués de Cubas was at the circuit, as were the representatives of the FEA. We invited both to a meeting in the

Aged about two, with my older brother Alexander. [Associated Press]

With my parents in 1962.

With Jean in our London flat, 1963. [Rex Features]

With other members of the 44 Independent Parachute Brigade Group platoon. I'm just visible at the back.

The Meadspeed workshop. David Reeves is 'The Thinker', Colin Gardner is on the left at the back and my partially dismantled U2 is in the foreground. [Courtesy of David Reeves]

Formula 2 at Zandvoort, 1968, leading Mike Beckwith and Brian Hart. [Ferdi Kräling]

Monza, 1968, as reported in *Le Notizie dello Sport*. The race carried on around the burning car. I'm in car number 11.

The four March founders with the original March 701 Formula One car. [Corbis]

The March six-wheeler with Martin Walters and Robin Herd. [Corbis]

Immediately after the 1969 British GP. Henrietta Guinness is in the centre at the front, Robin Herd is behind her and Jochen Rindt is on the right at the back.

Chatting to Niki Lauda (left) and James Hunt in 1971. [Jutta Fausel]

Ronnie Peterson struggling with our unsuccessful 1972 F1 car. [Ferdi Kräling]

Plotting with Bernie at the 1975 Spanish GP. [Ferdi Kräling]

More than 30 years later, no longer plotting but still much to discuss. [Ferdi Kräling]

FOCA in 1975. I'm kneeling with Peter Macintosh. Standing, from the left: Bubbles Horsley (who ran the Hesketh team), Ken Tyrrell, Colin Chapman, Frank Williams, Luca di Montezemolo, Graham Hill, Teddy Mayer. Behind are Bernie and Alan Rees. [Ferdi Kräling]

With Huschke von Hanstein, head of German motor sport and leading FIA figure during the FOCA–FISA war. [Ferdi Kräling]

Hôtel de Crillon, Paris, 1980: Frank Williams, Colin Chapman, me, Bernie, Ken Tyrrell and Emerson Fittipaldi announce the World Federation of Motor Sport right next door to the FIA headquarters.

Madrid 1980: Telling the FISA 'observer' he had to observe from outside our caravan.

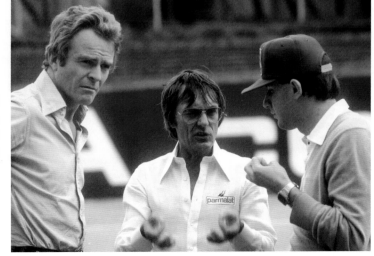

With Bernie and Marco Piccinini, the Ferrari team manager. [Ferdi Kräling]

Jean-Marie Balestre on the podium in 1985 with Alain Prost, Niki Lauda and Ayrton Senna. [Rex Features]

In front of the FIA headquarters in the Place de la Concorde (complete with flag) on the evening after my election as president of FISA in 1991.

cramped caravan that Bernie had hired for the race. Gérard Crombac, a French journalist and friend of Balestre, came in saying he was the FISA observer and must attend the meeting. Bernie ejected him and I stood in the doorway, telling him in front of the press that he could observe all he liked, but from the paddock – he was not coming in the caravan. With a mass of press outside and no air conditioning inside, the meeting got nowhere. We were adamant the drivers would race, with or without their licences. The FEA was just as adamant that no suspended team or driver could start practice until the fines had been paid.

Importantly, Spain wanted the race to go ahead, so did the Marqués de Cubas, who had the support of the Spanish establishment. So he announced that the Grand Prix was back under RACE's jurisdiction, which would then itself authorise the race. FISA and their FEA allies disagreed, and insisted that the revocation was invalid without the consent of the FIA General Assembly (which was technically correct). The FISA representatives were invited to leave the circuit and, when they protested, the Guardia Civil appeared and escorted them to the gates ('at gunpoint', according to some excitable reports). Practice then went ahead without Alfa Romeo, Ferrari and Renault, the three so-called *légaliste* teams. In the absence of the FISA, the event was to be supervised by the Spanish officials the FEA had originally appointed but under RACE's authority.

Back in the hotel, Balestre held an emergency meeting with the representatives of the *légaliste* teams. Marco Piccinini was there for Ferrari, Jean Sage for Renault and Pier Luigi Corbari for Alfa Romeo. These were the so-called *grandi costruttori*, known as the 'grandis' by us (although some British journalists irritatingly turned the word into 'grandees'). They gathered in Balestre's room and were deep into their discussions when one of them noticed water coming under the door. He had been running his bath and, in the excitement of the news from the circuit, had completely forgotten about it.

The flooding of Balestre's suite was a distraction compounded by an offer from Bernie to Alfa Romeo that if they broke ranks and raced with the FOCA teams, they could start the race from the front row of the grid. After all, he told them, as they had not been able to practise, it was only fair. A front-row start was beyond Alfa's wildest dreams at the time. To make good on his promise, Bernie would have had to secure the written agreement of the teams and officials. Typical Bernie, he no doubt thought he'd need to worry about this only if Alfa said yes and, whatever happened, he would at least have caused a diversion.

As soon as he heard of Bernie's offer, Marco made an emergency call to Enzo Ferrari, who was then 82 years old but still fully involved in the politics. Ferrari, in turn, called the president of Alfa Romeo. By now it was Sunday morning, but they had to make sure there were no defections from the *légaliste* teams. Ferrari's early morning call was successful and the race went ahead without the three manufacturers' teams. None of the parent companies was prepared to race in an event that FISA had declared illegal. Even though their officials were locked out of the circuit and were now making their announcements from a Madrid hotel, the international motor racing establishment was still powerful. Alan Jones won the race for Williams.

By chance, a major FIA meeting had been scheduled in Lagonissi, a resort near Athens, for the day after the race. Faced with a serious rebellion, Balestre wanted to show the FIA delegates a letter from Renault saying they would never join FOCA and also asked Ferrari to resign from our association. Marco managed to get the letter from Renault and rushed with it to the airport where Balestre's plane was about to leave for Athens. He had to persuade airport staff to knock on the plane's door and get it opened so he could deliver the letter.

Marco had already explained to Balestre that he had no authority to sign a resignation letter on behalf of Ferrari. Back in Maranello, Enzo Ferrari was saying: 'Don't let's be too quick to go against Bernie – after all, he's the one who produces the money.' This was certainly true – in the eight years since Bernie got involved, the prize fund had increased by a factor of ten. A few days later, Ferrari signed the resignation letter addressed to FOCA and sent his chauffeur to the local post office with instructions to register it, obtain the receipt then have the post office staff hand it back. As a result, although registered and officially posted, it was never dispatched. When Balestre visited Maranello a short time later, Marco was able to show him the resignation and the receipt for the registered letter to FOCA, yet still maintain Enzo Ferrari's good relations with Bernie.

Having run what we knew the FIA would call a pirate race, Bernie and I thought it imperative we should turn up at the FIA meeting in Greece the next day, despite not being invited and having made no plans to attend. We went to the airport, hoping to find a flight to Athens. It was about 8pm and there were no flights to Athens or anywhere close. Bernie wandered off into the bowels of the airport while I waited with our luggage, and he came back to say he'd found an American who was about to fly to Saudi Arabia in his private jet and had agreed to drop us off in Athens. Bernie had persuaded him it was on the way. What his pilots thought was not recorded.

We arrived at the FIA hotel about 25 miles from Athens in the early hours with the help of a taxi driver we found asleep at the airport. At 9am we walked into the dining room where the FIA delegates were having breakfast and found the atmosphere electric. They were all discussing the events of the previous day in Spain, which almost all had been following on television. The last thing they expected was that we would suddenly appear. Yet we were not entirely unwelcome – we had allies among the delegates, some of them even on Balestre's lost list of his supposed supporters.

Armed with that list, we had a good idea which delegates we might get at but were hindered by our exclusion from the meetings. We needed to find out what was going on, and knew that Balestre and his officials would be in constant touch with their staff and lawyers back in Paris. Other than the odd person-to-person phone call, the only way they could communicate was by telex, so we acquired a copy of every telex they sent or received from a very helpful young lady who operated the hotel's telex machine. We learned that Balestre had persuaded the FIA Committee to rule that the Spanish Grand Prix would not count for the World Championship and to confirm that FOCA would no longer be represented on the FISA Executive Committee.

Although the war itself was really about stopping the FIA and car manufacturers taking control of Formula One, the immediate battleground was the proposed ban on the aerodynamically important skirts. We had looked at the possibility of getting an injunction against the FIA to stop FISA (which, as already noted, was technically a FIA commission) banning the skirts on the grounds that a ban taking effect the following year (1981) did not provide the required two years' notice and would breach the stability rules. French lawyers, however, advised that the courts would be unlikely to agree because of a letter signed by most of the drivers asking for the ban to reduce cornering speeds for safety reasons. The problem for us was that the ban would reduce the cornering speeds of the British cars more than Ferrari or Alfa Romeo because the V8 Cosworth engine allowed a much better ground effect than the flat 12 Ferrari and Alfa Romeo engines. The 'grandis' would be giving up much less than us, so we proposed changes to the tyres that would affect all teams equally.

With the legal route in France seemingly blocked we turned to England, but the judge would not let us serve proceedings outside the jurisdiction of the English courts. He decided the French courts were the correct forum; otherwise, you might get an Italian team suing in Italy or a Japanese team suing in Japan with potentially contradictory results. The judge said with impeccable logic that the most efficient approach was to sue the FIA where it was based, in France. This was not what we wanted to hear because we now knew the French courts would probably accept the safety argument.

We had a number of allies among the FIA delegates at Lagonissi, one of whom, Ron Frost from New Zealand, suggested we come to the dinner that evening hosted by the Greek club. There was a strong desire for peace within the FIA and the climate was improving. But just as we were about to get on the bus, we learned that we had lost our position on the FISA Executive with immediate effect. We promptly cancelled our attendance at the dinner and told everyone it was clear we had to continue to operate outside FIA structures and would now return to London.

After we left, some delegates who were sympathetic to our complaints about rule stability put pressure on Balestre. As result, the FIA representatives for the USA, Germany and New Zealand were deputed by the FISA Executive Committee to meet us together with a senior sponsors' representative, Aleardo Buzzi, and seek a solution. Buzzi worked for Philip Morris, who sponsored both Ferrari and FOCA's McLaren using its Marlboro brand. After an appropriate show of reluctance, Bernie and I arranged to meet them in Lausanne.

Agreement was reached with this group on 6 June 1980. We signed a document which gave all sporting power to the FISA F1 Commission, with three representatives each for FOCA and FISA, two sponsors, three organisers and a drivers' representative. FISA's Executive Committee could send a decision back to the commission if it disagreed but could not change it, while commercial matters in Formula One were wholly reserved for the teams. We agreed to drop legal action, pay the fines and abide by a tribunal's judgment on the status of the recent 'pirate' Spanish Grand Prix.

It was essentially everything we wanted. We knew Balestre would not like it, so on the drive from Lausanne back to Geneva airport we decided to try to make it a fait accompli. In those days there was a telex room in the airport for businessmen to send urgent messages. We settled in there and had the entire agreement transcribed on to a telex tape and transmitted to all the members of FISA's Executive Committee, all the Grand Prix organisers and all the teams.

By the time it went out, Balestre was already in bed. When Michel Boeri, president of the Monaco club, received it he promptly warned Marco. Sure enough, at 4am, Marco got a call from Balestre, who used to make up for his early bedtime by rising at dawn or before. 'You have one minute to wake up,' he told Marco, 'then we must talk.' Balestre was furious. He said (with some justification) that the FIA negotiators had gone beyond their mandate and he was determined to tear up the agreement.

The next race was the French Grand Prix on 29 June, the most important on the calendar for Balestre as president of the French Federation. We took advice on whether we could disrupt it by sending only two cars. This would have accorded with the letter of our contract, but the French lawyers advised that we might well lose the resulting litigation because the quarrel would be seen as us resisting a safety measure requested by the drivers. But the rumour of a possible boycott reached Balestre and, to calm things, he called for a round table the day after the race to discuss all technical problems including cornering speeds and the proposed ban on skirts.

At the meeting, we once again argued that reducing tyre performance was the fairest way to reduce cornering speeds because it would be the same for all cars. By contrast, a skirt ban would affect the cars with flat 12 engines less than those using the Cosworth V8 and would therefore disadvantage our teams. The round table decided the discussion should go to a further technical commission meeting from which, in the event, nothing useful emerged. Our moral position was not helped a month later when Patrick Depailler was killed testing his Alfa Romeo at Hockenheim. The cause of the accident was said to be suspension failure, but there was a suspicion that a skirt had stuck in the up position, causing a loss of downforce (and hence grip) that took him by surprise.

Because Balestre's political control of FISA was so strong, we turned increasingly to the law and, by August 1980, Bernie was able to tell a FOCA meeting that we had five different pieces of litigation underway. As the weeks went by, we began to think that a breakaway series, or at least a credible threat of it, would probably be the most effective way to break the deadlock. We started contacting race organisers to build up a calendar for a

FOCA Formula One Championship and putting together sporting and technical rules (largely copied from the FISA versions).
Bernie already had contracts with most of the Formula One race
promoters and many of them were sympathetic.

In October 1980, ten race promoters signed an undertaking
that if no agreement were reached between Balestre and us, they
would honour their contracts and their races would be run 'with
or without the approval of FISA'. Finally, at the beginning of
November 1980 we were ready to announce the World Federation of Motor Sport, with its own World Professional Drivers'
Championship, and put out a press release to the world's media.

Balestre's response was to threaten sanctions against any circuit
that ran a race without FISA's consent. FISA, he said, would stop
the circuit running any other form of motor sport and he had the
power to do this under the International Sporting Code. A ban
would not necessarily be a problem for a street circuit such as
Long Beach (although there would be no support races), but
would be catastrophic for a permanent circuit that needed to run
lesser motor sport events all year round in order to be financially
viable. But the threat had major legal implications that Balestre
probably didn't foresee. In the medium term, we could probably
have claimed it was a breach of European competition law, something we were very focused on, but in the short term we could
immediately sue the FIA for interference with contractual relations on the basis of our existing contracts with race promoters.

We were now on much stronger legal ground. Bernie's Formula
One race contracts were all with FOCA's UK entity and governed
by English law; there was no safety argument and no need to go
to the French courts. We could go straight to the English High
Court. There was only one problem: the lawyers pointed out that
we could not ask for an injunction to stop FISA interfering with

our contracts for races that were part of the FIA Formula One World Championship and simultaneously set up our own alternative world championship. Our own competition would mean we were not going to compete in their championship and our contracts would be nugatory. It was either or. On 21 November, within a month of setting up the World Federation of Motor Sport, we announced at a press conference in the Crillon next door to the FIA that we were not going to proceed with it. We would simply enforce our existing contracts and race under the rules we had signed up to; namely, the rules with no ban on skirts.

There was a brief moment of euphoria in FISA's camp and the pro-Balestre sections of the press – they thought we had capitulated and he'd won. Then they discovered we had obtained injunctions against the FIA and each individual member of FISA's Executive Committee, restraining them from interfering with our contracts. Furthermore, we had leave to serve the proceedings abroad, outside the jurisdiction of the English courts. The injunctions involved blood-curdling official threats of fines, imprisonment and sequestration. Ignoring an injunction of the English High Court is a very serious matter in the UK. This greatly alarmed many FISA World Council members. All except Michel Boeri of Monaco started to refuse any engagement in the UK for fear of what might happen should they set foot there.

Now we were apparently in a strong position. We had the teams (except Ferrari, Alfa Romeo and Renault), we had draconian injunctions against the FIA and all the individual members of FISA's World Council and we had upwards of ten races on our calendar, all of which could respond to any threat from the governing body by saying they had a contract with us and therefore no choice but to run their event. But there was a major problem, albeit hidden. The sponsors were getting nervous. Big international companies like Philip Morris (Marlboro) and Goodyear did not want to be associated with a 'pirate' championship or any sort of revolt against the established order. Main boards were becoming involved and, however sympathetic those responsible for the racing budget might be, they warned that if it came to it, they would not be able to help us.

The money had already stopped flowing and with our teams entirely dependent on finance from sponsors, we were going to have trouble getting through the winter, never mind going racing next season. Then, in December 1980, Goodyear announced their withdrawal from Formula One. Michelin promptly declared that Formula One would not be without tyres but, as a French company very much closer to Balestre than to us, this was anything but comforting. The situation was becoming desperate.

13

THE CONCORDE AGREEMENT

Against this background, on 16 January 1981 Colin Chapman, the head of the Lotus car company as well as the Lotus team, Teddy Mayer, then head of McLaren, and I went to the Hahnenkamm downhill ski race in Austria. There had always been a lot of crossover between Formula One and ski racing, and friends in Austrian ski circles arranged a visit each year. We also got in a bit of skiing ourselves and even a bit of light-hearted racing, plus the regular wild party in The Londoner pub after the big race. Teddy was a very accomplished skier and former instructor and his wife Sally, who came too, was a former American junior champion. Colin was less skilled but what he lacked in ability he would make up for in determination and a love of speed. After each run he would appear a short time behind everyone else, covered in snow from his falls but loving every minute of it.

In the dining room of our small hotel near Kitzbühel was a mural showing two men painting a cow. Colin asked the waitress what was going on and she explained that in the Middle Ages, a nearby town had been under siege and had run out of food. Surrender was imminent but they had one cow left and each day they would paint it a different colour and parade it where the besieging army could see it, to give the impression they had plenty of cows.

'That's it!' exclaimed Colin. 'We must put on a race even though we've got no money.' FISA had just been forced to postpone the Argentine Grand Prix, the first race of the 1981 season (Argentina were FIA loyalists), so if we could put on a race when they demonstrably couldn't, the effect would be significant. We all went up to my room in a state of enthusiasm for Colin's idea and, sitting on the bed, called Bernie. I explained about painting the cow and what we needed to do. There was a short silence, then Bernie replied: 'You're all pissed.' This was partly true but he saw the point and eventually agreed that we must somehow put on a race despite almost all the teams being broke.

The following week, ever attuned to the political situation and the possibility of extracting an advantage for his company, Enzo Ferrari invited everyone to Modena. Despite all our conflicts, relations with Renault and Alfa Romeo had remained excellent on a personal level. Likewise with Enzo Ferrari, for whom everyone had great respect as the elder statesman of Formula One. The result of the discussions was the Modena Agreement. Much of what emerged from Modena was similar to the Lausanne Agreement of the previous summer (chapter 12), but instead of three members of FISA and three from FOCA the proposal was now equal representation on the F1 Commission for FOCA and the manufacturers, a sponsor from each side and only one FISA representative. The equal representation for the manufacturers came from a discussion shortly before the Modena meeting between Marco and Teddy Mayer arranged by Aleardo Buzzi, the senior executive of Philip Morris who had been at our Lausanne meeting the previous summer as sponsor of both Ferrari and McLaren.

The Modena Agreement was similar to the terms Balestre had refused the previous summer, at least as far as the powers of the F1 Commission and its relationship with his World Council were concerned, but there was now even less representation for FISA in the commission. It maintained the Lausanne position that they controlled the sport but commercial matters were strictly the teams' domain. The agreement, which was to be submitted to FISA, was announced on 20 January, just before all their main players were due to assemble in Monaco for the Monte Carlo Rally.

This put Balestre under intense pressure. If the Modena Agreement were accepted, it would be a defeat for him; but with every team including Ferrari in agreement, he was becoming isolated. Without the support of Ferrari and the major manufacturers, Balestre realised he was at risk of losing control. However, what he didn't know was that the financial position of the British teams was now so desperate he only had to wait and he would be able to dictate his terms, at least to us. We were very close to collapse.

This made it all the more important for us to put on the South African Grand Prix because the local organiser had a FOCA contract and had sided with us. The race was originally scheduled for 7 February and, encouraged by us, the South Africans had refused an attempt by FISA to postpone it until April along with the Argentinian race.

But Goodyear's withdrawal meant we had no tyres. They were no longer willing to supply, not even old stock, and there was no chance Michelin would step in without Balestre's approval. By pure luck, Bernie had a warehouse full of old Avon tyres left over from a race series he had been running in addition to his Formula One activities. The 1981 South African Grand Prix duly took place on 7 February, with all the teams running on Bernie's old tyres, and was won by Carlos Reutemann. FISA declared it a 'formula libre' race and it barely got a mention in the French motor racing press. The coverage of the FOCA–FISA conflict in the French and UK media was rather like the difference between the history books used in English and French schools – theirs contain battles no English child has ever heard of and vice versa, depending on who won in each case.

The fact that we could put on a race and FISA could not sent a clear message that did not escape Balestre or the main boards of the manufacturers. The 1981 Argentine Grand Prix had been scheduled for 11 January but had not been on the FOCA calendar, so none of our cars were prepared to run there. To overcome this, Alfa Romeo, Ferrari and Renault had said they would each run three cars, but the logistical problems were too great and they had to ask FISA to postpone it. A new date was fixed, 12 April, but the forced date change was a major setback for FISA, resulting in pressure on the manufacturers' teams from their sponsors as well as their own main boards. The increasingly strong message was: get this sorted out. When the 'pirate' South African Grand Prix was shown on television in Europe and elsewhere, the pressure on Balestre increased further.

Worse, from the point of view of FISA and the three manufacturers, the next race on the FIA calendar after South Africa was Long Beach in California. Chris Pook, the Long Beach organiser, had made it clear he would respect his contract with us and put on a race. The manufacturers' teams could participate if they wished but, if necessary, he would run the race just for our teams. Then Renault told Balestre they would have to run in California because of their American subsidiary. The reality was that we would probably not have been able to race in California for lack of money but, like the besieging army in Austria that was shown a different cow each day, neither FISA nor the manufacturers realised what desperate straits we were in. FISA started to lose its nerve.

As the pressure mounted, Balestre blinked first. Above all, he didn't want Ferrari to take the credit for a deal or the Modena Agreement to become a fait accompli. If there was to be an agreement, he wanted it to be his and for it to be named after the Place de la Concorde where the FIA had its headquarters, not Ferrari's home base. He sent out a telex saying the Modena Agreement was not valid, but he also sought a meeting and agreed to join Bernie and me for breakfast at the Crillon. He was ready to concede some vital points and was prepared to abandon his original demand that all commercial aspects of Formula One should be in the governing body's hands. This meant the teams (i.e. Bernie) could deal with the money, at least for the next three or four years.

The result was the Concorde Agreement, negotiated over three weeks by Ferrari's Marco Piccinini and me with the assistance of Ronnie Austin, a Paris-based English lawyer retained by Renault. To keep the negotiations away from Balestre, we met in the Cercle National des Armées, which is a centre for serving military officers, holders of the Légion d'honneur and elite civil servants, the idea being that even if he found out where we were, he wouldn't dare enter the building given his questionable war record. Ferrari used to joke that Marco and I were the parents of the Concorde Agreement 'but no one knows which one is the father and which the mother' – very Italian. Marco was later an outstanding deputy president (sport) supporting me at the FIA. More recently, he became Monaco's minister of finance.

Under the agreement, the teams were to keep control of the commercial side of Formula One for the next four years. This meant Bernie could continue to collect money from the promoters on behalf of the teams, and Balestre's ambition to take everything for the FIA was temporarily (as he thought) on hold. It was agreed that the FIA would continue to control the sport, but the rules were to be made by a Formula 1 Commission (constituted as in the original Modena Agreement) subject only to the FISA World Council, which could reject a proposal of the F1 Commission but not change it. The council could only send it back to the commission to be reconsidered. Surprisingly, this never gave rise to the obvious potential problem of stalemate, with a commission proposal being repeatedly blocked and sent back by the World Council. The teams were to have a member and deputy on the World Council (Bernie and me). Additionally, Ferrari (i.e. Marco) were to have the motor industry seat whenever Formula One was being discussed.

Balestre had not given up on his plan to secure complete commercial control of Formula One, but all the teams, including Ferrari, were united against him on this point. The Concorde Agreement was for four years, after which Balestre planned to try once again to take over the commercial side. Had this ever happened, legal problems would probably have emerged because of European competition law. But in the event, Bernie and the teams made sure the agreement was renewed in 1985 for two years and a new five-year version signed in 1987. Yet another five-year Concorde Agreement was signed in 1990, for the years 1992 to 1996 inclusive. The latter agreement covered the first five years after I was elected president of FISA, although it had been signed nearly two years earlier. Except for a gap in 2008 and 2009, it has governed Formula One ever since, albeit with modifications.

The potential legal difficulties under European competition law of a sporting body having control of the money as well as holding absolute power over the sport remained academic because the agreement gave the teams commercial control. The competition law point was only finally resolved 20 years later when, as part of its settlement with the European Commission, the FIA undertook not to exploit any section of motor sport commercially as a condition of retaining absolute power as the sole licensing authority for international motor sport with no rival regulators.

While all these conflicts were playing out, Bernie was building up the Formula One business. At the same time, he repeatedly asked the members to participate in the financial risk for races whenever the promoter wanted them to do this, but the teams always refused. Bernie eventually took on the (considerable) risks himself and this, ultimately, was the main reason he was able to make a fortune from Formula One. He was also working to get more coverage on television. In those days, it was not a question of fees but exposure for sponsors. Gradually, he got TV companies to move away from showing parts of the most interesting races to broadcasting the entire race to televising the whole season. It proved to be a very lengthy process. As early as May 1980, FOCA voted him a budget of $150,000 to begin the development of on-board cameras for television.

There was also constant work on rationalising the events. Traditionally, each organiser set its own schedule for practice and the race. Practice would go on for most of two days, all times counting for the grid. The start was usually given by an ageing figure from the national club, like the old boy in Monaco who would pose with the flag in front of the cars, wave it, then dash out of the way as they accelerated. The grid would be alternate rows of three and two cars, lined up beside each other. The race director would be a local motor club official in each country, usually with very limited Formula One experience.

All of this and more had to be sorted out. First, we had to have agreement on each point within FOCA then begin the long and painful process of persuading the organisers and then, finally, the F1 Commission. The slick, efficient procedures and safety precautions that are the norm at a modern Grand Prix took many years of tedious meetings and negotiation to achieve. Indeed, the process was not completed until I became president of the FIA many years later, but mercifully we were on our way at last. But the most fundamental change was that the Concorde Agreement had made it possible for Bernie to build one of the most successful businesses in modern sport.

14

BERNIE BUILDS HIS BUSINESS

When Robin Herd and I started March in 1969, the Formula One World Championship had been running for 20 years. It had a big following worldwide but as the Porsche deal in chapter 5 made clear, it was not nearly as important commercially as long-distance racing, which included events such as the Daytona 24 hours, Sebring 12 hours, Nürburgring 1000 km, Brands Hatch 500-mile race and, of course, the Le Mans 24-hour race. Although there had been a slight decline due to budget cuts by the car industry, long-distance racing was still streets ahead of Formula One.

When Bernie Ecclestone bought the Brabham team two years later, Formula One was very much the poor relation of sports cars and the so-called 'sports prototypes'. In our sport the financial prizes for success in a race were minimal. The real money, such as it was, came in the form of a payment to each team from the race promoter, negotiated individually and known as 'start money'. Sometimes the promoter was a commercial organisation, but major events, including Formula One, were usually promoted by the national sporting authority.

This arrangement worked against the teams' best interests. The promoter would know that a top team absolutely needed to participate in the event to earn World Championship points, which meant it could offer a reduced, take-it-or-leave-it fee. And a back-of-the-grid team would be told that the promoter didn't care whether they turned up or not. In both cases the promoters were in a strong position, which eventually pushed the teams to try collective bargaining.

Promoters countered this by also negotiating collectively, at least for the European races. I took part in my first meeting of this kind early in 1970, before the first race of the season. The teams turned up as a group because they didn't trust one another not to do side deals. Once the teams had seen the March cars actually run, they invited me along because I was a lawyer. That first meeting astonished me – I simply could not believe a world sport was run like this. The level of discussion and negotiation would have been OK for a village football club but that was about it. They would even undermine one another's points; for example, one asking for free hire cars, another saying 'but we've never had that', all in front of the promoters.

During this period, the payment system in Europe moved from individually negotiated start money and minimal prize money to one where rewards were dependent on a team's performance during practice and the race. Elsewhere, teams still dealt individually with the organisers because of travel costs, but this too eventually became a collective arrangement when Bernie started doing deals for the teams as a whole. The race promoters were all either the national motor sport authority itself or very closely connected to it. In this way, through the FIA, the promoters had complete control over the international calendar and the rules, as well as all commercial aspects of their events.

Shortly after Bernie bought Brabham at the end of 1971 he and I began to negotiate for all the teams. The organisation (such as it was) was called the Formula One Constructors' and Entrants' Association, and included 'entrants' because individuals were allowed to buy Formula One cars from a constructor and compete in the championship. A privately entered driver could score points but the points he scored for the Manufacturers' Cup would go to the company that built the car. The best example of a private entrant was Rob Walker, who won the 1961 Monaco Grand Prix with Stirling Moss and the 1968 British with Jo Siffert.

The association was managed by Andrew Ferguson, an ex-employee of Lotus recommended by Colin Chapman and trusted by everyone. Each team paid an annual subscription to cover the costs. It was very difficult to collect the money, and eventually we resolved that the prize fund would be paid directly to the association and shared out on the agreed scale to the teams after deducting 2 per cent for running costs. After a while, Bernie took over the secretariat with the agreement of all the teams and employed Peter Macintosh to run things. Peter had previously been in charge of the Red Arrows and had flown the spare plane to events. As the organisation took on more duties and scope and became more professional, Bernie increased his deduction to 4 per cent. By the 1980s it had doubled again to 8 per cent. Unlike paying a subscription, it was not painful because no one knew before the race what they would earn.

In his dealings with each promoter on behalf of the teams, Bernie began to get them to throw in the television rights as part of the prize fund. With one or two exceptions, they were of no value back then because it was very difficult for most races to sell the broadcast rights beyond the host country. Except for Monaco and perhaps the Italian Grand Prix, foreign rights were all but worthless because hardly any TV company wanted to show overseas races. Eurovision controlled all international rights within Europe and fees were either negligible or non-existent. At the same time it was widely believed in the 1970s that a promoter should not allow the race to be broadcast in its country because no one would buy tickets if they could watch it on television for free. Nowadays, everyone knows that's nonsense, but it was firmly believed back then. Because of these myths and timidity, television coverage throughout the decade of Stewart, Lauda, Fittipaldi, Peterson, Hunt, Andretti, Scheckter et al was scandalously sparse.

The objective at that time was not to increase revenue by selling the rights; the aim was to increase the coverage. The greater the coverage, the more money the teams could get from sponsors. With the rights in his pocket, Bernie bypassed Eurovision, who fought back in vain. Next, he began to withhold rights from broadcasters unless they guaranteed to transmit the entire race; and once he had persuaded a rapidly increasing number to screen individual Grands Prix in full, he began to push them to show the whole season.

The rights still brought in almost no money, but the coverage expanded enormously year by year. So did the audience because the season began to take on the narrative arc of a soap opera that could be followed from race to race. At last, by the end of the 1980s, the value of the rights themselves began to rise sharply and, by then, Bernie, on behalf of the teams, had all the TV rights to the championship – even Monaco, who were the last to relinquish them to him.

Ten years earlier, when the FOCA–FISA war started, the commercial rights were one of the things that disturbed the FIA. Although the FIA had never owned any commercial rights in the

Formula One World Championship, Balestre noticed that Bernie was acquiring more and more rights for the teams from the race promoters. Balestre felt that these rights should be taken over by the FIA.

As FOCA, we had raised the question of what were then Articles 85 and 86 of the Treaty of Rome (abuse of a dominant position) in the mid-1970s because the race promoters had such disproportionate commercial power. As a result of their membership of the FIA, they had complete control over both sporting and commercial aspects of Formula One. But no one in the FIA at that time took European competition laws, or what was then the European Commission's DG4, very seriously.

Part of the 1981 Concorde Agreement provided that all commercial aspects of the championship would be exploited by FOCA on behalf of the teams. In return, FOCA had to recognise that the rights to the championship belonged to the FIA. Balestre's intention was that these rights would go to the FIA when the agreement ended four years later. Had the agreement come to an end, things might not have been that simple. The promoters from whom Bernie had acquired rights would probably have pointed out that these had never belonged to the FIA, and an acknowledgement from Bernie and the teams that the championship rights belonged to the FIA could not change that.

Most importantly, the agreement gave the teams (effectively Bernie) the right to make all contracts for a Grand Prix. This simply recognised the de facto position that a promoter could not put on a race without the teams. In effect, this gave Bernie and the teams control of the calendar, the one element of the championship that arguably did belong to the FIA or, rather, collectively those members of the FIA that organised and promoted

Grand Prix races. However, Balestre insisted that the teams must individually submit an entry for the entire championship to the FIA. This further weakened the promoters, each of whom originally had the individual right to accept or reject an entry.

Had Balestre ever succeeded in acquiring all the commercial rights for the FIA, there might have been significant legal problems. Brussels could have challenged how such a monopoly operated under the Treaty of Rome. Moreover, Bernie had been very careful to make sure his contracts with race promoters and television stations never all expired at the same time. So any attempt by a third party such as the FIA to take over could be met with legal action claiming interference with contractual relations, the weapon FOCA had used back in the winter of 1980/81.

Bernie also wanted to control the advertising rights at each circuit during a Grand Prix. Initially, at least, this was nothing to do with making money – it was to stop advertising interfering with the television broadcast, or perhaps preventing a Grand Prix being shown at all in some countries because of objectionable trackside advertising. Circuit advertising also tended to be sold by the square metre and some circuits were plastered with logos, often of small local companies. It all looked messy and down-market, as well as sometimes breaching television guidelines. There was also the problem that circuits would offer advertising at rates below the increasingly large fees paid to the teams by their sponsors. Bernie realised that by cleaning all this up he could make each Grand Prix look better, protect the teams and, most importantly, keep the television companies happy.

But how to do this when he already had his hands more than full? The solution was Paddy McNally, who had been around motor racing for a long time. I first came across him when I went to buy two magnesium front wheels for my U2 from Robs Lamplough back in 1966. I found Robs and Paddy having dinner in a restaurant near Robs's place in Adam and Eve Mews in Kensington. They were both wealthy amateur racers and Robs later drove in that Hockenheim Formula Two race where Jim Clark was killed in April 1968. Later still, Paddy became *Autosport*'s Formula One correspondent, then went to live in Switzerland with his wife and joined the Philip Morris Formula One programme to look after their Marlboro circuit advertising.

With several years' experience of the business, he was the ideal person to take control of circuit advertising. Encouraged by Bernie, he set up in business and bought the circuit advertising rights from each organiser. By reducing the number of advertisers and repackaging the way these rights were sold, he turned it into a very successful business. He also created the Paddock Club, where sponsors could entertain their guests, fully understanding that you could charge outrageous prices if you provided an exemplary service. After some 25 years of this, Paddy retired a few years ago a very rich man.

Perhaps the most interesting development of all was how Bernie came to have the right to make all the race contracts for Formula One and thus, in effect, control the championship. To begin with, he dealt on behalf of the teams (with a bit of help from me). As already noted, he charged them collectively 2 per cent of the fee he managed to extract from the race promoter. This gradually increased to 8 per cent. He also offered to negotiate film and television rights in return for 30 per cent of what he could collect for them and, again, the teams agreed.

Then, in the late 1970s, two things happened. First, Watkins Glen, the home of the United States Grand Prix, failed to pay the agreed prize fund. The teams were understandably angry that they had raced but not been paid. Second, whenever race promoters said they couldn't afford FOCA's terms during negotiations, we would offer to take over all the finances of the race. We proposed paying the promoter a fee to look after all the sporting aspects, including the FIA's costs and calendar fee, while the teams assumed all the event's financial risks. If it rained, the crowd was small and the event lost money, only the teams would suffer. The race promoters always turned us down because, despite their pleas of poverty and a failure in many cases to promote Grands Prix properly, they were almost all doing well.

By the late 1970s we had pushed the prize fund to a point where a promoter finally took us up on the offer. As already noted, we found ourselves financially responsible for the 1978 German Grand Prix at Hockenheim. The organiser no longer wanted to assume the financial risk and Bernie asked the teams to participate. They refused, wanting their agreed fee no matter what happened with the race.

Yet it was quite an attractive proposition for a backer because you would know virtually straightaway, the day after the race, whether there had been a profit or a loss. And in Germany most of the tickets were sold in advance, so the receipts from the race were not at the mercy of the weather to the same degree as some other races. In the event, the backers made a profit and after such a profitable beginning, investment financing to promote the races became much easier to attract.

This same pattern was later repeated in Italy (Imola but not Monza), Brazil and other countries. Generally, those race promoters who were making good money kept the commercial risk. Others, particularly clubs for whom a Grand Prix was not part of their core business and who did not want to put their members' funds at risk or felt they might lose money, were glad to pass it

on. Each time this happened, the teams were invited to participate and they declined every opportunity.

By the end of 1977, I no longer had a team and was persuaded
to take on the job of securing funding and trying to make sure
the races didn't lose money. I made a number of mistakes, particularly with the 1978 German race, the first one I did. These
included infuriating the press by selling their traditional seats in
the so-called Press Tribune and giving them (as I thought) better
facilities. I also ordered far too many programmes – another costly
but useful lesson.

Apart from the errors, I made a lot of changes that worked at
Hockenheim. These included numbering all the seats in the vast
stadium (there turned out to be fewer than the circuit owners
thought) and increasing some prices substantially. From one section of the grandstands you could see the entire infield, so I more
than doubled the prices of the seats there. The officials of the
municipality that owned the circuit were horrified, saying it
would be bad for the town's reputation, but I pacified them by
promising to give each spectator a cushion. It worked, but at later
events I was more inclined to leave well alone.

Also, with the help of Peter Macintosh, who had been their
manager, I booked the Red Arrows display team for the race.
They put on an amazing show, going down below the level of
the highest grandstand seats to perform a manoeuvre just above
the infield. Standing on top of one of the transporters, I felt I
could reach up and touch the plane as it passed over my head.
The huge crowd was delighted and, extraordinarily for an out-
door sporting occasion, gave them a standing ovation. A senior
German official came to me afterwards and said he thought it
had been very dangerous. I tried to appear offended and said,
'But it's the Royal Air Force!' I think the pilots always made a

special effort if they were abroad, particularly in Germany, provided no senior RAF officer was about.

By the time I left Formula One at the end of 1982, the pattern was well established. The events where the organiser asked the teams to take the risk had all turned out to be profitable, at least to some degree, but the teams still refused to get involved. Their business, they said, was going racing, not event management. Bernie took it all on himself after my departure. Furthermore, after the Watkins Glen experience, the teams wanted him to take all the risks on the prize fund even where, as in that case, there was no commercial involvement in the race itself. Bernie guaranteed the teams their agreed money and they were happy for him to do his own deal with each organiser.

Eventually, Bernie moved his arrangements with the teams on to an annual footing. He would do a deal for an annual prize fund with the teams, then collect whatever he could from each organiser. By the time he came to consider an IPO, or initial public offering, of shares in his business in 1997 he was making a lot of money. It seems the teams had not really thought about his side of the business until that point. They, too, were doing very well, with massively increased sponsorship and the involvement of several major car manufacturers. But what Bernie paid them each season, although it had steadily increased, eventually became a great deal less than his total receipts from the promoters.

Bernie's deals with the race promoters by now included just about everything except the ticket sales, circuit advertising and hospitality rights. The latter by then belonged to McNally, who paid more for them than the promoter had been receiving but, by repackaging and linking some rights with the Paddock Club, was making a very good profit. Bernie owned the TV rights, the right to time the event – even the right to provide the safety car – and was collecting money for each. Some things, such as the timing, actually saved the promoters money because previously they would have had to pay timekeepers, but now everything was producing revenue for Bernie.

In the 1990s, he invested heavily in a multichannel TV system that, unlike the standard free-to-air coverage, was available only on pay TV. You could choose from six channels, one of which was the same live timing screen that the teams were given in the pits. You could even have natural sound, almost like being at the track. As a concept it was well ahead of its time, but it involved taking hundreds of people and some 200 tons of equipment to each race. I don't know the figures but suspect it made little if any profit. Bernie's deal with the teams meant he had to give them their percentage from the gross rather than after deducting costs. He eventually stopped it but today the whole thing could be streamed over the internet.

The internet rights to Formula One were one of the few things Bernie didn't fully exploit. For some reason, he always had a blind spot for it, even though I was urging him to put live timing on the web as early as 1995. It seemed to me that it would be a huge boost to the TV coverage and a potential source of revenue if you could have the same information as the teams right there on a computer beside your television. It was technically feasible even back in 1995. Of course, you could get live timing on Bernie's multichannel system, but unless you had two television sets you had to leave the live picture to see the timing. It seemed obvious that most people had a computer plus a TV, while almost no one would have two televisions in the same room, but Bernie did not agree.

However, neglect of the internet was a relatively minor matter back in the 1990s and by then, after 20 years of hard work, Bernie had a very significant business indeed.

15

A PEACE OF SORTS

Once things had settled down after the Concorde Agreement was signed in 1981, Bernie did a deal with several Las Vegas casino owners to hold a Formula One World Championship race in their town. The idea was to run it on a temporary circuit set up within the (very large) Caesars Palace car park. When the Caesars group came over to negotiate, we took them to a party in the Royal Albert Hall given by Essex Overseas Petroleum Corporation, who sponsored Lotus. Essex was an oil-trading firm then earning untold sums of money. The party was completely surreal – David Thieme, the company's owner, held a dinner on the floor of the auditorium for all the main Formula One people. His customers and staff were placed in the tiers of seats above. He flew in the three most famous French chefs of the time to prepare the dinner with the help of staff from a big London hotel, and hired top entertainers for later in the evening.

During the dinner the Caesars Palace casino manager, Billy Weinberger, suddenly turned to Bernie and me and said jokingly: 'Have you ever seen that film *The Sting*?' I understood what he meant – the whole thing was so weird you really could have thought we'd laid it all on just for him. He later took me to one of the London casinos where a large room full of people were gambling, and explained they were all there for the benefit of just one man who had won a great deal of money. Billy very discreetly pointed him out. The casino needed the right atmosphere and surroundings to keep him there until they could win it back.

Arriving in Vegas, Bernie had booked me into the Caesars Palace Fantasy Tower. I was surprised to find a large mirror on the ceiling directly above the huge circular bed. I called Bernie to ask what the mirror was for and he explained it was so one could comb one's hair in bed. I really should have worked that out for myself without having to call him for an explanation. In addition to the usual bathroom there was a Jacuzzi, big enough for several people, in the corner of the room. Apparently, at least one of the drivers took full advantage of all these facilities.

The next day we were having breakfast when Billy Weinberger took a call from someone who was obviously important. When the call finished, he told us the biggest gambler in the world had just said he was flying in for the race. I couldn't resist asking just how big the biggest in the world was. Apparently, when he had been in Vegas for the Leonard–Hearns fight, he had 'dropped' $8 million in Caesars and another $7 million down the Strip. It's the reason the big gambling centres run these events – they give the high rollers a reason to visit.

Nelson Piquet, driving for Bernie, won the Formula One World Championship at that Vegas race by a single point from Carlos Reutemann by finishing fifth. Carlos started from pole but ended up eighth, one lap behind. Bernie decided to join a big game that night with a group of elderly Chinese ladies and invited me to partner him. Fortunately, I declined. I watched him lose well over $100,000 but, with Brabham's World Championship win, he was still well ahead on the day.

Having made peace with us, Balestre had a confrontation with the drivers. He introduced a number of clauses the drivers didn't like in the application form for the so-called super licence they needed to drive in Formula One. We were not very concerned either way, but we encouraged Balestre knowing that a row with the drivers would keep him busy and also stop him using them against us in any dispute over the rules. They had, after all, greatly helped him over the skirt issue.

For the first time ever the drivers organised an effective strike and credit for that must go to Niki Lauda. At the start of the first day of practice for the 1982 South African Grand Prix, he had secretly hired a bus, persuaded all the drivers to board and took them to a Johannesburg hotel he had booked so that their teams could not make contact and put pressure on them in the usual way. What none of us knew at the time was that Ferrari were quietly giving the drivers legal and tactical advice via their driver Didier Pironi. Enzo Ferrari and Marco Piccinini were on manoeuvres again because they saw Balestre getting too close to us and wanted to move the fulcrum of the balance of power slightly away from our side. Helping the drivers give Balestre problems was all part of the process.

Niki and Pironi flew to the circuit from their hotel by helicopter to negotiate with Balestre and kept the other drivers informed. Eventually, they seemed to give in and the race went ahead, although a day of practice had been lost. But the offending clause that stopped the drivers changing teams easily (and was probably in restraint of trade and thus illegal) was quietly dropped. Balestre fined the drivers but they succeeded in getting the fines reduced in the FIA Court of Appeal, much to his annoyance.

This led him to abolish the right of appeal from the race stewards on the grounds that the public should not have to wait while the results of a race were discussed in a tribunal. Years later when I was elected, I reinstated the right of appeal. It was annoying if we (i.e. the FIA executive) lost, but an independent body to hear appeals was in my view essential. I don't think Balestre, despite being French, thought much of Montesquieu or the separation of powers. The idea that the executive, the legislature and the judiciary should be separate and independent of one another was not high on his list of priorities, yet it is just as essential to a properly run sporting body as it is to a country.

Despite the Concorde Agreement, peace with the FIA was short-lived. The teams running with the Cosworth DFV eight-cylinder engines were lighter but had less power than the continental teams with their 12-cylinder and turbocharged engines. The minimum weight limit, however, prevented the British teams from using this potential advantage. Clever minds can often spot a loophole, though, and two of them latched on to a clause in the regulations allowing the car's fluids (oil, water, brake fluid etc.) to be topped back up to their normal levels before a car was weighed at the end of the race. Brabham and Williams hit on the idea of water-cooled brakes.

The cars were fitted with a water tank and a device to squirt water on to the brakes to cool them. With the water tank full, the car complied with the minimum weight rule, but empty, it was significantly under the limit. There was an entirely justified suspicion among officials and rival teams that the water was being emptied soon after the start, perhaps even during the formation lap, so that the car could run for the entire race well under the weight limit. When other teams protested, the stewards decided that topping up the tanks with a large quantity of water in order to get the car's weight back up to the minimum after the race was illegal, despite the letter of the rule.

While this was going on, the political scene in France was shifting. In 1981 François Mitterrand had been elected president and Guy Ligier (the driver who said I'd pushed him off in that Spanish Formula Two race back in 1968, described in chapter 4) was now the owner of a successful independent Formula One team and allied with us. But, more importantly, at a low point in Mitterrand's political career when he was accused of faking an assassination attempt in 1959 (the so-called Observatory Affair), Guy had been an absolutely loyal friend and acted as his driver and bodyguard just when others were deserting him. Mitterrand had not forgotten and Guy was now in a good position in the French political establishment. This led Balestre to start to come over more to our side plus, in a funny way, I think he felt more comfortable with us than with the big car manufacturers. He'd had disputes with some of them in his *L'Auto-Journal* days.

As a result, when Brabham and Williams took the water tank question to the FIA Court of Appeal, Balestre was on our side. Meanwhile, Ferrari and the manufacturers, who were aware of the political changes, were watching him carefully. One of them even arranged for a photograph of Balestre in SS uniform to circulate, and also had a recording of him telling me on the telephone that we shouldn't worry about the water tank appeal – the FIA Court of Appeal was in his pocket and the judges detested Marco Piccinini, the Ferrari team manager. We would win, he told me. The people responsible told Ferrari about the recording and said it was made entirely by chance by an amateur enthusiast (a tale worthy of the *News of the World* in later years). It made me quite wary from then on about anything I really wanted to keep secret. Enzo Ferrari, however, told them not to publish the transcript, so no more was said.

When the water tank appeal was lost, the FOCA teams announced they would not participate at the next race, the San Marino Grand Prix at Imola, unless water-cooled brakes could be used. We argued that the FIA Court of Appeal had effectively changed the rule on topping up and done so without proper notice. But Tyrrell had just signed a sponsorship deal with a local Italian ceramics company and felt obliged to take part despite our boycott. Although the field was greatly diminished, the Italian crowd was happy with a display by the two Ferraris, while Tyrrell's presence ensured that there were enough cars for the race to count for the championship. It became clear to me that politically, FOCA was a busted flush, an instrument that would break in your hand at the key moment. The real power in Formula One lay with the FIA, which was coincidentally holding a major meeting in Casablanca.

We needed to be there, if only to keep the friendly elements onside, so Bernie, Teddy Mayer and I went to Morocco in a hired plane. By now Balestre was almost entirely in our camp and, as a result, had increasing problems with the manufacturers. In particular, Marco Piccinini didn't want Balestre too close to us, as this might perhaps have resulted in rules that Ferrari didn't like. So he set out to destabilise Balestre in much the same way as we had three years earlier. His main ploy was to get the Italian oil industry to use its Russian connections (which were strong) to influence the USSR delegate on the World Council.

The Russian delegate seldom did more than say something anodyne to get his name in the minutes before setting off for a good dinner at the Tour d'Argent. He always had an interpreter with him, who was rumoured to be a full-on KGB man. During the Casablanca meeting, he made a speech for the first time. His interpreter then spoke at length in French. We still don't know whether the first speech bore any relation to the second, but with some 20 or so votes in his pocket from the countries that made up the USSR in those days, he had to be taken seriously. Two decisions went against Balestre in Casablanca and he understood Ferrari's message.

We were due to report back to a FOCA meeting as soon as we got home, but Bernie had sent someone from the hotel to buy all three of us full traditional Moroccan outfits including a fez, a long shirt-like garment and shoes that pointed up at the toes. He insisted we should turn up for it dressed like that. After a few minutes of frivolity, we had to report that all the manufacturers' proposals had gone through because the failure of the Imola boycott meant the organisers, and hence FISA, no longer feared us. Any future threat to stay away would be seen as empty and would be ignored. The rest of the meeting was taken up with berating Ken Tyrrell for breaking ranks and going to Imola.

By 1983, the power imbalance between the teams with Cosworth V8s and the newly emerging turbocharged engines had become extreme and, from 1984, fuel consumption and later boost pressure were limited to keep power outputs under control before the turbo was finally banned in 1989. Among our teams, Bernie's Brabhams already had a turbo based on the four-cylinder BMW road car engine. Compared with the sophisticated Ferrari and Renault turbocharged engines it was relatively simple – it even used an engine block from the BMW 2002 road car – but was good enough to win the 1983 World Championship for Nelson Piquet and Bernie.

After five years of effort by Renault as the turbocharging pioneers, and Ferrari not far behind, it was extraordinary that a relatively low-key BMW programme would be the first to win the championship with a turbocharged engine. When Paul Rosche (he of the Formula Two engine eight years before) got back to Munich after his triumph, the BMW board of directors had arranged for a traditional Bavarian brass band to be on the airport tarmac to greet him.

Apart from doing an excellent all-round job, Rosche's department at BMW had heard of an old fuel formula in the archives of a German chemical company that had been developed in the Second World War when Germany was short of lead. Being lead-free, it complied with the Formula One octane rules but behaved as if it didn't. It had apparently been formulated for a very high-performance engine (probably a fighter plane) and was ideal for a turbocharged racing engine. It was rumoured that the original wartime technical specification was still marked 'top secret'. It gave an instant increase of nearly 100 horsepower. The BMW dynamometer could measure up to 1200 bhp but this was not sufficient to allow the engine to be tested at maximum power. The estimate was 1500 bhp when it was set up for qualifying. It must have been terrifying to drive.

The rest of 1982 was relatively quiet except that Bernie and I hit on the idea of moving the South African Grand Prix to Zimbabwe, then newly independent. We thought this might make an African Grand Prix possible, but without the South African problem. Our lawyer in South Africa was friendly with Humphry Berkeley, a maverick former Conservative MP who had the right connections and could introduce us to the new Zimbabwe government. We were not over-optimistic. Although there was a circuit, it was nowhere near what was needed, but maybe the newly independent government would develop it and finance a race as a matter of national prestige. I got the job of going there to investigate, accompanied by Berkeley and an associate of his from the UK.

Our first meeting was with the minister of sport, who was very welcoming and gave us tea but was clearly an expert in areas more connected with recent conflicts. His main civil servant, quite old and probably a survivor from the previous regime, said: 'This old head thinks this is a matter for the minister of finance.' I thought that sounded promising. A meeting was set up.

No fewer than three ministers turned up for the meeting, headed by Dr Nathan Shamuyarira, then minister for information and tourism. He had spent time in London and was very politically aware. He opened the meeting by saying, 'Tell me, Mr Mosley, are you any relation of the famous Oswald Mosley?' I thought Humphry Berkeley and the other person with us were going to die. They obviously feared the name was not top of the appreciation list in a newly independent Zimbabwe. I replied that, yes, I was his son but that up to now, in motor racing, everyone assumed I must be related to Alf Moseley, the coach builder from Leicester. I told Shamuyarira he was the very first to ask about my father in a motor sport context. There was much laughter from the Zimbabwe ministers and relief for Berkeley. However, disappointingly, the Zimbabwe idea went nowhere.

16

AN ATTEMPT AT UK POLITICS

The 1982 Imola race had shown the weakness of FOCA and made me realise it could never be a reliable power base in any conflict with the governing body. The teams could not be relied upon and the establishment would always win in the end. At the same time, I was beginning to think seriously about British politics. Politics was what really interested me and would have been my career from the beginning had it not been for my family name. It now seemed possible after my father's death in 1980. While he was alive it was not on – he would not have opposed me in any way but one never knew what he might do or say next.

My aunt Debo, the youngest of the Mitford sisters, was married to Andrew Devonshire, whose uncle was Harold Macmillan, the former Conservative prime minister. They invited me to Chatsworth to discuss the idea with Macmillan, who was by then living there more or less permanently. He and I talked late into the night after everyone had gone to bed, but I was distracted by his disturbing habit of lighting his pipe and not noticing that the match had burned down to his fingers. It looked so painful I could hardly bear to watch but he didn't seem to notice. He and my father were contemporaries and knew each other well in the period up to 1931. They had agreed about the need for Keynesian measures to deal with the economic problems of that time.

Macmillan's view was that no serious figure in politics would mind in the least who my father was and he thought that no voter would care, either. I later came to think he was almost certainly right but that the people in between – those who decide whether or not you get a seat – might be more of a problem. There was also the risk that my opponents would drag my father into any controversy.

Sure enough, nearly 30 years later when I suggested to a parliamentary select committee that a member of the public should be warned if their privacy was about to be invaded, an idiot *Daily Mail* columnist did just that. He wrote: 'A privacy law would suit Mr Mosley very nicely. Like his father he does not believe in freedom.' All I had suggested was that before a person's privacy was irremediably breached, he or she should be allowed to ask a judge to rule. No rational adult would label that a denial of freedom and what my long-deceased father had to do with it escaped me entirely. But it illustrated the sort of moronic tabloid nonsense I would have had to contend with in British politics.

Nevertheless, encouraged by what Macmillan had said, I decided to try. At the end of 1982 I stopped all my motor sport activity, including with FOCA, and began by helping the Tories at the 1983 Bermondsey by-election. The agent there was Ron Green; very experienced, very canny and the permanent agent in the Westminster North constituency. After the by-election, I became involved in Westminster North, where the sitting MP was Sir John Wheeler. Since I had decided on politics, I wanted to get on with it. But voluntary helpers are part-time, so it was not possible to throw myself as fully into political activity as I would have wished.

This was frustrating but I engaged on projects such as computerising the electoral register, commonplace now but unusual back in 1983. I got on well with the local party workers, particularly Ian Harvey, who was clearly very able but whose successful parliamentary career had been wrecked when as a junior minister he was caught with a guardsman in the bushes of St James's Park. Nowadays, they could have got married had they wished but back in 1958 homosexuality was still illegal in the UK and it finished his career.

One of the benefits of the decision to get out of motor racing was that I found myself with some free time at last. I decided to learn to fly a helicopter before I got too old. I loved it – it's the nearest thing one can imagine to a magic carpet and I had endless fun learning because the instructor, although very professional and competent, was not above showing me occasionally what the machine could do. After my first solo flight I thought long and hard but decided not to pursue it, realising I had the wrong temperament – you don't take risks with helicopters. Also, they are not suitable for part-time pilots. Had I continued, an accident would have been highly likely. I had fun, though, hovering outside the kitchen window of our little house near Bicester while the instructor held his hands up so Jean could see I was flying it.

The 1983 general election was the first time I could become fully engaged. It was a successful campaign and friendships were cemented. Ron Green and Ian Harvey, who was a key figure in Westminster North, were both on the more liberal wing of the party and this resonated with me. I was only a ward chairman but they encouraged me to go to Central Office and try to get on the candidates' list. When I met the person in charge of the list, a vice-chairman of the party, I thought him deeply unimpressive and, no doubt, he thought the same of me. But the really worrying thing was the other people waiting to see him, who struck me as extremely odd, to say the least.

Perhaps it was a day set aside for oddballs and they saw me as one of them but, whatever the reason, it was a far cry from Macmillan and his advice. With someone in charge like the man I had just met, I was certain it would take me a long time to get on the candidates' list and I would still be left with the problem of finding a constituency. There was a real danger of spending years looking for a seat. If the person in charge of the list was such an obvious dud, what would those further down the chain of command be like? Although I might strike lucky, I might also waste ten years. By then I would be in my fifties and it would be too late for anything else.

So in 1985, I went back to motor racing, but this time with the intention of becoming part of the establishment because it seemed the next best thing to politics. Returning to the Bar or some sort of business activity did not appeal, apart from which I had a lot of motor sport experience. It was probably the right decision. As things turned out, I think I was able to achieve far more in real (as opposed to motor sport) politics with the FIA than I could have in UK domestic politics, unless I had been extremely lucky and found myself in an important ministerial position. It had been an interesting diversion but I still hoped to do something significant with my life and didn't want to risk wasting years on British politics.

17

BACK TO MOTOR SPORT
AND FIA ELECTIONS

I had remained in contact with Bernie and Formula One and even went to the occasional race. In mid-1985, Bernie and I met Balestre for dinner at a restaurant near his home in the South of France, where we suggested I take over FISA's Manufacturers' Commission. The person currently holding the post was not very competent and Balestre recognised this. The commission was made up of the competition directors from all the major motor manufacturers, and it was important that they should feel their interests were understood and properly represented. It would mean me filling the car industry's seat on the World Motor Sport Council.

When we put the idea forward, I could sense Balestre was uncomfortable with the thought of bringing me into the heart of his fiefdom, but he didn't get on well with the car industry. When he edited *L'Auto-Journal* in the 1950s and '60s, he often ran campaigns against some of them. Now that he was about to become president of the entire FIA, not just its sporting commission, he felt he was on a par with heads of state rather than car company CEOs. The quarrels at the start of the decade had long receded – he had established something close to a modus vivendi with Bernie and probably thought I might be a useful link to the industry. Since I would be concerned with other forms of motor sport, not Formula One, he rather reluctantly agreed. Although he smelled danger, he felt he could not really refuse.

The appointment procedure was not very democratic. The manufacturers didn't want me and there was an election within the commission that resulted in 14 votes for the incumbent, five for another candidate and only three for me. But the vote was merely a proposal to the World Council. The final choice was the council's and Balestre kept his word, successfully urging my appointment. Bernie and I were now both on the World Council, but under the Concorde Agreement the manufacturers' seat was still occupied by Ferrari whenever Formula One was discussed.

Just before I began in my new role there was a bad accident during a World Rally Championship event in Corsica. The Finnish driver Henri Toivonen and his Italian-American co-driver Sergio Cresto were killed when their Lancia Delta S4 crashed and burst into flames. It was on a remote stretch of road and there was no one there to help them. The powerful and savagely fast Group B cars were virtually racing cars but used on the road and, apart from very high performance, were extremely vulnerable in a crash.

Balestre reacted by banning them, with effect from the following season. He claimed to be able to do this on grounds of safety, but his position under the regulations was weak. This time, though, his opposition was not the alliance of disparate elements and interests that made up FOCA but Peugeot, a major

French manufacturer whose team boss was Jean Todt. Peugeot sued him in the French courts and won FF400,000 (about €61,000) damages at first instance. This was a massive award by French standards, as their courts are reluctant to award financial compensation, and it put Balestre in a serious fix.

He asked me to persuade the competition managers of the other manufacturers to support the ban and vote against Peugeot. This was at my first meeting of the Manufacturers' Commission, where I had just been imposed as chairman, and the Peugeot representative on the commission was, of course, Jean Todt.

Improbably, I succeeded. Despite their own interests, even the competition managers who were running Group B cars seemed to feel the ban was probably the right thing to do. The rally community was very shocked by the deaths of two leading competitors in horrific circumstances. This, combined with big-company reluctance to challenge the establishment, which had caused us such difficulty in 1980 and 1981, proved decisive.

Balestre was waiting for the result of the vote in his office at the French Federation. When I told him the news I was given a full Gallic embrace. He was relieved, delighted, and sat me down for a long talk. He confided that he was very worried about Bernie and the difficulties he might still cause the FIA. I explained that when the English want to neutralise someone who is a bit of a revolutionary and might destabilise the establishment, they don't usually kill or imprison them. The very effective English technique is to bring them into the establishment and seduce them into a different approach to life. That way you get a friend rather than a martyr. I advised him to bring Bernie into the FIA. Although I thought this was sound advice, I was conscious that it would increase Bernie's, and thus my, influence within the FIA, but I also owed Bernie for his help in securing my position. After some discussion, Balestre accepted. With his usual control over the institutions of the FIA he made Bernie a vice-president of the FIA; not just FISA, its sporting arm, but the entire organisation. Bernie was now in charge of FIA promotional affairs, a turn of events that began a new phase.

I went out of my way to make the Manufacturers' Commission meetings effective and was greatly helped in this by Pierre de Coninck, the commission's secretary, who was also FISA's deputy secretary-general. He eventually found it impossible to continue working in FISA's administration as it then was and left, but when I was elected FISA president he came back as secretary-general and did an outstanding job for the entire 18 years I spent in charge of the sport.

We began holding the meetings at the airport rather than at FISA's Paris office, thinking that spending a good hour each way on the journey into the city was not an effective use of the time of 30 or so highly paid motor industry managers. We also tightened up the procedure, making sure all discussions were relevant and, wherever possible, documents had been circulated in advance. I gradually earned their trust and at the end of my first year they unanimously proposed me to the World Council. From then on I was re-elected unopposed each year.

I went every year to Japan because of the importance of the Japanese manufacturers in motor sport. These were enjoyable occasions because the meetings were usually high-level and interesting. Also, I adore Japanese food. On more than one occasion, Balestre came too and I mentioned to him that my great-grandfather, Bertram Mitford, had been one of the first British diplomats to visit the Imperial Court when Japan opened up in the mid-19th century. He had subsequently become an admirer of everything Japanese and written a number of books about the country, at least one of which is still on sale in most Japanese bookshops. He had seen the extraordinary change from a Japanese military using bows and arrows in the 1860s to one able to defeat the Russian fleet only 40 years later. Balestre insisted that I mention this to our hosts. I found that a bit embarrassing but he was right, it went down very well.

Although I was not involved in Formula One, I went to the 1989 Japanese Grand Prix to meet representatives of the Japanese car industry, who were always there in force. During the race, Alain Prost and Ayrton Senna collided. Prost could not continue but Senna did and went on to win. Balestre entered the stewards' room and pressured them into disqualifying Senna, which seemed to me quite wrong and a clear abuse of power. The following year at the same race, Senna deliberately took Prost off on the first corner. Balestre, who was not there this time, attacked Jan Corsmit, the Dutch race director, for not penalising Senna. But Corsmit had seen it as a racing incident so did not pursue the matter. I defended him, telling Balestre in front of the World Council that he should not second-guess the appointed race director.

I was increasingly fed up. I could never get Balestre to make decisions when issues arose and I was very unhappy about his interference with the stewards, particularly in the Senna case. I saw this as political interference with the judiciary, something utterly abhorrent to anyone with respect for the rule of law. And I had not forgotten what he told me about the FIA Court of Appeal during the bugged telephone conversation back in 1982, when he had suggested it was in his pocket. Over the winter of 1990/91 I decided I had to quit.

Then I realised that a fortuitously strange set of circumstances had perhaps given me an opportunity to take a different route. In

1986 Balestre had a triple heart bypass and, because of this, resigned as FISA president but remained president of the FIA. He then changed his mind and asked to be re-elected FISA president in October 1987, so his two presidencies were now out of sync and his four-year mandate as head of the sport was due to finish in 1991. This meant he would have to stand for re-election to his FISA post in 1991, but all other FIA office holders would still have two years to run before its next four-yearly election in 1993. As a result, he would be on his own, isolated without his usual list of cronies, all under an obligation to vote for each other and for him.

Although he would be weaker than in a normal election, Balestre was still considered unbeatable – not least by himself. But he had made a tactical error born of hubris and had left himself vulnerable to a challenger who had nothing to lose. All the various FIA office holders lived in fear of his sanctions – losing their country's World Championship Rally or Formula One race – but I was going to quit anyway, so thought I might as well give it a go.

My first requirement was a national sporting authority to put me forward but I knew that the British never would. My own country's backing was not essential, though – any national motor sport body could put me up. As it happened, Balestre had behaved badly to Ron Frost, one of his former allies, who at the time had been head of the New Zealand Federation. Balestre had taken away the traditional New Zealand round of the World Rally Championship and given it to the United States. This was the same Ron Frost who played a key role in 1980 when we made the short-lived Lausanne Agreement. I arranged to meet him during one of his trips to the UK and told him of my plan. Ron was in favour and spoke to Morrie Chandler, his successor at the federation. This was in June 1991 and Morrie immediately agreed to nominate me when the time came that September. It was a very courageous decision because Balestre was bound to react badly. The election would be held at the FIA General Assembly on 9 October 1991. I began campaigning.

My campaign line was that motor sport needed a new president of FISA. Balestre held three posts – the FIA presidency, the FISA presidency and the presidency of his national motor sport authority, the FFSA. This, I said, was a double conflict of interest. The FISA president had to mediate between national sporting authorities and the FIA president had to deal with difficulties between the FISA and a national authority. It was not possible for one person to do all this without a risk of a conflict of interest. And, that apart, the three jobs were too much for one person now that motor sport had gained such importance worldwide, particularly a man of 70. I also made the obvious points about independence of the stewards and the difficulty of getting any sort of response from Balestre, something from which the national presidents also suffered. But the real strength of my position was a general discontent with him, combined with the fear of retribution should anyone go against him.

Balestre didn't find out what I was up to until August. Apparently, he was in his swimming pool and Marco Piccinini, who was visiting him, casually mentioned the forthcoming election. Balestre was taken by surprise. There was a full-on, *'Quoi! Quoi? Quelle election?'* – he had forgotten that his four years as FISA president would be up in October. He also took this position and his FIA presidency completely for granted, often saying in interviews that he would only leave FIA headquarters in a coffin.

I had a long-standing arrangement to go on a family holiday in Italy but was able to campaign on the phone. We had rented a small house in the grounds of Cetinale, owned by Lord Lambton. Formerly a British government minister, he had retired there after the *News of the World* published pictures of him having fun with two young ladies back in 1973. I spent most of the holiday ringing club presidents all over the world and, interestingly, none told me I didn't have a chance, although a few said they would not vote for me.

At one point, Paul Channon, another well-known Conservative politician, visited. Over lunch, he and Lambton were surprised to hear that Balestre had not found out about my campaign until I had spoken to about half the FISA member countries. They said this indicated great hostility to him and that I would probably win. They said if someone in their party campaigned like that against Mrs Thatcher, she would have known within a day or two.

The main FISA positions were always held by the president of the national motor sport body in one of the member countries. As an outsider, I was still eligible if proposed by a national authority, but electing me would be a big change. Not only would it be completely unprecedented to have someone who was not already president of one of the national authorities, but I had also been one of FISA's main opponents less than a decade before.

I felt I needed to reassure the electorate that they would not risk being saddled with someone completely unsuitable if they elected me. So on 18 September I announced in a letter to all the clubs that, if elected, I would not serve a full four-year term but would resign and offer myself for re-election after 12 months. In this way, they could be rid of me quickly if they wished. I also emphasised that I was in a position to do the job without pay. The FIA is a non-profit organisation under the French law of 1901 that places strict limits on the amount officers of such a body can be paid. Fortunately, I had made a bit of money myself and now had access to family money after the death of my father.

On 25 September, Balestre sent a letter in reply, attaching numerous letters of support from motor sport luminaries including Monaco's Michel Boeri, Ron Dennis (McLaren), Piero Ferrari (Ferrari), Jean Todt (Peugeot) and Frank Williams (Williams), together with a certificate of good health. He also said he had letters from 31 national club presidents pledging their support, all of which were available for inspection. It's probably fair to say that it would have been unwise to refuse to send a letter of support if asked by Balestre to do so.

Balestre was absolutely confident of victory. On the morning of the election, Bernie suggested to him he should find a compromise with me, but he showed Bernie a list of all the countries and their voting intentions: only two were for me, with two more marked as doubtful. All the rest were for him. It seems he had not considered the possibility that, with a secret ballot, someone might tell him one thing but do another. Bernie, as ever, had a foot in both camps, understanding the old political adage that if you can't ride two horses at once, you shouldn't be in the circus. Had Balestre won, Bernie would have been his friend and backer.

Some of my supporters expressed the fear that the secretariat would number each dossier and record which delegate received it. With each ballot paper carrying its dossier number in invisible ink, the secretariat could then tell Balestre how each country had voted. From my dealings with the secretariat, I knew they would never be that organised or, indeed, capable of keeping it secret, but the perception was a danger. Everyone was terrified of reprisals if they were discovered to have voted for me should I lose. To overcome this fear, I insisted that the ballot papers should be made available randomly and separate from the dossiers. Fortunately, Balestre was so confident of his support that he did not refuse.

An African delegate who was secretly an ally told me he would walk twice round the room just before the ballot and drop two stones. Apparently, this was some sort of magic ritual in his homeland and would have a powerful effect on the outcome of the election. But to make absolutely sure of success he needed to sacrifice a horse. Could I help pay for the horse? I mentioned this to Jean, who was horrified. 'You can't – poor horse!' she said. But I explained no sub-Saharan horse would actually suffer – it was just a polite way of asking for a bung. I told the delegate my wife was a horse lover, so unfortunately I couldn't help finance the sacrifice.

The result was sensational and unexpected. The countries voted 43 to 29 in my favour. It was a terrible shock for Balestre, who nevertheless behaved with great dignity. Much of the motor sport press, particularly in France, was equally stunned. The FISA membership seemed pleased with the result but I realised that, now I was in charge, they probably wouldn't tell me if they weren't. Winning that election against all odds and prognostications was an extraordinary sensation. I felt that, at 51, for the first time in my life I had achieved something truly significant. Inwardly I felt triumphant, but was very careful not to let anyone see just how elated I felt. Above all, I was very conciliatory towards Balestre in the days that followed. It was a time for magnanimity, not triumphalism.

18

BERNIE'S £1 MILLION DONATION AND MORE POLITICS

Winning the FISA election forced me to make big changes in my life. I had to give up the motor racing business I had become involved in with Nick Wirth – a design consultancy, mainly dealing in computerised simulation. Nick is a brilliant engineer who has since been very successful, particularly in North American racing and, increasingly, in areas away from sport using some of the same technologies. The presidency also took some getting used to: instead of thinking of ways to persuade Balestre or his predecessors to do what needed doing, I could get on and do it myself provided the World Council agreed. I started running the World Council meetings as I had the Manufacturers' Commission. The various commission presidents were accustomed to giving long reports on their activities, covering all their various briefs from karting to truck racing, rallying to cross-country events. I abolished oral reports and insisted they should be submitted in writing and circulated at least two weeks in advance. This was mainly to give the council members time to consult the specialist experts in their home countries, but also to eradicate the boredom of listening to reports one could perfectly well read for oneself.

Any discussion was then based on questions arising from a written report which was also much better informed, the questions having been checked by specialists in the bigger clubs. Often, a report would be agreed without discussion. All this will seem very basic to anyone who has run a large organisation, but it was a big change. The meetings would usually be over in a morning, compared with two days under Balestre, but he was always generous enough to concede that things had improved.

As promised, I stood for re-election after a year and was unopposed. I then told Balestre I was going to stand for the full FIA presidency a year later in the autumn of 1993. I suggested we create a Senate and that he could be its president. This was actually Bernie's idea. Balestre concurred and did not stand again for the FIA presidency. After an abortive challenge from the RAC's Jeffrey Rose, I was again elected. The FIA may not be seen as a major world body in England but it certainly is in France, where it was founded in 1904, and beyond.

In addition to creating a Senate, I asked the General Assembly to restructure the FIA and its non-sporting commissions, all of which were theoretically on a par with the motor sport commission, FISA. The new idea was to have two divisions, one for motor sport, the other for road cars. This was all agreed and formed the basis of a major new effort for the ordinary motorist, whose interests had been largely taken over by the Alliance Internationale de Tourisme, the FIA's rival to which all the major motoring clubs belonged.

Eight years after abandoning the idea of British politics, I was introduced to John Smith, the leader of the Labour opposition, by his chief of staff David Ward. David was an amateur racer I had met through Jonathan Ashman, an official with the RAC Motor Sports Association. John Smith invited me to dinner at the House of Commons in July 1993 and I immediately liked him. Unprompted, he volunteered an insight into the problems I had experienced because of my father. He fully understood that one could never know whether a rejection was because of one's own shortcomings or for the other reason.

With John Smith's agreement, David undertook a project to establish an all-party group of members of the European Parliament concerned with motoring issues. It soon became apparent that David had great political expertise and could really make a difference, particularly on the road car side, but his scope was limited because he had a full-time day job with John.

Then, very sadly, John died suddenly during the 1994 Monaco Grand Prix. David was scheduled to attend and in the end came anyway because there was nothing he could do back at home. He spent the weekend thinking about his future. We met again the following Monday and I asked him to take charge of our Brussels office. Later that day he met Tony Blair to tell him he had decided to leave UK politics and work with me at the FIA.

At David's suggestion, I joined the Labour Party's 1000 Club. In 1995, he took me to meet Tony Blair, who made coffee in his Islington house and listened politely to our views on road safety. I invited Blair and his family to the 1996 British GP and they ended up spending the day in my room at Silverstone because the RAC wouldn't invite him to their official facilities. It was the first time I had met his wife. Until she mentioned it, I hadn't realised she had written a very impressive counsel's opinion for the FIA on some legal technicality. I had not made the connection with Cherie Booth, who I imagined to be some obscure but very intellectual Queen's Counsel. She was lively and interested and well up for fun, so Damon Hill took her and the children round the circuit at very high speed in a road car.

Following Blair's visit to the British Grand Prix, David was approached by Jonathan Powell, Tony Blair's chief of staff, who asked if Bernie might be willing to become a financial donor to the Labour Party, even suggesting the sum of £1 million. It fell to me to approach Bernie. I strongly urged him to agree because I wanted a friendly reception in Downing Street when we raised road safety issues, and suggested to Bernie that it would be easier to protect Formula One from political interference in a crisis – for example, a big accident – if we were already positioned close to the government. I was very conscious of the difficulties we had experienced after Ayrton Senna's death and the very real danger of politicians trying to get involved in our sport.

A meeting was arranged between Bernie and Blair in the House of Commons, this time organised by Michael (now Lord) Levy, who had become Labour's main fundraiser. At the end of the meeting, Levy took Bernie into another room and asked him immediately if he was willing to make a donation, but Bernie wasn't impressed by what must have felt like a premature shake-down and refused.

The matter was then dropped until early 1997 when Blair made it clear that he would not raise the top rate of income tax if Labour came to power. I rang Bernie to point out that Blair had just saved him rather a lot of money and he should perhaps think again about a donation. Rather unexpectedly, he agreed. David took the £1 million cheque to the House of Commons and handed it to Jonathan Powell. Contrary to the myth that has persisted ever since, the donation had nothing to do with tobacco sponsorship. It had been banned at British races since the 1970s, so the Labour manifesto promise to outlaw tobacco advertising was no threat to Formula One.

In the autumn of 1997, several months after the Labour victory, there was a major row. Someone tipped off the *Daily Telegraph* that Bernie had given Labour the seven-figure sum and, understandably, it instantly made a huge splash. David and I agreed that Downing Street should reply to inquiries by saying the party would follow the rules, publish the list of donors of more than £5000 on the due date and, if Mr Ecclestone had made a donation that qualified, he would be on the list.

David set off to Whitehall to convince Jonathan Powell but it was already too late. Downing Street did not react calmly – they were badly advised and admitted the scale of the donation long before it was required. Inevitably, the Tory press claimed the money was a bung for allowing tobacco advertising to continue in Formula One. No one thought to point out that this was an absurd accusation because there had been no tobacco advertising at the British Grand Prix, or at any motor sport event in the UK, since the 1970s.

By autumn 1997, however, a different tobacco problem had emerged. The European Commission produced a draft directive banning tobacco sponsorship. In September, David and I had a meeting with Tessa Jowell, then health secretary, together with Tony Banks, then sports minister, and civil servants from the Department of Health who seemed to radiate disapproval. Tessa started by saying that smoking was costing the National Health Service more than £1.5 billion a year because of tobacco-related illnesses. I replied that if we were going to talk money, it also brought in more than £11 billion a year in tax, on top of which most of the tobacco-related deaths were among pensioners, saving the Exchequer even more money.

In fact, David and I agreed with Tessa about smoking but I could not resist the temptation to irritate the ayatollah-like civil servants. I explained that the real question was what the British government could do to help us eliminate tobacco sponsorship from a global sport. We did not want this to happen piecemeal – it needed to be done worldwide and all at once. It became clear we needed to meet Blair.

A few weeks later, Bernie, David and I were outside Blair's private office in Downing Street. Bernie remarked: 'Just think, one minute you have all this, next minute you are queuing up at check-in like everyone else.' He manifestly preferred great wealth to great power. I confessed I found politics far more interesting than wealth (given a certain amount, which I was lucky enough to have). You can do more in politics than you can with money unless, of course, you happen to be a UK newspaper proprietor with both power and wealth.

In the meeting, we explained to Blair there was a move in the European Commission to bring in a ban on tobacco sponsorship in the EU. This did not pose any immediate threat to Formula One because the directive was flawed and would be struck down by the European Court (as it later was). However, this was, we said, the wrong approach. Tobacco sponsorship was certainly coming to an end but what was needed was a global agreement. Without it, races outside Europe would still have tobacco advertising that would be beamed to all EU countries on television. This would lead to myriad difficulties and could even interfere with Formula One's TV coverage in the EU. Any attempt by the FIA itself to ban tobacco advertising in Formula One would immediately be challenged in the courts, almost certainly with success.

We explained that neither Bernie nor the FIA had any reason to want tobacco sponsorship to continue. At worst, its loss would inconvenience some of the richer teams but we did want to avoid an EU ban conflicting with non-EU practice. We had a proposal to wean Formula One off tobacco on a voluntary basis quite quickly. As things turned out, had our plan been accepted in 1997, tobacco sponsorship would have stopped much sooner than it eventually did – but that's another story.

Blair immediately understood the legal reasons why the directive would fail and saw the sense in our proposals for a worldwide ban. Three days after the meeting, I bumped into Peter Mandelson at a Downing Street reception. I asked him if anything was happening. He replied in his characteristic way: 'Whitehall is reverberating to the sound of crashing gears ...' I understood this to mean our suggestions were being taken seriously and British tactics at the EU were being changed.

The £1 million story broke on the day Michael Schumacher was appearing before the World Council accused of deliberately pushing Jacques Villeneuve off the track during the 1997 European Grand Prix at Jerez in Spain. Unusually, the council was meeting at the RAC Motor Sports Association offices in Colnbrook rather than Paris, where the meetings were normally held. Bernie and I shared a car to the meeting. When we arrived we found ourselves surrounded by press and TV cameras. We didn't know what Downing Street had just announced, so things got even more complicated. In the resulting confusion our proposals to Blair got lost and the country was led to believe that Bernie had given Labour a large sum of money to preserve tobacco sponsorship in Formula One. It suited the Conservative opposition to promote this distortion and quietly forget that, when in power, they had always been more than friendly to the tobacco industry.

We met with Blair's advisers and various ministers but it proved impossible to get the true story out. Some years later, in April 2002, David managed to get a big feature in *The Times* setting the record straight, but the damage had long been done. After his initial donation, Labour had repeatedly approached Bernie to give more – a large sum each year until the next election. Foolishly, they then sought advice from Sir Patrick Neill, chairman of the Committee on Standards in Public Life, as to whether they could accept further money from Bernie if it were forthcoming.

Instead, they were shocked to be told to give back what they had already received. This advice was hugely unfair to Bernie, as it implied that there was something wrong with the original donation. Unfortunately, Blair's people were new and very naive in those early days, complete innocents compared with the Conservatives, who had happily accepted massive sums from the tobacco industry. I always felt bad about the way Bernie was treated over the issue. He would never have given the money had I not urged him to do so. The then Labour government distorted the entire story in order to preserve its political position, and the fact that the party had pressured him to give yet more money was quietly forgotten, even denied. But for this episode, I think Bernie would have been offered a knighthood. He might well have refused but, given what he has done for his country, it should have been offered.

On 20 January 2000 there was a postscript to the UK tobacco saga when Bernie and I were called to give evidence to the House of Commons Health Select Committee. The line the committee took was that we had a moral duty to rid Formula One of tobacco branding. In response, I pointed out that we had no power to stop the teams – they were independent businesses and tobacco sponsorship was not illegal. If we brought in a rule to stop it, we would immediately be challenged in the courts.

But, I said, apart from the legal position, the teams had another reason to refuse. I told them:*

... Their second point, and it is one on which the Committee might be able to help us, is that if the EU is serious about trying to stop the publicity from tobacco, they could do so overnight because the EU currently subsidises the growing of tobacco to the tune of 998 million ecus, the 1997 figure, which is probably in the order of two to three times as much money as the whole sponsorship of Formula 1. By contrast, they pointed out to me, not only are these 998 million ecus going to grow tobacco, the total EU budget for combating cancer is 14 million ecus and for health initiatives generally 37 million.

823 *[Chairman]* We have looked at this in some detail in this inquiry, as you might imagine.

(Mr Mosley) Good. I just wanted to make that point—

824 *[Chairman]* It is a very important point; we understand that.

(Mr Mosley)—that I had difficulty in convincing the teams that their position is morally difficult when confronted with this action by our Government.

Then later in the discussion (at 857) I couldn't resist starting again:

* http://www.parliament.the-stationery-office.co.uk/pa/cm199900/cmselect/cmhealth/
27/0012029.htm

… Every single member of the Committee has voted in favour of the 998 million ecus EU subsidy in the EU for growing tobacco by the mere fact of allowing this through the House of Commons. That is inescapable. Please do not let us get into the morality debate because we are all equally guilty, in fact I would submit the Committee is in a weaker position than I am because you could do something and I cannot.

[Chairman]: I think we might be trying to do something.

I have to confess I quite enjoyed the hearing. I was politely accusing them of being ineffectual hypocrites and I think some of them, at least, got the message.

While all this was going on, I remained a member of the Labour Party. Having joined in the mid-1990s at David's suggestion, I had made a lot of friends and useful political contacts. However, I felt I had to end my membership because of the invasion of Iraq. I thought it quite wrong for many reasons and I could not belong to an organisation that (officially at least) supported it. My Labour friends didn't think it was a good idea for me to join the huge anti-war demo in Hyde Park, but I nevertheless quietly attended.

In 2003, notwithstanding my opposition to the war, there was an intriguing interaction with the British military. They were interested in reducing the time taken to refuel and rearm the Apache helicopter. Doing this quickly was crucial because they were vulnerable when being refuelled anywhere near to the enemy. Also, shortening the time meant each one could fly more missions in a given period. The army sent some people to look at refuelling in Formula One, and eventually I arranged with them that Nick Wirth would go to the Army Air Corps base in Middle Wallop and see what he could advise. The result was a different approach and a substantial reduction in the time taken to refuel and rearm. As a reward, they brought an Apache, which was then very new, to Silverstone and demonstrated it at the 2003 British Grand Prix. Our ability to make a significant difference in an area far removed from sport showed how much Formula One technology had evolved in the previous three decades.

19

THE COMMERCIAL RIGHTS
TO FORMULA ONE

By the time I was elected president of FISA in 1991, the Formula One arrangements had evolved and Bernie was more in control than ever. The teams seemed quite happy and, as far as I was concerned, even if they and the organisers had ceded all their rights to him and the FIA had never really owned any of the rights to the races, it was still the FIA's Formula One World Championship. Yet, strictly speaking, the fact that the FIA had launched the championship in 1950 and supervised and regulated it ever since gave us no legal security. We couldn't claim to own very much apart from rights to the name, the race format, the technical rules and the International Sporting Code – and some of those could have been disputed or challenged in court.

Everything apart from the exercise of the sporting power as regulator had either never belonged to the FIA or was now governed by contracts. Even our right to decide the calendar was gone because the Concorde Agreement specified that an event could only appear on it if the promoter had a contract with the teams. They, of course, had long since delegated the right to make these contracts to Bernie. And in 1990, well before I had any thought of standing for election, a new Concorde Agreement lasting until 1997 had been signed.

Irrespective of who 'owned' it, the championship was effectively controlled by the teams because of their rights under the Concorde Agreement, and it had suited them to hand everything over to Bernie. On top of this, he had acquired the media rights (particularly television) that had always belonged to the promoters.

After my election to the full FIA presidency in 1993, I felt I ought to try to find a way of acquiring the rights to the championship for the FIA. It had developed enormously since the days when it was a collection of individual events with different formats run by FIA member clubs, loosely grouped together as a championship. Although this was still the pattern for our other championships, for example the FIA World Rally Championship, the Formula One World Championship was now a homogenous entity with all events run to the same format. It therefore needed to be treated as such. From my perspective as FIA president, it was our championship and we should own it, or at least keep control of it, even if its current pre-eminence had been achieved in spite of the FIA and not because of it.

The question was how. After internal discussions in the FIA, we decided on a long game. The FIA's receipts from Formula One exceeded its expenditure, which made the current situation sustainable. The FIA had the calendar fees from the race promoters plus annual entry fees from the teams. We also received a modest annual fee from Bernie in return for exercising sporting oversight. Balestre had demanded this in the late 1980s because by then the numbers of FIA personnel required at races had ballooned over the past decade.

I proposed an arrangement to Bernie that would fundamentally change the game. Where previously the Concorde Agreement was between the teams and the FIA and the teams then contracted with Bernie, the new idea was an agreement directly between the FIA and Bernie, an agreement between Bernie and the teams (for the money he paid them) and a contract between the FIA and the teams to govern rule-making, essentially the Concorde Agreement. It would be a triangular arrangement where previously it had been linear. Contractually, the teams had always stood between the FIA and Bernie, but this new structure would mean we in the FIA now had a contract directly with the person who held all the relevant rights to the races that made up our championship. To me this seemed a more logical arrangement.

The attraction for Bernie was that we would continue to oversee the championship for the relatively modest annual fee which Balestre had arranged in the 1980s (about FF40,000,000 linked to inflation, circa €6.1 million) plus, of course, the calendar and entry fees for the next 15 years. But, at the end of the 15-year span of our new deal (1 January 2011), Bernie would transfer all the rights, archives, footage etc. that he had accumulated over the years to the FIA. We would become the sole owners of the commercial rights to the World Championship as well as Bernie's rights in the underlying events. This seemed the best way to deal with what had become very complex arrangements. The legal difficulties of any attempt to untangle everything without an agreement would have been formidable, perhaps even impossible, and likely to threaten the championship itself. It was necessary to cut the Gordian knot.

Surprisingly, though, it was difficult to persuade Bernie to agree. After all those years I think he felt somehow allied with the teams. His original exit strategy entailed getting his business valued at some point and selling it to the teams at a significant discount. Indeed, in the early 1990s he had lengthy discussions with them about what became known as the 'Dying Agreement'. I was not involved but understood this concerned arrangements for the teams to acquire the business from his estate in the event of his death. In the end, I convinced him that his arrangements with the teams were a separate matter and that he would be better off working with the FIA, but it was a long process.

Inevitably, my relationship with Bernie changed after I was elected to head the sport then, later, the entire FIA. We remained friends and often met. Apart from swapping jokes and anecdotes about others involved in Formula One, there was a great deal of common interest between Bernie's business and the FIA. Both relied on the success of Formula One and needed to promote and encourage its growth. But there were also areas of conflict because Bernie maintained a steady pressure to wrest more control, particularly in the paddock at races. This did not affect me directly but caused difficulty for our staff.

Understandably, perhaps, Bernie always liked to interpret everything in his favour. For example, the fact that he had the promotional rights to Formula One led him to try to stop the FIA having the maker's logo on any of the technical equipment we used. He would also try to minimise the exposure of our own logo. I used to tell our staff he was like the person in the next seat on a flight who would take over the armrest if you left it clear for a moment – they had to be constantly on the alert to stand their ground. But on the whole relations were good. Things generally worked well, although never as closely as some of the teams seemed to think. One of the reasons the teams thought we were closer than we really were was that Bernie would go out of his way to give the impression he was in charge. For example, if I told him I was going somewhere he would often give people the idea he had arranged it. I was always quite relaxed about that sort of thing because I had known since 1982 where power over the sport lay if it really came to it.

Once Bernie had finally accepted, I put the proposed contract to the 1995 FIA General Assembly where it was agreed. Fourteen years on from Balestre's original proposals for the first Concorde Agreement, I had succeeded in the FIA's long-term quest to own the rights. And, crucially, this time Bernie himself had a contract with the FIA so, at least in theory, there should be no problem with him (or his successor) when the time for the handover came. Part of the arrangement was that he would not enter into any contract with a race promoter or television company that extended beyond 31 December 2010, when he was due to relinquish his rights to us. In practice, he could have sought our agreement if he had needed to sign a longer contract. We would then have become a party to it and participated.

Some of the teams were not pleased. Ken Tyrrell, in particular, was very unhappy, saying that Bernie had no right to do this. He said the championship belonged to the teams because without them there would be no championship. I thought that was nonsense: I told Ken you don't get to own a theatre just because you perform in it every night. If anyone might have a claim on them it was the promoters, who had originally owned the rights and run events in the championship for many years before Bernie started his business, but not the teams.

I didn't worry too much about the competition law point. I knew that the FIA would have difficulty exercising Bernie's commercial rights when they became ours in 2011 because we might then be considered to be in an excessively dominant commercial position under EU law, but I thought the FIA could deal with that problem if and when it arose. At worst, the FIA could sell the rights – perhaps even to Bernie, if he were still around. The important thing was to make sure there was still a viable championship in 2011.

Notwithstanding the uncertainties after 2010, there was an immediate and important benefit from the FIA's point of view. The deal drove a wedge between Bernie and the teams and put him much more clearly in our camp. I knew from the FOCA–FISA war that the teams could cause real trouble if they were properly financed, and that danger was significantly smaller now we had a contract with Bernie. The possibility of Bernie (or a successor) combining with the teams to run outside the FIA was eventually eliminated altogether in 2000, when our deal with the EU Commission meant we could stop non-FIA events running on any permanent circuit. But even with this, the convulsions caused by using our powers against a combination of Bernie and the teams would have been destructive. It was much better to have him with us.

Two years later, in 1997, on the basis of this 15-year deal, Bernie decided to float his business on the stock exchange and planned an initial public offering or IPO. His financiers, however, told him he needed a longer contract and he came back to us to ask for a ten-year extension to 2020. After an internal discussion, we agreed to do so for $300 million. Coming up with a figure involved an element of guesswork, because it meant trying to predict the value of contingent future rights in a market with an evolving championship and technology.

We pitched our figure high because we knew we could always

reduce it if Bernie balked. We also knew he was likely to get a large sum from his IPO. On the other hand, what we were offering would not take effect until the current contract expired, so not for another 13 years or so, and even then there were uncertainties about ownership of the various rights. For us at the time, the prospect of receiving a large sum of money for a ten-year extension seemed a good deal. When I first suggested this figure to Balestre, by then president of the FIA Senate, he thought it was unrealistically high. I got the full '*Quoi? C'est pas possible!*' treatment.

Although it was way beyond anything Balestre thought feasible, Bernie at first agreed, or at least pretended to. He could afford it if he succeeded with his IPO and he needed the FIA onside to keep the financiers comfortable – but I knew that once he had an IPO in the bag, he would probably try to renegotiate. This was how he operated. And as he himself always says, the old tricks are always the best ones.

With all this talk of flotation, some of the teams began finally to understand just how much money Bernie was making. As already explained, when they all refused to join in the risk-taking 20 years earlier, Bernie had himself eventually accepted the risks of promoters defaulting and guaranteed the teams an agreed amount of money for each race, which later became a fee for the entire season. But by the late 1990s, he was getting much more money from the Grand Prix organisers than he was paying the teams. He was also making money from television and other sources. On top of this, the teams realised that the FIA's 15-year deal direct with Bernie had changed things – he was now more allied to us than them. Some of them set out to stop Bernie's IPO unless they could participate.

It began with stormy meetings, at one of which, extending my theatre analogy, I pointed out that even if you dined in a certain restaurant each night, and even if you did so for years, that didn't in some way make you its owner or entitle you to shares in it. And, I said, it was our restaurant. Bernie was the chef, a very talented chef who had built the restaurant up, but it was still our restaurant. We had founded it in 1950, before any of them except Ferrari had any involvement, and that included Bernie.

Privately, Bernie used to say to me: OK, but if he left to open another restaurant down the road, then where would the FIA be? He had a point – quite a strong one – and I was always careful never to adopt a position that would provoke unity between Bernie and the teams before we had our contract with him. Together they could have been a problem, but as long as Bernie had a binding contract with us, the teams could do nothing. As already mentioned, this was another reason why the long-term deal we had just made with Bernie independently of the teams was so important. As it developed, much of the discussion took place in the shadow of an ongoing investigation by the European Commission and before its ruling eventually put us in an even stronger position.

20

THE CAR MANUFACTURERS
GET INVOLVED

Resentment against Bernie and the prospect of him becoming a billionaire grew. One of the team principals later boasted that he had single-handedly stopped Bernie's IPO, but this wasn't quite true. The real damage was done by a major car manufacturer with good connections in Brussels, particularly in the Competition Directorate then still headed by Karel Van Miert, and the resulting investigation stopped the flotation. Bernie nevertheless got his money, or some of it, in 1999 by selling a $1.4 billion bond, redeemable in 2010 at the end of his existing contract with the FIA. The money was secured on his media contracts and commercial rights. It put our $300 million proposal for a ten-year extension to take effect in 13 years' time into perspective and made it look rather optimistic. But inevitably the FIA was drawn into the proceedings that began as Bernie's dispute with the Competition Department of the European Commission.

After the dispute with the commission was resolved by means

of a novel approach to the length of our contract with Bernie (covered in greater detail later), we were able to offer a long-term deal for Formula One with the commission's agreement. This settlement piqued the interest of the major European car companies and I twice met Paolo Cantarella, then chairman of the European Automobile Manufacturers' Association, who suggested his members would like to make a collective offer. I encouraged him but he produced nothing concrete because, I suspected, his lawyers were saying the situation was risky due to Bernie's existing contracts and rights and the uncertainty about what we could actually sell.

The other problem was that we could only sell the rights we had with effect from 31 December 2010, when our original 1995 deal with Bernie expired. But back in 2000 it was difficult to predict what, if anything, the championship would consist of 11 years hence and, when it suited him, Bernie would mutter darkly about employing a scorched-earth policy towards the end of his contract.

When we subsequently negotiated a 100-year deal for the rights with Bernie after our agreement with the European Commission, we were faced with the problem of settling a price with him. I didn't want to do this myself because I knew people would say I was too close to him. I asked four of the main club presidents to do it instead – two lawyers (Rosario Alessi of the Automobile Club of Italy and Michel Boeri of the Monaco Automobile Club) and two businessmen (Otto Flimm, president of the German club, and John Large, his Australian sporting counterpart). The Italian and German clubs were both very large motoring organisations with millions of members.

It was a strong team and they finally agreed a price of $300 million with Bernie. This was the original figure we had proposed for a ten-year extension but, even with a gain of 90 years, Bernie still tried to reduce it. His proposal was to defer payment for seven years, despite knowing perfectly well that we were unlikely to be so stupid not to grasp that a dollar in seven years is worth less than a dollar today, even with a bank guarantee (the difference, of course, being a function of interest rates). It was a perfect example of one of his most cherished principles: it's always worth trying something unreasonable because sometimes people say yes. Our negotiating team agreed with me that his terms were unacceptable.

Meanwhile, having been invited to bid for the 100-year deal, the car companies kept prevaricating. In May 2000 we told them there was going to be a proposal to the World Council meeting in Warsaw at the end of June 2000 that we accept Bernie's $300 million. Cantarella asked us to postpone a decision until the autumn to give the car companies more time to consider, but when his request was discussed at the Warsaw meeting, the council decided to accept Bernie's money rather than give the car companies four more months. There was no guarantee they would even make an offer in the autumn and it was resolved, as so often in the sport, that the bird in the hand was worth more than the one in the bush.

After the council agreed, however, Bernie failed to complete because he was waiting to conclude his deal with German TV magnate Leo Kirch.

Kirch had taken over EM.TV, a television company that had previously secured a major equity stake in Bernie's holding company. It had acquired the rights to all manner of series, including the Muppets, and, at one point, the value of its shares was such that executives told the teams at an FIA dinner in Imola that their company was worth $16 billion. Shortly before EM.TV crashed a couple of years later, I saw an analyst's report from a well-known international investment bank marking the shares as a strong buy.

Although Kirch had taken over the company, I was told he needed another $1 billion or so to exercise the option to acquire control of Bernie's business. Bernie, it seemed, was waiting for Kirch to find the $1 billion to complete the deal, and expected him then to contribute his 75 per cent share of our $300 million. In retrospect, I think Bernie (or his family trust) made a major mistake in ceding control. He would have been better off issuing bonds private equity-style and keeping a majority of the shares. It would have saved him from the wranglings of a board of directors including the unpleasant individuals who tried to undermine me in 2008 then later turned on him. But that was not obvious at the time and, anyway, was not my concern.

The months passed without progress so in December 2000 I set up another meeting with Cantarella and invited him to reopen negotiations. I thought this would at the least put pressure on Bernie and perhaps even persuade him to complete his deal with us – notwithstanding that Kirch was prevaricating or could not raise the funds to exercise his option. Also, there was the possibility that the car companies might come up with a concrete offer now they'd had longer to consider it.

Throughout, I was talking to our lawyers about our legal position in the event of signing a deal with someone other than Bernie. I liked my restaurant theory but the fact was that when we talked of the rights to the Formula One World Championship, what we actually owned was nebulous. The name of the championship and its regulations had always been ours, plus the right to fix the calendar, but we were aware that the latter could be disputed because the teams had given Bernie the right to make the contracts without which there could be no calendar. Provided the teams backed him, he would retain de facto control of the calendar, no matter what deal was in place. Moreover, Bernie had acquired the most valuable commercial rights relating to Formula One from the original owners – namely, the race promoters and the teams. Those rights had never belonged to the FIA, leaving us with the unresolved question: who owned what and what could the FIA actually offer to sell to the European car giants?

Our lawyers from the big City firm Herbert Smith were not reassuring. They arranged for us to consult a top commercial Queen's Counsel, together with a trademark expert who is now a leading intellectual property QC. Trademarks had been something I had dealt with myself at the Bar, so I understood the complexities. It was not just a question of who owned what rights but also who owned the commercial goodwill in Formula One, including the right to exploit the name itself and the associated trademarks. It would have been difficult to argue that this was us. The essence of commercial goodwill is business and, even if we could have asserted that the FIA had initiated and run the championship itself (as opposed to the underlying events) for many years before Bernie started to build up the commercial side, the FIA had never itself run Formula One as a business. We realised it would probably be argued that the FIA had only ever been the sporting regulator, with no business interest in the championship.

Given his role in building the championship profile over the past three decades and running it as a profitable business throughout, there was a risk that the goodwill in the Formula One name (and hence commercial trademarks) belonged to Bernie. Reinforcing this argument was the fact that he had established a separate company to hold the commercial trademarks he used, as distinct from the FIA's own championship logo. Nevertheless, from my point of view it was still the FIA's championship, not Bernie's.

The QC advised us not to get into a legal dispute with him. The trademark expert agreed and added that there was a risk that the name 'Formula One' (and hence its variants 'F1' and 'Formula 1') could even be considered *terra nullius* – something that nobody owned and anyone could use.

I didn't tell Bernie any of this. I didn't want to give him the satisfaction of pointing out that (except for the *terra nullius* point) this was what he, a non-lawyer, had been saying all along. Also, had he fully appreciated the strength of his position he would undoubtedly have tried to haggle over the $300 million that had been so laboriously negotiated by the four club presidents. At one of the meetings with Bernie and his lawyers, when we had refused to accept his demand to include the FIA's copyright over the technical rules and the Sporting Code as part of the package he was buying, he rather pointedly asked what he was getting for his money. He said if we wouldn't include these (which we never did) he was getting nothing because he already owned everything else.

Then, a few weeks later, in March 2001, Kirch's option was exercised and Bernie received his money. Detailed negotiations on a contract then took off in earnest. Our team of Mike Kingston and Melanie Johnson from Herbert Smith were on one side; Kirch's lawyer, Dr Alexander Ritvay (from the German firm Noerr), Sasha Woodward-Hill from Bernie's office and two partners from the English firm Addleshaw Goddard on the other. The lawyers were permanently in session at Herbert Smith's offices in Paris for over a fortnight (breaking just once so that Sasha could get home to London overnight to feed her cat). The last 72 hours were almost continuous and particularly tense for our legal team; there were phone calls in the night on make-or-break points, and twice I said our team should walk out if a particular one was not conceded.

While I had a mandate to agree to extend the term to 100 years, it was important to ensure that the essential nature of the Formula One World Championship was fixed for the future by legal agreements. In particular, we insisted on veto rights to protect the Formula One values and format, its ownership and control – and to ensure continued media access for its hundreds of millions of fans worldwide. Our insistence on control over ownership and management apparently played a role in Kirch's eventual collapse because our veto rights prevented him using Formula One as security for a loan. Bernie and Kirch strongly resisted our attempts to protect the FIA's reversionary interest, but this is nevertheless included in the agreement. In the end we had a deal. It was lengthy and complex but we had done it.

In April 2001 the Hundred Year Agreement was signed and we received $313.6 million. The figure had grown because, as far as I was concerned, we had agreed everything the previous summer, so I insisted that they pay interest. The contract secured our full control of the sporting aspects of Formula One and ensured our annual fee would increase with the cost of living. The contract would come into force when our existing one ended on 31 December 2010, or earlier if both sides agreed.

By putting up the money that enabled the deal to complete, Kirch became the majority owner of Bernie's business. But this made very little difference to us because both the original 15-year deal (which was still in force) and the new Hundred Year Agreement contained clauses that required our consent if Bernie were replaced or there was a change of management. Later, Kirch followed its subsidiary EM.TV into bankruptcy and its shares in Bernie's business became the property of its major creditors – namely, their bankers. They eventually sold them on to CVC, a UK private equity firm that still holds many of them to this day.

Several times after the agreement was signed, Bernie, Kirch's banks and CVC initiated discussions with us to try to change the Hundred Year Agreement. They wanted to loosen or remove some of the FIA's retained rights, to make their investment more marketable and therefore, presumably, more valuable. They also wanted to enact it immediately, without waiting until 2011. But when I said we, too, would like to make a few changes, or at least receive a consideration for accepting theirs, they would never agree. So in the end the Hundred Year Agreement did not begin until 1 January 2011, after the 15-year deal came to an end. I don't think even Bernie will still be around when the Hundred Year Agreement ends on 31 December 2110.

Back in 2001, once we had the money I proposed to the FIA General Assembly that we put it into a UK charitable foundation which could promote road safety and other charitable objectives both through the FIA member clubs and on its own account. Gratifyingly, the assembly agreed. I was worried that someone might propose that the money should simply be split between the clubs and an opportunity to do the work of the FIA on a much greater scale would be lost. Almost as soon as the new FIA Foundation received it, we changed half the money into euros, paying just over 84 US cents for each euro. That was pure luck but produced a big gain when the euro rose above parity with the dollar.

Soon we had a fully functioning, well-endowed charity for safety work in motor sport as well as for road cars, paying for such things as crash-testing and safety belt campaigns. We were also able to cover safer roads, environmental research and other things we could never previously afford.

David Ward came back from Brussels to run the FIA Foundation and its income has enabled it to spend about

€10 million a year on things that matter. It is no exaggeration to say that the work its philanthropy has been able to fund has saved many thousands of lives over the past 14 years. Bernie always says we managed to sell him his own business and he only gave us the money for a quiet life. That claim is debatable but at least he has the satisfaction of knowing it has been very well spent.

The Hundred Year Agreement was intended to replace our original 1995 contract with Bernie, which was due to run out at the end of 2010. Back in 2001, Formula One looked fragile and we knew we might see it disappear for any of a number of reasons. However unlikely, there was always the risk that the teams would get together and organise a breakaway championship, particularly if a rich entrepreneur were prepared to fund it, and there was no guarantee that public interest in Formula One would not decline or switch to some other form of motor sport. It was easy (and I think right) to take the decision to accept $313.6 million in 2001 rather than wait until 2011 when all of Bernie's rights in Formula One were due to become ours. Even if the championship had prospered, the lawyers warned of debate and possibly lengthy legal disputes about what would actually be transferred to the FIA in 2011. The Hundred Year Agreement put an end to those concerns.

More importantly, from a humanitarian point of view, we know that thousands of lives would never have been saved had we waited and not taken Bernie's money in 2001. If we had known then what we know now – namely, that Formula One would survive and prosper – the decision might not have been so easy. It would then have been money versus lives, many lives. Had it been left to me, I would still have taken the money and started our foundation – even with hindsight. The certain knowledge that thousands of people all over the world are now walking around happily but would be dead or disabled had we not founded it in 2001 is, to me at least, what really matters.

Whether Bernie deserved to become so rich from his 40-odd years working in Formula One is a question I am frequently asked. Any fair answer has to consider the historical context: when he started, Sports Prototypes were bigger than Formula One, and arguably the World Rally Championship was too. Either could have been built up commercially in the same fashion as Formula One had there been someone able and willing to risk their own money and do the work. Unfortunately, no one ever did. We endeavoured assiduously to seek a Formula One-style deal for the World Rally Championship, a goal that was part of our deal in 2001 with the European Commission. We got close (although for less money than Formula One) but never managed it. My personal view is that Formula One would today be in much the same state as the WRC and Sports Prototypes, and thus producing very little revenue for the FIA and the participating teams, had Bernie not been involved.

Last time I checked, the FIA was continuing what began as my fruitless search for someone to do a Bernie in other categories of motor sport. I hope they succeed in finding some suitable entrepreneurs. The only certainty is that if someone were prepared to bring the same level of financial risk-taking, audacity, industry and intelligence to the World Rally Championship, long-distance racing, the World Touring Car Championship or even some completely new form of motor sport (for example, the FIA's new Formula E introduced by my successor, Jean Todt) that Bernie brought to Formula One, they would have a good chance of ending up as rich as he is in 20 years' time.

21

THE SPORT: FAR MORE
THAN FORMULA ONE

Only a week after being elected FISA president, I went to the 1991 Japanese Grand Prix. Japan had been instrumental in my election. It felt very strange suddenly being the person in charge and, even years later, I never really got used to it. But all my old acquaintances in the teams seemed pleased and the atmosphere was good. In Japan I told the press I intended to keep out of Formula One. It was well able to run itself, I said, and there was a great deal to do in the rest of motor sport. I had a meeting with the drivers and, among other things, expressed disquiet about wheel-to-wheel contact. Gerhard Berger came to see me afterwards and explained it was impossible to compete in modern Formula One without bumping wheels, which impressed upon me how out of touch I had become.

After the race, Ayrton Senna admitted on TV that he had deliberately taken Prost off the previous year. This was something everyone suspected but had always been denied. My election, I think, made him feel less constrained, more free to be candid and criticise Balestre. But Ayrton's team principal, Ron Dennis, was understandably alarmed because Balestre was still very powerful. Although I was now head of the sport, it was only a commission of Balestre's FIA and he could still try to withdraw Ayrton's licence. Newly elected, I might still be too weak politically to defend him, quite apart from the fact that, however great the provocation, self-help of the kind he had indulged in was a serious breach of the rules. The risk to life was obvious. But Senna refused to retract. He said he was speaking the truth and saw no reason to censor himself just because Balestre might not like it.

Ron asked me to talk to Ayrton. I invited him up to my suite and saw him alone. I told him that there are two kinds of people in sport: amateurs and professionals. An amateur does something because he feels like it; a professional does what is necessary – what he had just done was amateur. After thinking for a moment he said, 'You are right,' and his eyes started to well up. 'But that bastard took my win away. Racing has been my life since I started karting at six years old and he robbed me of a Grand Prix win and possibly even the championship.'

I told him I agreed. What had happened was completely unfair and was one of the reasons I stood against Balestre in the election, but he should not have exposed himself to sanctions, however strongly he felt. He should not needlessly risk his career. Ayrton was very smart and took my point – in the end, reason overcame emotion. We agreed some weasel words sufficient to avoid any danger of repercussions and he got the team to put out a statement. This was the first time I had sat down with Senna and talked to him.

In my new role I now had the opportunity to take a closer look at American racing. It had developed almost entirely independently from motor sport in Europe and the rest of the world, partly because of the distances involved but mainly because the USA is so big it does not need the involvement of other countries to put on major events. To me, it was all quite alien, although some American specialities such as drag racing thrive in parts of Europe.

American racing is divided into different types of competition, each with its own sanctioning body. The most important are probably NASCAR (the National Association for Stock Car Auto Racing) for so-called stock (i.e. road) cars, and the NHRA (National Hot Rod Association) for dragsters. There is also a big single-seat series called IndyCar, which was diminished when it split into two rival championships several years ago. In addition to all this, America also has many different forms of oval racing for a variety of competition cars. There are some 1200 permanent racing layouts, ranging from small local quarter-mile ovals, drag strips (a straight piece of tarmac on which two cars try to out-accelerate one another) and road circuits, to massive facilities like Indianapolis and Daytona. The sanctioning bodies in the USA all belong to ACCUS, the Automobile Competitions Committee for the United States, the American national sporting authority at the FIA. If an American driver wants to race outside the United States, he or she needs an international FIA licence issued by ACCUS.

The first time I saw a top fuel dragster run at an NHRA championship drag race, I was standing beside Nelson Piquet, still in a wheelchair after his accident during practice for the 1992 Indianapolis 500. With over 5000 horsepower and engines running on nitromethane (virtually a liquid explosive), they race down a quarter-mile straight, reaching more than 300 mph in less than five seconds. Neither of us had ever seen anything like it. We just looked at each other after the first run. Later that day, I was invited to join the starter, who stands between the two competing machines. Standing that close when they take off is like being in the middle of an explosion; it shakes your body to the core and the noise is overwhelming.

The NHRA probably has more competition licence-holders than any other national or international motor sport body. It was started in 1951 when increasing numbers of young people were holding impromptu drag races on public roads. The idea was to get drag racing off the streets and, at the same time, allow all sorts of cars to compete safely on dedicated facilities. NASCAR, by contrast, had its origins in the days of bootlegging, when specially modified cars were needed to outrun the sheriff. I was introduced to one ancient NASCAR team owner who was said to have been a legendary bootlegger in his day.

It was founded by Bill France in 1948 and his family still own and run it today. Last time I was in Daytona, Bill France Jr was firmly in charge. When the racing became rather processional, he turned to us in the tower and said: 'It's time for that Frenchman again, Jean-Claude Debris.' He then took the microphone and announced: 'Debris on the circuit, debris on the circuit.' Out came the yellow flags, the field closed up and the race became exciting. It was not obvious where the debris had been but it certainly improved the spectacle. Although NASCAR also races on road circuits, the cars come into their own on ovals such as Daytona.

Oval racing is part of American motor sport culture. The Indianapolis Motor Speedway was built before the First World War. In those days, even racing cars would not go round corners properly, so ovals were built with banking, allowing the cars to get round the bends without having to slow down too much. Today, of course, the problem is cars are often too fast, even on corners with no banking. Modern racing cars running on the Indianapolis Oval average well over 200 mph. Nelson Piquet explained to me that you went out, got used to the speed until you could do the entire lap with the accelerator flat on the floor. Then, still without lifting, you start to reduce the aerodynamic downforce on the car. This gives you greater straight-line speed but reduces the car's grip. The limit is when the car becomes unstable in the corners.

Despite the very high speeds and the fact that you can see the cars for the entire lap, oval racing has never really caught on in Europe. When Formula One cars ran at Indianapolis, they only used one corner of the oval and raced on a purpose-built road course on the infield.

In the early 1990s I visited Zhuhai, where they were planning to build the first significant circuit in China. It was only a short drive from Macau and, on arrival, we went to the town hall and set out with the deputy mayor in a motorcade to look at the site of the proposed circuit. Zhuhai was a big city but I was puzzled to notice there was no traffic. When I asked him why, the dignitary pointed up a side street where all the traffic had been stopped so that we would not be delayed. When I told Jean about this she thought it outrageous: 'Think how angry you would be if you were held up in London because some sportsperson was visiting,' she said.

In addition to their plans for circuit racing, we asked Guy Goutard, who had been president of the Rally Commission for many years, to discuss with the Chinese national motor sport authority the possibility of holding a WRC event in China. It was already obvious in the early 1990s that China had a great economic future and we thought a major rally would encourage motor sport. They had some ideal terrain and could make military and police personnel available to ensure safety. The Australian ASN was able to provide the necessary organisational expertise and the event went ahead. Having been warned by us about the speed of the cars, the authorities' safety precautions were initially over the top. The army even requested people with homes on the route to leave for 24 hours while it was on.

Later, during a visit to Beijing, I visited the head of the police to thank them for their help with the event. We had one of those very formal meetings where you both sit in chairs with an interpreter in between. The police chief had several deputies on his side of the room. I had our people on mine. Apparently, he had more than a million police under his command. After the formal polite exchanges and my thanks, I couldn't resist asking him how it had been for disciplined organisations like the police and the army during the Cultural Revolution. I could sense the embarrassment of my delegation at this apparent breach of protocol but, far from being offended, he was really interesting on the subject and revealed that, earlier in his career, he had been involved in the trial of the Gang of Four.

Eventually, an outstanding Formula One circuit was constructed near Shanghai, where the Chinese Grand Prix is now held each year. It was built on a swamp, a significant engineering feat that followed a spectacular ground-breaking ceremony at which I had to make a little speech. Going back a couple of years later, it was difficult to believe what they had achieved having seen the site when they started.

The World Rally Championship was, with Formula One, one of the two great FIA motor sport championships. But it had been neglected and had never been developed beyond a collection of events loosely put together as a championship each year by FISA. It was still run much as Formula One had been before Bernie and I started working for reform – any change would be opposed because of the vested interests of the organisers. It had a bigger fan base and conceivably greater worldwide potential than Formula One, but desperately needed the same sort of management.

In a rally, the cars travel on an ordinary road to a so-called special stage. This is a section of road or track closed to ordinary traffic which cars race down, one at a time, against the clock. Each car has a crew of two, driver and navigator. The navigator organises everything, makes sure the car arrives at each special stage on time and gives the driver information about the next corner and other hazards. With a single rally consisting of hundreds of kilometres of special stage, it is impossible for the driver to remember the course in the way a racing driver does a circuit, hence the need for so-called pace notes. The cars are road-legal because they have to travel on the public highway between stages.

The huge commercial advantage rallies have over circuit racing is that no expensive infrastructure is required. Almost any country could run a world championship rally on its ordinary roads and tracks, provided it could make sufficient army or police personnel available to back up the race officials. If necessary, the officials can come from other countries to run the event, as they did initially in China. Formula One, on the other hand, needs a very expensive track with a full range of spectator facilities before you even start.

The sport's commercial potential is glaring, so I persuaded Bernie to come to a world championship rally in Portugal because I hoped he would like what he saw and maybe apply his business skills to the WRC. We got off to a bad start when the former world champion who was driving our car got lost and took forever to find the rally despite the help of a former world champion navigator. Eventually we arrived on a hillside overlooking a special stage. I suggested climbing out of the car to watch, but Bernie put one beautiful Italian loafer on the ground, gave the mud a withering look and hopped back into the car. Rallying was not for him.

We eventually did a deal with Bernie but it never really took off. In any case, once we made our settlement with the EU Commission, he had to give up any involvement in the WRC. The commission wanted us to encourage the commercialisation of the championship on a similar basis to Formula One, but for competition law reasons this had to be with someone other than Bernie. John Large (former president of the Australian ASN and a successful businessman) negotiated on our behalf. A deal was struck with David Richards, a former world champion rally navigator who by now was running the very successful Prodrive car preparation business. This envisaged the FIA eventually receiving €100 million. In the end, David sold the business to North One Television, but they struggled with it and are now no longer involved. What a shame that a terrifically exciting sport, with a vast international fan base and immense commercial potential, never attracted a figure to harness and market it, as Formula One did with Bernie.

Although a major world championship with a global following, the WRC always felt different. It was out in the countryside, so you got much more of a feel for the country you were visiting than with Formula One. On top of this, there were local competitors, because the structure of a rally with a large number of cars running individually against the clock makes this possible.

It was strange to go to an event in the southern hemisphere in July and find myself in snow-covered fields.

As well as rallying, in the early years of my presidency and before we did our deal with the European Commission, I tried to mobilise Bernie's commercial expertise to drive various types of motor sport. It never worked because, fundamentally, he could not engage with them as he had with Formula One. Although I persuaded him to do a certain amount, he inevitably trod on the toes of people already running businesses in particular sports. Some of this was quickly resolved – for example, we had a good, if relatively small, championship for the kind of cars that run at Le Mans and other long-distance races, but he met with problems in other areas such as truck racing.

We could never overcome the difficulty that lengthy events such as rallies and long-distance races are no good for live television. I saw great potential in using the latest technology, particularly for rallies where the internet would allow an individual team and driver to be followed in real time on the web using on-board cameras, but we could never find anyone to exploit it properly. As already mentioned, Bernie, unusually for him, had a blind spot for the internet. He just didn't get it and still doesn't.

The fundamental problem with trying to run the sporting side of the FIA is that it has such a variety of categories, most of them very different from one another. Everything for four or more wheels is FIA; three wheels or fewer is the FIM (Fédération Internationale de Motocyclisme). This means the FIA governs all international karting, truck racing, touring car racing, rallying (on ordinary, but closed, roads), cross-country racing (including deserts), rallycross (part tarmac, part grass), off-road racing, drag racing, sports car racing, GT and prototype racing, quite apart from Formula One and all other forms of single-seat racing. It's like trying to run a federation for every conceivable ball game from soccer to tennis, baseball, American football, rugby, squash, bowls, golf and so on.

One of our problems was protecting competitors and officials from misconceived laws. A potentially serious problem arose when the new European arrest warrant (EAW) was announced. I realised at once that it was a serious threat to anyone responsible for, or involved in, a dangerous sport in the EU. Ostensibly designed to deal with terrorism and serious crime, it set the barrier far too low and exposed those responsible for dangerous sports to possible arrest for incidents of which they had no knowledge, still less control. For example, there could be an accident involving spectators at a rally or a hill climb somewhere in the EU. Inexpensive to run and very popular in many parts of Europe, hill climbs are speed competitions in which cars race, one at a time, against the clock, climbing a stretch of mountain road which has been closed to traffic. They often attract large numbers of spectators. If it were on the FIA's international calendar, the local organiser might try to escape responsibility by claiming that the fault lay with the FIA.

The local prosecutor could charge an FIA official with involuntary manslaughter, the maximum penalty for which would usually exceed the EAW minimum. A UK or French magistrate would be obliged to order arrest and extradition to the relevant country. There the authorities would say: 'Look, it's not serious – if you admit you are guilty you can be on a plane home tomorrow.' Should you reply, 'No, I'm not going to because I'm innocent,' they would explain that you could of course go to trial, but it wouldn't be for a few months. Meanwhile, you sit in their prison. It would also endanger participants. For example, the Italian authorities could have used it against Frank Williams and Patrick Head after the Senna accident.

This has to be seen in the context of the readiness of some EU countries to lock people up until they plead guilty. The danger of being pressured, even blackmailed, into taking the blame when you are not at fault was obvious. A meeting was arranged with a UK Home Office minister where I explained the dangers, particularly that the threshold was far too low. As implemented, it might, for example, expose a schoolteacher who had led a trip abroad on which one of the pupils had been hurt in an accident to the possibility of being locked up because of a refusal to plead guilty when blameless.

I was met with mulish incomprehension. Having to deal with Home Office civil servants and one of their junior ministers at first hand made me realise how endangered civil liberties would be in the UK if left to them. As for myself, I found a personal solution to the threat. In 2004 I moved to Monaco, technically not part of the EU. I saved a considerable amount of tax and my travel time to most European destinations was also substantially reduced. And Monaco is a very pleasant place to live. As things turned out in practice, the UK courts seem alive to the possibility of abuse and so far, I am relieved to say, my worst fears have not been realised.

22

MAINLY WORK –
BUT NOT ENTIRELY

Of course, my job as president of the FIA was not wholly made up of protracted and exhaustive meetings. One of the perks was the opportunity to experience rides in various competition cars and interesting planes, like the Red Bull Alpha Jets or an antique helicopter from the Museum of Army Flying. It may seem frivolous but it was also quite instructive as well as entertaining. For example, slick tyres (tyres with no tread and therefore more rubber in contact with the ground) were first used in 1970, after I had stopped racing. Driving a competition car on slicks for the first time showed me how much more smoothly and predictably a car would slide sideways on them, but also how extremely treacherous they can be when cold.

On the rare occasions I went to a Formula One race, I was sometimes allowed to drive the safety car round the circuit during the preliminaries. The specially modified AMG Mercedes had amazing performance compared with an ordinary road car, although was very slow by Formula One standards. I really enjoyed it but was always worried I would crash. Mercedes had a spare at the races, but I could imagine all too well the delighted mockery heading my way if I destroyed the safety car.

At the other extreme, and also instructive, Tim Keown, who was then chairman of the RAC, let me drive a very old car belonging to the club – I think it was a 1901 Mors. It made me realise that good brakes and steering are not necessarily safer. If you can hardly steer and require a very long distance to stop, you adjust your driving accordingly. Part of that is slowing down to a speed at which you would be very unlikely to get hurt.

The two most interesting experiences were a ride in the McLaren two-seater, courtesy of Ron Dennis, with Martin Brundle at the wheel, and a ride with Colin McRae in a WRC car. I felt slightly uncomfortable in the McLaren two-seater because, once in it, you couldn't get out unaided. Part of the bodywork was bolted in position over you. I asked Martin to be sure to stop by a marshal's post if it caught fire. But the ride was familiar, basically the same as I remembered from my time in the 1960s, only faster. Even with me in the car, I believe Martin was fast enough to have been competitive in the Formula 3000 race. It was pleasant and very exciting. Mika Häkkinen, who was driving for McLaren at the time, had offered to drive me but Ron Dennis, probably wisely, vetoed it – he realised Mika might well try to frighten me for a bit of fun and end up having an accident. The only comparable experiences were being taken round Interlagos by Emerson Fittipaldi in a Porsche 917 and round Riverside by Chris Amon in the March CanAm car. A prized memory of being driven round Monza in a 1925 Alfa Romeo Grand Prix car by Vittorio Brambilla, when I had the role of riding mechanic working the petrol pump, was slightly different. Nothing could have demonstrated more the progress racing car technology had made in 70 years.

The ride with Colin McRae in a WRC car was on Malcolm Wilson's test stage in Cumbria, high above Lake Bassenthwaite. Colin knew the track perfectly so didn't need a co-driver with pace notes and could take me instead. His car control was amazing. Sitting next to him and observing what he could do when he was at the limit on an unpaved forest track was an unforgettable experience – anyone who thinks they can drive would quickly reconsider given an opportunity to sit next to a world-class rally driver when he or she is trying.

After a couple of times round the test track, he stopped the car back at the transporters and suggested we swap places. I thought that brave of him. When we got out of the car, Carlos Sainz, who was also there testing for the Ford team that day, said: 'Now you've driven the car, surely you agree that the air restrictor is too small? We need more power, 300 bhp is not enough!' I had to tell him I was far too slow to appreciate any lack of power but was very flattered that he should think I could tell the difference. All a bit silly at my age, perhaps, but as they say: grow up means give up. And I don't think any genuine motor sport enthusiast would have refused any of those rides, given the opportunity.

In the World Rally Championship, the manufacturer teams were spending absurd sums. On the Greek Acropolis Rally, for example, a top team would use up to 30 vehicles plus three helicopters. They would also keep a fixed-wing plane in the air solely to maintain radio communications between helicopters, vehicles and their central command post. All this to look after a team of two competing cars! But it was necessary because each car was serviced before it went on to a special stage and again as it came off.

This seemed mad. It was ludicrously expensive and surely contrary to the purpose of rallying, which the manufacturers always said was to improve performance and durability. After a certain amount of consultation, I suggested scrapping pre- and post-stage servicing and substituting two or at most three service parks per day. I also felt teams should no longer spend weeks on 'reconnaissance' before a rally. But first I had to get this through the World Council.

One organiser argued against prohibiting reconnaissance (preparation for a rally) because the hotels in the region would suffer. I pointed out that they could pay the hotels if necessary, but it was absurd to waste fortunes running these very expensive cars simply to boost hotel occupancy levels. Guy Goutard, the president of the Rally Commission, came to see me with César Torres, head of the Portuguese club and an FIA vice-president. Both were former competitors and major figures who were greatly respected in the rally world, not least by me. They argued passionately against change, citing tradition and the classic structure of rallies. I told them I agreed, but if costs drove the competitors away, all the tradition in the world would not save our championship.

Eventually my arguments persuaded them and reconnaissance and servicing were drastically reduced. The drivers came on board, too, agreeing that two runs through a stage would be enough for the co-driver to make accurate pace notes. None of the predicted problems arose and much money was saved – no one would turn back to the traditional ways now. We also stopped organisers setting schedules on public roads that could not be met without breaking speed limits. But, on the other side, we had to threaten to stop holding the British round of the World Rally Championship in Wales unless the overzealous local police agreed not to operate temporary speed traps in breach of their own guidelines. Perhaps a foolish desire for publicity inspired their implied threat to make an example of some of the most famous drivers in the world.

That's not to say speed wasn't a major concern – in fact, all over the world we endured alarming problems with crowds' proximity to dauntingly quick cars on the special stages. Understandably, they wanted to watch some of the best drivers in the world going as fast as they could against the clock. Of course it's very exciting and young people, particularly, like to stand as close to the cars as possible. But if a driver loses control and the car goes off the road, spectators are at risk unless they are standing somewhere safe – on top of a high bank for example. The drivers are all at their personal limit and mistakes happen.

When we sent a safety vehicle down the stage to ask the spectators to move, they would often revert to their previous, dangerous positions before the competition cars arrived. I decided the solution was to start using helicopters. Balestre had opposed the idea because it was expensive and no one had been killed recently. 'Where are the bodies?' he asked. I said that was like refusing to stop small children playing on a motorway because none of them had yet been killed. I insisted and the World Council agreed. To prove our point, we now have chilling video footage of cars going off exactly where a group of people had been standing before our helicopter team persuaded them to move.

All this change required a cultural shift by the organisers. In my Manufacturers' Commission days I had visited the French round of the World Rally Championship, where the organiser had allowed someone to set up a *buvette* at the end of a very fast downhill stretch in the middle of what would have been the escape road if one of the cars had a brake problem. Spectators, marshals and the odd policeman were enjoying a drink. When I told Balestre (as head of the French motor sport authority) he couldn't see any harm in it. When I told him I felt the only safe place in the immediate vicinity was up a tree, he was quite funny about my tree climbing in comments to the French press.

More than a decade later, in 2007, we held a round of the World Rally Championship in Ireland. We had been invited by politicians on both sides of the Irish Sea and the idea was that the itinerary would go backwards and forwards across the north–south border and help draw the two communities together. We knew both sides would work happily together in the rally; we had seen the same thing with international rallies in Lebanon and Bosnia despite local armed conflicts. A common interest in sport brings people together. I managed to get the FIA to approve World Championship status for the Irish event; no easy task when so many countries wanted a round. As a result, I was invited to Stormont, where a special stage was to be held in the grounds. The car I was in stopped at the back of the building. I didn't ask why – it's always best just to go with the flow.

Then we drove round to the front where, waiting on the steps, were Ian Paisley and Martin McGuinness. Anyone from the British Isles will understand why this was one of the most surreal moments of my presidency, but needless to say I was very pleased. Apart from anything else, I was exceptionally interested to meet them. We all went to Paisley's room (he was then first minister and McGuinness was deputy), where we had a cup of tea. The atmosphere was pleasant and at one point McGuinness joked: 'The last person to sit with us in that chair you are on was Tony Blair.' It was hard to imagine how things had been a few years previously. Afterwards, Martin McGuinness took me round the building and showed me the parliament chamber. It was a memorable and riveting visit even before I found myself sitting next to Ian Paisley at the dinner that evening. He was fascinating company and I was surprised to discover he had a great sense of humour.

During the last two decades of the 20th century, the historic racing car scene began to take off, broadly made up of enthusiasts who had bought the kind of car they would have coveted when young but could only afford much later in life. The problem this poses, of course, is the combination of middle-aged drivers and old racing cars with no modern safety features. Though beguilingly beautiful to look at, the cars remain as dangerous as they were in the era in which they were built. The hazards were clear but it seemed wrong to interfere – these were all grown-ups doing it for fun and presumably entirely aware of the risks. We had a duty to ensure young drivers were protected as far as possible from the risks, but I didn't feel it was our role to play nanny to a much older generation. As far as practicable, though, we imposed modern safety measures like current crash helmets and, significantly, the races take place on circuits that are emphatically safer than they ever have been.

My slightly laissez-faire attitude sometimes brought me into conflict with our safety and medical experts, particularly when it came to drivers who had actually raced in the past. I didn't feel we could tell the greats, such as Stirling Moss or Jack Brabham, that they could no longer wear the original (very unsafe) helmets and overalls they had donned when competing for the World Championship in the 1950s and 1960s. When they were driving their classic racing cars in modern demonstrations and competitions, they understandably wanted to use their original equipment. Fortunately, I managed to get the World Council to make an exception for them, despite the entirely sensible objections of the FIA's safety people. The FIA can now give a special dispensation to former Grand Prix drivers to wear their original overalls and helmets.

I can see the appeal of racing historic racing cars, but it has always seemed myopic and plain wrong to me that often unique and very special antiques are endangered in such a way. I felt they were part of the heritage of motor racing and the automobile industry. People in one hundred or two hundred years' time would think we were vandals for not preserving them more carefully. I tried to persuade the historic movement to race replicas rather than the originals but without success. Of course, there is something special about driving the actual car that one of the great drivers of the past had raced, but I felt it should be just driven, not raced. Thankfully, companies like Mercedes-Benz preserve their old racing cars and, although they take them out for demonstrations, they are never raced, so there will be something original left for future generations. I gather the FIA is now encouraging the use of replicas.

My brief was trans-generational, making sure Moss and Brabham were unencumbered at one end of the scale and, in my role with international karting, ensuring that expense did not block young people's ambitions of participating in motor sport. I was always conscious of the need to try to control the costs of karting because it suffers from the drawback that performance can be bought with money. A child with rich parents has a better chance than the less well-off, and the only way of thwarting this is a centrally operated, single-make series that completely levels the playing field. I was always in favour of it but, if you try to impose single-make championships, you come up against the commercial interests of the kart builders. There could also be competition law problems.

One of my regrets is that I didn't leave behind a clear, low-cost path from local-level karting to Formula One when I finished my presidency. The commercial interests of those who make a living from motor sport are the main obstacle. Everyone, from the kart suppliers at grassroots level right up to the people operating GP2 and Formula Renault 3.5 just below Formula One, has a vested interest. There was concerted opposition when the FIA backed a one-make, centrally operated Formula Two championship as a very low-cost alternative means of gaining a Formula One super licence. It was clearly in the interests of motor sport generally to reduce the cost of access to Formula One because the lower the cost, the greater the number of talented drivers who would have a chance, but the vested interests prevailed.

Although I didn't have the time to become intimately involved in karting, I did interfere directly once when I received a call to say that a British kart driver was being kept out of a big competition in France on the apparently spurious grounds that his medical certificate was not in order. I called the president of karting and asked him to check that the certificate was OK and, if it was, insist that the organisers allow the driver to compete. It worked and the driver rewarded us by winning his heat and the final. A few days later, the 15-year-old driver sent me an autographed picture by way of thanks. It was a picture of him on the front cover of a McLaren in-house magazine. I was really amused by the gesture and thought, with that much attitude, he'd go far. That was the first time I'd heard of Lewis Hamilton.

The kind of cars that race at Le Mans always caused us difficulties. They are essentially two-seater racing cars with bodywork enclosing the wheels, which share some of the technology of Formula One but are entirely different in other respects. The races are generally long distance – Le Mans, of course, lasts for

24 hours, but there is also a Sebring 12-hour race in America and various other long-distance races in Europe and around the world. Shortly after the FISA election I called a meeting of what was then the Sports Car Commission to see who would be running a team in 1992. There were so few firm promises that the commission even proposed cancelling the Sports Car World Championship.

As mentioned before, there were a number of famous long-distance races in the 1960s and, back then, this form of racing was more important and better funded than Formula One. But it was never centrally managed and most of the great races have now disappeared. Although technically under the FIA, the Le Mans race was so important that the organising club was able to make its own rules for this one event, and I never managed to persuade them to join fully in a central rule-making process. Their rules had to be submitted, of course, and we could veto anything dangerous or unfair, but we could not insist that the Le Mans people sit down with other organisers in an FIA commission to agree common technical rules.

The person responsible for making the technical regulations for Le Mans liked to announce them each year. It was his big moment, but it didn't make for stability or a universally applicable set of rules. For obvious reasons, stable rules common to all competitions in each category, and which do not change unpredictably, are important to anyone building racing cars. I made several attempts to sort this out but had no real success.

The evolution of the Formula One World Championship since 1969 when Bernie and I became involved compared with what has happened to some of the most famous races for so-called sports prototypes is the best answer to those who say the approach we took to Formula One was bad for the sport. The failure of those races to earn significant worldwide coverage shows that central rule-making combined with central commercial management are essential if you want global reach. Nevertheless, Le Mans itself got along very nicely with private entrants and small constructors, and the occasional big-budget manufacturer looking for a prestigious win without too much competition.

My successor, Jean Todt (who won Le Mans for Peugeot as a team manager), has apparently succeeded where I failed. The FIA's World Endurance Championship is now sufficiently attractive to persuade the Le Mans organisers to join in the normal process for agreeing technical and sporting rules internationally. This united approach can only be positive for long-distance racing. In Formula One, Monaco could easily have made a case for special rules for their very abnormal circuit but, had they done so, they and Formula One would have been much less successful.

It wasn't all work. Every year at the Monaco Grand Prix, Flavio Briatore would give a party on his large yacht. As a host, he was among the best; his gatherings were well organised and he laid on excellent food. The only problem was he specialised in billionaires, so anyone like me who wasn't one would feel quite poor in his guests' company. Sitting with a group that included Bernie's wife Slavica, Mohamed Al-Fayed, then the owner of Harrods in London, Ernesto Bertarelli and Lakshmi Mittal, the other side of Al-Fayed, Slavica remarked very quietly to me about Mittal's strange haircut. We both started laughing and Al-Fayed leant over to ask what was going on. I told him and he promptly turned to Mittal and said: 'They are laughing at your haircut.' Quick as a flash Mittal replied: 'I'm not surprised, I get it cut at Harrods.'

23

IMOLA 1994: SENNA'S DEATH AND ITS EFFECT

In one weekend during my first year as president of the full FIA in 1994, a succession of events occurred that had a profound effect on motor sport and, as it turned out, far-reaching consequences for safety on the roads. It reminded me yet again of all the tragedies I had witnessed in top-level motor sport, but now, at last, came a real opportunity to do something about it.

On 1 May 1994, Ayrton Senna was killed during the San Marino GP. The previous day during qualifying, Roland Ratzenberger, an Austrian driver in his debut season, had died in a horrifying accident. There were three other life-threatening incidents during the same weekend. The first involved Rubens Barrichello, the next a mechanic in the pit lane and finally a member of the public in the start-line grandstand.

Senna should not have died. Other drivers had crashed in the same place without serious injury. But part of the car's suspension penetrated his helmet. The FIA's chief medical officer,

Professor Sid Watkins, was a leading brain surgeon and professor of neurosurgery at the London Hospital. One of the innovations he had introduced since starting his role in 1978 was a medical car on standby with a doctor on board who was skilled in resuscitation. He knew that, provided the necessary resuscitation procedures were begun within two minutes, irreversible brain damage (which will generally occur if the brain is without oxygen for more than two minutes) could be avoided even if the driver had no pulse. The driver could then be put on a life-support system and his injuries properly assessed. Sid was in the car that reached Senna within the two-minute window after the accident and carried out the procedures, but it was immediately obvious to him that Ayrton was unlikely to survive. This was devastating for him because he and Ayrton were close friends.

Ayrton was by then one of the world's leading sportsmen. His rivalry with Alain Prost had gripped millions, mainly because they were so different. Prost was calm, down to earth, rational and calculating. Senna was spiritual and emotional. Prost once told me it was worrying driving against Senna because he was deeply religious – he thought God was with him in the car and was quite simply unafraid. For outright speed, Senna was unmatched, as his extraordinary succession of pole positions shows, but Prost may have been the better all-round driver. I don't feel qualified to judge.

There had not been a fatality at a Grand Prix since Riccardo Paletti was killed at Montreal in 1982, so the shock was immense. The media storm continued all week. With two deaths, one of them the world's most famous driver, the media wanted someone or something to blame. Several commentators said it was the elimination of electronic driver aids, a classic post hoc point. It was an intensely stupid inference but was nevertheless widely reported. It was obvious nonsense because that generation of drivers had all acquired their skills in the days before electronic aids. Indeed, the leading drivers including Senna were opposed to them, as explained later, but this was all forgotten in the general hysteria.

All the great and good of Formula One went to Senna's state funeral in Brazil. I decided to go to Ratzenberger's more modest one in Austria. After all, it was just as tragic for his parents and family as it was for Senna's. Although there was nothing I could really do, I felt it important to try to support his parents and partner rather than join the big names in Brazil. It was desperately sad. He had just started out in Formula One in a small team and had worked very hard to get there with the support of his family.

Two weeks later, Karl Wendlinger, another Austrian, suffered severe head injuries in practice for the Monaco Grand Prix. Pictures of the incident appeared all over the world. We now had a full-blown crisis. Commentators were asking what was wrong with Formula One; the big car manufacturers and sponsors were talking openly about pulling out; and there were even suggestions from politicians that Formula One should be banned. I found myself having crisis meetings with senior car industry executives, who always seem to be particularly numerous at the Monaco Grand Prix.

The media storm brought home to me just how global Formula One had become. I fully understood why people felt as they did, having been through this all too often myself, but it was not a time to let emotion take over. What was needed was a calm and systematic approach. Had I pointed out that the five serious incidents in one weekend at Imola, followed by another major accident two weeks later, were simply a statistical cluster, I would probably have been attacked from all sides as irresponsible. It was best not to say that. However, the crisis provided an opportunity to do something that needed doing.

Ever since I started looking at it closely following my election, it seemed to me that Formula One was more dangerous than it needed to be. But until the accidents happened, I had been unable to interest anyone in safety. The conventional view was that it was safe enough, too safe some said. Now there was panic. Annoyingly irrational, certainly, but the hysteria gave me the opportunity to start a revolution.

At very short notice we were able to introduce a number of measures to reduce the risks and, much more importantly, I decided we should set up an expert group to look at all aspects of motor sport safety systematically and scientifically rather than in the ad hoc way it had been dealt with in the past. I asked Professor Watkins to take charge. Apart from being our top medical officer and a world-class neurosurgeon, he was brilliantly clever and able to apply a scientific approach to non-medical problems. He also understood about keeping things simple. Once, sitting in an airport lounge, he told me about a revolutionary technique he had invented for getting a blood supply from one part of the brain to another. 'That's really clever,' I said. 'Oh no,' he replied, 'just O-level carpentry!'

Until then, a failure to apply basic science and scientific methods systematically had been a fundamental problem. A lot of work was done on such things as rollover bars, fire prevention and protection of the driver's feet. We had endless FOCA discussions on these and other aspects of safety before repeating them with the FIA in Paris. But it was all piecemeal rather than systematic.

Safety had also improved as a side effect of the adoption of new technologies, such as composite materials, but those benefits were incidental – the main objective of all that engineering work had always been to improve performance. A few individuals did their best, particularly one or two drivers, but drivers lacked the qualifications and knowledge to make real progress. Being able to drive a car fast does not make you an expert on how to minimise the risks if you lose control. The media listen to the drivers, who are quite rightly the public face of the sport, but the effect of this is to amplify the confusion and put pressure on the circuit owners. Some unwise and unscientific things were done in the name of safety before reason took over. Armco barriers, particularly in the wrong place as in François Cevert's fatal accident in 1973, are a classic example.

The lack of science is illustrated by the discussions between the teams and the FIA about reducing cornering speeds back in 1980, described in chapter 12. The question was whether to reduce grip and hence cornering speeds by changing the tyres or by curtailing the aerodynamics. Representing the FIA was, among others, Paul Frère, a recognised authority. He had driven in several Formula One races and in 1960 won the Le Mans 24-hour race for Ferrari (with Olivier Gendebien). He was the author of *Sports Car and Competition Driving*, then a standard motor racing textbook.

In one of the technical meetings he disagreed with Colin Chapman's suggestion that reducing the grip of the tyres would be the best way to reduce cornering speeds. Frère explained this would be dangerous because, if grip were reduced, a car would decelerate less quickly if the driver lost control. As a successful racing driver himself, he had the support of almost all the drivers. They knew from experience that the bigger the tyres, the more grip they had and the quicker the car would stop if it went out of control.

They were right, of course. The car would stop more quickly if it had more grip, but the problem is, if it hits something before it stops (the only thing affecting safety), it will hit it harder. Aerodynamics apart, any first-year engineering student can prove on a single sheet of paper that the distance for which a car spins, if control is lost when it is travelling at the limit of adhesion in a corner, is a function of the radius of the corner. Neglecting second-order effects and aero, it remains the same irrespective of grip.

It follows that at any given point before the car stops of its own accord, it will be travelling faster if it has more grip because it starts from a higher speed. And the impact, if it hits something, will therefore be greater. If it doesn't hit anything there's obviously not a problem, but our only real concern is what happens when it does hit something. All this is difficult for many drivers to accept, and the big-tyres-stop-quicker theory was explained to me yet again at a meeting with the Grand Prix Drivers' Association at Heathrow in 1999. When I offered to do the sums for them there and then, they said, amid laughter, they'd prefer to take my word for it.

The truth is counter-intuitive but is easier to understand if you imagine a Grand Prix starting on packed snow. Then it should become obvious that no one would be likely to get hurt because the cornering speeds would be so low. If low grip increases safety in competition driving, exactly the opposite is true for normal driving on an ordinary road. There, if the driver is being responsible, speed is limited not by the grip of the car but by various legal speed limits. So, in everyday motoring, the more grip the better. It increases the driver's chances of keeping out of trouble in an emergency.

I'm afraid this may be a bit tedious for the non-enthusiast, but it illustrates perfectly the well-meaning but relatively primitive mind-set we were up against at the beginning of Professor Watkins's work. Since then, two decades of applying science to safety by Sid Watkins and his team, working with all sorts of consultants and university departments, have transformed Formula One and the rest of motor sport. It will never be safe but by eliminating the folklore element we reduced the probability of injury. In all activities where safety has to be taken seriously – aviation, for example – the work is all about reducing the probability of injury while recognising that it will never be zero.

As part of its research, I had suggested to Sid that the group should look at government work on occupant safety in road cars. It seemed certain that with (at that time) some 50,000 deaths on the roads and up to eight times as many serious injuries each year in the EU, there must be several extensive research programmes for road safety in the countries of western Europe. These would inevitably include the protection of car occupants because they accounted for such a high proportion of the casualties. Official work on protecting car occupants was likely to be directly relevant to driver safety in Formula One. Compared with the FIA, governments had virtually unlimited resources and it seemed likely we would be able to learn a great deal in a very short time from their research programmes.

To our astonishment, we found almost nothing was happening. There had been quite extraordinary neglect. The crash-test requirements for road cars in the EU had not changed since 1974, largely due to the powerful car industry lobby that was firmly entrenched in Brussels resisting anything that might add cost. This revelation provided the incentive to begin work in Brussels on road safety and start the Euro NCAP crash-test programme, of which much more follows later.

Apart from the cars themselves, we also subjected the circuits to Sid's scientific approach. We began with really accurate plans that enabled us to use a computer program to look at each corner and ensure that our approach was uniform and consistent. Many of the major circuits were also used for motorcycle racing. What was suitable for cars was not always ideal for the bikes, but we co-operated closely with the FIM, the world governing body for motorcycle racing. Our principal circuit inspector was Charlie Whiting, which worked well because he was also in charge of the Formula One Technical Working Group and a member of Sid's safety group. As a result, he could deal with the safety issue in its entirety.

Right at the beginning, we had a particular problem at Monza, where inspections and our calculations showed conclusively that more run-off was needed at the *Curva Grande*. Slowed by a chicane in 1972, this was originally the very fast corner just after the start which I had discussed with Jochen Rindt back in my Formula Two days. The new work would mean cutting down 150 trees, a proposal the park authorities refused to countenance. The race organisers offered to plant 5000 trees elsewhere in the Monza Park, but still they refused. The World Council gave them a deadline: if the trees were not felled, there would be no race. The deadline passed. On holiday in the South of France, I called the FIA office and asked them to put out a press release saying the 1994 Italian Grand Prix had been cancelled.

I went into our sitting room and told Jean I had just cancelled the Italian Grand Prix. She looked at me as if I were mad: 'You *what*? No one cancels the Italian Grand Prix!' It seemed to me the obvious thing to do. If the World Council gave a deadline and those responsible took no notice, as far as I was concerned cancellation was inevitable. If we wanted the FIA to be taken seriously, particularly on safety, we had to act.

Predictably, the effect was dramatic. The press release provoked an astonishing political crisis in Italy. We were told the Northern League were even threatening to pull out of their coalition with Silvio Berlusconi if the problem wasn't solved. I started getting calls from what seemed to be someone in an Italian government office. Our number was supposedly ex-directory so, trying to sound like a local Frenchman, I kept telling them they'd got the wrong number. Eventually, however, it became clear I couldn't just forget about Monza and get on with my holiday. A meeting was set up and Berlusconi's right-hand man, Gianni Letta, plus a very senior Northern League politician came to Cannes to negotiate, accompanied by advisers. I suggested Cannes airport as they would be coming by plane.

To my surprise, they arrived in a motorcade. Apparently, the government DC9 couldn't get into Cannes with its relatively short runway, so they had landed at Nice. I was alone. We debated the question for some hours. It was all very polite, but I wouldn't budge. It was the same reasoning as for the Canadian Grand Prix almost 20 years earlier. Never compromise once a deadline passes. If you do, no one will ever again take your deadline seriously. At one point, Berlusconi himself joined the discussions by phone. 'Do me this favour,' he said, 'and you will always have a friend in the Council of Ministers.'

It was difficult. Gianni Letta (uncle of the recent Italian prime minister) is extremely clever and has great charm. I was very tempted to give in but felt it was my duty to refuse. The lack of run-off at the *Curva Grande* was not a problem for anyone except the drivers and the chance of one of them being killed or seriously hurt at this part of the circuit was remote, but that was not a risk for others to take on their behalf. The deputation left empty-handed. Yet everyone still wanted the race to go ahead. I discussed what to do at length with Gerhard Berger, who was able to represent the drivers. I said it was entirely up to them, but we would only reinstate the race if they all agreed.

In the end, the deal was one last race without the run-off, so we gave the circuit a year's grace to cut down the trees. Happily, no one was hurt and the missing run-off was not needed, even though there was a multiple accident on the first lap and the race had to be restarted. Gerhard finished second for Ferrari; Damon Hill won in a Williams. The trees were duly chopped and the run-off extended in time for the following year. The trees were never fine specimens and, when they finally came down, almost all turned out to be rotten.

Following all the controversy, Berlusconi invited Bernie and me to dinner after the race. He had a house in the Monza Park, so instead of flying back to the UK we found ourselves in a police helicopter being taken to a very strange gathering. It was mainly for friends of his from Hollywood. I found myself sitting next to Sylvester Stallone, who told me all about O.J. Simpson, then very topical. He was also interesting about the American film industry, of which I knew nothing. He was quite different from his screen persona.

At one point, Berlusconi, who spoke very little English, was trying to explain his legal difficulties to the entire table. 'The problem,' he seemed to say, 'is that all our little Jews are communists.' Or at least that's what it sounded like. We all froze in embarrassment. A guest at the dinner broke the silence – it was the leading South African businessman Johann Rupert, who quickly said: 'I think he means judges.' He had realised that what Berlusconi wanted to say was 'magistrates', but not knowing the word had tried to say 'little judges'. But he had used the French word for judge (*juge*) which sounds a bit like Jews. Everyone relaxed again – Johann's quick thinking saved the dinner.

Senna's death the previous May led to a major judicial inquiry in Italy whose focus was apportioning blame for the accident. Frank Williams and Patrick Head were prosecuted. In Italy, if someone is killed and anyone can be blamed, even to a minor degree, it can be a criminal offence, so something that in England would be mere negligence can be deemed a crime in Italy. If the degree of negligence is slight, it is not a serious crime but a crime nonetheless. Frank and Patrick were eventually acquitted, but it took about ten years before the case was finally finished.

I thought the whole thing a colossal waste of time. The important question in Senna's case was not why did he crash or who was to blame, but why did the crash kill him? On a public road it is obviously important to ask who was to blame for an accident but not on a racetrack, where everyone is at their personal limit in a sporting contest. They are bound to make mistakes and a crash is the likely outcome. Losing control and going off the road is an inevitable part of the contest. It's like hitting the ball out in tennis. The job of the authority (sporting or legal) is not to inquire endlessly as to who was to blame (other than, sometimes, as a minor sporting infringement), it is to try to make sure that, when the inevitable crashes occur, no one gets hurt.

The Italian Olympic Committee picked up on this and on the undesirability of the authorities getting involved and prosecuting those organising or participating in a dangerous sport if someone is accidentally hurt. In 1997, it organised a major conference on the subject *La Colpa di Voler Vincere* (Guilty of Wanting to Win), with the then president of the European Olympic Committee, Jacques Rogge (later president of the IOC), and Francesco Zerbi, then president of the FIM, plus a number of legal and political experts. They invited the FIA to participate and also asked if I could persuade an expert on English law to come and explain the very different way the English common law approaches the problem of dangerous sport.

I thought of Sir Maurice Drake, then a prominent English High Court judge. When he was at the Bar I had been one of his pupils. He very kindly agreed to come to Rome and gave what everyone thought was a brilliant exposition of the English approach and the law of negligence. It made a great impression on our hosts and the representatives of dangerous sports. I took advantage of the time I spent with him to ask why (as I had noticed from the press) he seemed to be getting such a high proportion of the most interesting cases coming before the High Court. He explained that he was in charge of the list. I felt quite envious – if only I could choose the interesting questions like that.

Meanwhile, the problem of cornering speeds in Formula One had not gone away. They were constantly increasing and tending to negate our efforts to improve safety on the circuits. Sitting in an office at the French Grand Prix, I thought back to the discussions about skirts and tyres in 1980. I knew the answer was to decrease the grip of the tyres. I did a few sums to convince myself once again that the conventional wisdom was wrong and that, in competition (as opposed to road) driving, less grip meant more safety. By chance, Robin Herd was in the pits doing a bit of consulting for one of the teams. As it was more than 30 years since my university days, I was not totally confident about my maths and went to find him to ask him to check the calculations. He confirmed the sums were right.

The simplest way to reduce the grip was to reduce the size of the tyre contact patch, and the easiest way to do that would be narrower tyres. But if we decreased the maximum tyre width, the straight-line speeds would increase because a very high proportion of the aerodynamic drag of a Formula One car comes from the wheels and tyres. So, for a smaller contact patch we needed some form of tread, just as Colin Chapman had pointed out to the FIA and Paul Frère back in 1980. But it had to be a clear rule and easy to check. Hiroshi Yasukawa, the head of Bridgestone's Formula One programme, came up with the answer: parallel grooves all the way round the circumference of the tyre – easy to define, easy to measure, and the same for everyone.

We brought in grooved tyres for 1998. Some drivers objected, still believing that less grip was dangerous. When first tried, the grooved tyres were pronounced undrivable and hopelessly slow, but the problems were soon solved. The traditionalists always disliked grooved tyres (strange, because treaded tyres had been the norm for 80 of the previous 100 years) but at least the engineers could do the sums and understand the thinking.

The grooves were only necessary when there was competition between tyre manufacturers. With a single tyre supplier, the FIA can simply ask for a bit less grip. After all, it's the same for all the teams. But if you have competition between two or more tyre companies, which we had until recently, the grooves were a fair and very effective means of keeping cornering speeds under control. Although it was 30 years and more since Jim Clark's death at Hockenheim and Roger Williamson's horrific accident at Zandvoort had made such a deep impression on me, safety was at last at the top of the agenda, and science was being deployed to further it. And, before long, this thinking would extend far beyond the track to everyday cars on the roads, changing the culture of the global car industry and saving countless thousands of lives.

24

CONFLICT IN FORMULA ONE

Even before that harrowing weekend at Imola in 1994, my resolve to stay out of Formula One after the 1991 election had been short-lived. Electronic systems, developed to assist the drivers, had become a genuine and growing concern. They were expensive but, more importantly, they were going to render much of a driver's armoury of skills redundant. Pretty soon we would get to the point where there would in effect be a second driver in the car in the form of a computer, which would take over an ever increasing number of the tasks traditionally carried out by the driver. This is precisely what you want for road cars, where the more that can be done to assist the driver, the fewer the accidents and the better the traffic will flow. But motor sport is supposed to be a test of driving skill rather than a means of getting from A to B safely and efficiently on the roads.

Ayrton Senna found the increasing use of electronics worrying, even depressing, because he recognised that the new technology was bound to devalue the driver's skill. At Christmas 1992, he sent me a card on which he had written by hand:

To Max,

92 wasn't particularly great! Perhaps this is the time for a
change. Rather soon before is too late. F1 cannot continue like this
any longer, it's got to change!
Ayrton Senna

Apart from anything else, I was impressed that he could write English that well – it's one thing to speak a foreign language, quite another to write it with only one very small mistake.

I took this as a plea to get rid of the electronic aids and we knew that other top drivers felt the same. I fully understood that motor racing had always involved a machine as well as a human, and that the greatest driver would be helpless without a suitable car, but the World Council and most people in motor sport felt that it was for the driver to make the most of a mechanical car without assistance. It was the essence of his skill. Inside the FIA, we thoroughly agreed with Senna.

Having found a consensus in 1993 that the drivers should drive the cars without electronic assistance, we set out to ban the new systems. The result was a big discussion with the teams about so-called driver aids. I proposed the ban to the F1 Commission and had a precise piece of text prepared, but the teams at the forefront of electronic development objected to the wording. They didn't want any real restriction. In the end, I offered them a very simple rule: 'The driver must drive the car alone and unaided.' They liked that. There was no definition of the driver aids we were trying to ban and they thought the rule would be unenforceable because it was so vague. They had missed the obvious lawyer's point that, without a definition in the rules, a 'driver aid' was whatever the stewards (and ultimately the FIA Court of Appeal) thought it was. Those who take an interest in such things know very well that the less clear the law, the greater the power of the judges. Sometimes the rather narrow outlook of some team principals could be helpful.

We were now armed with a very broad rule. But then it was explained to me by one of the teams that we could never genuinely check because it would take thousands of years to penetrate the software source codes. Our response was: you are going to have to give us your source code. It's no different from opening the bonnet of a car – if you want to race, we have to be able to check that your car complies with the rules. If we don't have your source code, then we can't verify that it contains no illicit driver aids and your cars won't leave the pit lane. Two of the teams were dilatory, claiming the source code was proprietary and belonged to a major manufacturer. So we fined them; and we eventually received all the codes.

Now we needed proper computing know-how if we were to get on top of this new technology. We began by recruiting Alan Prudom, who had previously worked on the computer control systems for nuclear power stations. He brought a whole new level of expertise and could certainly match the sort of people the major Formula One teams were hiring. Alan was able to access the information in a team's electronic equipment even when it was hidden, which was to become very relevant.

One unfortunate aspect of the 1994 ban on driver aids was the suspicion that Benetton were still using the now banned traction control and launch control. Launch control was a special program to govern all the parameters when the race started so as to optimise the car's acceleration. There had to be enough power to allow just the right amount of slippage between wheel and road but not enough for full wheel spin. It was very clever but now illegal. In order to check, we seized a number of electronic devices at the 1994 San Marino Grand Prix, among them those used by the Benetton team. Unfortunately, in all the confusion and stress following that disastrous race weekend and its aftermath, I made the mistake of authorising their return to Benetton before they had been fully checked.

Later in the season, we seized their electronic devices again and our IT experts discovered a hidden launch control program. Benetton claimed it had never been deployed that season but that removing it from the software was too complex. They said it had been hidden to prevent it being switched on by mistake. Having given back the Imola boxes, we could not prove one way or the other whether they had actually put the illegal aid to use that season. There was strong suspicion that they probably had, however, and we decided to publish the finding, confirming its existence and that it had been switched off. Other teams were quick to say that removing the now illegal programs over the winter had been an easy task, an assertion that stoked considerable press excitement at the German Grand Prix.

Another concern was the sheer volume of communication that was now common between cars and the pits. Modern Formula One cars have hundreds of sensors, all streaming data back to the teams. We were not particularly worried about this, but we were concerned about information coming back the other way that might be used to help drive the car. We introduced very restrictive rules about what could pass from pit to car, likewise with verbal radio communications. Plainly, a team would not want its rivals to listen to radio discussions with their drivers, so these transmissions were routinely encrypted. But we insisted that our staff in the tower should be able to listen to everything to make sure there was no cheating. Today, the teams allow non-critical conversations to be broadcast, which enhances the TV coverage, and all communications are open and accessible to both the FIA and the broadcasters.

At one point, when discussing cost, I asked the teams if all this information from the sensors was really necessary. The banks of computers behind the pits and the personnel to analyse it in real time were clearly very expensive. Oh yes, they said, it is expensive but it's for safety. I asked why they couldn't just have a warning light to tell the driver to stop if there were a safety problem. They admitted they could, but said even if the computers were not really about safety, the equipment so impressed the sponsors that it brought in more money than it cost. I had no answer to that.

The ban on electronic driver assistance was the first real divergence between what was needed on the road and what is useful in racing. Just as this technology was undesirable in a sporting context, it was ideal for roads (our Brussels campaign for electronic stability control on road cars finally bore fruit on 1 November 2014, when ESC became compulsory on all new cars sold in the EU). Devices such as electronic stability control, for example, save many lives in everyday motoring. Some journalists and even teams argued that it was absurd to prohibit devices in Formula One that were becoming commonplace for road cars. To most of us in the FIA, that was missing the point. Reducing the need for driver skill in Formula One diminishes the sport because driver skill is an essential element of motor sport. But reducing the need for skill on the roads (where it is often in short supply) enhances the safety of all road users because it lessens the likelihood that an error will cause an accident.

We also had a problem with Formula One fuel at the beginning of the 1990s. There was a strange smell in the pit area and it was noticeable that the personnel fuelling the cars in the garages were wearing elaborate protective clothing. The cars were supposed to use fuel that a motorist could buy from the pump but, when I asked what exactly that meant, I learned it could mean almost anything. Long-established FIA regulations specified little more than a maximum octane rating. High-octane fuel was synonymous with high performance in popular perception but meaningless when fuel company chemists got going. An early example of this was the fuel in the BMW turbo engine back in 1983 described in chapter 15.

Pump fuel can have several hundred components and, worse, these vary according to the time of year and the latitude of the country where you buy it, as well as the characteristics of the local refineries. This does not matter for road cars, as their relatively low-performance engines are able to accommodate the differences, but in a racing engine at very high rpm and high compression ratios, the composition of the fuel becomes a critical performance factor. And with a vast number of components, the possibilities for making a special fuel just for Formula One and claiming it was pump fuel were obvious. For example, one of the favoured additives was norbornadiene, something you might find in rocket fuel. Its purpose was to increase the speed of combustion in these very high-revving engines.

We could not deny the fuel companies scope to develop new and improved pump fuels because this sort of research was an important reason for their participation in Formula One. Yet we needed to make sure it was a fuel that might genuinely be sold at the pump in the future. The obvious answer from an administrative point of view – a standard fuel – would have deprived Formula One of a lot of sponsorship.

The oil companies helped us produce some elaborate regulations. Provided a fuel complied, you could be sure that it was genuinely a potential pump fuel. But given the unavoidable complexity of the rules for pump fuel and the huge number of possible components, how do you quickly check that the fuel you have just sampled at a race is legal? You could send it away for detailed analysis but you would risk having to exclude a car long after the race results were published.

We hit on the idea of asking the fuel companies to submit a sample well before it was used in a race, so that it could then be fully analysed and checked for conformity. The next step was to use gas chromatography to take a 'fingerprint' of the sample. With the relevant instrument among our equipment at each Grand Prix, we could then compare the 'fingerprint' of the fuel taken from the car with that of the sample we had already analysed and thus check very quickly if the two were identical.

The first time a sample failed it was from a car using Elf fuel. When the stewards took action, a rather tiresome PR lady from the fuel company told the press we didn't know what we were doing and our equipment was primitive. She was backed up by top Elf management (the same people who were later involved in a major French political scandal), who were very aggressive and even started legal proceedings in Paris against the FIA.

Inevitably, and annoyingly, this created a media storm. Fortunately we had a 'B' sample, which we sent to the world-renowned SGS laboratory in Germany and they confirmed our result. Interestingly, when analysed, the Elf fuel was actually legal under the rules but was not the same as the sample they had submitted, so did not comply. There was no question of them trying to cheat or use an illegal fuel. They had merely made a change without resubmitting it. After that, everyone knew our equipment worked and we could detect even very small differences and thus guarantee the cars were using pump fuel.

Running the sport was an endless succession of complications like that, particularly in Formula One. Trying to make sure everyone plays within the rules is extremely difficult. Teams routinely change as many as 100 elements on their cars between races in a constant search for more performance, and all the top ones have dozens of highly qualified engineers. Many of them have doctorates in engineering and related subjects. They are constantly at work and part of their remit is to push to the very limit of the regulations. Against this, the FIA has a small group of engineers, computer experts and fuel specialists led by Charlie Whiting, who is the head of the FIA technical department as well as the race director.

None of this is cheating – it's perfectly legitimate to go to the limit of the rules – but inevitably there are disputes, sometimes between a team and FIA experts, sometimes between the teams themselves. The race stewards resolve disputes but there is also a right of appeal to the FIA International Court of Appeal. Its members are senior independent lawyers, all from different countries and with a good knowledge of motor sport, who are nominated by their national motor sport authorities and elected by the FIA General Assembly.

As budgets increased in the 1990s and the cars became increasingly sophisticated, there was a tendency for the teams constantly to introduce new devices that tested the boundaries of the rules. These would often be very expensive to design and develop, and risked being ruled illegal when first used at a race, wasting the money spent. So, early in my presidency, we invited the teams to start submitting their latest ideas in strict confidence at the design stage. Charlie would look at the design and offer an opinion as to its legality. This was on the clear understanding that he was only giving an opinion, not a ruling, but nevertheless an indication of the line the FIA technical department would take. It was a sort of prior notification – a concept I tried to introduce years later in my dispute with Britain's tabloid press.

If Charlie and his group thought it illegal but the team disagreed, they were welcome to take the device to a race and try their chances with the stewards. Conversely, Charlie might OK something but another team might protest. Again, it would be up to the stewards. Sometimes he would discuss a borderline idea with me. I never ceased to be fascinated and surprised by the ingenuity and originality of some of the concepts. I think one of the reasons Formula One attracts such brilliant engineers is the short time between conceiving an idea and seeing it applied in real life. By contrast, in most areas of engineering – for example, aviation or defence – the time lapse between a novel idea and its practical application can be many years.

We also told the teams that if they didn't inform us about a new device which we later discovered and ruled illegal, we would presume they didn't tell us because they intended to conceal it and therefore cheat. This system worked surprisingly well. Charlie received literally hundreds of submissions but there were almost no instances of his opinion being challenged by a team or overruled by the stewards or the Court of Appeal.

Breaking the rules could potentially have lethal consequences. At the 1994 German Grand Prix, Benetton had a massive fire in the pit lane. An investigation showed that the team had removed a filter from the refuelling system on Jos Verstappen's car. This reduced the time of a pit stop by about a second but its absence had allowed dirt to jam open a valve, hence the leak and the fire. Benetton got away with it (just) so far as we were concerned by claiming a junior employee had removed the filter and that someone from the fuel rig manufacturer had given permission for this.

To our considerable surprise, a representative of the fuel rig manufacturer confirmed the story.

Michael Schumacher, then also driving for Benetton, was already racing under appeal because of an incident at the British Grand Prix two weeks earlier. He had been shown a black flag (a signal to stop and come into the pits) following an incident at the start of the race, but had not stopped. He claimed not to have seen the black flags, even though they were placed on either side of the start line. The stewards imposed a modest fine, but we thought it very serious if he had indeed deliberately ignored a flag signal because the flags are primarily used for the safety of drivers and marshals. The matter was brought before the World Council. After a detailed hearing, the defence was not believed and Schumacher lost his second place at Silverstone and was banned for two races. With the suspension under appeal, Schumacher was able to start the next race, his home German Grand Prix.

Controversy escalated further for Benetton when, a month later at Spa, Schumacher's 'plank' (a device to keep a minimum gap between the car and the ground in order to reduce downforce and hence cornering speed) was found to be too thin. The team claimed it had been damaged when he went sideways over a kerb but could not explain why, in that case, all the wear lines were in the direction of travel. Despite having George Carman QC, then England's most high-profile lawyer, to defend them, it was clear they had run the car too low in order to gain downforce and hence performance.

Schumacher was excluded again, this time wiping out a victory. When he also lost his appeal against the two-race ban from Silverstone, his big lead in the championship disappeared. Even so, he eventually became world champion for the first time that year by a mere one-point margin over Damon Hill after yet another controversial incident at the final race in Australia. Schumacher went off the road while ahead of Hill and had apparently damaged his car. When Hill went to pass him, he came across the track and the two collided. Schumacher was out immediately; Hill tried to continue but couldn't. Schumacher was widely accused of deliberately running into Hill, but the stewards decided it was a racing incident. Hill maintained a very dignified silence and kept out of the controversy. My private view was that Michael had been very lucky not to be penalised and thus lose his World Championship win. But the stewards had looked into the incident and come to the opposite conclusion. It was a matter of opinion and it would have been wrong to interfere, particularly after criticising Balestre for doing just that a few years before.

25

MORE TROUBLE
IN FORMULA ONE

At times I felt almost besieged – as soon as one problem was solved, another immediately materialised. The next was a legal dispute with British American Tobacco over the appearance of their cars, which at least demonstrated that not all problems were buried deep beneath the bodywork. The point of conflict was the team's desire for two distinct liveries on their two cars for two different brands. Despite a call from Kenneth Clarke, former Home Secretary and Chancellor of the Exchequer who was then a BAT board member and a Formula One enthusiast, we said no, it's a two-car team and the rules say the cars should look substantially the same. BAT insisted on arbitration, as was their right under the Concorde Agreement.

Each side appointed an arbitrator – Anthony Grabiner and Jonathan Sumption, both top lawyers – who in turn appointed a neutral chairman. Our case was brilliantly argued by David Pannick QC and, against expectations, we won. BAT had a point in that multinational companies with several brands might be more likely to come into Formula One if they could promote two of them rather than one. We should have had a discussion and perhaps a rule change, but big companies sometimes too readily seek to impose their will without bothering to negotiate with a mere governing body.

We had yet more difficulties at the 1997 European Grand Prix, the last of the season, run on the Jerez circuit in southern Spain. Unusually, I was there and watching from a room in the control tower with (strangely) the opera singer Placido Domingo. During lap 48, we looked on as Michael Schumacher seemingly turned into Jacques Villeneuve's Williams as it tried to overtake him. Michael was summoned to a hearing at the World Council, which happened to be convened on the day the story of Bernie's £1 million donation to the British Labour Party broke. A media scrum surrounded Bernie and me when (unusually) we arrived together for the hearing and, although Schumacher lost his second place in the championship, the next day's papers were full of Bernie's £1 million with barely a mention of Michael.

Schumacher was also asked to spend seven days helping our road safety campaigns, a sort of community service for his offence. He did this willingly (and continued to help our campaigns long after the Jerez incident was forgotten). The only awkward moment came when he and I turned up for a road safety event in Warsaw and almost got caught (I'm ashamed to say) not wearing seatbelts in the back of the limo. We got them on just in time to avoid being photographed without them. He became the FIA's number one ambassador for road safety and proved very adept at dealing with the media on safety matters. His example encouraged other drivers to join our campaigns.

Michael was an extraordinary talent. He also had an exceptional work ethic and would go back to the pits after dinner in the evening to talk to and encourage the mechanics working on his car. This was unusual and certainly contributed to the loyalty his team felt for him. He had a bad-boy image and was certainly very determined when racing. But in private he was charming, intelligent, somewhat insecure (surprising, given his extraordinary ability) and very interesting to talk to about Formula One. I used to have the occasional quiet dinner with him when I was in Geneva, close to where he lived. I always learned something from those conversations.

Schumacher won a second successive World Championship with Benetton in 1995 and there was pressure on him to complete the hat-trick when he joined Ferrari in 1996. (Ferrari had not won the drivers' title since Jody Scheckter in 1979.) Even with Jean Todt now running the team, it took Ferrari some time to get going and things turned even more difficult for Michael when he crashed and broke his leg during the 1999 British Grand Prix at Silverstone. His championship chances slipped away during subsequent races, although he was able to return for the final two events and help his team-mate Eddie Irvine in the title fight with McLaren's Mika Häkkinen. At the penultimate round in Malaysia, it was Ferrari's turn to pose us a major problem.

All the cars, not just Ferrari, had a panel on each side of the chassis for aerodynamic reasons. These were nicknamed 'barge boards' by the teams because they looked as if they were there to protect the cars when they bumped into one another. In fact, it was an aerodynamic device. Like almost all the other parts of the cars, the panels were subject to strict rules. One particular dimension was determined by the 'shadow' the board cast over a sort of lip at its lower end when viewed from directly above.

One of the McLaren staff thought the lip on the Ferrari looked slightly too big and tipped off the FIA officials at the Malaysian Grand Prix. The cars were measured, found to be illegal and excluded, thus losing their first and second places. Ross Brawn, then in charge of engineering at Ferrari, in a surprising moment of frankness admitted to the media that the boards did indeed exceed the maximum permitted dimension. The boards were impounded and brought back to FIA headquarters pending the inevitable appeal.

The boards were grubby and covered with race debris but when, out of curiosity, I looked at one in my office it was clear that the lip was indeed too big. However, it was also immediately obvious that if the board had been at a slight angle to the chassis, rather than vertical, the dimension would have been legal because the 'shadow' would have been smaller. Someone from Ferrari came to check the boards prior to the appeal hearing and, sure enough, they noticed the same thing. They took the point and won the appeal – the FIA had no evidence concerning what the angle had been now the boards had been taken off the car.

With hindsight, we should have impounded the entire car. Inevitably, some commentators suggested we had influenced the court to favour Ferrari. We never did but it was impossible to convince a partisan Formula One fan that the appeal system was genuinely fair – and the criticism came the other way round when, for example, we acquitted McLaren at the first 'spygate' hearing, of which more later. Sadly, one of the cleaners got hold of the boards and cleaned off all the race debris, so what would have been a souvenir for the FIA head office is no longer so authentic.

A short time later, I was very surprised when, at a reception at the Turin motor show, Gianni Agnelli thanked me for the decision. That he thought I had, or even could have, influenced it one way or the other really worried me. I tried to explain that the FIA International Court of Appeal consisted of senior lawyers who all had knowledge of motor sport but no connection with me or with any competitor. A judge was not even allowed to be from the same country as any party to the appeal. I also told him that, out of more than 30 members of the court, I only knew two personally. I did my best to persuade him that the court was entirely independent of the FIA administration but I'm not sure he was entirely convinced.

The court had, of course, been completely reconstituted since the days when one of the car companies had somehow managed to record Balestre telling me on the telephone that he controlled it. Initially, a French lawyer managed the court, then David Ward took over, but from 2007 it was supervised by an independent external lawyer, usually Ken Daly from Sidley Austin. The judges were all elected by the FIA member organisations and were the sort of people who would have been outraged had I, or anyone from the administration, contacted them, directly or indirectly, to suggest what they should decide. Anyone with knowledge of the UK Bar, for example, would have known that the idea of me calling up either of the two British judges (Anthony Scrivener and Edwin Glasgow, both eminent QCs) to suggest what they should decide would be nothing short of absurd. Given all that effort, it was disappointing that anyone should think the court was not fully independent.

Some of the Formula One teams fed this deceit by constantly carping about the court and questioning its independence with the media. So, shortly after David took over we decided to open the court to the press. This was strongly opposed by Maître Loitron, the very distinguished French lawyer on whom we relied for guidance on questions of French law. He said we'd regret it and, as luck would have it, the very first case open to the press was indeed a bit of a disaster.

In 2001, after finishing fourth, Jarno Trulli's Jordan had been excluded from the United States Grand Prix for a breach of technical regulations. But the steward who needed to sign the order had left early to chair a meeting next day in Europe, so someone else had signed his name on his behalf. Eddie Jordan and his team discovered this and appealed, claiming the order was a forgery. Things were further complicated when Eddie paid the deposit accompanying the notice of appeal with dollar bills so old they were no longer legal tender. When the case came before the Court of Appeal, the FIA had to throw in its hand because of the irregularity of the signature. Fortunately, only one journalist turned up for the hearing and he wrote a very funny account of it. But the principle of open justice was now established and the press could see for itself how the court worked. After a few more hearings, the media began to recognise the professionalism and independent legal expertise of the court.

When the 2001 attack on the New York World Trade Center happened, we were in the middle of a South American congress in Peru. The whole of North American airspace was immediately shut down and everyone from Europe who had travelled via Miami, the conventional route, was stuck in South America. Fortunately, I had avoided Miami (always a wise precaution) and flown direct to Lima from Madrid. Although it was a shocking act of terrorism, the degree of panic was surprising, not just in America but elsewhere. Even Michael Schumacher went round the drivers the following weekend at Monza urging everyone to refuse to go to the next race at Indianapolis for fear of an incident.

The suggested boycott didn't materialise but I was quite

annoyed. It was our job, not Michael's, to call off a Grand Prix if there were a threat. Also, given the level of hysteria, I thought a big sporting event at Indianapolis, in the heart of the American Midwest, would be one of the safest places you could imagine in the coming weeks. The security might be over the top (indeed, warplanes flew overhead during the race) but the risk of a terrorist incident would be negligible – and so it turned out.

However hard you try to be even-handed between all participants, I don't think it will ever be possible to convince the most committed Formula One fan that the system is fair if a decision is taken which is perceived as disadvantageous to their favourite team. A good example of this was the 2003 tyre controversy. The rules stipulated a maximum tread width for the tyre. We discovered, however, that Michelin had so constructed theirs that it conformed when measured in the garage but took on a mushroom-like shape when the car was running, making the contact patch wider than permitted. We stopped this as we thought it was a clear infringement. To this day, McLaren fans accuse the FIA of having done it to help Ferrari, who were on a different make of tyre. It reminded me of Lyndon B. Johnson's maxim about a jackass in a hailstorm: 'Nothing to do but stand there and take it.'

Apart from the larger conflicts, there was a never-ending succession of smaller disputes. These were almost always accompanied by outraged comments from the supporters of whichever team was perceived to have come off the worst. The supporters often included journalists, some of whom would not even bother to pick up the phone and ask for the FIA's side of the question. Aside from the technical and sporting disputes, there were arguments whenever we tried to reduce costs in the interests of the less well-funded teams.

After more than ten years of this, I started to ask myself if I really wanted to go on. I was spending all my time trying to solve other people's problems, and often getting roundly abused or even sued for doing so. Was this really the best way of spending my time now I was into my sixties? Much of the job was fascinating and I could at least exert considerable influence. But, in the end, Formula One was not my personal problem and exercising power for its own sake was never my thing. The aggravation was beginning to outweigh the appeal.

But sometimes I could at least get my own back on a journalist. My son Alexander had a maths doctorate and had won a prize from Linux for his work on open-source software for computers. As a result, he was able to help me by finding a way to make fun of a Formula One magazine that kept writing inaccurate and hostile articles about me. He set up a site that looked similar to the magazine's own website and arranged that anyone searching for the magazine, or the name of its editor, would be taken to our site and find my counterattack. Sometime later, Bernie (whom I suspected of being much closer to the magazine than he admitted) invited the editor and me to lunch to make peace. Bernie asked him why he had always been so hostile to me. He said it was because I had sent people to go through his dustbins. Bernie surprised him (and me) by saying, 'That wasn't Max, that was me!'

26

A BREAKAWAY?

By 2002 the costs of competing in Formula One had become prohibitively and perilously excessive. In the 1990s, a very serious accident, particularly one involving spectators, seemed the greatest threat to Formula One but, in the following decade, inordinate cost seemed to me increasingly the problem most likely to destroy the World Championship.

So much of the expenditure was profligate. For example, qualifying cars were a particularly crazy waste of money. Teams were preparing special cars just to qualify for their grid position, fitting special engines that delivered great power but lasted only about 50 km – just enough for one or two really fast laps and a good grid position. Those who could afford it also set their cars up with special bodywork and little or no cooling for engine and brakes. This gave much better aerodynamics but meant the car could do very few laps before overheating. Overnight before the race, the car would be completely rebuilt, with a fresh engine, proper bodywork and the normal cooling systems. It would then be able to run for 300 km in the race. I thought this absurdly expensive and quite unnecessary. Why not simply qualify the car you race?

At the FIA's invitation, the teams spent the autumn of 2002 discussing cost reduction in their own private meetings. There were plenty of possibilities quite apart from the qualifying cars, yet nothing was agreed. One of the team principals joked that they couldn't even agree which sandwiches to order, so in January 2003 I met the teams and announced the FIA was going to exercise its right to put the cars in *parc fermé* after qualifying. The cars would then be released in time for the race.

This meant a team could not change its car after qualifying and any team that hoped to finish the race would have to qualify with its car in race trim. Before doing this, I had made sure that some of them were in favour. However rational your arguments, it is never wise to take them all on at once. When I made my announcement, the atmosphere in the meeting was extraordinary. One of the team principals seemed to go into a sort of catatonic trance and I began to worry that he might have a seizure, but ultimately all was well and the meeting ended with acrimony but no casualties.

Because the power to put a car in *parc fermé* was already in the rules (where it had probably been since before the Second World War), we could just do it. We didn't need a rule change, so didn't need the agreement of the teams, but McLaren and Williams disputed our right to act. They announced that it was not, as we claimed, a procedural measure and we were effectively changing the rules. They held a press conference with an international TV link and announced they had started arbitration proceedings against the FIA under the Concorde Agreement to stop us.

They explained that by preventing the mechanics from working on the cars on Saturday night we were putting the drivers' lives at risk, and claimed we were misusing a very old rule that was there for a different purpose. It was a concerted effort to thwart our attempts to stop waste and save them money. At one point, Frank Williams (who always remained a friend even when he disagreed) called me and said: 'But Max, I've been changing my engine on Saturday night for the last forty years.' When I said this was straight from the 'we've always done it that way' school of management, he could see the funny side despite the conflict. In the end, after some sensible discussions on detail, a rule was agreed and the arbitration proceedings were quietly abandoned.

Interestingly, shortly after this rule – sorry, procedural measure – came in, we had the first Grand Prix for more than 40 years in which every car finished. So much for the safety argument – I always thought it was much better that team personnel should get a good night's sleep before the stresses of race day, pit stops and so on, rather than be fiddling with the cars most of Saturday night. Nowadays, I don't think you would find one person in the paddock who would want to go back to qualifying cars.

Still on costs, in May the following year I called a meeting of the Formula One engine manufacturers during the Monaco Grand Prix. Seven major car companies were now involved in supplying engines for the World Championship. Norbert Haug, in charge of the Mercedes racing programme, confirmed that, between them, the manufacturers were spending more than €1.5 billion (billion, not million!) annually, just for the engines. Everyone in the meeting agreed this was grossly excessive.

From a philosophical point of view, it was quite difficult to convince engineers from the big car companies to agree to restrictions. For example, the then CEO of Honda had explained to me one evening in Japan that they were intrinsically wrong and, apart from a limit on capacity, the only restrictive engine rule he would readily agree to was a ban on oval pistons. As a young engineer, he had successfully developed oval pistons for Honda's racing motorcycles and knew how fiendishly difficult the work had been. (Oval pistons allow more valves, thus better breathing and more power.)

Like most brilliant engineers, innovation was what motivated him. I entirely understood this, but I knew Formula One could not afford to give engineers free rein and a blank cheque. Even if the big car companies were prepared to spend lavishly in the good times, come the first downturn they would stop and Formula One would be left with a major problem.

Following the Monaco meeting, the seven manufacturers held a series of meetings among themselves and came up with a long list of proposed restrictions on engine architecture, dimensions and materials, with the objective of reducing the scope for innovation and research and hence costs. But Ford and Renault wanted to go further and produced a minority report suggesting even greater restrictions for even greater reductions in costs. That struck us as sensible, so we announced we would accept the minority report.

Two of the car companies threatened arbitration, saying any restrictions that had not been agreed by all seven were illegitimate. Unanimous agreement was needed for short-notice changes (the argument I myself had used against the FIA 25 years earlier). They asked for a meeting. I joined them in a hotel room in Fontvieille in Monaco, where one of them began by announcing they were going to court the following day to get an injunction to stop us. I stood up to go, asking why they had wasted my time when they intended to litigate. They said well, not literally the next day, but they would sue if we didn't back down.

We didn't really do backing down so I pointed out that it was more than just Formula One at stake for their employers. It was obviously not a core business for them but it was the FIA's premier championship and we didn't want it needlessly interfered with. The more restrictive rules would not penalise them in any way; they would merely reduce the temptation to waste money. They were the same for everyone. However, I continued, what went on in Brussels was a core business for them and our co-operation there was useful to the car industry. We effectively held the ring politically between them and the more extreme consumer organisations that lobbied in Brussels against cars and carmakers.

So, before starting arbitration proceedings and applying to a court for an injunction, would they please explain to their respective main boards that we were always as helpful as possible in Brussels provided, of course, our help was consistent with the interests of the millions of motorists who belonged to our various member organisations. However, our goodwill and co-operation could easily be withdrawn. They left the meeting somewhat put out, but in the end agreed to the enhanced restrictions. Eventually, things got back to normal and we were all friends again.

Disappointingly, not even the more draconian restrictions significantly reduced spending. All we really achieved was a decrease in the power gained per million dollars spent. Our next idea, after the usual discussions, was to freeze the engines – a complete ban on changing anything in the engine that moved or could only be reached by opening the engine. The engine builders could no longer spend money on developing the moving parts or cylinder heads etc.

But even this didn't really solve the problem. With no modification allowed to any internal part of the engine, the rich teams spent massive amounts on bringing air to it instead. They set out to develop the interior aerodynamics of the air boxes. The experts had assured us that any gains from this or from the exhaust system would be negligible. They were wrong. One should be very careful of experts. That so much power could be gained in an area no one had really bothered about until then was instructive but nevertheless annoying.

Finally, we hit on a measure that did save a great deal of money. This was to restrict the number of engines a team could use during the season. Where it had been quite usual to use two (and in some cases three) engines per car per weekend, now the engine could not be changed until it had done two (and eventually more) entire race weekends. Again, there was very strong opposition when this was first proposed and some of the engine builders told us this would increase costs, not reduce them. Their main argument was that, by forcing the teams to run each engine for longer, we would increase the time test and development engines had to spend on the dynamometer and hence their cost.

This was true but the extra cost was trivial compared with the saving made by reducing the number of engines used during the season. Our theory was that a rebuild costs pretty much the same whether you do it every 500 km or every 5000 km, and it turned out to be correct. In the end, the rule was eight engines per car per season. When the rule was first proposed, we were told the failure rate would increase; but we were confident the opposite would apply and it would actually decrease. Failure is most likely to occur towards the end of an engine's life and, as there would be fewer end-of-life moments per season, there would be fewer failures. Again, our theory was proved right; seen from the outside, nothing changed despite the massive reduction in engine costs.

One of the team principals who had fought almost all of our cost-reduction measures was kind enough to say later that, without them, his team would probably no longer be in business.

Another of our initiatives, the introduction of a standard engine and transmission at the end of 2008, never attracted enough support. What it did do, though, was provoke an emergency meeting of the new Formula One Teams' Association, FOTA, following which the car manufacturers supplying engines for Formula One agreed to cap the costs. These came down to €8 million for the 2009 season and €5 million for 2010. I thought even these figures unnecessarily high, but they were at least a major improvement and, incidentally, the biggest cost saving FOTA ever achieved.

I still think a standard engine was a good idea. Carmakers already shared components and technologies for road cars. So why not share the basic Formula One engine and demonstrate technical excellence with the ancillaries (energy recovery etc.), where there was so much potential for road-relevant research? Sacrilege to a traditionalist, perhaps, but we would essentially be treating the engine as a commodity and channelling all the R&D effort into the new energy-saving technologies. Costs could have been kept well under control and it might have led to interesting developments in future technologies for the ancillaries. But the basic idea of moving away from refining known technology, and putting engineering effort into revolutionary ideas for energy efficiency, never really appealed to the teams. Understandably, perhaps, they saw this as an unnecessary risk. They just wanted to go racing – if possible, with the best car.

Looking forward, we are likely to see continued refinement of known technologies combined with new techniques for energy efficiency. This means there will probably be no more independent commercial suppliers of Formula One engines, such as Cosworth. It will almost certainly not be economic for them to pay for the necessary R&D. I'm not sure this is a good thing in the longer term. It might risk giving great power over Formula One to two or three car companies, with the ever-present danger that one or more will suddenly decide to stop racing, perhaps for reasons that have nothing to do with motor racing itself. I always felt Formula One needed at least one independent engine supplier, so as not to have to rely entirely on the car industry. It remains to be seen if I was wrong.

Technically, the new engines that came in for 2014 are interesting, but with major manufacturers now involved in engine development, it would have been wise to have a cap on the cost of supplying a team with engines for a season. The car industry should not be allowed to pass on road-relevant research costs to the teams.

Talk of a breakaway by Formula One teams rose in volume throughout 2002 because they thought Bernie was not giving them enough money. If he gave them more they'd only waste it, was Bernie's rejoinder, but in essence both were right. Arguably, Bernie was not paying them a fair proportion, but their belief that a bigger slice of the Bernie money would make all their financial problems disappear was patent nonsense. Without financial discipline they would continue to waste money, as the battles over cost reduction had already shown.

As part of their preparations for a breakaway the teams had approached two of the big international sports management companies, asking for proposals and business plans. Interestingly, both said it was essential that there should be only one championship. If Bernie asked the FIA to sanction a rival championship and called it Formula One (which, arguably, was his right and our obligation), the rebellion, they said, would be fatally flawed. It would not be possible for a breakaway to command the fees and television time essential for its success if it were one of two competing championships.

Needless to say, this is exactly what Bernie had planned should the need have arisen. He would have held a championship for GP2 cars and asked us to sanction it as a world championship. GP2 was then a commercial racing series that Bernie controlled and was just below the level of Formula One (rather like the FIA's Formula Two back in the 1970s). It was perhaps three or four seconds a lap slower than Formula One and was the series from which most of the new drivers came. Quite apart from our contract with Bernie, our arrangements with the EU Commission meant we would not have been able to refuse. And he would almost certainly have had the right to call it Formula One. I believe it could have been a reasonably credible championship series.

The FIA was not directly involved but we were nevertheless watching with interest. Would 'Grand Prix World Championship' (GPWC), the teams' organisation, try to run entirely outside the system or would they ask us to regulate their championship as a rival to Bernie's? In 2002, GPWC engaged investment bankers Goldman Sachs and law firm Denton Wilde Sapte to prepare the plan. The result was a bulky, highly confidential document that, needless to say, quickly found its way to me. I was intrigued to see that it envisaged GPWC 'appointing' a regulator.

It seemed the three-year battle we fought with the EU Commission on precisely this point had not been noticed by GPWC or by their advisers. The fundamental element of our settlement with the commission was that there would not be multiple competing motor sport regulators (see below). So it was obvious to me and to the FIA lawyers that the whole plan would fail unless they first came to the FIA to authorise and regulate their series, something they did not seem to have planned. In the event, however, the teams did not stick together. As usual, Bernie split them by paying Ferrari over the odds, then picking off the rest.

The teams' advisers were doubtless influenced by the way in which independent operators had been able to set up in tennis and cricket without the relevant international governing body, or in boxing with four or five rival bodies. Unlike motor racing, those sports do not need massively expensive racing circuits that depend on licences from the governing body for their everyday business. They can hold an event almost anywhere. In motor sport, even rallies need the local government, police, insurance companies etc., none of whom feel comfortable without the blessing of the established sporting authority and its safety experts. There was an obvious lack of research into the basics, quite apart from the failure to note the FIA's deal with the European Commission.

Having been secretly shown the business plans from the two sports management groups, I was convinced the proposed GPWC series was doomed even if they asked the FIA to regulate it. Both plans assumed they would be able to charge race promoters and TV companies the same fees Bernie was getting. In the first year of their new series, the GPWC plan projected an income of €775 million, rising to €1473 million in year five. That was claptrap – it was never going to happen. Even if Bernie failed to set up a rival championship as the two sports promotion companies advising the teams had feared, the race promoters and television broadcasters would both have been in an impossibly strong bargaining position. They would have been able to dictate terms that were very much less favourable to the teams than Bernie's. On top of that, Bernie could almost certainly have stopped them calling it Formula One even if the FIA were sanctioning the series.

That the teams could not run entirely outside the FIA structures became clear during the FOCA–FISA war more than 20 years earlier. Then, Balestre's killer weapon was the FIA's ability to prevent a circuit running one of FOCA's non-FIA races by stopping all FIA licence-holders using the circuit. That would have been decisive had we as FOCA not been able to counter it in the courts by suing the FIA for interference with contractual relations. But now, relationships had fundamentally changed. The teams had no contracts in place – Bernie had the contracts with the circuits and we had a contract with Bernie. Most importantly, we had come to an agreement with the EU Commission that would stop any legal threat based on competition law.

On the other hand, although we could stop them running outside the FIA structures, we had to be prepared to sanction any international championship that satisfied the FIA's criteria for safety and sporting fairness, even a direct rival to Formula One. The breakaway teams could have written their own detailed sporting and technical rules just as, say, Formula Renault could. But the International Sporting Code would have applied over and above these rules, just as it does in Formula One. So, too, would the FIA criteria for safety and fairness and its system of stewards and International Court of Appeal.

I pointed all this out at a dinner Flavio Briatore arranged with Patrick Faure, then a very senior Renault executive. When I explained that no circuit could afford to lose all its other events, Patrick's response was, 'Then we will buy the circuits', which didn't strike me as very realistic. Imagine going to the board of an international automotive conglomerate and asking them to buy a number of racing circuits with very high overheads so that their Formula One team could race on each circuit once a year with no other competition activity. Worse than that, one of the directors might ask what the quarrel with the FIA was all about. One can picture the board's reaction when told their team was fighting the governing body because it was trying to reduce the cost of Formula One so the teams could race on smaller budgets.

The reality was that the teams, although now better financed, were far weaker than Bernie and I had been in 1980 during the FOCA–FISA war – and the FIA was now far stronger. I could remember vividly how difficult that had been from the other side. I never found out whether, more than 20 years on, the teams intended to run their breakaway under the FIA system or entirely outside it. I don't think they had thought it through properly and doubt they knew themselves. There's a tendency for outsiders and even some team principals to ignore the vitally important structural subtleties of the sport.

Then Professor Burkhard Göschel, a BMW main board member and its head of research, became the chairman of GPWC. We had met briefly on other occasions and he came to Nice airport on 7 August 2006 together with a senior BMW lawyer, Jürgen Reul, for a serious discussion about Formula One and relations between the FIA and the car manufacturers. This was a revelation. Instead of the usual tiresome debate, I found myself talking to someone who was brilliantly clever and focused on what really mattered.

We quickly agreed that before discussing rules it was necessary to decide what the objectives were – what we were trying to achieve. It was hardly ever possible to get the teams to adopt this approach because each was always either seeking an advantage for itself or busily resisting change of any kind. I quickly found common ground with Professor Göschel about the sort of technology that should be developed in Formula One. He was committed to the search for energy efficiency and way ahead of the teams he led. As already mentioned, for some time I had wanted to move the sport's huge R&D expenditure away from endlessly and pointlessly refining known technologies (gearboxes, for example) to a search for energy efficiency, in particular limiting power by restricting fuel instead of a wholly irrelevant limit on engine capacity.

To my delight, Professor Göschel agreed. What's more, he knew far more about the relevant technologies than I did. He talked about wasted energy and how, broadly speaking, only about a third of the fuel bought at the pump actually propels the car; the other two-thirds is wasted as heat lost from the radiator and energy out of the exhaust. He was as fascinated as I was at the prospect of recovering and using some of this energy, and the possibility of using Formula One to stimulate the research. Moreover, he was fully informed about the latest work in these areas. It was a great moment. After years of trying fruitlessly to convince the teams, here was someone in charge of their group who was an established world expert in exactly the area that I believed we needed. I was convinced that with his knowledge and backing, we might really achieve something.

Having agreed the objectives for the new rules, it was just a case of finding the most efficient way of achieving them. Professor Göschel, too, saw the meeting as a success. A few months later he told *Autosport*:

After this meeting, Jürgen Reul and I thought we had made a big shift. We were so excited we went to the beach in Nice in our suits and ties and with our briefcases in hand, it was very warm and everyone was sitting in their bathing suits, so on the beach we both had a glass of red wine.

For my part, I gave Flavio Briatore a call after the meeting and told him I thought we had a breakthrough. Tellingly, he did not seem as pleased as I thought he would be.

When we started looking seriously at where Formula One should be going, it seemed obvious that energy efficiency should be the performance differentiator. Simply running the engine faster to get more power was obsolete, likewise aerodynamic research that had no relevance to the real world. Peter Wright, by now one of the FIA's top technical advisers, and former Jaguar team principal Tony Purnell turned these thoughts into a very interesting proposal to allow Formula One cars to achieve the same performance with only 50 per cent of the fuel consumption, all this by means of fully road-relevant technology including movable aerodynamic devices. It would have sent a positive message about Formula One that many sponsors would have found attractive. Most of them nowadays are very environmentally conscious and, with intelligent rules for engine supply and use, we could have achieved this at the same time as reducing costs.

A combination of the teams' conservative approach to radical technologies and Bernie's belief that very loud noise is an essential element of Formula One made it a struggle to bring in a high-efficiency engine. Such engines are inherently quieter because a greater proportion of the fuel is used to propel the car rather than produce ear-splitting noise. I always disagreed with Bernie about the noise. I thought for the less than 0.1 per cent of the audience who watched a race live, the attraction was the extraordinary and almost violent speed of the cars, while for the 99.9 per cent who watched on television the noise was almost entirely irrelevant.

Nearly ten years later, new engine rules introduced in 2014 incorporated many of the elements we wanted, although the variable aero is missing and there was an unfortunate compromise that resulted in a six-cylinder engine rather than the more modern and efficient four originally proposed. Also, vitally important restrictions on costs were missing. Nevertheless, it will be interesting to see how things develop and it's pleasing to see Formula One finally more in tune with major research areas for road cars. With any luck, this will make the car manufacturers slower to pull out when the next economic downturn comes. It will also encourage more of the sponsors to stay in Formula One. Almost all these big companies are concerned about corporate social responsibility and find it much easier to support a Formula One that makes a real contribution to research into energy efficiency. Making a very loud noise with inefficient and obsolescent engines is not a priority for modern society.

Also in 2006, we persuaded the teams to accept (albeit very reluctantly) an energy recovery and reuse system (KERS) similar to the hybrid systems increasingly seen in modern road cars. KERS was revolutionary in Formula One terms, but was plainly relevant to all wheeled vehicles. Recovering energy currently lost as heat when a vehicle brakes and reusing it to propel the car is necessary whether the car is driven by fossil fuel, hydrogen, electricity or any other means. We hoped that bringing the technology into Formula One would accelerate its development, and that has indeed happened.

But even KERS could only save part of the one-third of the fuel that propelled the car. The other two-thirds mentioned as wasted by Professor Göschel was still to be looked at. Before we could start trying to convince the teams with the professor's help, they fell out among themselves as usual. The breakaway eventually faded but so did the search for energy efficiency, at least temporarily, when Professor Göschel moved on. Work in this area continued within the FIA and thanks to pressure from my successor, Jean Todt, Formula One finally acquired more efficient engines in 2014 and now uses up to 40 per cent less fuel while achieving the same speeds.

KERS was dropped in 2010, but under pressure from sponsors, who understand more about image than most of the teams do, it was brought back a year later. KERS is now firmly established in Formula One and increasingly on the roads. The arguments I had with two major car company CEOs ten years ago, when I was trying to convince them it was certain to be used in road cars, now seem part of ancient history. It seems extraordinary today that, back then, most major European manufacturers thought KERS pointless. The CEO of one very big company told me it was no good on a motorway! Toyota was way ahead of them.

Formula One KERS systems are like those on hybrid road cars. They depend on converting some of the energy that is otherwise lost when a car brakes into electrical energy stored in a chemical battery, to be used when the car needs to accelerate again. In this way, with a road car, some of the petrol a motorist pays for is effectively used more than once. The problem is that the rate at which energy can be fed into a chemical battery is very limited. Unless the braking is very light, most of the energy is still lost as heat. For really high amounts of energy in and out you need a flywheel or perhaps a super-capacitor.

A major regret in all this was my failure to bring flywheel technology into Formula One. Flywheels can store large amounts of energy for a short time by spinning very fast and had been in development by parts of the car industry for some time. The safety problems had been overcome and, because of their ability to absorb and release large amounts of energy very quickly, flywheels were ideal for Formula One. I believe they will have a big role in future road vehicles, where the ability to store a lot of energy quickly is necessary if it is not to be lost.

Had we been able to introduce flywheels or other high-energy-in/high-energy-out systems to Formula One, there would have been a huge boost to the development of the relevant technology. A flywheel for a car needs to be small, light and fail-safe, even when running at extreme speeds. Making mechanical devices small and light is what Formula One is really good at, and the fail-safe technology already existed. But in order to fit a flywheel in a Formula One car without giving a non-flywheel car an aerodynamic advantage, we needed to increase some of the minimum chassis dimensions slightly and there was no way to get the teams to agree to that. Interestingly, car companies involved in long-distance racing are less conservative than the Formula One teams, and flywheels are now appearing at Le Mans and other endurance races.

Uniquely among the Formula One teams, Williams saw the potential and began a significant flywheel R&D programme in parallel with their Formula One commitment. They also achieved a tie-up with a major manufacturer. The Williams flywheel technology (since sold to GKN) has now been successfully deployed in long-distance racing, and is likely to be seen increasingly on road cars and heavy vehicles in cities, including buses. Eventually, apart from minor losses in the system, all the energy currently lost in heat when a vehicle brakes will be recovered and reused, even when it brakes hard. To its shame, Formula One will not have played the key role it should have in making that happen quickly.

27

RESIGNATION

By 2004 I was beginning to tire of spending all my time trying to solve other people's problems. None of the things I was trying to put right in the sport affected me personally. I had taken on the job so I had to do it, but I had been working under considerable pressure for 13 years, much of the time in the teeth of fierce opposition, sometimes even litigation, from the very people I was trying to help. The utterly irrational opposition to the elimination of qualifying cars in Formula One discussed earlier is a prime example. Moreover, as far as I was concerned, the constant attempts to cheat, or at least game the rules as set out, were wasting a lot of time to no useful purpose. Leading the FIA had been fascinating and a great privilege but the time had come to quit.

A particularly irritating meeting of the F1 Commission at the end of May 2004 had convinced me that my decision to resign was the right one. Unusually, there was an FIA General Assembly on 1 June, which was the right occasion to make the announcement. Having first told the senior members of the FIA staff and some of my closest associates, I duly announced my resignation to the FIA membership in the assembly. For the previous 13 years, Formula One had been the key that opened so many political doors. It had enabled really significant changes to road safety but the necessary structures were now in place.

Formula One for its own sake had no appeal any more and I went to very few Grands Prix. There is always a certain satisfaction in making something that dysfunctional work (if you can), but after a while I began to wonder if there were not more interesting ways to spend my time. It seemed to be always the same old arguments with the same old people. In some other role I could perhaps try to help people who actually wanted to be helped. And I felt the rest of motor sport, not just Formula One, probably also needed someone fresh.

I had been lucky enough to be in a position to work unpaid because of family resources and money I had previously earned. I have never been entirely comfortable with the concept of inherited wealth. It seems somehow wrong (though no more so, I suppose, than winning the lottery) but without it, or the prospect of it, I would not have been able to do any of the things that I now see as significant in my life. For various reasons, almost all the family money came to me, which I could justify if I did something useful with my time and passed at least as much on to the next generation as I had been fortunate to receive myself. But it seemed utterly pointless to continue as president of the FIA if I was no longer enjoying it. Eleven years was enough; I no longer had the patience and I was determined to quit.

I confirmed my resignation to the media during a press conference at the French Grand Prix a day or two later. Inevitably, some commentators suggested the resignation was some kind of elaborate ploy. It wasn't, and there was immediate pressure from the FIA Senate to rescind it because there was no obvious successor. They said I should at least continue until the end of my current mandate, in the autumn of 2005. The only dissenter was Bob Darbelnet, the head of the American AAA, the biggest of the FIA clubs with nearly 50 million members. He had his heart set on the presidency for himself and came to my office immediately after my announcement to ask if I thought he could succeed me. I couldn't bring myself to say anything negative, even though it was not clear to me how he could deal with the sport. Who could he get to do that part of the job? He knew nothing about motor sport and it seemed unlikely that anyone capable of running the sport would be prepared to work under him.

In the end, I had to agree that there was currently no obvious successor and would therefore see out the remaining year of my term so one could be found. I approached Jean Todt about putting his name forward with my support in 2005. His extraordinary record in both racing and rallying spoke for itself, and I was confident that he would be as enthusiastic as I was for road safety and the interests of the ordinary motorist. He had, after all, founded the Institut du Cerveau et de la Moelle Épinière (Institute of the Brain and Spinal Cord), a major research centre in Paris of which I became a founder member at his invitation. As it specialised in brain and spinal injuries, the institute's research was very relevant to the FIA's safety work. Jean and his friends raised the money and Professor Gérard Saillant, who succeeded Professor Watkins as head of the FIA's medical team, was in charge.

I also spoke to Sebastià Salvadó, the president of Catalunya's RACC, one of the most successful of our member clubs and the promoter of the Spanish Grand Prix. He is outstandingly able and would have been ideal, but a combination of being several years older than me and the magnitude of his job running the RACC led him to decline.

Just as I was beginning to worry, Jean Todt accepted my proposal and all seemed set – I would finally be able to stand down in October 2005. But then Jean was offered the job of running not just Ferrari's Formula One team but the entire company, including the road cars and Maserati. Quite understandably, he wanted to accept and postpone our deal, yet maintained that he would probably be ready to stand at the end of the next presidential term in 2009. We decided this would be the plan and I would carry on for four more years.

Looking back this was a major mistake on my part. I should have said to Jean that I was going to stop come what may. If he were willing to refuse the Ferrari offer and stand for election for the presidency of the FIA in October 2005, I would support him fully. But, if not, I would retire anyway and it would be up to the members of the FIA to choose a successor without any suggestion from me.

Except for our successes with road safety, my last four years were to prove every bit as difficult and frustrating as any of the previous 14. The only real motor sport achievement in that time was the introduction of energy recovery and the concept of energy efficiency as a performance differentiator in Formula One. Apart from that, I spent my time trying to solve other people's problems in the usual, exasperating way. If Jean's time as president turns out to be a success, I suppose I would have to say it was worth hanging on, but from my own point of view it was four years too many.

The next major problem – exactly the sort of thing that made me feel it was time to quit – came at the 2005 United States

Grand Prix. Arguments about costs, plus ongoing plans by the Formula One teams to form a breakaway championship, meant there was real tension. This came to a head at the race. Seven teams were on Michelin tyres, three on Bridgestone. Michelin had experienced no difficulty the previous year but their tyres proved to be unsafe on Turn 13, a very long fast corner, and the only one from the Indianapolis oval to form part of the Formula One circuit. Surprisingly, Michelin were unable to solve the problem. They had no safe back-up tyre at the race and apparently none in stock. The seven Michelin teams, backed by Bernie in alliance with Flavio Briatore (then team principal at Renault), demanded a chicane before the corner. They said this would slow the cars and eliminate their problem.

At home in Monaco, I refused. This was partly for sporting fairness: Bridgestone might well have packed a different tyre had they known a chicane would be used. They had brought a tyre that was able to withstand the stresses of Turn 13 and this might well have involved compromising its performance elsewhere on the circuit. Michelin had apparently not made any such compromise and might have had an unfair advantage if the circuit were altered to suit their tyres.

But the decisive reason was that changing the circuit without following our own safety procedures would leave the FIA exposed if there were an accident. Imagine trying to explain to an American judge hearing a case involving injuries to spectators that you had changed the circuit without following any of your own standard safety procedures and checks. Doing so because some competitors had brought the wrong tyres would certainly not impress the court, indeed quite the reverse – it would give the impression that those running Formula One were either incompetent or irresponsible.

We made various proposals to solve the problem, any of which would have allowed all the teams to race without us having to break our own rules. These included repeated tyre changes (the Michelin tyres were safe for a limited number of laps), running through the pits each lap (with the usual speed limit) instead of Turn 13, running at the bottom (the flat part) of Turn 13, or observing a speed limit in Turn 13 (with drive-through penalties for breaches). The seven teams – McLaren, Renault, Williams, Toyota, BAR, Red Bull and Sauber – rejected every one of our solutions. The measures we proposed would all have placed the Michelin teams at a disadvantage, but this was to be expected as they had brought the wrong equipment and could not run at full speed on all parts of the circuit for more than a few laps at a time. But running at a disadvantage was certainly better than not running at all. Their sponsors were paying them to race and that is what they should have done.

They also had a duty to the spectators, both live and watching on television. Looking back, I think Bernie and Flavio knew all this perfectly well but never believed for one moment that we would allow the race to go ahead with only six cars. They were convinced that, faced with seven teams who were prepared to stick together, we would have no alternative but to back down.

Perhaps if I had been there I could have made them understand why that was never going to happen. I spoke on the phone to all the main players including Bernie, Tony George (head of the Indianapolis Motor Speedway), Flavio and even, I think, Ron Dennis, but perhaps it would have been more effective had I been there in person. Then they might have accepted one of our compromise solutions for the 'Michelin Seven' rather than not run at all. Any of the solutions we offered would have added to the entertainment, even if they potentially left the Bridgestone cars in the first six places.

In reality, though, this was never truly about an unsafe tyre. The seven Michelin teams, led by Bernie and Flavio, probably saw it as a golden opportunity to strengthen their position. The teams were, after all, in one of their breakaway modes and Bernie may have seen it as an opportunity to appear to be in charge and on their side. With the threat of a breakaway, he and CVC, the private equity firm that owned his business, probably thought they needed to improve their relations with the teams. One way to achieve this was to present the FIA as the common enemy.

On Sunday morning it seemed the organisers would put in a chicane with or without the FIA's consent. Tyre bundles were being moved to form a chicane, allegedly on Bernie's instructions. Charlie Whiting, as the FIA race director, intervened and put a stop to it. Charlie and I agreed that if the organisers installed a chicane despite his ruling, all FIA personnel would leave the circuit immediately and we would declare it a non-championship race authorised by the local sanctioning body and not by the FIA. At least that way we would be covered if there were an accident. Also, the sporting unfairness would not matter if it were a non-championship race because no team would be obliged to compete and the World Championship would not be affected.

The international television coverage kept showing huddles of team principals and others in different parts of the paddock. They were supposedly having important meetings and there was much coming and going, possibly predominantly for the benefit of the cameras. But, in the end, all they could do was refuse to race or compete in a locally organised non-championship event. I decided the only course for the FIA was to ignore the threats and simply follow the start procedure on schedule. The teams could then do as they pleased.

It was almost the FOCA–FISA war all over again – it's very difficult to take on the governing body in big-time international sport. The competitors and commercial people may have the ear of the media but when it comes to a championship, a sport's governing body has the power and makes the decisions. As I had learned in the early 1980s, the FIA is where the real power lies in Formula One. But it should only ever be deployed in extreme situations and when absolutely necessary.

In the event, the cars all went out for the warm-up lap, then the 14 cars from the seven Michelin teams peeled into the pits instead of going to the grid. I learned later that they had told their drivers this would make the FIA buckle and, after a slight delay, agree to the chicane. I was watching all this on television and was quite surprised when the cars went out on the warm-up lap. I hadn't known they'd decided to do this.

We followed our plan, turned out the red lights on schedule and the race started with only six cars. Fortunately, all finished. As happens in America, lawyers acting for spectators started a class action, suing us and everyone else, including Michelin and the teams. We won. They appealed. We won again. But Michelin, quite rightly, did later make a generous gesture to the spectators, refunding their tickets and giving them free ones for the next year's race.

We summoned the seven dissident teams to the World Council, where David Pannick QC defended them very ably. We found them guilty but later exonerated them when new evidence became available which meant that, technically, they had committed no offence under our rules despite their abortive rebellion.

Paradoxically, the wider American public became aware of Formula One for the first time as a direct result of this incident, illustrating the old adage: there's no such thing as bad publicity. Formula One had never previously made all the American news bulletins, even in the case of serious accidents, because, except for Mario Andretti, the drivers were never national figures there and, fortunately, Mario never had a big accident in Formula One. There were the usual silly comments from some of Formula One's self-appointed experts. One particularly stupid pundit pronounced it the end of Formula One in the United States. Needless to say, we were back at Indianapolis the following year, but this time with the right tyres.

A few weeks later, Édouard Michelin, great-grandson of the founder of the company, made a press statement in which he was very critical of the FIA over the Indianapolis incident. I had high regard for him because he was passionate about advanced automotive technology and had explained some fascinating ideas to me at a recent Geneva motor show. But his criticisms were annoying because what had happened at Indianapolis was entirely caused by his company bringing the wrong tyres. It was not our fault.

Having made such a monumental mistake, Michelin had expected us to break our own rules and change the circuit to solve the problem they themselves had created. He also criticised the FIA's move towards a single tyre supplier for Formula One, apparently not realising this was a teams' initiative, not ours. I put out a rather aggressive press release saying he showed 'an almost comical lack of knowledge of modern Formula One', which apparently caused great offence. A few months later I came to regret my tone when he died in a boating accident in Brittany.

Another difficulty came early in 2009, when I heard claims that

Nelson Piquet Jr had been instructed to crash his car during the 2008 Singapore Grand Prix in order to bring out the safety car. It seemed an extraordinary stroke of luck that it had to come out just after Piquet's team-mate, Fernando Alonso, had refuelled because it gave him a big advantage. It forced the field to bunch up, allowing Alonso to move up place after place as other cars had to refuel while he was able to keep running. It looked fishy straightaway and aroused immediate suspicion. Renault had refuelled Alonso's car unusually early in the race and, apparently by luck, done so at the ideal moment, just before the safety car handily came out and gave him the edge to go on and win. But there was absolutely no concrete evidence of anything untoward.

Now, suddenly, we had some sort of confirmation that all the suspicions might be well founded. But could it be proved? It was an extremely serious matter because, although unlikely, someone could have been killed: a track worker or the driver of another car or a spectator, even several spectators, if part of the car had gone into the crowd. If we held an inquiry, though, it was obvious that everyone in the team would simply deny it. Without real evidence, we would get nowhere. Very reluctantly, I decided we could do nothing for the moment. But we could wait and, sure enough, as we shall see, a few months later there was a breakthrough.

The same year a major technical dispute erupted when Brawn, Toyota and Williams appeared with a radical new design for the rear underside of the car known as the diffuser. This is a device to create significant downforce from the airflow and exhaust gasses at the back of the car. They had read the new bodywork regulations as permitting them to create a second channel in the diffuser, thereby increasing the downforce it generated and improving the car's performance.

Ferrari were among the teams that had not spotted this possibility. They began an intensive campaign to have the so-called double diffuser banned. They started lobbying the FIA and ran a campaign in the media accusing the others of cheating. They ignored the fact that, as explained in chapter 24, any team was entitled to turn up with a new device at a race, whatever the FIA technical department's opinion might be (though in this particular case our technical department thought the device legal). A team that disagreed could then protest to the stewards and invoke the normal procedures. It was nonsense to suggest that we could somehow ban it, as they must have known.

At the first race of the season, the Australian Grand Prix in Melbourne, Ferrari lodged an official protest. Very conveniently, their usual English QC just happened to be on holiday in Melbourne at the time and was able to present their case. They lost in Melbourne, lost at the next event in Malaysia and then lost on appeal in Paris. Ferrari were furious and their fury was directed at me because they had expected me to intervene in some way. I had refused to do so and, anyway, I couldn't even if I had wanted to. The rules didn't allow it. Ironically, what Ferrari chairman Luca di Montezemolo wanted me to do then would not only have been illegitimate, but precisely the sort of dictatorial behaviour of which he was later to accuse me. The technical rules were published and it was for the stewards and the International Court of Appeal to interpret them. The FIA president was not and could not be involved.

Instead of admitting that their designers had missed an opportunity, they had to find someone to blame, so they turned on the FIA and me. Needless to say, the (mainly British) fans who had always accused us of favouring Ferrari didn't notice any of this. But it was undoubtedly a factor in Luca's hostility towards me during the summer of 2009 – slightly disappointing, even small-minded perhaps, but no big deal to me.

So much for my determination to stay out of Formula One back in 1991, but all the trouble was part of the job. If you take it on you have to accept the consequences. Like racing back in the 1960s, I didn't have to do it. Only this time it was my wife, Jean, who was pointing out that it was all entirely voluntary. I did not really need reminding that if had stuck to my decision to retire in 2005, I could have avoided a whole range of problems that made my last mandate so troublesome.

28

MONEY AND THE
FORMULA ONE TEAMS

In January 2008, I invited the teams to Paris and pointed out that with six major car companies still involved (Ford had already pulled out) Formula One was particularly vulnerable to any change in their fortunes. This was at a time when the industry was riding high off the back of record sales and profits in 2007. The collapse of Lehman Brothers and the world financial crisis lay in the future. But I pointed out that the level of costs was unsustainable even for those companies and that with other pressures, such as new EU emissions limits, their resources would be pulled away from Formula One. I added that a third factor was the increasing likelihood of a worldwide recession that was probably coming and would have an effect on the motor industry. If we didn't reduce costs, we risked losing teams, particularly the car manufacturers'.

The teams were all there, even Bernie came, and, for once, no one disagreed. I explained that the experience of the previous five years had shown conclusively that it was impossible to control costs by technical regulation alone. Again, no one disagreed. I added that, having repeatedly tried and failed to reduce spending by technical regulation, we had to stop making the same mistake over and over again. A radical solution was required to bring costs properly under control.

I suggested that the only fair and effective way was to impose a cost cap – to limit the amount each team could spend. Apart from the obvious money-saving benefit, it would spur greater sporting fairness because a team spending more than its rivals had an unsporting advantage. It was no different to being allowed to run with a bigger engine. With a cost cap, the rich teams would no longer be able to spend more on R&D and exotic materials than the smaller teams, with all the competitive advantages this was according them. The top teams would still attract massive sponsorship, but most of this would now be profit for their shareholders.

Another major benefit of a cost cap would be that the cleverest engineers would have a chance of winning, not just the best-funded ones. I always bore in mind Keith Duckworth's dictum that an engineer was someone who could do for a pound what any idiot could do for £100. Moreover, the big car companies would never let their engineers design a new road car without a budget. In the real world, everything has to be done to a price and still be competitive. After some discussion, everyone except Ferrari's Jean Todt seemed to like the idea.

The first obvious issue we faced was whether we would be able to enforce a spending cap if one were agreed. I said we certainly would because, for a tiny fraction of the money that was currently being wasted, we could hire two former tax inspectors for each team to do nothing but watch every move they made. It shouldn't be too difficult to come up with a more sophisticated monitoring system than that. We agreed to set up a working group of the teams' financial officers under Tony Purnell. Tony had all the relevant expertise, having built up and sold a very successful electronics business and then run a Formula One team, Jaguar. At his suggestion, two partners from Deloitte, Patrick Maher (Forensic and Dispute Services) and David Noon (Internal Audit and Risk Management) joined the teams' representatives. After several meetings, the group produced a complete and robust scheme in May 2008 and the independent expert accountants from Deloitte confirmed it would work. Still Ferrari dissented, but they were in a minority of one and I was confident they would not be able to stop the plan.

While this was going on, I had a meeting with ACEA (the European Automobile Manufacturers' Association) at the Geneva motor show and explained the cap to them. It's one of the few occasions when you can find all the CEOs of the major car companies together in one room, and those with no involvement in Formula One listened patiently. Someone immediately said enforcement would be impossible because R&D expenditure would be so easy to conceal. I replied this was a question for experts, for forensic accountants. They would decide whether we could enforce a cost-cap rule. It was futile to discuss that in this meeting. We needed to address the principle not the particular: if it could be done, should we do it?

Carlos Ghosn, the CEO of Renault and Nissan, immediately saw the point and agreed. Interestingly, he also sided with me at a lunch some time later, arranged by Bernie and Flavio, where they had hoped he would tell me my cost-cutting plans were misconceived. They were surprised to discover he opposed their objections and supported us. He is one of those rare people who get straight to the central point, to the things that matter, without wasting time on irrelevancies. No wonder he has been so successful.

I also quietly had my sights on what I saw as a fundamental unfairness in the finances of Formula One. Bernie had a long-established technique for dealing with the teams. First he would sign up Ferrari by giving them the most money; then he'd sign one or two of the top teams; then divide what was left among the remainder. The rich got richer, and thus more competitive (unless very badly run), while the poor faded. He believed (rightly as it has turned out, at least until 2014) there would always be another billionaire if one of the poorer teams disappeared. I thought that, although the most sponsorship would naturally go to the most successful team, the money Bernie controlled should be divided equally. Bernie did not agree – he derided this idea as 'communism'.

A financial memorandum of understanding signed by Bernie and the teams in 2006 formed part of a new draft Concorde Agreement prepared by Bernie's lawyers. It was a schedule of great complexity and about 20 times as long as the equivalent in the previous (1998) agreement. Bernie wouldn't give the FIA a copy, saying it was none of our business – we should just sign it without seeing it. But I couldn't possibly sign the agreement without seeing the financial schedule officially and getting the OK from our lawyers. I was also planning to try to secure a more equitable distribution of money, which led to the biggest row Bernie and I ever had in the World Council.

The extract below from the minutes of the meeting of 25 June 2008 cannot convey Bernie's anger. During the exchanges, he more than once folded his papers and made to leave but each time thought better of it, all this in front of the entire World Council, the commission presidents and FIA staff – upwards of

50 people all told. We usually avoided public disagreement by discussing things beforehand, and almost always one of us would see the other's point. Sometimes it was me, sometimes it was Bernie, who is usually rational contrary to the impression he sometimes gives. I try to be, too.

But in this instance I had broken off contact after he sided with those who were trying to get rid of me following the *News of the World* story. I wouldn't take his phone calls and there was no discussion before the meeting. I think Bernie genuinely believed that his arrangements with the teams were none of the FIA's business, no matter what their impact on the fairness of the sport might be. He thought that the deal with the European Commission meant we should leave commercial matters entirely to him, whereas I was quite clear that, although we must not participate commercially, we still had to make sure all the arrangements, including the money, were fair.

Above all, he did not seem to want to understand that if we were to sign an agreement, it was essential that we should see and agree with all of it. The question of whether or not we could interfere with his arrangements with the teams (which, of course, were part of the agreement) was an entirely separate point.

This is an extract from the World Motor Sport Council minutes of 25 June 2008:

Concorde Agreement

The President said that, despite the comments in the press, the facts were as follows: in February 2007, Formula One Management [FOM] had sent a proposal to the FIA for part of the Concorde Agreement, namely the section that dealt with regulations and how these were agreed. In May 2007, the FIA had, after discussions with its lawyers, sent a counter proposal to FOM. Since then there had been no progress until a few weeks ago, when Mr Ecclestone had proposed to sign a red line version [a draft showing all the proposed amendments in red] of the 1998 Concorde Agreement.

The President had agreed and asked Mr Ecclestone to send a red line version. He had not done so yet.

The President said that the red line version should include Schedule 10 which covered the financial arrangements and which had always been part of the Concorde Agreement and therefore had to be agreed by the FIA if it was to sign the Concorde Agreement. He understood that there had been lengthy negotiations between FOM and the teams about the content of Schedule 10 and although he had had sight of a proposed Schedule 10, he had not been sent it officially for the FIA's approval. He added that if a new Concorde Agreement could not be achieved, the FIA's current commercial agreement with FOM would simply continue. He concluded that this was not a criticism of FOM in any way but the delay was not due to the FIA. He undertook to look at the red line agreement including all the Schedules as soon as the FIA received it in order to progress matters.

Mr Ecclestone said that the President had stated that he would not sign a new Concorde Agreement and that he simply wanted the current commercial agreement to continue. All the current competitors had signed the new proposed Schedule 10. He felt that the current Concorde Agreement met all of the FIA's objectives as well as those of all the teams.

The President said that it was inaccurate to say that he had stated that he would not sign a new Concorde Agreement, as it was not his decision but that of the FIA as a whole. He had set out his position in a letter of 16 May to all the FIA clubs in which he had stated that the FIA would only sign the Concorde Agreement if it was in the interests of the FIA. This had always been his position and until he had seen the whole of the proposed revised Concorde Agreement, including the commercial arrangements in Schedule 10, he could not make a proposal. He said that there would probably be no difficulty in obtaining the FIA's agreement to the new Schedule 10 but he had noted some radical changes between the document he had seen unofficially and the Schedule 10 that was agreed in 1998. For that reason the FIA needed to be sent this document officially so that it could give its opinion. It also needed to be sure that it was fulfilling its commitments to the European Commission.

Mr Ecclestone said that all the signatories to the new Schedule 10 were happy with it and that the FIA did not have a say in the commercial arrangements.

The President said that Mr Ecclestone was wrong to say that the FIA had no say in the commercial arrangements. The FIA's arrangement with the European Commission was clear: the FIA was, as the regulatory authority, not allowed to play an active role in commercial matters. It was, however, allowed to ensure the financial arrangements between FOM and the teams were fair or practical or otherwise if these arrangements were to be incorporated in an agreement to which the FIA was a party.

Mr Ecclestone said that if all the signatories were happy, there was no reason for the FIA to be concerned.

The President said that his information was that not all of the signatories were indeed happy with the agreement.

Mr Ecclestone said that they had all signed the agreement.

The President said that the FIA had been given different information. The FIA needed to have sight of the final document signed by all the teams; it was not enough just to be told that it had been signed.

After some discussion, **Mr Ecclestone** undertook to send the FIA the red line version including the signed Schedule 10.

<u>Governance of Formula One</u>

The President proposed that the FIA also discuss with the teams the governance of Formula One. Currently there were elements which in his opinion could be enhanced. For example he felt that even if the World Council has been able to timely deal [sic] with issues that took place during race weekends or such as the McLaren/Ferrari case in 2007, possibly a separate judicial body* may represent a more effective solution. There would, of course, be a right of appeal from such body to the International Court of Appeal.

This was agreed.

---

* Just such a judicial body to replace the WMSC as a tribunal was introduced by Jean Todt shortly after he took over.

To me, it seemed obvious that the FIA had the right to look at the commercial terms of an agreement to which it was a party, even if it had no right to participate in any profit that might be made under it because of the deal with the European Commission. Our duty to supervise the sport plainly required that there should be nothing grossly unfair which could distort the championship. Suppose, for example, Bernie decided to give all the money to one team? Surely we could and should object to that? We never received the promised red-line version.

Bernie sought to reinforce his position by holding a meeting of the teams to discuss costs in the absence of the FIA. He called Luca di Montezemolo, the Ferrari chairman, and suggested all the teams should meet in Maranello. Bernie took Donald Mackenzie from CVC with him, as well as some of the UK-based team principals, and they all travelled together in one of Bernie's jets. The meeting did not go entirely according to plan: after a short discussion, Luca explained that no other sport lets the promoter take half the total income. He then turned to Bernie and Donald, thanked them for coming and said the teams now wanted to continue their discussions on their own. Bernie was so surprised by this that he phoned me as they were leaving (we were now back in contact) and said he and Donald had just been thrown out of the meeting. It certainly shocked him – such a thing had previously been unthinkable – and it meant he could no longer rely on the teams as a power base. What with them saying he was taking too much money out of Formula One and the FIA asking to look at the proposed financial schedule to the Concorde Agreement (which the teams had apparently accepted), Bernie must have felt a bit beleaguered.

But for me, everything for the previous three months had been coloured by the *News of the World* story, much more detail of ·

which comes later. In the immediate aftermath of the publication, a number of people behaved very badly. Some were insidiously disloyal; others brazenly exploited an opportunity to get rid of someone they disliked. But three of the most significant team bosses, Jean Todt, Frank Williams and Dietrich Mateschitz, the owner of Red Bull, were supportive. After Jean had shown such loyalty over my personal difficulties, forcing a cost cap through with or without Ferrari did not feel right and the story essentially put a stop to my 2008 cost-reduction plans.

As predicted, the economic crisis developed during the 2008 season, culminating in a full-blown financial panic when Lehman Brothers collapsed in September. Faced with falling car sales, Honda announced their withdrawal from Formula One at the end of the 2008 season, Toyota and BMW followed a year later. Toyota left Formula One with the distinction of having spent more money per championship point than any team in history. Its representative in meetings with the FIA was someone called John Howett, who was always very critical of what I was trying to do. He was reputedly an expert on MOT testing but he seemed to me to be out of his depth in Formula One.

With the financial crisis and imminent withdrawal of manufacturers, there was a genuine danger too few teams would survive to maintain the credibility of Formula One. Indeed, even some of the remaining teams were rumoured to be in financial difficulty, a crisis I tried to address at another meeting with them in Monaco in December 2008. Once again, it was agreed that costs had to come down and some ideas, all of which involved technical restrictions, were put forward. I was both surprised and frustrated – they had acknowledged the previous January that we could not cut costs by technical restrictions alone, but still they returned to the same old facile 'solution' despite the global financial crisis. I reiterated that piecemeal reform was no answer: we needed a concrete figure for maximum permissible expenditure, together with foolproof methods for checking that no one was breaching the agreed limit. We knew this was possible because the procedures for monitoring had already been agreed by Tony Purnell's expert group.

But we were stuck in an impasse and I could make no progress. The teams refused to meet FIA representatives, saying they wanted to deal with cost reduction internally, without us. I knew this wouldn't work: rules, not informal agreements, are the only way to suppress the teams' natural instinct to seek competitive advantage. In February 2009 I had a one-to-one meeting with Luca di Montezemolo. In response to my concern that we would lose more of the car manufacturers because of the financial crisis, he tried to assuage me by promising to obtain letters from the CEOs of the competing car companies guaranteeing their continued participation in the championship.

It did not take long to discover that Luca could not deliver on his promise – he could not even obtain a guarantee from Fiat, of which he was then still chairman (although the real boss was Sergio Marchionne). Without those guarantees of participation, Formula One was in serious danger, not mitigated by Luca's assurances that the remaining teams would run three cars if more manufacturers pulled out. He could not even produce guarantees for that, so with no new teams and a real likelihood that others would follow Honda's example (as indeed happened when Toyota and BMW left at the end of that year), we might soon be left with 14 cars or fewer.

I felt I could not just sit idly by amid this complacency and naked self-interest and watch them sleepwalk towards possible disaster. After much consultation and with the agreement of the World Council at two separate meetings, I proposed some very radical new rules to reduce costs and allow new teams to enter. These included allowing teams that agreed to run within a specified cost cap (and submit to the necessary rigorous checks) to have technical advantages to bring their performance up to a level close from that of the top teams. This would have been no different from allowing GP2 teams to make up numbers, something we would have had to do (and for which there were precedents in the 1950s and 1960s) if several Formula One teams had folded, but the speed differential would have been smaller than with GP2, thus reducing the risks.

Apart from maintaining full grids and giving us better competition, this would have demonstrated the important point that, when viewed from the grandstands or on television, there was no visible difference between a $60 to $70 million team and one spending $300 to $400 million.

We knew, of course, that the top-spending teams would not agree. A Formula One with an open approach to technology but strictly limited expenditure was anathema to them. They were used to throwing money at problems and competing on an equal basis with just two or three other big-budget teams. The last thing they wanted was an attack on the status quo that provided for more teams with the same resources in a sport where engineering excellence rather than money was decisive.

Sure enough, they bitterly attacked the proposal, saying this first phase would lead to two-tier racing. In reality, they already had two- or even three-tier racing because the smaller teams had insufficient money to compete with them. FOTA announced that the proposals were 'dictatorship' and an example of my 'autocratic' style. However, publishing the rules and allowing the minimum 20-day period required by the International Sporting Code before the opening of entries, at last brought FOTA to the negotiating table. They knew we had received upwards of 20 applications from new teams wanting to compete under the proposed new rules. After detailed investigation of the applicants, we eventually selected three.

I met the teams at Heathrow on 15 May, although my personal situation (my son Alexander had been found dead ten days earlier) was making things very difficult for me. It was soon clear that the main teams had not come to negotiate or discuss but intended simply to dictate terms. When I raised the question of a cost cap (fundamental to our plans and the reason we had applications from new teams for the first time in many years), John Howett tried but failed to lead a walkout. Apparently, they had agreed beforehand they would leave the meeting if I raised the question of a cost cap, but it was obvious the walkout plan was childish and no one else stood up.

I kept my temper (just) but I took the gloves off with Briatore, to the point where he accused me of being rude. He was right but I felt it merited. I thought he had ambitions to take over Formula One and I believed this was why he seemed to be encouraging dissent, while I was simply trying to solve a problem. Meanwhile, the atmosphere deteriorated further when I was passed a note from our lawyers announcing that Ferrari had launched legal proceedings against the FIA in Paris, something that, until then, the Ferrari representative had failed to mention. It was not a productive meeting.

Predictably, the French courts threw out Ferrari's legal challenge and we had another meeting in Monaco a week later, on 22 May. This time, FOTA were prepared to talk. They asked for three things: clear rules of governance, stable regulations and a more gradual reduction in costs. This seemed entirely reasonable and I agreed. I offered to reintroduce the governance and stability provisions of the old Concorde Agreement (which had expired 18 months previously, on 31 December 2007) in order to cover the first two points, and to discuss their ideas for a more gradual cost reduction in detail for the third.

When the deadline for entries was reached on 29 May, eight FOTA teams submitted 'conditional entries', effectively saying that they would enter only if their preconditions were met. But Williams entered without seeking to impose preconditions, explaining that they had a legal obligation to do so because of their sponsorship contracts and that not entering was anyway unthinkable given their 30 years of competing in Formula One. FOTA then decided to 'expel' Williams, an indication of how emotional and irrational things had become.

The conditions attached to the eight entries purported to reject outright the published 2010 rules. Under the International Sporting Code, the FIA had until 12 June to accept or reject entries. On 11 June, we had yet another meeting with FOTA in London. This time everything was agreed except the mechanism for the cost cap. Given that the target figures for their and our cost caps (or 'resource restriction agreement', as they preferred to call it) were virtually the same, we agreed to put our respective financial experts together the following Monday to finalise the methodology.

We understood Ferrari's reluctance to publish figures but saw no real difficulty because all the detail of the FIA method for checking and enforcing the cost cap had been worked out by Tony Purnell's expert group in the first half of 2008, with only Ferrari dissenting. We were also happy for the teams to self-certify, with outside auditors involved only if there was genuine suspicion of cheating. We also planned to offer a very substantial reward to any whistle-blower who brought us evidence of illegitimate spending by a team.

No sooner had this been agreed than elements within FOTA that were not present at the London meeting rejected the agreement. The following Monday our financial experts were confronted with a blank refusal to discuss any of the FIA cost-cap provisions, notwithstanding the 2008 arrangements agreed by the CFOs of all the teams in Tony Purnell's group. The teams later prepared their own so-called 'resource restriction agreement' and announced they would police it themselves. It soon failed for the very obvious reason that only an independent body can adequately police such a thing.

After effectively breaking off negotiations (which I had thought were beginning to go quite well) the teams announced their breakaway series a few days later during the 2009 British Grand Prix. The media were very excited but I was completely confident. I jokingly called the leaders 'loonies', which caused great offence – because, I suspect, it was so near the truth. For the same reasons that the 2005 breakaway would never have worked, I was quite sure this one was fatuous too. The teams could make a fuss, beat their chests and hold press conferences for several months, but any attempt to carry out their threats would collapse as the 2010 season approached.

It all got very emotional. Even teams that wanted to reduce costs said they should do it themselves and not involve the FIA, while the very rich teams were opposed because it would erode their competitive advantage. They knew a team-run system was bound to fail, allowing them to maintain the gap between themselves and the teams with less money. It seemed strange to me that the smaller ones had not spotted what was going on, but it's very easy to get swept along when everyone is being emotional. Luca was also distracting them by focusing on the percentage of Formula One income Bernie paid them instead of the massively wasteful way the richest teams spent it.

I still think Flavio, who was nominally leading the teams, had his own ambitions within FOTA and perhaps for Formula One generally. He may even have thought this was an opportunity to take over Formula One but, unusually for him, Bernie seemed blind to what Flavio was up to. And in my view Flavio, in turn, was managed by Luca.

In one acrimonious meeting I told Toyota's John Howett he would find his P45 (an employee's leaving document) on the fax machine one morning. Later that year Toyota did indeed shut down its Formula One team. But my problem was that I, too, wanted out. Having postponed my resignation in 2005 because of Jean Todt's new job at Ferrari, there was no way I was going to stand for election again when my mandate expired in November 2009. Indeed, everything was by now in place. In January 2009, I had met Jean at Le Bourget airport and told him I was determined to stop at the end of the year. I asked him to confirm our understanding that he would definitely stand for the FIA presidency the following November. He confirmed that he would and I promised to back him. I had also told the senior FIA staff in January 2009 that I was not going to stand for election again. I had even amended my *Who's Who* entry back in April to show 2009 as the last year of my FIA presidency.

Yet if I wanted to prove my point about a breakaway, I would have to stand for re-election. It had been made clear to me within the FIA that I would be re-elected if I stood again. Jean Todt would probably have been quite happy to wait until I could finally quit later in 2010 but, although I was entirely confident the breakaway would have been over by February 2010 at the latest, to stand again would have put back my plans by another year. And central to my personal plans was my desire to give News International, the publishers of the *News of the World*, my undivided attention. I had already waited more than a year.

Although I was convinced the smaller teams were being very badly treated financially, my sympathy for them had been ground down by their apparent support for the proposed breakaway. After all, I had gone out of my way to try to improve their situation, even in my last year when I could (and probably should) have just taken it easy and let things ride, but they had chosen to back the big teams that were effectively ripping them off. If they were not prepared themselves to stand up to the richer teams, or at least refrain from supporting them against the FIA, there was not a lot of point in my giving up another year to fight their battles for them.

As explained in chapter 26, despite their emotional objections to the way Formula One was being run, the breakaway teams would have had no choice but to submit their sporting and technical rules to the FIA and accept its system of stewards and Court of Appeal. In essence, it would have been back to square one under the FIA, but without Bernie's money. As reality dawned over the winter and the more excitable team principals calmed down or left, I was quite certain all would have been back to normal for the 2010 season. Even so, I was not prepared to put my personal plans on hold for another year just to prove that point.

I don't think CVC, the private equity group that now owned Bernie's company, ever truly understood any of this or, if they did, their bankers certainly didn't. As a result, the teams' announcement of a breakaway seemed to cause something close to panic within CVC. As Donald Mackenzie, its co-founder and co-chairman, said later when giving evidence in Bernie's Constantin Medien case,* they were impressed and alarmed by the teams' apparent anger. Also, as is clear from that judgment, CVC and the banks were obsessed with the Concorde Agreement, even more than I realised at the time. It was a classic case of everyone focusing on something relatively unimportant and missing the main point.

In retrospect, it's strange that, as far as I can remember, no one from CVC or the banks ever sat down with me or anyone in the FIA and asked for a detailed explanation of how the sport was governed. It was extraordinary because, after all, we were the governing body. I think they believed that Bernie ran Formula One and presumably they felt talking to him was sufficient. He probably encouraged that view, and it was true as far as the race contracts and small day-to-day things like passes went, but when push came to shove, it was the FIA that held the power and made the decisions. It was a lesson I learned in the FOCA–FISA war and others should have taken on board before Indianapolis in 2005.

That the teams could induce something close to panic in CVC surprised me. Donald Mackenzie had been calm, even stoic, when earlier breakaway threats had been made, but the world financial crisis seemingly had put them under pressure. It was rumoured that several of their businesses were in temporary difficulties and their bankers were worried. To stabilise Formula

---

* German media company Constantin Medien were due money if the Formula One shares were sold for more than an agreed sum. They sued Bernie in the High Court, claiming that the sale of shares to CVC was at an undervalue. They lost.

One, at least in the eyes of their banks, they needed a new Concorde Agreement to be signed without delay.

To the outside world, and particularly in high-finance circles, the Concorde Agreement had achieved almost mythical status. It was seen as the glue that held Formula One together. Fundamentally, this was nonsense. All the Concorde Agreement really did was tie the FIA's hands when it wanted to make changes to the Formula One rules. It also set out the commercial terms for the teams. Tying the FIA's hands and fixing the money had, after all, been our principal objectives when FOCA first negotiated the Concorde Agreement with the FIA back in 1981.

True, the Concorde Agreement meant the teams were contractually bound to race in the championship each season, but what else were they going to do? Bernie had all the TV and race contracts, and we, not the teams, had a binding contract with Bernie. One of the reasons for making both the Hundred Year Agreement and the earlier 15-year agreement with Bernie was to stop him (or whoever ended up owning his business) getting together with the teams to try to run outside the FIA's structures.

In any event, the teams' undertakings to compete were virtually worthless. There was no way to enforce them. An ordinary independent team would only stop competing in Formula One if it ran out of money, in which case there would be nothing left to sue. The car companies were the only participants with significant assets and therefore worth suing, but they were always careful to ensure that their Formula One team should sign the Concorde Agreement, never the main company. The team was disposable so it could break its agreement to race. It would always owe the main company more than the value of its assets and could be wound up if there were trouble. Bernie often tried to get the parent companies to sign up but they always refused. This was also the reason Luca failed to deliver the guarantees he had promised back in February 2009.

I always believed that Bernie and CVC would have been better off without a Concorde Agreement. Then the teams would have had to enter each year, like participants in any other international motor sport competition. They all needed to race in the Formula One World Championship because that's what their sponsors wanted and, more importantly, except for the American IndyCar championship, there was no other comparable series. Any attempt to set one up was bound to fail for all the reasons already mentioned – and moving to IndyCar would have presented far too many technical, logistical and financial difficulties for it to be more attractive than Formula One, even if the FIA were in sole charge. IndyCar's position in ACCUS and hence the FIA was another obstacle.

With no Concorde Agreement, the FIA had much more control over the Formula One rules, which would have allowed the introduction of a cost cap as I had planned in 2008 when Concorde had expired and had yet to be renewed. A well-judged cost cap would have made the teams profitable, demand for places in the World Championship would soon have exceeded supply, and each team would have had what amounted to a valuable franchise. Bernie and CVC might even have had to pay the teams less money in total.

The problem was that the financial world did not understand the fundamentals of Formula One (some of the analysts' guidance in the EM.TV and Kirch days around the year 2000 was positively hilarious). To the financiers, a Concorde Agreement was a sine qua non. Just how limited is the financial world's understanding is clear from the judgment in Bernie's Constantin

Medien case.* You begin to see how the big investment banks regularly manage to lose billions by getting into things they don't fully understand.

Following my disagreement with Bernie in the World Council in June 2008, the FIA had still not been given a complete draft of a new Concorde Agreement a year later. As a result, the 2008 and 2009 seasons ran without it. We could see no urgent need to sign. We only wanted to sign an agreement if Formula One and motor sport in general had some advantage from doing so. But with CVC under pressure from their banks and increasingly anxious to get it signed, Donald Mackenzie and Rolly Van Rappard, two of CVC's three main partners, saw my refusal combined with the standoff with the teams as a major problem. They asked for a meeting in June 2009, to which Bernie came too.

They said I must resign my presidency of the FIA immediately to stop the breakaway, because they were at risk from their banks. I replied I didn't have to do anything of the kind and that it was immaterial to the FIA whether we had CVC the other side of the table or a couple of people from their banks. It made no difference – the original 1995 agreement was still in place and the Hundred Year Agreement would follow on 1 January 2011. Who we dealt with didn't matter – we were well protected by our contracts.

I did tell them I was not going to stand again in November but made it clear I would remain president and in charge until then. I told them they had no choice but to accept this. I added that I intended to get the Concorde Agreement signed before I stood down rather than leave my successor with a mess, and then told

* http://www.judiciary.gov.uk/wp-content/uploads/JCO/Documents/Judgments/constantin-median-v-ecclestone-ors.pdf

them I very much hoped the new president would be Jean Todt, whom I intended to support. This seemed to dismay them. I was fairly sure they had someone in mind for the FIA presidency and they definitely did not want Jean. I didn't bother to ask who they were thinking of because I knew it would be someone unsuitable and, anyway, it was for the representatives of some 130 countries to decide, not Bernie and CVC.

When, as planned, I informed the FIA World Council a few days later that I was not going to stand again, Luca di Monte-zemolo, still Ferrari president, made some disobliging comments to the media after the meeting, despite an earlier agreement not to criticise one another. Irritated, I replied in kind and was widely quoted in the Italian press. I was briefly tempted to stand again just to make a point and prick the breakaway bubble, but realised I should not allow irritation to goad me. It was annoying that Luca claimed he had got rid of me and that some of the more gullible media actually believed him. The fact that my departure in November 2009 had been planned for years was completely ignored.

It was tempting to stay on just to show that Luca was talking nonsense, but there's a limit to how much time it's worth spending on something like that. After an exchange of insults (Luca called me a dictator, I said he was a mere *bella figura*), he rather disarmingly phoned and said: 'Let's be like football and call it a draw.' We had, after all, known each other for nearly 40 years. I knew that what had really upset him was the double diffuser dispute earlier in the season, and I didn't want an entirely impersonal technical matter to destroy what was left of our friendship.

Some weeks were then spent negotiating the Concorde Agreement. Ken Daly at Sidley Austin acted for the FIA. It was in place well before the November election. The negotiations were made easier because the FIA and the teams both wanted a relatively short-duration contract. Each suspected that CVC would want to sell its Formula One business as soon as the financial crisis was over and at that point CVC would need a much longer contract with both the FIA and the teams. The financial sector's almost superstitious belief in the need for a Concorde Agreement and its consequent role as an essential element in a sale or IPO would demand a longer contract. This would give both the FIA and the teams an opportunity to extract significant money from Bernie and CVC. Relations with CVC eventually returned to something like normal and I felt I was leaving the FIA in reasonable shape.

Immediately after my announcement at the June 2009 World Council that I was not going to stand again, Ari Vatanen, a former MEP and world champion rally driver whom I knew well, visited me in Monaco. He said he was going to stand for the FIA presidency and would like my support. I told him I was backing Jean. There followed a rather disagreeable election campaign, with Ari's camp making all sorts of claims – for example, that Jean was being allowed to use the FIA plane for his campaign. It was all completely untrue but created a needlessly unpleasant atmosphere. Ari even visited me for a second time in Monaco, seemingly to give me instructions about how to conduct the election. The inference that it might not be fair irritated me and I showed him the door.

In November 2009 I presided over my last FIA General Assembly. I had arranged for a French *huissier de justice* (a sort of bailiff) to be present and supervise the voting, to put its fairness beyond question. There was a small diversion when Ari's son (he brought his family with him to the assembly) saw one of the club presidents put two ballot papers in the box. Ari immediately jumped up to protest vehemently but he had failed to acquaint himself with FIA statutes: a club that was responsible for both sport and touring in its country had a vote for each. Jean Todt defeated Ari in the election by a very substantial majority.

Jean had taken on a difficult job and later told me he found it much harder than he had imagined. But he threw himself into it and has worked tirelessly ever since. Among other things he has, I believe, visited all the member countries of the FIA, a huge task on its own. Work occupies his entire day and beyond. The critics who sit on the sidelines for the most part have no idea what goes into a job like that. Interesting though it was, I felt a huge burden had been lifted when I stood down. It was not just the work, but also the feeling of responsibility whenever there was a serious accident. Now I was like an ordinary member of the public, hoping no one would get hurt and no longer having to ask myself could I perhaps have done more to prevent it.

29

CHEATING

At all levels of motor sport, cars are quite often excluded for breaches of the rules. The rules are complex and it's easy to fall foul of them. But cheating, for me at least, is something different. It's knowingly and deliberately breaking the rules in order to gain an advantage and taking steps to conceal what you are doing.

There is a view in some parts of motor sport, even Formula One, that cheating doesn't matter as long as you don't get caught. And, when someone does get caught, there's always a group of apologists ready to excuse the team and claim that everyone does it so it doesn't matter. The bigger the team, the louder the chorus will be.

A very unpleasant aspect of this is the pressure it puts on an honest competitor. If cheating is endemic, the honest competitor has either to start cheating too or endure constant defeat by unscrupulous rivals. This may seem obvious to someone from outside motor sport, but it is less glaring to some insiders. Eliminating deliberate rule-breaking must surely be a fundamental task for any governing body in sport.

The complexity of the cars in both racing and rallying provides many more opportunities for cheating than most sports afford. For me, the dividing line between deliberate rule-breaking and criminal financial fraud is a narrow one. Most cheating in top-level sport is fraudulent and brings or is intended to bring financial gain. Without being moralistic about it, it is difficult to see this as anything but crime.

Back in my March days, one of our mechanics reported he'd unthinkingly put his hand over the air restrictor on the engine of our works Formula Three car. To his astonishment, the engine had continued to run. The air restrictor was a device to limit power by requiring all the air entering the engine to pass through a hole of a certain size. The scrutineers would check that no air could enter the engine other than through the hole. To do this, they would seal the hole and then pump air out to check that the restrictor assembly could maintain a vacuum, thus proving that no air could reach the combustion chamber other than through the hole. When the scrutineers checked, the engine was always switched off because it obviously could not run when they had blocked the hole.

When the engine on our car was checked in the usual way, the scrutineers had found it held a vacuum as the rules required. So if the restrictor were blocked, no air could get in and the engine could not run. Yet our engine had run with the mechanic's hand blocking the intake. Something was clearly very wrong.

Back at the factory, I asked him to dismantle the engine and investigate. It turned out that the engine supplier had fitted a very sophisticated valve system that was opened by oil pressure. When the engine was running, the valve was open and admitted extra air through a concealed hole in the manifold, giving an illegitimate power increase. But when the engine was not running there was no oil pressure and the valve was closed. As a result, when the scrutineers checked, they would find a perfect seal and no extra air reaching the engine.

I was very annoyed because it was our works team and we were legally responsible for the car, yet the engine supplier had not told me about his device. Had the scrutineers somehow found it rather than our mechanic, I would have been branded a cheat for the rest of my life. No one would have believed I didn't know. I was so annoyed that I reported the engine supplier to the UK motor sport authorities instead of merely telling him not to do it, as I would have done had he asked me if it was OK.

But this was quite amateur compared to the Toyota factory team in the 1995 World Rally Championship. We caught them with an extraordinarily sophisticated cheat device. Again it involved letting extra air enter the engine, bypassing the restrictor. It was almost impossible to detect because it disappeared as soon as you gained access to the restrictor to check. The restrictor on a rally car was much harder to cheat than on a Formula Three car because the rally car had a turbocharger. On the engine side of the turbocharger, the air was above atmospheric pressure, so any leak would lose rather than gain power. If extra air was to be allowed in illegitimately, this had to be done in the very short distance between the air restrictor and the turbocharger.

Toyota's device was a carefully machined circular element in the air restrictor assembly that could be pulled out against a very strong spring. When the component was examined, the spring held this circular element in place. The machining was perfect and it was impossible to see the join. The restrictor appeared normal and the hole was the correct size, but when the car was running it had a (legitimate) steel-reinforced pipe taking cold air to it. The secret device was pulled out against its spring so more air could get to the turbocharger and then held in place by a jubilee clip round the cold air pipe. The steel reinforcement was strong enough for the pipe to hold the device open against the spring. But if the cold air pipe was removed to allow the scrutineers to access and check the restrictor hole, the jubilee clip had to be undone and the device would immediately spring back into the closed position. All would appear to be in order.

It was like using a sophisticated computer algorithm for some illicit purpose and programming it to vanish without trace if anyone tried to look at it or investigate.

Jacques Berger, a young engineer who had come to work for FIA, found it. He called me because a senior FIA official at the event was saying the stewards should do nothing since we could not afford to lose Toyota from the World Championship. I felt there was a principle at stake and insisted on action. Toyota were excluded from the championship and were particularly unhappy when I explained the device to the media.

Back in my days running the Manufacturers' Commission, rallying presented a major difficulty following Balestre's ban on the ultra-fast Group B cars mentioned in chapter 17. From then on, only Group A cars could be used in the World Rally Championship. Group A were basically road cars that had been modified for rallying but not excessively so. Among other things, they were required to have a standard production turbocharger. (As explained in chapter 12, this is a device to pump air into the engine using a turbine driven by exhaust gasses. It increases efficiency and reduces fuel consumption but in a road car must also be suitable for quiet driving in city traffic.) For a car to be eligible to compete in the WRC, at least 5000 identical examples had to be produced including the standard turbocharger. This was to

The 1995 Benetton pit fire. The *Sun*'s headline was: 'The Ignited Colours of Benetton'. [Corbis]

Explaining the highly ingenious Toyota device to cheat the air restrictor used in the World Rally Championship.

Flavio Briatore with Nelson Piquet Jr and Fernando Alonso. Fernando won the 2008 Singapore GP after Nelson was instructed to crash deliberately. [Getty]

With the starter at the American national drag racing championships.

Ayrton Senna on the starting grid of his last race. [Getty]

Sid Watkins, head of the FIA Medical Commission and professor of neurosurgery at the London Hospital. He led the work to improve safety in F1.

[Rex Features]

With Michael Schumacher at a road safety event. He became a key participant in our campaigns.

A common sight on the World Rally Championship before we introduced measures to protect spectators. [Ferdi Kräling]

A typical NCAP crash test in laboratory conditions. [Global NCAP]

The Apache helicopter and some of its ammunition on the main straight at Silverstone. On the left: Brigadier Richard Folkes, head of the Army Air Corps, and Geoff Hoon, Secretary of State for Defence. Our drivers seem ready to swap jobs with the army pilots. [Getty]

About to visit Bernie in his mobile office in the paddock at the 1996 British GP with Tony Blair. Perhaps Blair was already thinking about the £1 million? [Corbis]

A more relaxed meeting with Bernie in an Austrian ski resort.

With Martin McGuinness, Ian Paisley and two rally officials at Stormont for the Irish round of the 2007 WRC.

Press conference with Bernie and Ferrari chairman Luca di Montezemolo after the June 2009 World Motor Sport Council. [Getty]

Thanking Martin Brundle for driving me in the McLaren two-seater. Jürgen Hubbert, head of passenger cars at Mercedes, and Ron Dennis are in the background on the right.

Outside the High Court flanked by my lawyers Dominic Crossley (left) and David Sherborne, immediately after victory over the *News of the World*. [Press Association]

With Lord Hunt, then head of the Press Complaints Commission, after publication of the Leveson Report in November 2012.

establish that the turbocharger fitted to the rally car really was a production item and not one specially made for competition.

The problem with the stipulation was that an ordinary production turbocharger restricted engine performance too much for rallies, while a turbocharger suitable for rallying made the car very difficult to drive in everyday use. Cars appeared at the rallies with big turbochargers and there was a suspicion that some manufacturers had not produced the necessary 5000 cars equipped with them because of their unsuitability for everyday use on the roads. However, it was considered impossible to prove. The question was: how could we even find, still less check, the 5000 cars?

I suggested asking each manufacturer for a list of the chassis numbers of the 5000 cars they had produced and sold with the big turbochargers. We would then take a random sample of cars that was big enough to give high statistical probability of revealing that not all the 5000 had been equipped with the big turbocharger, if this were indeed the case. Expert statisticians said that there would be a very high probability of finding a car with the wrong (i.e. standard, road-going) turbocharger if we looked at a random sample of 100 from the 5000 cars supposedly fitted with the big turbocharger.

The plan was to trace each of the 100 cars in our sample through to the final customer (or showroom if it had not yet been sold) and pay a visit to ask if we could check the turbocharger. Faced with this, two car companies admitted they had not fitted their competition turbocharger to 5000 cars. One was European, the other Japanese. I felt really sorry for the Japanese competition manager. I had done this with the best of intentions but the consequences for the individual can be severe. OK, he shouldn't have cheated, but it's still somehow very sad to have messed up someone's career. He probably felt he had to do it, which is why cheating is so pernicious.

Formula One's tradition of cheating spanned its entire history, a favoured method being to run under weight. In the early days, some teams would qualify with a light car and then conceal lead in it at the end of the session before it was checked and weighed. When the officials finally caught on (long before my time in the FIA), things became more elaborate. The new trick was to bring the car in at the end of qualifying, take off the engine cover and other bits of bodywork and swap them for much heavier pieces before the car could be weighed. As a guest in one pit in the early 1980s, I went to move an engine cover blocking access to the loo, expecting it to be feather light. To my surprise I needed both hands and quite an effort to move it. It was the scrutineering – as opposed to qualifying – cover.

When the FIA got wind of this and sent officials to watch and make sure the same bodywork went back on the car after the last visit to the pits, the driver would stop out on the circuit and the mechanics would go to fetch it in a truck, taking the heavy bodywork with them. These tricks finally stopped when weighing equipment was installed at the entrance to the pit lane so the cars could be weighed at random, as they are today.

A very ingenious but illegitimate way to run under the weight limit was invented by the BAR Honda team in 2005. Their fuel system included a hidden tank that could hold five or six kilos of fuel. At the last refuelling stop, the hidden tank would be filled along with the rest of the system and would then remain full until the end of the race. However, when the fuel was drained at the end of the race so that the car could be weighed without fuel to make sure it was not under the weight limit, the hidden tank was so arranged that its fuel stayed in the system. As a result, the car appeared to be over the weight limit and thus legal when without the fuel it would have been under the limit.

In effect, the fuel was being used as ballast to make the car legal when weighed, yet except for the last part of the race this fuel was available so the car could run under the weight limit. The advantage was bigger than it sounds because the car would have a lower average weight for the race than it would otherwise have had.

When this was discovered, the scrutineers reported the matter to the stewards. After very long deliberations, the stewards inexplicably decided that no action was necessary. Fortunately, the FIA as well as the teams had a right of appeal to the FIA's International Court of Appeal. This court is independent of the FIA administration and made up of senior outside lawyers. The FIA's right of appeal was hardly ever exercised. The team hired David Pannick QC to appear for them in the Court of Appeal. Perhaps British American Tobacco, their sponsors, remembered his brilliant performance for us against them in the double-livery arbitration described earlier. By then Pannick and the head of his chambers, Ian Mill QC, had become the go-to lawyers for Formula One teams in trouble.

We argued that the hidden tank amounted to cheating and the team should be excluded from the championship. The court was not satisfied it really was deliberate, however, and imposed a more modest, but nevertheless severe, two-race ban. The ban included the Monaco Grand Prix. Litigation was threatened but did not materialise.

At the beginning of July 2007 I received calls in quick succession from Ron Dennis, the McLaren team principal, and Jean Todt, his Ferrari opposite number. Ferrari had received an email from someone working in a Surrey photocopy shop headed

'Industrial Espionage'. They very nearly didn't open it (each team gets lots of strange emails) but when they did, they could hardly believe what they were reading. Attached were full details of their current Formula One car, including all its most secret design data. A lady had come into the shop with 780 pages of technical documents and asked the person behind the counter to put everything on CDs. It was the complete technical details of the current Ferrari Formula One car plus other important information. A Formula One fan working in the shop had realised its significance and emailed the digital version to Ferrari.

This was not the first time someone had stolen technical information from Ferrari. Sometime before, they had been tipped off that an engineer working on Toyota's Formula One car in Germany was using their data. Ferrari informed the German police, who dealt with the matter. Paddock gossip spread that the police were amused to find the Ferrari prancing horse on the screen when they started the Toyota engineer's computer. For whatever reason, Ferrari never alerted the FIA and we only heard of the incident indirectly.

The photocopy shop evidence was much more serious. It involved the entire IP of the current Ferrari Formula One car, 780 pages of drawings and technical data, plus full information about how the car was operated. It revealed all the technical secrets, everything necessary to build and run the latest Ferrari, and was an absolute gold mine for any other team. When I heard this, I could see the reason for Jean Todt's call. It also helped us solve a mystery about a feature of the Ferrari to which McLaren had drawn our attention at the start of the season. When it was examined, our technical department did not think it broke any rule, but we could not work out how McLaren knew about it.

Following the tip-off, lawyers acting for Ferrari under a court order had raided the home of McLaren's chief designer, Mike Coughlan. The lady in the shop was his wife and had left her name and address with the material she had asked to be copied. The lawyers recovered CDs containing the entire technical IP of the current Ferrari Formula One car. The 780-page printout had, in the meantime, apparently been destroyed. Although Ferrari had already brought the matter before the English High Court when applying for the search order, they had also complained to the FIA. We clearly had to act. It almost goes without saying that if a team acquires all their main rival's current technical information and intellectual property, they gain a huge and very unsporting advantage.

McLaren were summoned to the World Council and brought Ian Mill QC to defend them. They claimed they had held an internal enquiry which showed their chief designer had been acting entirely alone and no one else in the company knew of, or had anything to do with, the Ferrari IP. This was my first encounter with the one-rogue-employee defence, later made famous by Rupert Murdoch's newspaper the *News of the World*. McLaren backed this up with a document apparently signed by most of their engineers confirming they had no knowledge of Ferrari's documents.

The council did not believe the defence story could possibly be true. We were all convinced of McLaren's guilt but, during the discussion after we had listened to McLaren and their legal team, I and two other lawyers on the council pointed out that we had no hard evidence that what they had told us was untrue, still less that McLaren had actually made use of Ferrari's IP.

It seemed quite obvious that McLaren had used the information and their chief designer had not (as they claimed) acquired it just as a curiosity for his private collection. But this was not the same as proof. If we were to convict without concrete evidence, they would go to a civil court with their expensive lawyers and almost certainly win. Very reluctantly, we had no option but to acquit. Back in the Crillon, the hotel next to the FIA headquarters where I always stayed, I had a call from a very unhappy Sergio Marchionne, CEO of Fiat. A short time later, Luca di Montezemolo, chairman of Ferrari, called. Both were outraged that McLaren had got away with it. Wearily, I explained the legal difficulties.

Later that summer, Fernando Alonso, who was driving for McLaren, fell out with Ron Dennis over Lewis Hamilton, the other McLaren driver. Alonso told Flavio Briatore, his manager, that emails existed confirming other engineers in McLaren knew about the Ferrari IP. Flavio told Bernie, who in turn told me. If this were true, it would show McLaren had indeed been using the material and had misled the World Council. Eventually, I was shown copies of some emails which were very compromising.

To prove Alonso's allegations, we needed copies of the emails and wrote to all three McLaren drivers (Alonso, Hamilton and their test driver, Pedro de la Rosa) offering them a deal. We explained that if they came forward within a specified time-frame with details of everything they knew, they would not be individually pursued for participating in a breach of the rules. On the other hand, if they did not come forward and were later discovered to have had any knowledge or evidence about use by McLaren of the Ferrari IP, they could be found to have 'brought the sport into disrepute' and their licences would be at risk. This was the only way to pursue the case because, at the time, ordinary team employees and even the company bosses did not have FIA licences, so we had no direct authority over them.

Our threat to their licences produced the compromising emails and McLaren were summoned back to the World Council. This time we had the evidence and they were obviously guilty, despite Ian Mill's best efforts. The emails showed beyond any possible doubt that others besides Coughlan had had access to the stolen material. But what should we do? If we excluded the team from the 2007 World Championship we would wreck a great battle between Lewis Hamilton and Ferrari's Kimi Räikkönen. Worse, a ban would possibly have to be for 2008 as well as 2007 because the 2008 car was already being designed during that summer and further investigation might show it, too, incorporated stolen Ferrari IP. But a two-year ban might put McLaren, with 1300 employees, out of business.

I and other lawyers on the council were for a ban. 'Hard cases make bad law,' we said. The majority, however, wanted some other penalty, mainly because of the championship. I felt that McLaren's possession of all Ferrari's IP meant that Hamilton had an unfair advantage over Räikkönen, which had already skewed the championship contest, but the majority view prevailed. Happily, Kimi won the 2007 World Championship by a single point from Lewis, so the distortion didn't matter in the end.

In spite of all the evidence, McLaren continued to maintain that only their chief designer had seen the Ferrari secrets and, they said, had kept everything to himself. This irritated the council because it was obviously untrue and had now been proved to be untrue. Eventually, it was Bernie Ecclestone who suggested a $100 million fine. Those who wanted a ban, including me, reluctantly agreed.

Even today, I still think a ban would have been better. McLaren would certainly have appealed and might have gone to a civil court or, more probably, to the FIA Court of Appeal, where they would have had a completely new hearing in front of outside independent lawyers. Those avenues might well have led to a better solution. A financial penalty, no matter how astronomic, is seldom appropriate for a sporting infringement, particularly one giving an unfair competitive advantage. It leaves a feeling that the advantage has somehow been bought. It should never be forgotten that the value of the stolen IP was significantly greater than $100 million – at least if you consider what Ferrari must have spent to acquire it.

In an amusing postscript, McLaren successfully argued in front of a UK tax tribunal that the cash part of the fine (around £32 million) was a legitimate business expense because, they said, cheating was part of their motor racing business and the fine therefore incurred 'wholly and exclusively as part of their trade'. When the tax authorities appealed to the UK's Upper Tax Tribunal, a High Court judge had no difficulty in ruling that McLaren had engaged in conduct that was not 'in the course of its trade'. It's a pity that McLaren didn't tell the World Motor Sport Council that they believed cheating was a normal part of their business.

The result made headlines and inevitably attracted the attention of critics and rent-a-quotes. You could understand hired PR people trying to put a spin on what McLaren had done but a few supposedly independent commentators were suggesting we had somehow picked on them, completely ignoring the fact that the team had knowingly stolen not just the odd drawing or piece of information, but the entire technology of Ferrari's current Formula One car, and then repeatedly lied about it when challenged. Furthermore, we had been given evidence that McLaren's spy in Ferrari, Nigel Stepney, had been sending them a constant stream of SMS messages. The Italian police had provided Ferrari with a list, although only the time, date and location, not the content. The number increased substantially during race weekends, making it highly probable that Stepney was keeping McLaren up to date with information about Ferrari's actions and strategy during each Grand Prix. Indeed, some of Coughlan's emails within McLaren referenced the strategy that Ferrari was planning to adopt.

It seemed to me that to maintain, in the face of all this, that we had engaged in a witch-hunt against McLaren, or that we had in some way behaved improperly, was beyond absurd. Given the evidence and a complaint, what were we supposed to do? Simply ignore it? Or pretend it had nothing to do with the World Championship? Refusing to acknowledge that McLaren's behaviour was very wrong indeed and trying somehow to suggest that the FIA was itself to blame for the whole thing struck me as quite simply cretinous.

McLaren didn't appeal against the fine, probably realising there was a risk that the FIA's International Court of Appeal might cancel it and substitute a sporting penalty, in all likelihood a ban. The fine, though large, was something they could handle but a lengthy ban could have been catastrophic for the company. We also excluded McLaren from the Constructors' Championship. Their loss of revenue from the prize fund as a result of their demotion from second place to last in the Constructors' Championship counted as part of the $100 million and went to the other teams rather than to the FIA. This is because McLaren had been lying second to Ferrari in the championship before they were excluded, so all the teams below McLaren (i.e. all except Ferrari) moved up a place and got more money. Thus the fine gave us about $60 million for grassroots motor sport, but also distributed some $40 million among the remaining teams. The penalty, significant though it was, did not stop McLaren winning the Formula One drivers' title the following year with Lewis Hamilton by one point from Felipe Massa.

Had McLaren come to the first hearing, put their hands up and admitted their guilt, the fine would have been very much lower. Had they turned up without lawyers and said to the council: you are all ex-racers, can you honestly say that, given an opportunity like that, you would not have been tempted? It was the stubborn, obviously untrue insistence that they were innocent, reinforced by a large and expensive legal team, that led Bernie to joke that Ron was fined $5 million for the offence and $95 million for being a c***.

Knowing that the size of the fine would attract a lot of media coverage, I asked our lawyers to prepare the detailed reasons as quickly as possible. They actually worked all night on the document so that it was ready for distribution first thing the following day. Hostile elements in the press immediately took this as evidence that the decision had been pre-cooked. Having worked so hard only to find their efforts criticised in this way, our legal team remarked that, as always, no good deed goes unpunished.

One of the most exasperating aspects of the whole saga was the suggestion in various blogs and articles that this was all part of some vendetta of mine against Ron Dennis. A lot of people think I dislike Ron. This is not true. Of course, he could be annoying in meetings but only because he was defending what he saw as his company's interests. And he was prepared to do this when other team principals who might have secretly agreed with him were not. It could be annoying but it was his job as he saw it and I had no personal problem with that. I often thought he was wrong (for example, when he fought hard to retain the absurdly expensive qualifying cars) but that did not make me dislike him.

Any reasonable person would admire Ron's achievements, one of Formula One's great success stories. The only real black spot is that he allowed his company to lie repeatedly to the FIA about 'spygate', and again over the incident at the 2009 Australian Grand Prix (see below). I thought McLaren deserved better leadership than that.

While I had no problem with Ron, he may have had one with me. Tom Bower, in his book about Bernie, says that Ron commissioned a psychologist to do a report on me. If true, it's very funny, but I would never have gratuitously had a go at him or indeed anyone when I was acting as an elected official. At the insistence of Norbert Haug, the Mercedes Formula One chief at the time, Ron and I shook hands publicly in the Spa paddock in September 2007 but neither of us was comfortable doing so. It felt like a PR stunt.

To date, the FIA's share of the fine has aided the national motor sport authorities in 107 countries with more than 330 projects. And the money was not completely spent until very recently. Part of the decision was that we examine the 2008 McLaren car to ensure it used no illegally acquired Ferrari IP. McLaren said they welcomed this and we could look at whatever we wished. They may not have anticipated we would take them at their word and send a forensic IT team to back up our technical people and go through 1.4 terabytes of their emails and other documents. The IT experts found further damning evidence. Confronted with a 23-page report which showed conclusively that they had seen the Ferrari information (including references to their 'mole in Ferrari' and waiting until the 'FIA aggro' was finished before using a particular device), McLaren finally came clean. On 5 December 2007, Martin Whitmarsh wrote to the World Council on behalf of McLaren, apologising for what had happened.

None of this took place in secret – on the contrary, the media were kept fully informed – yet even today, eight years later, you can still read articles by the odd lazy or incompetent journalist suggesting McLaren did nothing wrong and were penalised without evidence. The Greek chorus never rests.

McLaren's owners promised to make management changes and on that basis we felt we had to drop the matter. The alternative was in effect to shut the team down. A few months later, Martin Whitmarsh, who had taken over the team principal role from Ron Dennis, invited me to lunch at McLaren to patch things up. Paddy Lowe, McLaren's engineering director, was at the lunch and it was a friendly affair. When alone with people I had known for years, I always became very conscious of the consequences of what the governing body does. Martin confirmed that a ban would have been more than serious. I couldn't help feeling it was all so unnecessary – it could so easily have been nipped in the bud if McLaren had alerted Ferrari as soon as the stolen IP was offered to them. That, after all, was the obvious and honourable thing to do, as Martin Whitmarsh indeed acknowledged in his letter.

The unsolved mystery is what motivated Nigel Stepney to hand all that information to McLaren in the first place. Did he have some sort of grudge against Ferrari? Or was he induced to do so and, if so, by whom? Is it really credible that he gathered together and secretly copied hundreds of pages of secret information to pass to Coughlan in Barcelona and then sent a constant stream of SMS messages to McLaren, all without having a strong reason to do so? One can speculate but I doubt we shall ever know. Stepney died in 2014 when he stepped in front of a lorry on the M20 motorway.

Meanwhile, it emerged that a McLaren engineer had taken some of their IP with him to Renault. It was orders of magnitude less extensive than the Ferrari IP acquired by McLaren but, most importantly, it was not an action by the Renault team; it was an individual taking information with him when changing jobs. Renault immediately made a full admission rather than engage top lawyers and set out to mislead the World Council. We, nonetheless, conducted a full investigation and a hearing to make sure we had the full picture, including an analysis of every piece of McLaren information that Renault had seen. It was soon clear that the information was never used, and indeed couldn't have been useful. Renault had broken the rules by not preventing the information from being taken across, but to reinforce the point that, in sport, a quick and honest admission is an essential part of the process when rules are broken, we imposed no penalty. Amazingly, some of McLaren's supporters in the media have suggested that the treatment of Renault was inconsistent with what happened to McLaren.

In contrast to 2007, McLaren themselves adopted the open and honest approach after the 2009 Australian Grand Prix. The race finished under the safety car with Jarno Trulli in third place and Hamilton fourth. Trulli had overtaken Hamilton while behind the safety car, which is against the rules unless invited to do so in order to regain position. As a result, the stewards docked Trulli 25 seconds, dropping him from third to 12th and moving Hamilton up to third. During their inquiry, the stewards asked Hamilton if he had waved Trulli past. Hamilton said he hadn't, although he had previously given a TV interview saying he had.

The FIA subsequently discovered a recording of the team telling Hamilton by radio to let Trulli past. At the next race, there was another stewards' hearing and the recording was played to Hamilton and Dave Ryan, the McLaren sporting director. Both continued to deny that Hamilton had invited Trulli to overtake, despite the recording and Trulli's testimony that Hamilton had waved him through. This new evidence led the FIA to reinstate Trulli's third place, and to bring charges against McLaren because of the persistent lying. Misleading the stewards is a very serious matter, doubly so when the objective is to take a fellow competitor's podium finish.

The following day, Hamilton called a press conference at the Sepang circuit in Malaysia and admitted he had indeed waved Trulli past. I believe it was his father who (in my view rightly) suggested he do this, not the team. He apologised to his fans and the media for twice lying to the stewards and depriving Trulli of his podium finish, saying he had been pressured to do so by Ryan. Hamilton was strongly criticised in the media but at least he had abandoned the lie.

McLaren sacked Ryan, who was a long-standing McLaren employee and greatly respected in Formula One. Many in Formula One were very surprised to hear that Ryan had told Hamilton to lie to the stewards without first consulting the team. At the subsequent World Motor Sport Council hearing, Martin Whitmarsh turned up alone and quite simply apologised for what had happened. The result was a very mild (perhaps too mild) three-race ban suspended for 12 months. The absence of lawyers and, more importantly, any attempt to deny what had taken place or mislead the council worked strongly in McLaren's favour. I felt the verdict had at least helped give the lie to the allegations of an FIA vendetta against McLaren.

What a contrast the whole affair makes with Stirling Moss's honesty in defence of Mike Hawthorn at the 1958 Portuguese Grand Prix, which eventually enabled Hawthorn to win the World Championship by one point ahead of Moss. But at least this time the McLaren apologists in the paddock and beyond kept quiet. They had looked very foolish when the full facts of the Ferrari spying episode emerged at the end of 2007 and their accusations of a witch-hunt were shown to be nonsense. Now, with no dissembling from the team, even its most one-eyed supporter could understand what had really happened.

In 2009, two years after 'spygate', I faced my last great cheating scandal. Nelson Piquet Jr, who had been driving for the Renault team alongside Fernando Alonso, fell out with team principal Flavio Briatore and was fired. It was typical of what happens in Formula One when a driver is not getting results: the team blames the driver who, in turn, blames the team. Shortly afterwards, Nelson's father, a three-time world champion and an old friend, came to see me in Monaco and told me the full story of the crash at the 2008 Singapore GP. I didn't tell him I had already heard some details of this, if only as a rumour. I said we needed a sworn statement from Nelson Jr.

A few days later, a former senior Scotland Yard detective who was now working for Quest, the security organisation run by former Metropolitan Police commissioner Lord Stevens, took the statement. It confirmed the story that Nelson Jr had been instructed by his team to crash on a particular lap in a particular part of the circuit where his wrecked car could not easily be reached. This was to make sure the safety car would have to be deployed immediately after Alonso had refuelled, thus giving the team the colossal advantage that allowed Alonso to win the race. But I knew his statement, even if sworn, would not be enough on its own.

By coincidence, Flavio Briatore invited me to lunch at the Rampoldi restaurant in Monaco to make peace after our conflicts over costs earlier in the summer. We had a friendly lunch and agreed such things were not personal. I said nothing about my conversation with Nelson Sr in the same restaurant a few days earlier, or the sworn statement that we now had.

The problem was we still didn't have sufficient proof. With something this serious, the lawyers said we needed proof to the criminal standard, in other words 'beyond reasonable doubt', rather than proof on the balance of probabilities which would apply in a civil case. We also knew that, if we simply charged the team on the basis of Nelson Jr's statement plus the circumstantial evidence, they would say he had invented the story to get his own back for being fired. They would continue to claim it was pure luck that they decided to refuel Alonso's car unusually early in the race, as they had told a number of sceptical journalists at the time. We needed much more.

We decided to use the stewards' powers to call members of a team in for questioning during a Grand Prix and put the plan into action at the Belgian Grand Prix in Spa. It was essential that it should be a surprise. If the team had been forewarned or we had sent someone to the factory to ask questions, it would have been easy for everyone involved to deny all knowledge of any sort of plot.

We arranged for an expert barrister, accompanied by the senior former Scotland Yard detective, to enter the paddock secretly at the Belgian race. The idea was to question members of the Renault team separately before they were alerted or had an opportunity to confer. We made sure no one in the paddock knew what was going on except the race director, Charlie Whiting. The ploy succeeded and the interrogators got the necessary additional evidence.

When we charged the team, the Renault board appointed a senior English barrister, Ali Malek QC, to mount an internal investigation. He carried out a detailed inquiry and called me two weeks later to say Renault were not going to contest the charge. He also said that Flavio Briatore and Pat Symonds, the technical chief, would be leaving the team immediately. It seemed to us that was exactly how a big company should handle that kind of situation. The FIA does not have a police force and should not have to fight to get the truth out. Formula One is supposed to be a sporting contest and has to rely on the participants wanting to keep it that way.

Because of the way the company had dealt with the matter, it was clear there was no case against Renault itself. They had done exactly what they should have done. We invited Flavio and Pat to the World Council to answer charges of having personally brought the sport into disrepute, but neither came and both were banned from Formula One. Flavio challenged this decision in the French courts and won a partial victory. The court did not like our procedures (commenting that the FIA didn't have direct supervisory authority over team employees, because they didn't have licences) and set the penalties aside. But it made no finding of innocence and did not exonerate Flavio or Pat.

In the end, Flavio never answered the charges directly. Had he taken it to the FIA Court of Appeal he would have been entitled to a complete rehearing in front of entirely independent lawyers. His own lawyers could have argued that he himself was innocent and knew nothing of the plot, as he has continued to claim ever since. Instead, he chose to go to a civil court on a technical point, thus depriving himself of a fresh hearing and an opportunity to plead innocence in front of an independent tribunal.

Our outside lawyers thought the French court's judgment was hopelessly flawed, mainly because it's fundamental in so-called domestic disputes that you exhaust the available internal remedies before going to the ordinary courts. In other words, Flavio should first have gone to the FIA's Court of Appeal as was his right. He could have gone to a civil court later if he was still not happy. Had I still been president, we would have appealed and I'm quite sure we would have won. The judgment was so weak and badly reasoned that it almost fell apart in your hand. But by then we'd had the election and Jean Todt had taken over. He's more risk-averse than me and did not want to take any sort of chance in the courts. He reached a compromise of sorts with Flavio and his lawyers, but the end result changed nothing of substance. I still see Flavio from time to time. As we agreed that time in the restaurant, these things are not personal.

30

CRASHING THE CAR
INDUSTRY

Although the FIA is popularly associated with motor sport, the original purpose of its constituent clubs in the different countries was to protect the interests of the ordinary motorist. The FIA's function in its early days was to co-ordinate these efforts globally, and it secured international conventions on such things as traffic signs and the pedal layouts in early motorcars (some had the accelerator in the middle!). Of all the things I did or attempted to do in my 16 years at the head of the FIA, the one that gives me the most satisfaction is our work on road safety because it has undoubtedly saved thousands of lives.

When I was elected in 1993, I had already been responsible for motor sport as president of FISA for two years. I now had responsibility for the road car side of the FIA as well. This had been largely moribund since the Second World War because the FIA concentrated on motor sport. The big motoring clubs all belonged to a rival global organisation, the Alliance Internationale de Tourisme, or AIT. Those with a sporting division also belonged to the FIA in order to keep their place in international motor sport, but the remainder, for example the AA in the UK or the ANWB in the Netherlands, tended to be AIT only.

Given its active involvement during the first half of the 20th century, I felt the FIA should still be working for the ordinary motorist, particularly on safety. After all, the FIA member organisations had tens of millions of motorists on their books, spread across 130 countries. With thousands dying on the roads each year and governments doing little or nothing about it, road safety was an area that should be an urgent FIA priority.

As noted in chapter 18, David Ward came to work for the FIA full-time after the death of the Labour Party leader John Smith and took over our activities in Brussels. The AIT already had an office in Brussels but didn't want the FIA to share it because its member organisations, particularly those with no sporting division, were nervous of motor sport. The AAA in America had even given up the sporting power for the USA following the Le Mans disaster in 1955, and many motoring and allied organisations (such as the UK's Caravan Club) seemed to have a rather old-fashioned view that motor sport was irresponsible.

David set up a separate FIA office close to the European Parliament and it became a real force. After he had been there for a year or two, nothing much happened in Brussels to do with cars without our involvement in some form.

Eventually, the big clubs with no motor sport division decided to abandon their rather ineffectual Brussels AIT office and asked if they could join us. They had begun to realise that motor sport, far from being a handicap, helped with politicians because it opens doors. Ask a politician to a seminar on road safety and he probably won't come. Invite him to his country's Grand Prix and you are much more likely to get a chance to talk to him. We eventually absorbed the entire AIT into the FIA.

Backed by Alan Donnelly,* a friend of David Ward and senior Labour MEP, I was elected honorary president of the European Parliament Automobile Users' Intergroup – an all-party group of MEPs interested in motoring issues. This enabled us to build a valuable network of contacts in the parliament. As explained in chapter 23, following Ayrton Senna's death in 1994 we had discovered that, astonishingly, there had been no new legislation for the protection of car occupants since 1974. Proposals were in the pipeline but not due to take effect for many years. The European Commission wanted improved standards for entirely new models from 1998 but not until 2003 for all new cars in the showroom. The car industry was running a determined campaign to weaken them and make them less costly and easier to comply with. With only one or two consumer groups to oppose them, they were succeeding.

The FIA began a campaign in Brussels to stop the car industry watering down the new EU legislation. We knew the European Parliament's role would be crucial because the Maastricht Treaty had just given the legislature stronger powers to propose amendments to the commission's directives. One of David's last tasks for John Smith was an analysis of the major changes brought about by Maastricht. As a result, he knew all about the parliament's enhanced powers, which were only slowly being understood in Brussels.

* Alan Donnelly was then socialist leader of the European Parliament Economic Committee, rapporteur on the car industry and chairman of the European Parliamentary Committee for Relations with the United States Congress. He later became leader of the European Parliamentary Labour Party, holding the position from 1997 to 2000.

As a senior member of the parliament's Economic Affairs Committee, which had responsibility for the crash-test legislation, Alan became the rapporteur for the draft directive. This put him in the driving seat to toughen up the proposed standards, using the parliament's new powers. With the help of officials from the UK Department for Transport, David supplied Alan with over 50 draft amendments to the EU legislation. These dropped the weaker front- and side-impact crash tests proposed by the industry and replaced them with more realistic and demanding tests. One MEP joked that, although he had great respect for Mr Donnelly's ability, even he did not believe Alan had drafted these highly technical amendments himself. The MEP was right, of course. One of the experts in the UK Department for Transport who helped us had raced against me in Clubmans Sports Cars in his younger days.

In 1995, Alan persuaded his committee to hold an open hearing on the issue, which ensured that the discussion would get public exposure despite its highly technical nature. Now we needed a way to make a detailed technical discussion about the dimensions of crash-test barriers and the height of side-impact points a hot political topic for the media. We set out to dramatise the issue so that our solid evidence in favour of more stringent and realistic crash tests would have a chance of being voted through by the parliament.

We invited Gerhard Berger, a leading Formula One driver and former team-mate of Ayrton Senna, who was then driving for Ferrari, to join the FIA's delegation to the European Parliament hearing. Alongside our technical experts, Gerhard explained he was safer crashing in his Formula One car than in a typical road car, despite the racing car's much higher speeds. This was because the FIA had started to apply realistic crash tests. His evidence attracted real attention and, to our delight, an outraged industry representative even heckled us in the meeting. Thanks to Gerhard, quite obscure details of crash-testing were shown on primetime German TV.

International coverage was extensive, including, for example, a full-page feature in *The Times* written by Kevin Eason, who later became its Formula One correspondent. The detail was hard to follow but the message was clear: the car companies are trying to avoid making your car safer in order to boost their profits. Apart from the general media coverage there was strong support from MEPs.

Alan's proposed amendments were unanimously accepted first by the parliament's committee and then by the entire plenary meeting of the parliament in Strasbourg. With parliament now strongly backing the FIA's position on the draft directive, the European Commission had to decide whether to object or accept the parliament's amendments. The responsible commissioner was Martin Bangemann of Germany.

Fortunately, I had a perfect opportunity to persuade him because Alan had proposed him for an honorary degree from Newcastle University. I decided I had to go from Brussels to Newcastle for some reason the very same day of the ceremony and offered him a lift in the FIA plane. I managed to convince him of our case for road safety and he immediately saw the point of realistic crash tests. He decided to support the parliament's view and stop any further negotiation with the car industry. In truth, it wasn't a problem for the industry. Provided they all had to adopt higher standards, there was no competitive advantage or cost disadvantage for any individual company. With the final hurdle crossed, the amended directives were to start coming into force three years later, in January 1998, and finally take full effect in 2003. This marked the start of major improvements to car safety across Europe.

Apart from the debate over new EU laws, various organisations and governments were crash-testing cars and publishing the results as information for consumers. But the tests all used different and confusing standards and therefore, understandably, no one took much notice. A uniform and pan-European approach was required, exactly the sort of issue where I thought the FIA should be taking the lead. I persuaded the FIA Senate to agree a £1 million budget for crash-testing, justifying it on safety grounds for the enhanced protection of the millions of motorists who belonged to the FIA's member organisations.

I also pointed out to the Senate that if there were ever another major accident like the one at Le Mans in 1955, we would need friends in politics if we were to protect motor sport. It would be too late to start wooing politicians after the event; we would need them onside immediately, already well briefed about the lives that were being saved because of what motor sport was doing for the ordinary road user. If we had a big accident without all this in place, we would risk politicians banning motor sport. It had been banned in some countries following the 1955 Le Mans catastrophe, and the public were much more sensitive to death and injury now than they had been in 1955, only ten years after the end of the Second World War.

In 1995, with our campaign beginning to take off, officials from the UK Department for Transport (DFT) and the Transport Research Laboratory (TRL) approached the FIA about the possibility of creating a New Car Assessment Programme (NCAP). The first NCAP had been founded by the US government in 1978 and gave consumers independent safety ratings of car models based on laboratory crash tests. The TRL's Professor

Adrian Hobbs had been given the go-ahead for a research project to crash-test some popular UK cars and hoped it could develop into a permanent NCAP.

We encouraged Adrian and his DFT officials to make it a European rather than solely UK programme. It would be easier for the FIA to support the project if it was more international in scope, and we thought that it would encourage some other governments and partners to join. Thus was born the European New Car Assessment Programme (Euro NCAP), for which I was asked to serve as chairman. As we anticipated, Euro NCAP quickly gained support from the governments of the UK, Sweden and the Netherlands, as well as FIA clubs and consumer organisations. At last, and after a great deal of investment, hard work and persuasion, the FIA was now playing a leading role in European road safety.

In addition to the legislation, we needed to get the European Commission on our side for this project. A number of commission experts agreed with us because they had been forced to dilute the original draft legislation by heavy car industry lobbying. They were now delighted with the tougher standards introduced by the parliament as a result of Alan Donnelly's amendments. They liked the idea of an NCAP providing EU citizens with information on vehicle safety. Luc Werring, the head of the road safety unit in the commission's Directorate General for Transport, played a key role by supporting an FIA-led application for a road safety grant for Euro NCAP.

Predictably, the Brussels-based ACEA tried to block this by lobbying officials in the Industry Directorate. This intervention initially delayed commission support, but Luc Werring resubmitted our grant proposal at a moment when his opposite number in the industry unit was absent and the grant was approved.

Euro NCAP's first test results were released to the media at a launch in 1997 and gained huge publicity across Europe. The Rover 100 (originally the Mini Metro) performed particularly badly – its zero-star result sent sales through the floor and within six months Rover had decided to terminate production.

The industry reacted with fury. Britain's Society of Motor Manufacturers and Traders hired an ex-MP to try to rubbish Euro NCAP's work. A very senior executive from Renault asked for a meeting at the next Grand Prix and told me they would pull out of Formula One if we continued. I invited him to go right ahead. Later, however, David and I met the then CEO of Renault, Louis Schweitzer, a former senior French government official, who had an entirely sympathetic view and saw the potential for Renault. He completely changed the company's approach to passenger safety and Renault eventually produced the first ever five-star car, a level of passenger safety not thought possible in the mid-1990s. Even the new, tougher EU legislation was only a little better than the equivalent of one of Euro NCAP's stars. Safety has been a major selling point for Renault ever since and other manufacturers have followed their lead. The conventional wisdom that 'safety doesn't sell' has long since been discredited.

By 2011 nearly all passenger cars on the roads of the EU complied with the new 1998 crash-test standards. These regulations had created a mandatory minimum level of safety and Euro NCAP was by then providing an incentive to build cars that far exceed the legislative standards. This has transformed the safety of cars on the roads of Europe and many neighbouring countries. Five-star cars are now the norm rather than an exception.

Recognising this success, the European Commission described Euro NCAP as the most cost-effective EU road safety initiative of the previous 20 years.* In the UK, the Department for Transport estimates that half the improvement in road safety in the last 15 years is the result of improved passenger car safety. Across the EU since 2000, road fatalities have dropped by just under 50 per cent, resulting in a reduction of over 100,000 in the number of road deaths that would have occurred had things continued with no change. As much as 40 per cent of this improvement is due to the combined effect of the 1998 EU crash-test standards and the creation of Euro NCAP.

As these figures began to emerge, I felt we had achieved something really worthwhile. All the meetings, travelling, early-morning starts and heated arguments seemed justified. This was a truly crucial triumph. You could achieve a certain amount in motor sport, but these figures were many orders of magnitude more significant. You never meet the people who are alive and uninjured as a direct result of all that effort, but you know they are out there and that is deeply satisfying.

In January 2006, the work we had all done on road safety in the previous 12 years was recognised by the French government. The French foreign minister held a reception for us at the Quai d'Orsay and awarded me the Légion d'honneur. He made a very kind speech recognising what we had done for road safety internationally. The European Commission invited me to join its CARS 21 High Level Group for the European car industry – many of the CEOs of the big car companies were also members and by now relations with the industry were friendly. I think behind the rhetoric many of them secretly agreed with much of what we had been doing to improve safety standards. No one could really be happy with thousands of avoidable deaths on European roads.

* EU Commission's *Communication on Road Safety* (17/3/2000 Com2000 125 final)

Less pressing but nevertheless important was the environment. There was a great deal of work to do in Brussels. We ran a campaign to reduce sulphur levels in fuel, essential for really low emissions because sulphur damages catalysers. We were opposed by a determined oil industry because reducing the amount of sulphur in fuel increases refining costs. They were much more united than the car industry but the zeitgeist was against them, particularly in northern Europe.

We also secured a legal requirement for catalysers to work in freezing conditions. That is why the unpleasant smell in urban areas on cold mornings has gone. The car industry was not pleased. One big manufacturer showed us the new cold rooms in their R&D centre and, only half-jokingly, told me, 'This is all your fault!' But in the end the extra cost was the same for everyone and the improvement in air quality on frosty days is palpable. In a similar way, the CEO of a major car company told me, again half-jokingly, that the irritating beeping in modern cars if the seatbelt is not fastened was my fault. This was partly true because the beeper is important for a good NCAP score. But if it persuades more people to fasten their belts it will save lives.

In 1995 we started a carbon sequestration project with Edinburgh University, with the objective of making Formula One carbon neutral. It was intended to be purely symbolic because the amount of carbon produced by Formula One was negligible in the real world. However, we wanted to draw attention to the CO_2 problem that was already apparent, even then. But despite being able to say Grand Prix racing was now greener than athletics (because we were removing all Formula One's CO_2 from the atmosphere but no one was removing the CO_2 produced by the exertions of athletes), it proved impossible to interest the media. In 2014, the IPCC took up the idea, suggesting that trees should be planted on a huge scale to avoid irreversible climate change. We had persevered and the project continues to this day, but even the most rational campaigns don't work until their time comes. They need to resonate with the public. Euro NCAP might well have failed had we done it ten or 15 years earlier.

31

GLOBAL ROAD SAFETY

Soon after the EU applied Alan and David's front and side crash-test standards for which we had lobbied so hard, the United Nations adopted them as Regulations 94 and 95 respectively. This was very significant because the standards have gradually been adopted in an increasing number of countries (most recently India in January 2015), making them today the benchmark around the world. We don't have figures for the number of lives this has saved and continues to save but we know it is very significant indeed.

Harmonisation reduces costs and helps consumers by making safer products more widely available, but promoting it is often a challenge, particularly as Europe and the US have a different approach to regulatory systems (type-approval versus self-certification). Even though the resulting standards do not differ much, they have never been fully harmonised. Nevertheless, in 1996 the EU and the US launched the Transatlantic Business Dialogue to try to encourage regulatory harmonisation. Automobile standards were included in the talks and the EU and US

Department of Commerce held a major conference on the subject in Washington in April that year. Alan Donnelly was invited to participate in his role as the European Parliament's rapporteur for the automobile industry and David Ward arranged for the FIA to host the conference dinner.

As the joint host of the dinner together with Martin Bangemann, the EU industry commissioner, I was able to give a speech in favour of harmonisation and propose a new approach to the UN's automotive regulation system. We proposed that the relatively obscure UN working party in Geneva be reorganised as a World Forum for Motor Vehicle Harmonisation and, crucially, that it should have the specific goal of consumer protection and high safety and emission standards. This, I explained, would 'result in less expensive cars and bring benefits to the ordinary motorist'. These suggestions were well received, not just by Bangemann but also by Ricardo Martinez, head of the US National Highway Safety Administration.

Following the Washington meeting, the EU and the US held further negotiations and the UN adopted a new regulatory agreement in 1998. This supplemented rather than replaced the existing 1958 agreement but, importantly, it now included the United States. As we had recommended, the name of the working party was changed and the new agreement included provisions for consumer protection and high safety standards. Since then, the 1998 agreement has produced a number of important global technical regulations for key safety issues, such as pedestrian protection and electronic stability control (the anti-skid technology), all very important progress not just from an FIA perspective but also from a human perspective, avoiding thousands of casualties in countries all over the world.

In 2004, after some ten years as chairman of the European

New Car Assessment Programme, Euro NCAP, I stood down in favour of Claes Tingvall of the Swedish Road Administration. Claes is a world-renowned road safety expert and originator of the pioneering 'Vision Zero' road safety concept. His idea was that the target should be a world with no injuries at all on the roads. I was always much more comfortable with this than the more usual approach of saying we must halve the casualties. That seemed to me to imply that half the current number of deaths and injuries was acceptable – not a good message.

Despite standing down as chairman of Euro NCAP, I still had a role in vehicle crash-testing. With David Ward I became involved in the idea of bringing the different NCAPs around the world together, and we started a pilot Latin NCAP project in South America, testing popular cars in Argentina and Brazil. The results were shocking. The top-selling cars all performed very badly, with weak body shells that collapsed on impact and no airbags. It was zero stars all over again and 20 years behind the levels now seen in Europe thanks to the 1998 regulations and Euro NCAP.

The Latin NCAP pilot project led to the launch of Global NCAP in 2011, and I became its inaugural chairman. In 2012, it held its first annual meeting in Melaka, Malaysia, and attracted support from all the NCAPs active around the world. The meeting also featured the launch of another pilot programme for an ASEAN (Association of South-East Asian Nations) NCAP at a crash laboratory built on the edge of the rainforest. It was remarkable to witness an event that was so similar to and yet so different from the original launch of Euro NCAP at the UK's Transport Research Laboratory back in 1997.

The Latin and ASEAN programmes made such remarkable progress that by 2014 both had been able to award five-star scores to some vehicles and make safer cars available more rapidly than Euro NCAP in the 1990s, far faster than would have been possible with legislation alone. It demonstrates the extraordinary power of consumer information to encourage the industry to build better cars. Also in 2014, Global NCAP launched its 'Safer Cars for India' project, testing several popular Indian models and exposing their defects. These startling results were reported throughout India, making an enormous impact, and we visited Delhi in November 2014 for meetings with the government to discuss the problems.

On the same trip we visited China for the Global NCAP annual meeting, where we were amazed by the CATARC test centre and greatly encouraged to hear talk of Vision Zero as a target for road safety in China. Meanwhile, in India the media coverage stimulated consumers to insist that cars should meet the UN crash-test standards and, in January 2015, the government announced the construction of an Indian test facility and the introduction of the UN regulations in 2017. Two decades after Alan Donnelly, David Ward and I first started work on car safety in Europe, it has gone global and shows no sign of diminishing.

Through the FIA Foundation, we were also able to back the International Road Assessment Programme, IRAP. This evaluates the safety of roads in much the same way as NCAP measures the safety of cars. The relationship is analogous to the way in which the FIA specifies measures for the safety of circuits as well as for the cars that race on them. IRAP has demonstrated that there is a very big difference in the casualty rate per kilometre between roads that have modern design elements and those that do not.

So great is the difference that IRAP is able to make an unanswerable business case for governments to accept the relatively modest cost of making roads safer because of the cash savings which result from fewer casualties. In the EU, the average cost to society for each life lost is generally reckoned to be €1 million, taking into account all the direct and indirect costs of removing an economically active person from society early in life. And that's before you look at the human suffering which cannot be quantified in monetary terms. Many of IRAP's requirements are simple and inexpensive – for example, putting the right road markings in the right places – yet have a very big impact on casualty rates. IRAP has been extraordinarily successful and is now active in over 70 countries worldwide. Its chairman, John Dawson, is one of the FIA Foundation's trustees.

We were fully active in Brussels from 1994 until my mandate as FIA president ended in 2009. I continued to undertake all sorts of lobbying activities with David and sometimes Alan, and seemed to be in Brussels almost constantly. By contrast, I only went to two or three Formula One races each year. In 2000, Alan Donnelly left the European Parliament and I persuaded him to become the FIA's permanent representative in the Formula One paddock. Just the person, I thought, to handle the politics. This he did consummately well.

In 2001, I was elected chairman of Brussels-based ERTICO (Intelligent Transport Systems Europe), which brings together car, electronics and telecommunications industries with representatives of (then) 14 EU governments, local authorities, police, IT companies, the car industry and infrastructure operators. Its purpose is to encourage the introduction of electronic and allied systems for better road safety and traffic management. My work there made me aware of the almost unlimited potential of electronics for car safety and the efficient control of traffic.

I am continually surprised by how long the authorities take to adopt new technologies. More than ten years later, cars that drive themselves are only appearing slowly. Advanced technologies for traffic management – for example, cars that 'talk' to each other – have not yet appeared at all, at least not for everyday use. The increase in road capacity that could come from cars being joined electronically does not seem to feature, and even the electronic accident avoidance measures that are now entirely proven are not being introduced as energetically as they should be.

Hoping for early adoption of some of these technologies for road safety, in 2003 I co-founded eSafety Forum with Erkki Liikanen, then EU commissioner for enterprise. Its purpose was to promote modern electronic technology for road safety. He completely understood the potential but, as happens with the European Commission, his mandate came to an end in 2004 and he went back to Finland, where he became chairman of the board of the Bank of Finland and a member of the governing council of the European Central Bank, positions he has held ever since. Had he stayed on at the commission, we might have had some radical proposals for road safety and traffic management. Instead, in 2012 the EU got the Liikanen report on structural reforms of the EU banking sector. The financial crisis had shown how much this was needed but he was nevertheless a great loss to the cause of road safety.

Also in 2003 the European transport ministers (including those from what were then the enlargement countries) met in Verona for a conference on road safety. Among those present was Ms de Palacio, a vice-president of the European Commission and the commissioner in charge of the common transport policy. I found myself on the platform and in a position to say what I thought. So I criticised not just those who were present but politicians in general, saying they never worked seriously on road safety yet were always ready to turn the world upside down for terrorism that killed far fewer people.

I went on to point out that, terrible though the attacks on the World Trade Center in New York had been, the deaths were fewer than the numbers killed every month on the roads in the US at that time and only just equalled the approximately 3000 deaths recorded every single day on the roads worldwide. The problem, I said, was that the politicians seemed to have no imagination. If they had to be present a few times when the police have to visit a family to tell them one of their number has just been killed in a road accident, they might take road safety a little more seriously.

The politicians and the commissioner were not happy with this but, given the opportunity, I thought it important to spell out just how useless they had been with thousands of people needlessly dying and being seriously injured on the roads. The measures needed to reduce casualties drastically were well known and many were already in place in countries like Sweden and even the UK. Two of the transport ministers came up to me afterwards and said they fully agreed, as did a number of senior police. The police are always supportive on road safety, no matter which country you go to, because they see what actually happens and have to deal with the aftermath.

The following year, I was elected ERTICO's president and spokesperson. Two years later, jointly with EU commissioner Viviane Reding, I became patron of the eSafety Aware Communications Platform. This was a public–private initiative to promote accident-avoidance technologies. It was another attempt to convince politicians and the public that modern electronics are going to be the key to so many road safety and traffic management problems.

One of our campaigns included a spectacular demonstration of the effectiveness of electronic stability control. Two parallel slalom courses were set up on a surface that had been made extremely slippery. Two identical cars were lined up, one with a world-class competition driver, the other with an ordinary driver. With the electronic stability control switched off in the expert driver's car, the ordinary driver always won easily. The system is an incredibly effective safety device in difficult situations and quite cheap to fit to a car which already has ABS.* Our campaign was successful and ESC became compulsory on all new cars in the EU from 1 November 2014. It has already been widely adopted and, according to independent studies, avoided some 190,000 accidents and saved more than 6000 lives across Europe. Global NCAP is now looking at mounting a campaign for worldwide introduction.

All this time, David Ward was busy in the United Nations and the World Bank, working on road safety. In 2007, encouraged by David, General Kiryanov, the head of road safety for Russia and president of the Russian Automobile Federation, an FIA member club, organised a major event for the Make Roads Safe campaign at the Tavrichesky Palace, the original seat of the Russian Duma in St Petersburg. Delegations from all the CIS countries (those formerly part of the USSR) were present. The hall was unchanged since Lenin made his April Theses speech from the same podium on the tasks of the proletariat in the

---

* ABS is an anti-lock braking system that prevents a car's wheels locking up, no matter how hard the driver presses the brakes. Preventing the wheels locking increases the rate at which the car will slow but, perhaps more importantly, it also allows the car to be steered round an obstacle with the brakes full on. Without ABS, the car will simply slide into the obstacle with all its wheels locked when making an emergency stop.

revolution, all those years ago. I found it an intriguing place from which to make a speech about road safety.

David was able to progress from this to ensuring that the Make Roads Safe campaign achieved a first-ever United Nations Ministerial Conference on global road safety in 2009 in Moscow, hosted by the then president of the Russian Federation, Dmitry Medvedev. This led to the United Nations General Assembly proclaiming a decade of action for road safety, from 2011 to 2020. It's pleasing to look back to the moment we began the whole thing in Brussels more than 20 years ago and see the progress that has been made. When the result of that first election to the presidency of FISA was announced in 1991, I had no inkling of where it might all end. Had I been told, I would have been very surprised indeed to learn just how far-reaching our achievements would be.

32

TROUBLE WITH
THE EU COMMISSION

At the FIA we were always aware that our position as sole regulator of international motor sport was a source of resentment and perhaps vulnerable to a legal challenge of the kind we ourselves, as FOCA, had planned back in 1980. So, on the advice of our lawyers, Stephen Kinsella and Ken Daly, we sought clearance of our rules from the European Commission. We knew this would be helpful should anyone challenge our activities under EU law. I had it very much in mind that we had planned just such a challenge against the FIA back in 1980 when we were at loggerheads with my predecessor, Jean-Marie Balestre, and even earlier in the 1970s when we had problems with the Formula One race organisers.

More than a year passed with no response from the commission so, in January 1997, Alan Donnelly arranged for me to visit the then commissioner for competition, Karel Van Miert. It was a friendly encounter and Van Miert and I were soon on first name terms. At the same time, I had a conversation about road safety with Neil Kinnock, who was then transport commissioner. At first he seemed very onside with what we were trying to do to improve cars and roads, but a short time later his attitude changed, probably because of the fallout from Bernie's £1 million gift to the Labour Party.

After the Van Miert meeting, the commission suggested sending an official to a Formula One race to get a better understanding of how it all worked. Our lawyers told us to be careful, but we all assumed the commission was acting in good faith. The commission official thought the most useful race for him to attend would be the Monaco Grand Prix. Although Stephen told him Monaco was atypical and Spa (an hour or two from Brussels) would be much better, he insisted on Monaco. We went out of our way to help him when he came down for the race weekend in May 1997; David Ward took him round the paddock and pits, explaining everything. We now know he had been sent on a jolly and to do a bit of spying. At one point he rather mysteriously said to David that we didn't realise what we were up against.

Having enjoyed a very privileged weekend in Monaco, the official left without paying his hotel bill, which came to FF16,900 (€2576). I thought this impolite, to say the least, but when I complained the commission accused me of attempting to damage his promising career. I was very surprised that the commission thought it appropriate for one of its officials to accept hospitality, never mind just take it. As far as I know, no note of the visit ever appeared on the commission's file. What a contrast with American NHTSA officials who accepted an invitation to discuss vehicle safety over breakfast in our Washington hotel but insisted on paying their own bills. Even basic hospitality such as breakfast was off-limits to them, and in their case there was no question of anything contentious.

The official later returned to his native Greece, where he became head of the national competition authority. Unfortunately, there was a problem involving a Greek dairy company that complained to the police that it was being blackmailed in a competition case. In 2006, the promising official was arrested with two others, one of them in possession of €200,000 in marked notes, apparently part of a €2.5 million bribe. As a result, he had another stay in accommodation he had not paid for – this time in Greece and for rather longer than he spent in Monaco.

Not long after the official's visit, the commission began to show signs of hostility towards us, so Stephen pointed out to them that no complaint against the FIA had been lodged. Amazingly, its reaction was 'and don't you find that suspicious?' When one finally came in, a relieved official told Stephen they had 'a number of complaints'; when Stephen pointed out it was just one complaint, the commission's response was 'Well, one is a number.'

The complainant was a man who ran a business filming the FIA truck racing championship and apparently supplied footage to any television station that would take it. We were told his production costs were covered by some of the truck manufacturers. He was unhappy that, in an effort to increase television coverage of motor sport other than Formula One, we were trying to get Bernie (who at the time was the vice-president of the FIA responsible for promotions) to deal with television for all other FIA championships.

It seemed pretty clear to us that Van Miert welcomed the complaint and the probable reason lay in Belgian domestic politics. Coincidentally, in 1997 Belgium banned tobacco advertising and, as a result, there was a threat to cancel the 1998 Belgian Grand

Prix. The rumour was that Van Miert's colleagues in the Belgian Socialist Party had asked him to 'do something' in the wholly unrelated competition area where he had considerable power. Whatever the reason, Van Miert now became aggressive. The car industry lobbying and the Belgian Grand Prix problem probably explain the promising official's rather mysterious warning to David.

In November 1997, the commission published two notices in its *Official Journal* detailing summaries of the FIA's notifications and inviting third-party comments. Then in December it sent us warning letters. In essence, the European Commission was saying the FIA had a dominant position in motor sport and was abusing it. The letters set out the commission's view of possible infringements of EU competition law. They are supposed to be confidential, so we were very surprised to find details of the letters a day or two later in a number of newspapers, including the *Financial Times* and the *Wall Street Journal*.

It was quite obvious that the commission had deliberately leaked them. We complained but the officials categorically denied it; yet when we investigated further we discovered they were lying. A commission official had called journalists from the major business newspapers into an office and handed them copies of the letters. It was quite clear the whole thing had been set up and planned in advance.

Even before we had replied to the commission's warning letters, in January 1998 Van Miert gave an interview to the *Wall Street Journal* saying the FIA's case was 'the single worst case of antitrust violation' he had ever seen. For him to make such a statement before he or his officials had seen our response – or had any opportunity to consider the case – was a gross breach of the rules. But our protests achieved nothing.

In June 1998 there was an FIA General Assembly in Stockholm, where I took the opportunity to tell the assembly what was going on and asked for authority to do whatever was necessary to respond to our treatment by the commission. There was a strong sense of outrage and the assembly agreed unanimously. This was very significant and confirmed my decision to take the gloves off. I was now in a position to launch an all-out attack on the commission should this become necessary.

I could also threaten the nuclear option (although none of us wanted to use it) of saying the FIA would treat the EU as a single country when allocating events counting for the FIA championships. The remaining 115 FIA member countries would then continue to arrange their affairs as they always had. The FIA was, after all, a world body. It would be for the EU to decide if it wanted to be part of the international motor sport community, in which case it would have to comply with the international rules – our rules. The EU's position would then have been analogous to that of the USSR before it broke up, with one country holding a number of votes. Our event calendars always had to be representative, and treating the EU as a single country would have meant that more major events would be held outside the EU and the number of Formula One World Championship races in the EU would have been significantly reduced. There would have been more than one, but certainly not ten out of 16, as was the case in 1998.

Meanwhile, the commission had continued to lie about leaking the letters, even when confronted with incontrovertible evidence. Finally, on 6 April 1998, it admitted the warning letters had indeed been given to the press. Astonishingly, though, it seemed there was nothing we could do about it. Our complaints were simply ignored until our lawyers suggested that the commission's actions amounted to a 'decision'. This meant we could treat it like any other decision and submit an appeal against it to the European Court of Justice.

So, in May 1998, the FIA lodged an action against the commission in the European Court of First Instance. The judge supervising the case could see what a mess Van Miert and the commission had made. He called a meeting in Luxembourg and pointed out that it would be disastrous for the commission to lose. He suggested it should settle, publish a press release (drafted by our lawyers) apologising for the leak and Van Miert's prejudicial statements, and pay our legal expenses. In July 1999, the commission duly issued a formal public apology to the FIA and paid an unprecedented €40,000 towards our legal costs.

The previous month, the commission had issued its Statement of Objections. We decided to put the entire statement and our response on our website. The commission objected but we pointed out that, in contrast to the warning letters, this was not a leak – the SO was just like any other letter it might have sent us and our property to do with as we pleased. Publishing the commission's Statement of Objections was unprecedented (and, as far as I know, still is) but it allowed us to hold up its case to ridicule. An entertaining postscript was that when we had finally settled everything, the commission asked us to take it all down from our website.

A useful development came in 1999 when allegations of financial mismanagement resulted in the entire commission, including Van Miert, resigning in disgrace. With Van Miert removed, we soon had a new competition commissioner, Mario Monti (later Italian prime minister). He was a well-known professor of economics and was more realistic and far more intelligent than Van Miert who, powerful though he had been, was only ever a small-time Belgian politician. We were optimistic because Monti understood motor sport and the special difficulties and dangers it faced. His Italian background helped: as a small boy he had been in the back of his parents' car when they gave Fangio, a family friend, a lift back to Milan after he had won the Italian Grand Prix at Monza. Monti Jr was holding the cup.

Despite that promising development, the same hostile officials were still in charge and the commission's attitude did not seem to have changed, so we decided to up the pressure. In February 2000, we called a press conference in the commission's own Borschette press centre and revealed its idea that there should be several regulators for international motor sport, all competing with one another. A reasonably intelligent ten-year-old would see that the only way regulators could compete would be by reducing costs and hence safety. The commission had also said each Formula One team should be free to deal with its own television rights. It seems they hadn't reflected on the practical difficulties this would cause or considered the next logical step: each of 22 players in a major football match dealing with his or her individual television rights. We handed out a five-page letter I had written to Monti calling for an inquiry and saying the commission had 'displayed incompetence amounting to abuse'.

Our criticisms received wide publicity. This was an entirely new experience for DG Comp. The major companies it dealt with were invariably terrified of an adverse decision. Big public companies with shareholders and boards of directors could never attack the commission as we could. Once I had a mandate from the FIA General Assembly I effectively had carte blanche, subject only to following the advice of our lawyers at all times. The commission was clearly shocked by the attack – but what it didn't know was that Ken Daly had actually toned down some of my more aggressive comments. However, the essential criticisms were still there. It tried to respond with a letter signed by Monti, but it was now clear that Monti himself had become aware of the problem. Once he took charge, an intelligent dialogue became possible.

Apart from the commission's strangely irrational approach before the arrival of Monti, another disquieting element was constant pressure on Bernie to reach a deal with the cameraman who filmed the truck racing, as well as with a French race series organiser who complained some time later. The pressure came from an Irish official who had been in charge of our case from the beginning under Van Miert. All his suggestions would have involved payments to those who had complained.

Although I could understand an official wanting to get a complaint off his desk, it seemed to me improper that he should encourage one party to a complaint to pay off another. Either EU competition law was being broken or it was not. If it was, the commission should take action. If it was not, the commission should tell the complainant he had nothing to complain about. In neither case would a payment by one to the other, brokered by the commission, be appropriate. It would be easy in such cases to feel one was being shaken down with the help of the commission. In the same class was the failure of the commission to see anything wrong in its promising Greek official helping himself to thousands of euros of free hospitality at the Monaco Grand Prix. On top of all this, a woman fundraiser working for the business school at Nyenrode University, in Holland, approached Bernie for money. It turned out that this was where Van Miert was now working following his retirement from the commission. Perhaps the commission saw all this as quite normal, but we didn't.

After a further six months or so of detailed exchanges, we reached a settlement with the commission under which the FIA would not participate commercially in Formula One but would retain an exclusive power to authorise international events, issue competition and circuit licences and enforce its rules. This power was recognised and endorsed by the commission on the basis that the objectives of the rules were safety and fairness, and there would be no attempt by the FIA to exploit its powers for profit.

The commission also accepted that competition between bodies enforcing safety rules would inevitably lead to one body demanding measures that were less expensive, and therefore probably less safe, than its rival in order to get the business of a circuit or event promoter. The idea that motor sport safety might become the responsibility of public authorities fell to pieces as soon as the practicalities of attempting it internationally were considered. And that was without looking at the record of the public authorities in vehicle safety before the FIA got involved.

The quid pro quo for the FIA's authority was that we had to be completely neutral between rival series of races or rallies and also between individual events. We had to be prepared to authorise, for example, a rival series to Formula One (or any other motor sport competition) provided our standard requirements for safety and fairness were met. We could charge a fee for our services in regulating each championship but we must not share in any profit. This was to avoid us being in any way tempted to favour one championship over another.

We made changes to the International Sporting Code to reflect this agreement. Crucially, once these had been made, the commission approved the code as not anti-competitive under EU law. This confirmed the FIA's power, in an extreme situation, to ban a circuit, a driver or car manufacturer from all international competition. Having this power recognised and accepted by the commission meant that if we were ever faced with an attempt to run a series outside the structures of the FIA, we could bar it and all its participants from all the permanent circuits without any danger that we could be successfully sued under EU competition law. Thus, as explained earlier, if some of the Formula One teams had indeed got together to run their own championship they would have had to run under the FIA and its Sporting Code, including the system of stewards and the FIA's International Court of Appeal.

Moreover, the FIA's contract with Bernie further strengthened our position and would prevent him getting together with the teams and attempting to operate outside the FIA. He still wanted to extend its life beyond 2010 but the commission would not agree an extra ten years. Indeed, they considered the existing 15-year deal too long. They asserted that under EU law, we could not make a contract with a particular entity for more than three to five years.

But there was nothing to prevent us selling outright whatever rights we had in the Formula One World Championship, which we could do without breaching competition rules. So, with our lawyers, we hit on the idea of a long lease. As the length of a lease grows, we argued, it becomes increasingly close to a freehold or an outright sale. As there was no competition law objection to an outright sale, we suggested we sell the rights for a hundred years.

This, we explained, would be virtually indistinguishable from an outright sale but, like the owner of leased land in the UK, we would retain certain veto controls over Formula One, in particular the right to ensure sporting fairness and minimum safety

standards as well as media access by the public. This was analogous to the way in which the great leasehold estates in England
retain all sorts of rights to enforce rules about what their lease-
holders may and may not do. It was also consistent with our
mandate for safety and fairness.

The Brussels legal establishment thought this couldn't possibly work – if five years was the limit, they said, a hundred years
was outrageous. But they had not really understood the concept
that our outstanding Brussels legal team, Stephen Kinsella and
Ken Daly, had come up with. More importantly, the group by
then working on our case in the commission and Mario Monti
himself had fully understood the concept and agreed with it. Our
lawyers later received a prestigious award for their work on our
case from the relevant branch of their profession.

Meanwhile, Van Miert had retired to his home base in
Belgium. He produced an autobiography, *Markt-Macht-Wettbewerb*
(Market-Power-Competition), sadly not available in English, in
which he revealed that Bernie had sought a meeting with him.
He said that when they met, it turned out to be like a sort of con-
fessional, with Bernie telling Van Miert he secretly hoped
eventually to become president of the FIA. I can just picture the
scene and, had I been there, it would have wrecked everything.
One of Bernie's regular complaints about me was that I could
never keep a straight face. In Balestre's day I used to have to
knock papers onto the floor during World Council meetings so
that I could laugh unobserved under the table. I learned to do
this in my Bar days, at a planning inquiry where an expert witness began his evidence with the words, 'I've been in sewage all
my life.' It was typical of Bernie to wind up someone like Van
Miert with an obviously absurd story. But then he never could
resist that sort of thing.

Agreeing not to profit commercially from any of the FIA championships was a small price to pay for the official right to be the sole regulator of international motor sport. The FIA had only ever charged a fee and expenses for putting an event on the calendar. Commercial exploitation had always been left to the event organiser. It was only Bernie's systematic acquisition of the Formula One organisers' rights that had changed any of the practices of the previous 80 years. Regulating international motor sport was the raison d'être of the FIA's sporting division. Also, as a general principle, there is much to be said for keeping a regulatory body away from the commercial side of big-time sport. The sort of international committee you need for sporting rules is not necessarily the right body to take decisions involving the allocation of events and massive amounts of money.

While all this was going on we decided to open up a second front with Brussels, this time involving the international sporting community. Although motor sport was not part of the Olympic movement, the FIA always had excellent relations with the International Olympic Committee. It was the Italian Olympic Committee, for example, that organised the Rome symposium on dangerous sports in June 1997, at which Sir Maurice Drake spoke and which alerted the Italian authorities to the dangers of the inappropriate use of the criminal law in sport.

In October 1997 we informed the IOC about the growing problem with the EU Commission's Competition Directorate and the dangers it presented for sport in general. The IOC president, Juan Antonio Samaranch, called a preliminary meeting on the question of sport in the EU and invited the FIA and three other major sports federations to Lausanne. We suggested we should form a united front and explain to the commission that sport should have a special status and was not just another commercial activity. What was needed was recognition of the special status of sport in the EU treaty, and there was now an opportunity to achieve this because a new treaty was being planned to deal with EU enlargement.

At the next meeting, Samaranch said he had discussed getting sport into the treaty with Helmut Kohl, the German chancellor, who had promised it would happen at the next EU summit. But David explained that a treaty change was not straightforward – it required an Intergovernmental Conference and unanimous agreement of the EU member states. Having Chancellor Kohl on board was not enough, because at least two, perhaps even three, countries (including the UK) were against any increase in EU competencies.

Samaranch was plainly displeased but at least the IOC now understood the realities of the situation. We invited him to a meeting we had arranged for the international sports federations in Downing Street with Tony Blair, Chris Smith, then Secretary of State for Culture, Media and Sport, and Jonathan Powell, Blair's chief of staff, which proved a success and helped change the UK position on sport in the new treaty.

In October 1998, the European Commission launched a consult- ation on the 'European Model of Sport'; and in February 1999 the FIA hosted a workshop in Brussels for the motor sport ACNs and ASNs to discuss and agree a draft memorandum on the FIA's position. Following this, the FIA published its memorandum on 'Sport and the EU' as our contribution to the EU-wide con- sultation. The memorandum advocated recognition of sport in the EU treaty but always subject to unanimous voting. It also called on the commission to recognise the self-regulatory func- tion of sports governing bodies as well as their global role. And it proposed a voluntary code of practice for sports governance. All this was, of course, directly relevant to our dispute with the commission's DG Comp.

In December 2000, during the French EU presidency's summit, the EU adopted the Nice Declaration on Sport. This recognised the self-governance of sport 'on the basis of a democratic and transparent method of operation', and also set out the solidarity principle that top-level sport should help encourage participation and the growth of grassroots sport. The declaration stated: 'These social functions entail special responsibilities for federations and provide the basis for their competence in organising competitions.' This was very much what we wanted and effectively overruled the commission.

In the summer of 2000, the FIA established a Governance in Sport working group which prepared a draft 'Statement of Good Governance Principles for Sports Governing Bodies'. The following February, the FIA, the European Olympic Committee and Herbert Smith, the UK law firm that had represented the FIA in Brussels, jointly hosted 'The Rules of the Game', Europe's first ever conference on the governance of sport. The conference was attended by more than 170 delegates and adopted the principles proposed by the working group. The main speakers were Mario Monti, the competition commissioner, Jacques Rogge and me together with Stephen Kinsella, who had been instrumental in setting up the conference and formulating the proposed rules. Jacques Rogge, who was elected IOC president later that year, subsequently told us that the feedback from the National Olympic Committees and international sports federations had been very positive. The conference report is still in use as a reference on sports governance.

The FIA occupied the middle ground between the National Olympic Committees and the football federations. We had good relations with FIFA, the Fédération Internationale de Football Association (its president, Sepp Blatter, was at one time involved with Formula One as director of sports timing for Longines), and we shared its concerns about a regulatory role for the EU, but we also supported the IOC's interest in EU sports programmes. The FIA helped develop a compromise and in June 2004 the EU agreed a revised text for a draft constitution that included the federations' article on sport. The Lisbon Treaty, including that article, was agreed in 2009. As a result, sport was no longer menaced by suggestions that its governing bodies should be treated as if they were ordinary commercial entities.

I occasionally reflected on the idea that the FIA should propose a new division of the Olympic movement for mechanised sport, a third leg to take its place alongside the Summer and Winter Olympics. In that way, all the different modern powered sports could be represented in one great competition every four years. It was an intriguing idea and certainly very ambitious, but I never made the approach or mentioned it despite the many meetings I had with Samaranch or Jacques Rogge, his successor. Perhaps I should have but there always seemed to be too many other pressing issues.

33

THE *NEWS OF THE WORLD*

On a Sunday like any other in March 2008 a phone call from the FIA's press chief, Richard Woods, informed me something entirely private I had done two days earlier was all over the *News of the World*. The newspaper is now closed but it had always been notorious for publishing any sort of salacious material it could get its hands on. I had no inkling that they were planning a story about me – there had been no phone call from them to seek a comment or any reason to suppose they were up to something. The first I heard was Richard's phone call at around 10.30 that Sunday morning, when the paper was already in nearly three million homes.

It was not a paper I ever read so I went to the nearest newsagent and bought two copies – one for me, the other for the lawyers. It was the main story on the front page and inside there was more, plus photographs that seemed to have been taken from a video. It was not immediately clear how the video had been made, but it was evident that they were pictures of an S&M encounter I had had with five ladies two days earlier. It was entirely consensual, harmless and light-hearted, and ended with a cup of tea and, for some, a glass of wine. Importantly, it was something that everyone present had agreed beforehand would remain entirely confidential and a secret between the participants, whom I considered to be friends.

Having got hold of the paper, I had to show it to Jean. Her immediate reaction was that I'd had it printed specially by a joke shop – it's the sort of thing I might well have done. She had no idea that once in a while I got up to that sort of thing. Until that morning it had been a very small part of my life; something I did occasionally when the mood took me.

Worse even than the photographs and standard tabloid text was the newspaper's claim that what had taken place had involved 'Nazi' role-play. The outrageous headline, covering almost the entire front page, read: 'F1 Boss Has Sick Nazi Orgy with 5 Hookers'. The Nazi accusation was an outright and deliberate lie. It had never crossed any of the participants' minds that what we were doing had any Nazi connotations whatsoever. But I knew immediately that the *News of the World*'s Nazi characterisation would be used against me.

The only German element was that I spoke the language for some of the time to one of the ladies who is German. She was the sort of modern German citizen who would have been outraged had she been asked to enact some sort of Nazi scene, just as I would. We spoke German because another of the ladies liked to be given orders in a foreign language she didn't understand. I know it sounds odd, but then S&M and much else to do with sex is indeed odd. What took place was just classic S&M, as the *News of the World*, of all papers, would have known perfectly well. Yet they were trying to pretend it was a scene from a Nazi concentration camp.

It emerged later that the newspaper's journalists had invented the Nazi allegation in an attempt to give their story a public interest element. Without some sort of public interest justification, it would have been quite blatantly illegal to publish the story in the UK, and even more so the photographs that had been taken secretly in a private place without the consent of any of those involved.

As a general rule, sexual activity between consenting adults, even if not to everyone's taste, is considered a private matter in the UK and in most civilised countries. Unless there is some genuine public interest in publishing (something more than it merely being of interest to some of the public), it is illegal to invade someone's privacy by publishing pictures or a description of something done behind closed doors that everyone has agreed to keep confidential.

The newspaper's editor, Colin Myler, knew he was on very thin ice legally, particularly in publishing the pictures. He had a problem because the pictures in no way supported any Nazi allegation. He had no public interest fig leaf. So he took enormous trouble to make sure I didn't find out before the story was on the streets. He admitted later in court that he feared I would ask a judge to stop the story (by way of an injunction) because it was a clear invasion of privacy. He knew the request would in all probability have been granted.

Because of the danger of an injunction, the story was kept secret among a small group of editorial staff and, to reduce still further the chance that I would find out before it was published, the newspaper even went to the trouble and expense of producing a 'spoof' early edition with a completely different front-page story and no mention of what was to come in the main edition. They did this in case someone bought the first edition at around 10pm on the Saturday night and tipped me off. Then I would have been able to seek an urgent injunction from the duty judge. All these elaborate steps were taken on the basis that, once the story is on the streets, the victim will not sue. The reasons why people don't sue, no matter how serious the invasion of privacy, became clear at my first meeting with the lawyers.

Given my antecedents, the newspaper's front-page headline with the 'Nazi' story was, of course, particularly offensive and damaging. I was very surprised by this attack – it was plainly illegal and I could not see why the paper should want to break the law in order to damage me. I had never done any harm to its owner, Rupert Murdoch, or to those who worked for him, yet they had deliberately set out to damage me in a particularly malicious way. Possibly they hoped to sell a few newspapers, although I was not one of their usual celebrity targets. It seemed odd that they should pick on me when they were running a profitable business and surely did not want needlessly to stir up trouble. However, they were probably very confident I would not sue. That their actions might ultimately have wider consequences is unlikely to have crossed their minds.

Whatever their reasons, as far as I was concerned this was a declaration of war. Murdoch's company had attacked me gratuitously and in a most vicious and dishonest way. I could never undo what they had done, or remove the story from the public mind, but I decided to respond by whatever lawful means were open to me. At the very least I hoped to make it more difficult for them to do the same thing to anyone else. I already knew they were in the habit of 'exposing' private sexual activity by people who lacked the resources to take them on, although I didn't at that time know of the resulting suicides. But I resolved to try to put a stop to this sort of thing once and for all.

The immediate aftermath was very busy. Straightaway it was obvious that one of the participants had made the video using a hidden camera. Looking at the pictures, we later worked out which of them (later named Woman E) was responsible. But, for the moment, I didn't know how it had reached the *News of the World*.

After the paper came out on the Sunday, my solicitor, Dominic Crossley, had immediately retained David Sherborne, the go-to barrister for privacy and defamation. Two days later we met in his chambers.

I quickly discovered some disturbing facts about bringing a claim for invasion of privacy. Because the paper had behaved illegally we would almost certainly win if we brought proceedings, but that was by no means the whole story. By suing, the entire case would be heard in open court. Everything private would be exposed all over again, with a full press gallery reporting every detail. The coverage becomes positively parasitical and newspapers like the *Daily Mail* would be there, slavering over the details. Worse still, this would happen when the original story had begun to fade from the public mind. No wonder victims were so easily discouraged from fighting back.

On top of this, there was the question of cost. I would be out of pocket whatever the result. Even if I won, damages in privacy cases were very low and would almost certainly not cover the difference between the costs awarded by the court and my solicitors' bill. And if by any chance I lost, it could cost me £1 million because I would have to pay the costs of the *News of the World*'s lawyers as well as all my own.

But the most inimical and unjust deterrent of all was the discovery that the newspaper would almost certainly make something called a Part 36 offer, which has the effect of making the winner liable for all the costs if the damages do not exceed the offer. The newspaper's legal team could offer a modest amount by way of settlement, but enough to exceed the likely damages. As a result, if I continued with the action and (as was likely) recovered less by way of damages than they had offered, I would pay all the costs even if I won my case.

I began to understand why the *News of the World* went to so much trouble to make sure I didn't find out what they were doing and restrain them with an injunction. They knew they were breaking the law but could be confident I would be so inhibited by embarrassment and the costs that I would not sue them. No one sued for breach of privacy once the story was out on the streets. If you didn't find out beforehand and obtain an injunction, the law would not help you – on the contrary, it would simply add to the damage you had suffered by allowing further publicity from proceedings in open court and charge you royally for doing so. It was as if you sued someone for breaking your leg, only to find the court's remedy was to break the other leg and send you a large bill into the bargain.

In addition to finding out about the legal risks, I also had friends and relations urging me not to sue, though Jean and both our sons were not among them. It should not be forgotten that, at this stage (before Leveson and the phone-hacking scandal), UK tabloid newspapers and Murdoch's in particular were extremely powerful. Their influence included close relationships with senior police officers and politicians, in addition to Murdoch's enormous wealth. Bernie told me he had been telephoned by an Australian friend of Murdoch, asking: 'Does Max know what he's taking on?' Bernie replied that he thought I probably did, but he wasn't sure about Murdoch.

As far as I was concerned, Murdoch and his *News of the World* had started a war. You can't fight a war without casualties. I was determined to fight and I intended to do my best to see that, in the end, their casualties were heavier than mine. In particular, I intended to try to put an end to the *News of the World*'s business model, which primarily consisted of illegally publishing private information about individuals for no better reason than financial gain. I thought it scandalous that they did this safe in the knowledge that hardly anyone would be prepared to tolerate the additional publicity or be able to afford the financial risk of taking them to court. I was very aware it might take a long time and cost a lot of money, but that's how wars are.

I resolved to see it through whatever the cost. I told the lawyers I would not accept any Part 36 offer, no matter how big. I was going to force Colin Myler and his reporter, Neville Thurlbeck,* into the witness box and expose them for the liars they were. If I ended up paying all the costs, so be it. At this stage I knew nothing of the further information that would eventually emerge about illegal activities at the *News of the World*.

As it was, they never made the Part 36 offer. It seems they thought that once I understood how much additional publicity there would be from a trial, and that it would cost me tens of thousands of pounds even if I won, I would not go through with it. And they certainly thought the ladies, named Women A to E in the legal proceedings to protect their identities, would refuse to come to court. It became clear later that they had completely underestimated the people involved. Also, I suspect they didn't want me to accept their offer and be able to tell the world I had won. Their arrogance in those days was such that they would have found even that small reverse hard to swallow.

---

* In 2014, Thurlbeck was sentenced to six months' imprisonment for conspiring to intercept communications and the unlawful interception of voicemail messages.

That arrogance cost them a million pounds – a seven-figure mistake, by Murdoch's lawyers. Had they made the offer, it would certainly have been for more than the very modest (even if record) damages awarded by Mr Justice Eady, so I, not the newspaper, would have ended up paying the £1 million costs. But the lawyers, I suppose, had even bigger worries at exactly this time because of the chairman of the Professional Footballers' Association, Gordon Taylor.

Taylor was one of the phone-hacking victims mentioned in court when the *News of the World*'s royal reporter, Clive Goodman, and the paper's private investigator, Glenn Mulcaire, pleaded guilty to phone hacking at the end of 2006. The *News of the World* management were desperately trying to maintain their lie that only Goodman, their 'rogue reporter', had hacked phones. They were trying to pretend that no one else at the paper was involved, but Taylor sued them, claiming they had hacked his phone. Moreover, he had evidence that the hacking was done by someone other than Goodman and that there were a very significant number of additional victims. Had the Taylor story become public, it would have shown that illegal phone hacking was a fundamental part of the *News of the World*'s business and being conducted on an industrial scale.

We later learned that it was at the beginning of June 2008, about five weeks before my case came to court and after receiving leading counsel's opinion, that the *News of the World*'s in-house lawyer Tom Crone sent James Murdoch the notorious 'unfortunately it's as bad as we feared' email referring to the hacking of voicemails. Having received that email, the only way James could later claim he was not fully informed about the extent of phone hacking was to say he never read it. Needless to say, I find his explanation absurd.

A few days later, notwithstanding his claimed lack of knowledge of the contents of the email, James authorised a settlement with Taylor for a reputed £700,000, far in excess of any damages Taylor could conceivably have won had he pursued the case in court. If James didn't know about the phone hacking, it follows that he didn't know why he was paying all that money. Yes, it's an unlikely tale but presumably it was either that or admit to covering up criminality. The newspaper's secret was protected by a stringent confidentiality clause in its settlement contract with Taylor.

Given the management's simultaneous battle with Taylor, they certainly had their hands full. Nevertheless, in the middle of all their worries about Taylor, the *News of the World* probably realised within a day or two of the story appearing that I was likely to sue. They were not expecting this. Their calculations were always based on the cynical assumption that their victim would be deeply ashamed, retreat into hiding until things died down and be too intimidated to fight back.

But, if I sued, they knew they had a major problem because the 'Nazi' element was a lie. Without it they were in a hopeless legal position on privacy – what took place was merely lawful consensual sexual activity between adults. It might be unconventional but it was entirely legal. If you could publish pictures like those, you could publish a video taken with a camera hidden in a hotel room of two celebrities making out. If there were no public interest in publishing the story, the victim's right to privacy under the Human Rights Act prevailed.

Their Nazi invention was intended to give their story a supposed public interest defence. The idea was that, as head of a world body with members from a great variety of ethnic backgrounds, I should not be doing something that was (falsely) described as 'Nazi'.

Having concocted then published the 'Nazi' falsehood, they now desperately needed to find a way to back it up in court. The solution was typical of their approach to journalism. It involved one of their tried and tested techniques: they would attempt to blackmail the women, or at least some of them, into confirming the story. Blackmail was, after all, one of the *News of the World*'s standard practices, as we were all to learn a few years later when the criminal trials started.

As a seasoned Murdoch man, Neville Thurlbeck, the paper's chief reporter who had written the story, knew exactly how to go about this. He obtained the email addresses of two of the participants and wrote to them, saying he would publish their pictures openly and without pixelation the following Sunday. He attached the unpixelated pictures to his emails so they could have no doubt about what he was threatening to publish.

On the other hand, he explained, if they co-operated with him he would pay them £8000 and give them what he called 'anonimity' (sic). He knew the girls were vulnerable to this sort of blackmail because of what he had learned about them and their families from Woman E. He also knew three of them had significant careers. They all led very normal lives apart from their unusual sexual interests.

Criminal blackmail was so much a part of the *News of the World* and News Corporation ethic that Rupert Murdoch could not see anything wrong with Thurlbeck's approach when his paper's conduct in my case was put to him during the Leveson Inquiry into the UK press, set up by the prime minister in 2011 following the revelation that the *News of the World* had hacked into the phone of a murdered teenager. He told the inquiry: 'A journalist doing a favour for someone in returning (sic) for a favour back is pretty much everyday practice.' No doubt under pressure from his lawyers, he later put in a second witness statement devoted almost entirely to this matter in which he finally admitted Thurlbeck's conduct was wrong.

Three days after the story broke, I arranged to meet Woman A. Before doing so, I needed to ensure we were not observed or overheard or, worse still, photographed together. I asked Quest, a security firm headed by Lord Stevens who had the necessary expert personnel, to provide counter-surveillance. It was all very cloak and dagger. Quest told me to collect Woman A from an agreed spot in Hyde Park using a taxi and then go to a mysterious garden off the Kings Road which they already had covered. While there, they gave both of us equipment to ensure future communications were secure.

With Woman A's help, I quickly identified who had made the film, later known as Woman E. She was a close and trusted friend of Woman A. They saw a lot of each other and sometimes looked after each other's children. For Woman A, it was a horrifying betrayal. In the world they shared, confidentiality was fundamental. Among other details, Woman A knew Woman E's husband worked for MI5, the UK's internal secret service. He was a surveillance expert and a former Royal Marine. Later, I arranged for his employers to be informed that he had set the whole thing up with the *News of the World*. MI5 immediately got rid of him.

Sitting in the Kings Road garden, Woman A was adamant that she and the others would stand firm. Neither the blackmail nor the bribes would work. That was very courageous as she, like the other three, had a great deal to lose if the newspaper published her name and photograph. She also said they would all be prepared to give evidence if I took the paper to court and they could do so anonymously. The lawyers were surprised and delighted when I told them this. It was vital because I particularly needed to prove the Nazi allegation was false. This was important, not just to destroy the newspaper's public interest defence but also for my own reputation.

The women, of course, could confirm that nothing Nazi had occurred or had been discussed or even remotely contemplated. Having the participants there was also going to be bad for the newspaper, who would have liked people to think I was abusing women who were vulnerable or had in some way been coerced. The last thing they wanted was for it to become obvious that these were successful and independent women who happened to have slightly unconventional tastes. The *Daily Mail* went on peddling the abused women thesis long after the facts became known. In truth, the ladies were more into what they did than I had ever been, but I don't think the *Mail* has ever worried very much about the truth.

When we finished the discussion, one of the Quest operatives hailed a taxi in the Kings Road. He called Woman A and me and we jumped in so that I could take her to a mainline station to get a train home. Then, in the taxi, her mobile phone rang. It was Woman B, who had just had a phone call at her workplace from Thurlbeck. He was threatening her even more strongly than he had in his emails. He said he would expose her if she didn't co-operate and she was very alarmed that he had traced her to her place of work. Woman A told her not to worry, we were preparing a counterattack.

Meanwhile, the legal action was well under way and the lawyers had put together an application for an injunction to get the video and pictures removed from the *News of the World*'s website. The need for an injunction arose because, having initially agreed with my lawyers to remove the article, pictures and video from their website, they decided a few days later to put it all back.

The application was heard by Mr Justice Eady on the Friday, with judgment reserved to the following Monday. When the judgment came, Eady refused the injunction, saying that he did so 'with reluctance'. He said there was no public interest in their continued publication but the pictures had already had such wide circulation (the newspaper claimed millions of hits globally) that to make an order to stop them now would be futile. The judge said he did not want to be like King Canute trying to hold back the waves.

Had we appealed, I think we would have won – after all, each new publication of the pictures is a fresh invasion of privacy – but there was a vital element in this first judgment that we could not put at risk. He had granted an expedited trial. This was extremely important. Had the trial come on in the normal way, I would have had to wait 18 months or so before I could prove the *News of the World*'s editor and his journalists had invented and then lied about the Nazi element. With an order for a speedy trial, a full hearing could be scheduled in July, about three months after the publication, an almost unprecedentedly quick timeframe for a full High Court trial. An appeal would have made that impossible.

A delay of 18 months would have made everything academic as far as the FIA went, as, by then, my mandate would have finished and my long-planned retirement from motor sport started. For the same reason, we did not sue for defamation over the Nazi allegation. This would also have taken upwards of 18 months to come before the court and they would have tried to have both cases heard together. With an expedited trial in our pocket, the best course was to stay with it. In the short term, the most important thing for me was to show the Nazi story was untrue. The newspaper was going to have to try to stand it up to have any hope of winning the privacy action. And we knew they would fail – it would fall to pieces in court because it was a lie. This would achieve my first and main objective.

When Thurlbeck's attempts at blackmailing the women didn't work, the newspaper published another story the following Sunday in an attempt to back up the first one. It was also clearly intended to intimidate me and underline that you don't take on the *News of the World*. Intimidation of anyone who challenges them is an established tabloid tactic, also used regularly by the *Daily Mail* as became very clear during the Leveson Inquiry. This second series of stories was another Thurlbeck effort. He wrote what purported to be an interview with Woman E, supporting his Nazi story. He then met her in a hotel near her home and offered her £8000 to sign it.

This was not as generous as it sounds because he had originally promised her MI5 husband £25,000 but only paid £12,000 once he had the story, another standard tabloid trick. Woman E signed her so-called interview at Thurlbeck's request but he then rewrote it extensively, claiming later in court he had telephoned her each time he changed it. The paper also included statements from someone purporting to be an expert on Nazism. When we checked out their so-called expert, a Dr Keith Kahn-Harris, we discovered that his principal expertise (on which he had written extensively) was heavy metal music. Perhaps even more revealing was an article on his website titled 'How to talk about things we know nothing about'. He was an example of the way they had dredged up all sorts of people to criticise me on the basis of their invented story.

When neither blackmail nor intimidation worked and they grasped that I was pressing on, the newspaper's management was beside itself. They set out yet again to demonstrate that you don't take them on. This time they wrote to the president of the FIA's Senate in Paris, enclosing copies of both the original edition of the newspaper and the follow-up edition from the second Sunday. They also included the secretly filmed video and invited the Senate to circulate everything to the entire FIA membership.

This was to land them in a criminal court in France when I invoked French privacy laws and the French authorities prosecuted the newspaper and some of its personnel. The *News of the World*'s publishers were eventually convicted and fined. This also resulted in what must have been a very embarrassing appearance for Crone (taking time off from his employers' desperate rearguard action on phone hacking), Thurlbeck and a senior lawyer from Farrers (a firm of solicitors in London which has allowed its reputation to be destroyed by being prepared to act for the *News of the World*) in front of the *juge d'instruction* in Paris. It must have been very obvious to them in the corridor outside that they were in a full-on criminal environment, with policemen handcuffed to prisoners also waiting their turn. As it turned out, that was perhaps a taste of things to come for some of them in the UK.

Having launched proceedings against the newspaper and its editor, Colin Myler, as well as Thurlbeck, I now had to think about the FIA. There were calls for my resignation from a few motor sport figures who disliked me, hoping in a rather contemptible way to take advantage of the situation. Urged on by one of them, Bahrain very publicly cancelled my planned visit to their Grand Prix. This was surprising. I had always had good relations with the crown prince, HRH Salman bin Hamad bin Isa Al Khalifa, to give him his full name. He was the driving force behind getting Formula One to Bahrain. I even took part in the ground-breaking ceremony for the Bahrain circuit with him and had been to at least one Bahrain Grand Prix. His letter finished with the words: 'I don't want to add to the difficulties in which you find yourself.' I couldn't help wondering why, if that were true, a copy of his letter had been given to the press, but then discovered this had all been done by Bahrain's rather stupid London PR agency, not by the country itself.

There was very extensive coverage of all this in the press. Looking back now at the cuttings, it's quite amusing to note how almost all the papers said I would have to resign and would not even last the weekend of the Bahrain race. The pressure was considerable but these demands that I resign were utterly nonsensical. So an element of my sex life had been exposed – so what? I thought the uproar was childish and probably, in many cases, hypocritical. And the suggestion that all this was more important than working to save thousands of lives on the roads struck me as mind-numbingly stupid. Clearly I would have to ask the FIA membership but there was no question of just walking away.

Cancelling my Bahrain visit was frustrating because I had not wanted to go in the first place. A quick phone call would have settled it if they really were worried that my presence would distract from their Grand Prix. I had already decided to cancel because of everything that was going on and I believed the message had reached them. I made no announcement because I didn't want to appear to be changing anything as a result of the newspaper story. But by deliberately making such a lot of noise about cancelling their invitation they, or rather their PR advisers in London, seemed to be wilfully trying to embarrass me. An equally public official invitation to attend the 2009 Bahrain Grand Prix (which I refused) did not really make amends.

I later learned that, in my absence, there had been some action at the 2008 race. Bernie called Alan Donnelly to a meeting in his office where Fred Goodwin, then CEO of the Royal Bank of Scotland, was waiting. The bank sponsored one of the teams and Goodwin was a well-known figure in the paddock, sometimes appearing wearing bizarre multi-coloured trousers. As a sponsor, his message was unequivocal – Alan had to tell me to resign. Alan quietly explained that I would do no such thing. When RBS went bust a few months later, becoming the biggest corporate failure in UK commercial history, there was a suggestion that Goodwin (unsurprisingly now out of a job) would make an ideal replacement for me as president of the FIA. Many FIA officials had seen Goodwin in the Formula One paddock with his curious trousers but would probably not have thought his record in commerce was a good qualification for the FIA. Goodwin himself was a bit more realistic than his supporters and called me to say it was all rubbish.

At almost exactly the same time, and in complete contrast to Bahrain, HRH Prince Feisal Al Hussein of Jordan, unprompted and unexpectedly, issued an official invitation to attend Jordan's round of the World Rally Championship – a courageous and principled decision in the circumstances and one I greatly appreciated. I particularly enjoyed the way his invitation was an implied reproof to those in motor sport who were trying to take advantage of the *News of the World* story. It was fascinating to see how different people behaved in these (for me) difficult circumstances. It told you a great deal about the character of each.

Back in Monaco, I met Michel Boeri, who was then president of the FIA Senate, and Marco Piccinini, who had until recently been the deputy president (Sport). They felt I should take a 'so what' attitude to the revelations. This was very much my own feeling. People tend to be much more grown-up about sex on the Continent and understand that even the most normal people probably would not want their bedroom activities on the front page of a newspaper.

There's still the odd person in England who thinks that anything but the most mundane sex is somehow intrinsically wrong, but happily they seem to be a dying breed. Paul Dacre, the editor of the *Daily Mail*, is the personification of that outdated attitude, saying in a speech to the Society of Editors that what I did was 'unimaginable depravity'. You do wonder what he would consider ordinary, or even imaginable, depravity and on what basis he sets himself up as a sort of Kensington Taliban, trying to tell other adults what they should or should not do in their bedrooms. The bestselling book *Fifty Shades of Grey* shows what an utterly preposterous figure Dacre has become, declaring himself unable to imagine something vast numbers of his readers were soon to be happily consuming. Even to the *Daily Mail* and *Mail Online* staff, Dacre's lack of imagination must seem very strange.

Apart from agreeing with my 'so what' attitude to the revelations, Marco and Michel suggested the FIA should hold its own inquiry to investigate whether there was any substance to the Nazi allegation. I was very much in favour because I knew this could be done quickly, before the High Court case, and would begin the work of exposing the *News of the World*'s lies. Anthony Scrivener QC was retained to conduct it. As a former chairman of the English Bar Council, judge in the FIA Court of Appeal and one of the UK's most prominent lawyers, he was the perfect person. His inquiry confirmed the Nazi allegation was entirely false.

Some of those in motor sport who disliked me for whatever reason inevitably seized on the newspaper story as an opportunity to try to oust me from the presidency. Most people in the FIA, like Marco and Michel, were supportive and sympathetic but Bernie, to my surprise, popped up on the other side. Having sold a majority stake in his company, he now had a board of directors and was apparently under intense pressure from some unpleasant individuals appointed by the new owners.

It seems they had decided I ought to resign because of the 'Nazi' slur. Whether the story was true or not didn't seem to trouble them, and none of them bothered to meet me or pick up the phone and ask what the truth was. It was out of character for Bernie to go along with them, however great the pressure. I was astonished and could not imagine acting like that had the boot been on the other foot. He could easily have told them he had checked with me, that I had made it clear that the Nazi part was completely untrue and I was taking the newspaper to the High Court to prove it. That, surely, would have been the end of the matter, or at least enabled him to ignore the troublemakers.

But there was more to come from Bernie despite nearly 40 years of friendship. He and Flavio Briatore (who inexplicably had decided to become involved) called a meeting of the Formula One teams in Barcelona at the Spanish Grand Prix, three weeks after the Bahrain race and four weeks after the first story hit the streets. They urged all the teams to sign a letter calling on me to resign. Apparently, Adam Parr (then in charge of the Williams team) enraged Bernie by saying he would only consider signing if he first saw everyone else's signature on it. After Bernie and Flavio failed to get their letter signed, CVC's little group went round the paddock at the next race, the Monaco Grand Prix, trying to persuade individual teams to say publicly that I should resign.

They roused support from the BMW and Mercedes teams, neither of which, again, had bothered to ask for my side of the story despite having had friendly relations with me for many years. I found this extraordinary because one of the first things you learn running any sort of organisation is to listen to both sides before doing anything. However, both teams rushed out press statements referring to the Nazi story and calling for my resignation.

The temptation to throw the stone back was irresistible because their glasshouse was so large. I put out a release reminding everyone of the involvement of both companies, and those behind them, in some of the worst aspects of the Nazi regime in Germany at a time when I was still in the nursery. They were extremely offended. The team principals concerned had apparently failed to reflect on their respective company histories. To be fair, I think the press releases were probably the work of rather stupid media advisers who, at best, understood only Formula One. Certainly, no one in either main company would have started that discussion. Some of my allies thought I had gone too far but I thought it served both teams right. They had no need to intervene.

When the CVC deputation arrived at the Ferrari motor home during the Monaco Grand Prix, they suffered a reverse. They asked Jean Todt to sign a declaration saying I should go. It seems they thought this would be straightforward because he's Jewish. But he would have none of it – he is a friend and had taken the trouble to find out the facts. He told them what they were doing was wrong and why, then sent them on their way.

Instead of scuttling round the paddock trying to undermine

me, CVC's directors should have been supporting my efforts to cut costs. The real threat to their business was not some fabricated story about my private life but the unsustainable costs for the teams.

What was dispiriting about that CVC offensive was the lack of understanding of motor sport it displayed. These people were supposed to be involved at the highest level, yet anyone who knew the basics could have told them they were wasting their time. A vote of all the Formula One teams would have been no more than an irritation, like the intervention by Bahrain. What mattered was what the FIA member organisations thought. After all, it was they who had elected me. The Formula One teams have no votes in FIA elections and what they thought did not really matter.

For this reason, in the week following the first *News of the World* story, I decided to seek an extraordinary General Assembly of the FIA. When I told Bernie, he advised me strongly against doing this, encouraging me to resign rather than risk a humiliating defeat in a General Assembly. I couldn't agree. The FIA member clubs had elected me, so it was up to them to decide what I should do. If I lost the vote so be it, but it would be wrong and cowardly to walk away without giving all the countries that had repeatedly supported me for nearly 17 years an opportunity to express their view.

The General Assembly was held on 3 June 2008 and the countries voted in my favour by 103 to 55, with seven abstentions. Most of those against me (at least the ones who spoke) were opposed to me in any event because of the internal disagreements you get in any large body, particularly an international one. With the *News of the World* trial just over a month away, it was an important victory. It demolished the newspaper's claim that I was an unsuitable person to lead the FIA and that their story was therefore, at least to some degree, in the public interest. The international community had spoken and the *News of the World* was seen for what it was – a disreputable scandal rag of limited importance inside the UK and no importance whatsoever outside.

When the vote was announced, my enemies were mortified. A few days later, Bernie tried yet again to get the teams to speak out against me, this time at the Canadian Grand Prix. Once again, Williams and Ferrari refused to join in and Dietrich Mateschitz, the owner of Red Bull, went out of his way to support me. Bernie tried hard to get Ferrari's backing for his campaign, even visiting Luca di Montezemolo in New York on his way to Montreal. Luca refused and was reportedly greatly annoyed when, in his absence, the contrary impression was somehow given during the team meeting that followed.

Having called the meeting, Bernie phoned Alan Donnelly as my representative and said he should attend so he could inform me about the teams' view (I don't think Bernie had anticipated the difficulty about Luca). Alan rang me and I suggested he should just ignore them. In fact, Alan diplomatically told Bernie he was on his way back to the hotel and couldn't make it. In the event, Bernie failed once again to get the vote he wanted.

What was so strange about this Canadian campaign was that Bernie ought to have known that, now the FIA General Assembly had voted and Scrivener had found in my favour, it was pointless trying yet again to get the teams to come out against me. Even if he had not appreciated at the time of the Barcelona meeting that the FIA would simply ignore them, as would I, it must surely have been obvious now. At most, a vote of the Formula One teams would have been a minor point to help the *News of the World* in the forthcoming trial.

This set the scene for the confrontation with Bernie at the World Council meeting on 25 June 2008, described in chapter 28, when he questioned the FIA's refusal to sign the Concorde Agreement without seeing the financial schedule. However, at the World Council meeting a few months later, on 7 October 2008, Bernie expressed regret that he had joined with those who were trying to oust me. Once he had said that in public, I believed that as far as he, the FIA and I were concerned, it was the end of the matter. Bernie always maintained that pressure from his board of directors was the reason for his actions. I found that difficult to believe but no other explanation has ever been offered.

Unfortunately, the following January the *Daily Express*, another UK tabloid, announced that Bernie had launched what it called a 'scathing attack' on the FIA and quoted him as saying my private life had influenced my decision-making. I found that disappointing. It was untrue, as he well knew, and saying it served no purpose. I knew the journalist would not have written the story without a recording of what had been said. But finally, in an interview in March 2009, Bernie was quoted as saying: 'I have only one regret in my entire life – I'm sorry about how I treated Max. A friend is someone who helps you when you are in the s***. Max would do that for me and that's why I'm upset about it.' When I read it, as far as I was concerned that really was the end of the matter.

In a way, I should have liked to resign as soon as the *News of the World* story first appeared, because I could then have given Rupert Murdoch and his acolytes at News International my immediate and undivided attention. But I was determined to continue to November 2009 and finish my mandate, as I had planned back in 2005. I was not going to be pushed out of office by the gutter press.

There is no doubt that the support of the FIA General Assembly greatly weakened the *News of the World*. The FIA meeting was always going to be crunch time, at least as far as international opinion was concerned. I never for one moment doubted that holding it was the right thing to do – and it would still have been the right thing to do even if I had lost the vote.

34

MOSLEY v NEWS GROUP NEWSPAPERS

On 7 July 2008 I arrived at the High Court for the first day of the trial. I was slightly taken aback by the scale of press interest. A huge bank of photographers mobbed my legal team and me as we approached. I had expected interest, but not at this level, and we had to take elaborate precautions to get the young women involved in and out of the High Court without them being photographed.

The *News of the World*'s barrister, Mark Warby QC (now a judge), put forward a case that seemed largely irrelevant nonsense. At the time I couldn't understand why, but of course we now know the newspaper was in the thick of the Gordon Taylor cover-up, as explained earlier. No doubt their in-house lawyer, Tom Crone, who was in charge, was preoccupied. We have only recently found out just how desperate Crone must have been to keep the Taylor settlement secret. All this was going on at exactly the same time as they were briefing counsel and preparing their defence to my claim.

Warby was particularly unimpressive in cross-examination. He began by asking me to confirm that I had been at the Chelsea flat that afternoon. This allowed me to point out immediately that it was indeed a flat and not a 'torture chamber', as his clients had alleged. Competent cross-examiners try to open with a difficult question to get the witness on the back foot. Warby did the opposite, and hardly got off his own back foot for the rest of our encounter.

He questioned me at length about my political views in my late teens and early twenties. Someone had plainly done some research but fortunately I had never said or done anything, even 50 years ago, that embarrassed me or was of any use to his case. Perhaps Warby's clients were hoping to show I had had right-wing views in my youth and would consequently be inclined to have some sort of Nazi fantasy in my sex life. If someone with left-wing parents was into S&M, presumably the *News of the World* would tell their lawyer to say he was re-enacting Stalin's gulags. It is difficult to think of a more stupid approach, particularly with nothing concrete to back it up. I felt a bit sorry for Warby, who was no doubt under instructions to put this hogwash forward.

He asked long rambling questions and several times I invited him to frame a clear one so that I could try to answer it. His questions were often irrelevant but James Price, my QC, never interrupted because he could see Warby was getting nowhere. For example, at one point he went on at length about the 'uniforms' the girls were wearing, which happened to include camouflage dresses reaching to mid-thigh and little else. When Warby persisted in asking which period of German history their clothing brought to mind, I said: 'I have never seen any German wearing mid-thigh camouflage – it is just nonsense. Did you have a particular period in mind for the mid-thigh camouflage uniforms?' Warby, at a loss for anything to say, could only manage, 'Ha, ha, ha.' My response to this rather un-QC-like performance was: 'Well, you know, you made the point Mr Warby, not me.'

He had a very weak case but he struggled on with his client's attempts to claim that Marks and Spencer blazers, a modern Luftwaffe jacket and camouflage dresses reaching barely to mid-thigh with nothing underneath were somehow Nazi. I constantly had to resist the temptation to say something unkind. I had to keep reminding myself I mustn't irritate the judge, who was the only person I needed to think about. Convincing him had to take precedence over making fun of Warby's case, however tempting it might be.

The *News of the World* also badly underestimated the women. Warby got off to an unfortunate start with the first one, Woman D. She suddenly burst into tears when he was about to begin his cross-examination. She is a sensitive person and was perhaps a little overwhelmed by the atmosphere and pressure of a big case in the High Court. Instead of offering sympathy, he suggested she was putting on an act. She plainly wasn't, and soon recovered herself. It's never a good idea to risk appearing a bully in such a situation, and I don't think Warby really meant to, but that's how it looked. His cross-examination got nowhere and it was the same story with the other three participants giving evidence.

The longer he went on, the more it became obvious that there had been nothing remotely Nazi in what took place. The only other line open to the newspaper was to try to suggest I had somehow exploited or abused the girls. This fell to pieces when, one by one, they made clear how much they enjoyed the activities in question. One of them has a PhD in hard (not social!) science from a top UK university; another had a very responsible job. It was possibly not what Warby's clients were expecting and a bit beyond their narrow minds. Although Warby had an impossible case to argue, he did manage to satisfy his employer's wish to provide material for the *Daily Mail* and the rest of the gutter press.

The editor, Colin Myler, and chief reporter, Neville Thurlbeck, both gave evidence. There was steadily increasing embarrassment when Myler was shown photo after photo taken from the video (which he claimed to have reviewed before allowing publication) and each time asked to point to a 'Nazi' element. He couldn't, of course, because there wasn't one. James Price was relentless and very effective. I almost felt sorry for Myler.

He was also in real difficulty when asked why he didn't have the German dialogue translated, and why the story claimed the girls were wearing Nazi uniform when one of the newspaper's own internal emails said there were no Nazi uniforms and that two of the girls were wearing ordinary Marks and Spencer blazers. Even the German girl's jacket was only an imitation of a modern German air force uniform.

It did not take long to reveal that Myler and his editorial assistants had not been interested in the truth of their story; they just wanted to run it. Myler at least tried to tell the truth on oath in the witness box despite his failure to do so in his newspaper. But Thurlbeck stuck stubbornly to a little list of points he had brought with him. He did not impress the judge, particularly when he tried to claim he had not set out to blackmail the women despite being confronted with his own emails doing just that. Even when giving evidence on oath, he had little regard for the truth, as was made clear in Mr Justice Eady's judgment. More recently, Thurlbeck ran a blog telling the world repeatedly that he had never hacked a phone, only to plead guilty when his lies finally caught up with him. He is, to put it bluntly, a bit thick and a nasty piece of work.

There was a sensational start to the fourth day when the *News of the World*'s star witness, Woman E, who had worn the hidden camera, failed to appear. They needed her to back up the interview in which they had quoted her as saying a Nazi scenario had been planned. It had already become evident that the story published on the second Sunday, which purported to be an interview with her, had simply been invented by Thurlbeck. It also became clear that inventing stories (in addition, of course, to blackmail and phone hacking) was an important element in his work as the newspaper's chief reporter. Warby told the court she was unwell. The judge asked if he had evidence of this. Of course, he hadn't. We all realised the truth: she was not prepared to commit perjury for the *News of the World* as they had plainly hoped she would.

I suspect they knew they would probably lose the case unless I withdrew at the last moment, but they seemed to have decided to try to use it to deter anyone who might wish to hold them to account for a breach of privacy in the future. Warby emphasised repeatedly the most private and (his clients would hope) embarrassing aspects of the case. He did this particularly in his closing speech and I could only assume on instructions. As a former barrister, I can understand that sometimes one has to argue a case on difficult facts. One of the traditions of the Bar is that you accept any case – the analogy given is that of a London taxi that has to accept any fare. But that is entirely different from setting out to embarrass a claimant and demonstrate to others what they would face if they took on News International.

I thought Warby's approach to my case unworthy of a member of the Bar. He must have known none of his grandstanding would impress the judge. By the time of his closing speech, the *News of the World*'s case had been dismantled by both evidence and legal argument. This was merely providing material for the gutter press to print in the next day's editions. This may have served his clients but it was not going to rescue his case.

As James Price QC, who was representing me, said in response to Warby's closing speech:

> What my learned friend has just said in public appears to have been said as much for the benefit of the press, as for your Lordship. We will be inviting your Lordship to reflect the outrageous things that have just been said in your Lordship's award of aggravated damages. This is quite deliberately designed to increase the humiliation of the claimant for having had the temerity to bring this action against the News of the World, and it just shows what a newspaper can do. If it can get past the interim injunction stage by preventing the claimant from having the opportunity to bring it before a judge and stop the publication, it can then castigate the claimant in public, and that in future is most likely to stop people having the temerity to sue the News of the World, and that, we shall invite your Lordship to reflect in the award of damages.

I hope that in reflecting on his performance Warby has come to realise he should have refused to go along with his clients' plan. The code of conduct of the Bar does not allow a barrister to 'compromise his professional standards in order to please his client'.*

* Article 307(c), Code of Conduct of the Bar of England and Wales, 8th Edn.

In my view, Warby's closing speech, when he must have known the case was lost, did compromise those standards. But at least I knew the judge would see exactly what the *News of the World* and its lawyers were up to.

It later became public knowledge that what Thurlbeck wrote and Woman E signed for the second *News of the World* story was false, quite apart from the additions made by Thurlbeck without her knowledge. After the judgment, she surprised us all by appearing on Sky News to confirm there had been no Nazi element that afternoon in the Chelsea flat, that the *News of the World* had made it all up and she bitterly regretted making the secret film for them. There was no doubt now why she had refused to give evidence.

Two weeks later, the judge, Sir David Eady, handed down a 54-page decision in my favour. He said that I 'had a reasonable expectation of privacy in relation to sexual activities (albeit unconventional) carried on between consenting adults on private property' and found 'that there was no evidence that the gathering on 28 March 2008 was intended to be an enactment of Nazi behaviour or adoption of any of its attitudes'. He added that 'there was no public interest or other justification for the clandestine recording, for the publication of the resulting information and still photographs, or for the placing of the video extracts on the *News of the World* website – all of this on a massive scale'.

However, as predicted by my lawyers right at the beginning, the damages, although at £60,000 a record for a privacy case (which it remains to this day), did not cover the difference between what the newspaper was ordered to pay towards my costs (about 82 per cent of the total) and my lawyers' bills.* But

* My solicitors' bill was £510,000, the proportion the *News of the World* had to pay was £420,000, leaving me £30,000 out of pocket despite the £60,000 damages.

that was of secondary importance. What mattered was that the judgment had made it absolutely clear that the Nazi allegation was a lie. It also established the principle that the article was an unlawful invasion of privacy. I made a quick little speech for the media on the steps of the High Court, accompanied by my lawyers and the Quest personnel. Myler followed and clearly still didn't get it. The judgment was widely welcomed. It became very clear the general public was on our side and felt it was high time the *News of the World* got its comeuppance.

Predictably, the *Daily Mail* editor, Paul Dacre, was outraged. In a speech to the Society of Editors, he made a disgraceful and cowardly attack on the judge. He also arranged for an obnoxious article about Eady to appear in his paper. He has a large collection of second-rate hacks and aging harpies to set on anyone who displeases him. Attacking a judge in a personal and offensive way about something he or she has done in a judicial capacity is about as low as a journalist can get. A judge cannot answer back. What a disgusting and contemptible fellow Dacre is. Perhaps he cannot help himself, but it's extraordinary and shameful that the Rothermere family is prepared to tolerate him as an employee.

As the doyen of the gutter press, Dacre led the chorus of fury, although others were equally unhappy. The judgment had made it more risky for them to indulge in gratuitous breaches of privacy for no better reason than titillation. The *News of the World* even had a former Archbishop of Canterbury, Lord Carey, available to criticise the judgment and attack me. His article described my conduct as 'indecent' and 'unspeakable' then repeated the tired old canard: 'If a politician, a judge, a bishop or any public figure cannot keep their promises to wife, husband, etc., how can they be trusted to honour pledges to their constituencies and people they serve?' He completely ignored the fact that some of the most successful and revered public figures of the last two centuries were often less than faithful to their partners. No one would deny that a married couple should be faithful (unless they agree otherwise) but infidelity is a matter for the couple. As my wife said when she read Carey's article, 'Of course I don't like what has transpired, but it's none of his business.'

Carey claimed the judgment was an attack on press freedom and was 'socially undermining', whatever that's supposed to mean. It is surely nonsense to suggest that entirely lawful sexual activity in private involving a very small number of consenting adults could 'undermine' anything. But suppose those adults really were doing something wrong: it should be obvious that delivering details to three million homes might encourage others to do the same. This very elementary thought seems to have eluded Carey. Perhaps the Murdoch shilling clouded his judgment.

I know Murdoch's money was involved because I wrote to Carey to ask him and he admitted to having a paid contract to write for the *News of the World*. To my mind, this is truly shaming, particularly for someone claiming to be a Christian leader. The paper's business was selling sex, partly by writing about it, partly by advertising pornography. And its information about sex was often acquired by criminal means, including phone hacking, bribery and blackmail. In my case, the newspaper used both bribery and blackmail, as Carey knew perfectly well from the judgment of Mr Justice Eady on which he based his article. It seems extraordinary that he would accept money from such a source – in my view, his conduct amounts to living at least partly off the proceeds of immorality. Not what you expect from a retired clergyman.

Most civilised people understand that consensual sexual activity in private between adults is a matter of taste and concerns only those affected. In the modern world, some religious extremists try to tell grown-ups what they can and cannot do in their own bedrooms but responsible religious leaders do not. When the *News of the World* invited the then incumbent Archbishop of Canterbury, plus the leaders of the Catholic and Jewish religions in the UK, to comment on my case, all refused.

Before the case came on, James Murdoch circulated an internal newsletter to his staff saying what a great job they had done on the story – understandable, perhaps, for someone who claimed to be too stupid to seek an explanation for the massive amount of money he authorised his company to pay to settle the Gordon Taylor case. Later that year, despite knowing of the judge's finding that their chief reporter had tried to blackmail two of the women involved, the *News of the World* applied for the 'Newspaper of the Year' award on the basis of their story about me. They said they were fighting for a 'high principle'. Presumably by that they meant the right to continue to act as Peeping Toms then blackmail and intimidate anyone who objected. This remarkable contempt for the courts and the rule of law was later to give the Leveson Inquiry a very clear insight into the morals of the Murdoch family and those who work for them. That the *News of the World* never appealed the judgment in my case shows they understood exactly what they had done.

The vote at the FIA General Assembly and the decisive win in the English High Court were both very important, and indeed essential as a basis for me to continue my response to Murdoch, but I knew this was just the beginning. I would be handicapped for the next 18 months or so because of my work at the FIA, but then I would be able to focus entirely on the issue.

While all this was going on we had to deal with *Bild*, the German equivalent of the *Sun*. They reproduced the *News of the World* pictures and the story without checking the facts. It was a level of journalistic insouciance right up there with their British counterparts. My German lawyer, Tanja Irion of Irion Kanzlei für Medienrecht in Hamburg, instituted proceedings against Axel Springer Verlag. At her suggestion, the public authorities also launched a criminal prosecution (*Strafanzeige*) against each Axel Springer director. That got their attention and they eventually settled by publishing an interview with me putting the record straight and paying €200,000 to charities of our choosing.

When my son Alexander died of a heroin overdose in May 2009, the press found out quickly, almost certainly from the police, some of whom in those pre-Leveson days used to earn squalid little bribes for such information. There was immediate press interest. When I arranged to meet Jean and some of Alexander's friends in a restaurant near our house, a journalist tried to follow me. I had with me a surveillance expert from Quest, who easily outmanoeuvred the journalist so that he had to pretend to be a passer-by and go on his way. Quest then watched the restaurant although you would never have known they were there.

The Press Complaints Commission code required journalists to show 'sympathy and discretion' at times like that but, as we know, tabloid journalists and their newspapers seldom took any notice of the PCC or its code. On one occasion, I had journalists sitting in the cafe opposite the mews house where I was staying in London, but once again it was easy to avoid them and they eventually gave up.

A day or two later I went to Alexander's house to go through his things. There was a young man sitting on a doorstep nearby. It took about five minutes to figure out he was a journalist when, after a short delay, more of them plus some photographers gathered outside the house. It was like watching vultures assemble. There was no back way out so I called Dominic Crossley, who soon appeared on a scooter and gave them all a letter saying that, if they did not leave immediately, we would apply to the High Court for injunctions against their newspapers.

From behind a curtain I watched them get their mobile phones out, presumably to call their news desks. After the *News of the World* case, they knew my lawyers did not make empty threats. Having made their calls, they all put their phones away and left. This was all very fine, but what do you do if you cannot afford top lawyers? I wondered if they had any idea what a death like that means to the immediate family. Could they really not imagine the utter desolation and despair we were feeling? I suspect they probably could but simply didn't care. It's quite worrying that people like that are sharing the streets with the rest of us.

Journalists and photographers even tried to get close to Alexander's funeral. One appeared disguised as a rambler, but was immediately spotted by the people from Quest because his outfit was brand new. Quest did a great job keeping them away but, again, what do you do if you can't afford Quest? We could have called the Press Complaints Commission but it took time for them to act, if indeed they acted at all. Once the journalists and photographers are present and you are being harassed you might as well call the Salvation Army. Of course, harassment is a criminal offence but I'm told calling the police is futile.

When Rebekah Brooks and Andy Coulson, two former editors of the *News of the World*, went on trial at the Old Bailey for phone hacking and other alleged offences, their very expensive lawyers tried desperately to claim Article 8 (privacy) rights on their behalf to prevent their sexual relationship becoming public. I wondered if they saw the irony or reflected for a moment on the feelings of those whose phones their newspaper had hacked precisely in order to deprive them of that same privacy and in blatant disregard of the law? Or whether they had the wit to contrast the care with which the court considered the Article 8 rights of Mrs Coulson and her children with the way in which, as editors, they would go to great lengths (even, in my case, a 'spoof' edition) to prevent any court reviewing their decisions to indulge in blatant and illegal breaches of privacy?

A civilised society requires respect for privacy. Those who really suffer when privacy is invaded are the victim's family. They are usually completely innocent yet are the ones whose lives are exposed and who have to suffer the pointing fingers and knowing looks. I often wonder if the individuals responsible for the gutter press – people like Murdoch and Rothermere – ever stop to think of the damage they do and the pain they cause. Or do they only care about the money they make?

'If you hadn't done it, there wouldn't have been a story' is the standard response to the victim when the tabloids have damaged a family with one of their so-called exposés. That of course begs the real, indeed the only, question, which is whether it is right to publish. The law and civilised society say it's not, but the tabloids have no respect for the law except, possibly, when it finally feels their collar. My experience and that of my family has led me to use every lawful means open to me in an attempt to prevent the tabloids doing to other families what they have done to mine. I very much hope that, when nothing further remains to be done, I will have contributed in some small way to that end.

After all this, we still hadn't discovered who had initiated the whole thing. Was it just the MI5 man and Woman E? Did they genuinely not foresee the consequences of what they were doing? Did someone put them up to it? Of course I had enemies, particularly in Formula One, but would anyone go that far? The conventional wisdom in Formula One has always been that someone was behind it. I am not entirely convinced but I admit there are suspects. Eventually the truth will come out.

35

STRASBOURG

As long as I remained president of the FIA, I had little time to pursue the broader issue of privacy and the press, but I decided to bring a case in the European Court of Human Rights because I knew it would take a long time to reach a conclusion. Our case was that the absence of any law in the UK to compel a newspaper to put an allegation involving breach of privacy to the subject meant there was effectively no remedy in the UK. Once the information had been published, it could never be made private again. The only effective remedy was an injunction to prevent it being published in the first place, but you could only ask a court for an injunction to prevent publication if you knew about the story in advance. Even then, if you wanted to get it stopped, you had to be able to convince a judge that you were more likely than not to win a case for breach of privacy when it came to trial.

It followed as a matter of very simple logic that if Article 8 of the European Convention on Human Rights (dealing with respect for private and family life) was to have any force in the

UK, prior notification was essential. Once the story was out, not only could it never be made private again, the UK courts could offer no remedy because anyone suing would have the breach of privacy repeated in open court and then be given a large bill of costs. It followed that the UK should either exclude Article 8 from the Human Rights Act or introduce a law requiring you to be warned if a story was going to be published that might invade your privacy. If the invasion could be justified under Article 10 (guaranteeing the right to freedom of expression and to receive and impart information) you would not be able to stop it. We were only concerned with cases where it could not be justified.

In practical terms, this would be a small although vital change. In 2009 the editor of the *Daily Mail*, Paul Dacre, told the House of Commons Culture, Media and Sport Select Committee that 'in 99 cases out of 100' the victim would have knowledge of the story. So we were talking about only the 1 per cent where a newspaper deliberately conceals its intentions from the victim. Presumably, they do this when they know their story is an invasion of privacy and would almost certainly be stopped if put before a judge. With serious investigative journalism, the person concerned always knows about the story because the journalist invariably asks for a comment. Needless to say, the press opposed my application. The last thing the tabloids want is human rights to interfere with the profits they hope to make through the illegal publication of private information.

Astonishingly, given his disgraceful behaviour towards the judge in my case, Dacre was also chairman of the Press Complaints Commission Code of Practice Committee, the body that made the rules governing the conduct of the press. That a person like him could hold such a position shows how morally bankrupt the PCC had become.

In March 2009 I took time off from the FIA to appear before the same select committee as Dacre and explained the case for prior notification. I think some of them could see that there was something worrying about an editor who wanted to invade someone's privacy being the sole arbiter of whether or not to publish very private and potentially life-ruining information about an individual, while denying him or her any reference to a judge or other neutral outsider. Even more worrying, you would think, would be the absence of any remedy in law after publication, no matter how outrageous the breach of privacy, because of the cost and publicity disincentives to suing.

But there was much talk of censorship by judges, as if I were asking for some draconian new power for the courts. The fact that judges have always been able to order a paper not to publish (and sometimes do) was completely ignored. In reality, the only issue was whether the victim should always have knowledge and so *be able* to approach a judge. This simple point was deliberately obscured by talking about 'chilling effects' and glossing over the fact that, in all serious investigative journalism, the victim has knowledge, if only because of the need to put the allegation to him. The fact that a judge would never give an injunction if the effect might be to prevent lawful comment was also ignored.

Despite my attempts to explain, the committee did not seem to appreciate that the 1 per cent would only involve instances like mine, where the case for an injunction was so clear that publication was deliberately kept secret, even to the extent of publishing a 'spoof' first edition to prevent the victim – me – going to a judge. But this was back in 2009, when parliament and the government were terrified of the tabloids and for all practical purposes danced to the tunes of Murdoch and Dacre. Before appearing at the committee, I told a very senior MP how much

I appreciated the invitation but, given the power of Dacre and Murdoch, I knew I would be wasting my time. The surprisingly frank reply was, 'Well, there is an element of "don't even go there".'

Once I started to look at why the politicians were so frightened of the press, the reasons became clear. No political party was likely to win an election without the support of Murdoch and his newspapers, including the *Sun*. After the 1992 election it even boasted in a headline 'IT'S THE SUN WOT WON IT' when John Major was re-elected against the odds and the Conservatives won another five years in government.

In 1995 Tony Blair, then newly elected leader of the Labour Party, went all the way to Hayman Island in Australia to woo Murdoch. When challenged about this by an old Labour stalwart, he cited Faust's pact with the devil, as described in his autobiography, *A Journey*. A few years later David Cameron made a similar pilgrimage to visit Murdoch on a yacht near Santorini in Greece. Extraordinary that the 'Leaders of Her Majesty's Most Loyal Opposition' should feel compelled to make supplication to a foreign newspaper owner because they were convinced they would not be prime minister without bending the knee.

Such overt political influence was backed up with dossiers on the private lives of many MPs. These were kept confidential but the newspapers made sure the MPs knew they existed. The experience of Chris Bryant, the Labour MP and former minister, whose private life was exposed after he put Rebekah Brooks on the spot over making illegal payments to the police for privileged information, was there to remind them what would happen if they stepped out of line. Had I been an important politician, the *News of the World* would never have published their story about me. They would have told me that someone had given them the video but, not to worry, they would make sure it stayed secret, leaving the implicit threat in the air. The media barons and their editors use their power like old-style dictators and modern mafiosi. They are self-serving, unaccountable and vicious.

The Strasbourg hearing of my case came on in 2011. Lord Pannick QC appeared for me. This was the same David Pannick who appeared for the seven teams who had refused to race at the 2005 United States Grand Prix when their tyre supplier, Michelin, brought the wrong tyres. With him in Strasbourg were David Sherborne and Dominic Crossley, who had been my legal team in the *News of the World* case together with James Price QC. When we first went to see him to discuss the case, David Pannick surprised David and Dominic by announcing that he had once appeared before me. Of course, it wasn't really just me, it was the FIA World Council.

Early on in this first conference he made the very valuable point that we didn't need to go through all the layers of English courts and exhaust all domestic remedies, as is generally the rule before going to Strasbourg. This was because in my case there were no domestic remedies. We were complaining about the omission from UK law of any requirement for prior notification in privacy cases and pointing out that the result was a newspaper could simply ignore the right to privacy set out in Article 8 of the European Convention on Human Rights.

The hearing was quite short but there was a lot of media interest. Several UK newspapers had put in submissions that ignored our central point that, in the absence of prior notification, Article 8 is a dead letter, probably because it is almost impossible to dispute. They concentrated instead on their (in my view) wholly irrational fear of what they said would be the 'chilling effect' of a decision in my favour. They also implied I was seeking a law to allow a judge to stop a newspaper publishing a story, which was disingenuous because the courts could already order a newspaper not to breach privacy and quite often did.

The case was called *Mosley v The United Kingdom*. That amused me. It seemed so odd, somehow – me suing a country. The government at the time was still in a state of obsequious compliance with the wishes of the tabloid press. They sent a very modest but pleasant legal team and Pannick had much the best of the argument, as one would expect. As the judges were filing out, I caught the eye of one or two and got the distinct impression that they were on our side. However, the decision went against us.

It's interesting to read because it is logical and makes sense until a certain point when the argument suddenly no longer seems to follow. It appeared to have been changed after it was first written. I am convinced the judges were warned by the British elements that, if they found in my favour, there would be a massive anti-Europe media storm in the UK. The tabloids already took every opportunity to attack the court and the Human Rights Act and invariably confused the Council of Europe with the EU and vice versa. A decision that might stop newspapers breaking the law whenever they felt like it would have caused outrage. Their reaction to Leveson a year or two later seemed to prove the point.

Perhaps some of the judges felt the greater good required the court to avoid giving ammunition to the anti-Europe campaign in the UK. After all, this was May 2011, still two months before Murdoch's hold over Westminster was broken. The decision coincided with media hysteria that had developed over a so-called 'super-injunction' that the footballer, Ryan Giggs, had obtained to protect his privacy. The newspapers were prevented from publishing details but the information was available on the internet. There was a strong suspicion that much of the leakage on to the web was being organised by elements in the tabloid press in order to bolster their arguments against injunctions. They kept saying that the injunctions did not keep the information secret but merely hampered the written press. Privacy was still a dirty word. It was another age. The *Sun* and the *Mail* were delighted that I had lost, a little prematurely as it turned out. We asked the Grand Chamber for another hearing, but they refused. A battle had been lost, but the war would continue.

36

EXPOSING A CRIMINAL ENTERPRISE

I could not do much to pursue all this or look more closely at News International until my FIA mandate and all the associated work came to an end. But once Jean Todt was elected in November 2009, I was finally free. I could now devote all my time to the issue of privacy and, equally importantly, look properly at the practices of the *News of the World*. On 4 February 2010 there was a debate and professional development forum on privacy and the media in Gray's Inn. The panel I was invited to join included Sir Ken (now Lord) Macdonald, the former Director of Public Prosecutions, Alan Rusbridger, editor of the *Guardian*, and other significant figures. Sir Alan Moses, then a Lord Justice of Appeal, was in the chair.

It was an interesting evening and there were many senior lawyers and judges present. For the first time in more than 40 years I met contemporaries from my Bar days back in the 1960s, several of whom were now judges. I commented that the way the

Press Complaints Commission was allowed to operate was like having the Mafia in charge of the local police station. The room seemed to agree with that but I wasn't sure how my jokes about Paul Dacre's sex life would go down with such a grown-up audience. I was in two minds whether to make them, but as usual couldn't resist. I was relieved when the laughter came.

During the question-and-answer session, there were interventions from the floor including Anna Ford and Tom Stoppard, who both had experience of the way the tabloids operate. For the first time, I heard about the Gordon Taylor settlement and that the publicist Max Clifford was also suing. It was now obvious that News International's 'one rogue reporter' line was untrue and that criminal phone hacking was endemic at the *News of the World*. But how could this be proved?

I met Nick Davies, the *Guardian* journalist who was later to break the Milly Dowler story that led to the closure of the *News of the World*. He told me that when the police arrested Glenn Mulcaire, the private investigator who actually carried out the majority of the phone hacking for the *News of the World*, they had seized a vast treasure trove of notes and other material. This undoubtedly contained evidence of the extent of the newspaper's criminality. Nick had written a terrific and hair-raising article about it the previous July (2009) but the Metropolitan Police, who had all this material stored somewhere in bin bags, were not prepared to look at it. The reaction of the police to Nick's story was to wait for a few hours, then announce there was nothing new.

If someone were disingenuous enough, they could claim this was strictly true. The police had already been holding the material for three years, so they were being truthful when they said it was not new. The problem was that they were stubbornly refusing to examine it or, if they had looked at it, were doing nothing – presumably in order to protect their friends in the tabloid press. Like the politicians, the police were terrified of the tabloids. An unfavourable article could destroy a police career just as it could a political career. Two of the great institutions of a modern democracy – parliament and the police – were effectively being subverted, if not controlled, by Murdoch. And Murdoch was not even a British subject.

In the summer of 2010, Nick Davies told me he was beginning to be seriously worried that the truth might never come out. His revelations about criminality in Murdoch's News International a year previously had produced no result. He also told me the *New York Times* had a team in the UK investigating. Apparently, they were very clear about what was going on, but would this make any difference? The evidence was all in Mulcaire's notes, but these were in the hands of the police with no means of access.

In the meantime, it emerged that Max Clifford, who had said at the Gray's Inn event that he would never surrender and would fight them on the beaches etc., had settled his phone-hacking claim. He was rumoured to have accepted in the region of £1 million, with the usual absolute confidentiality clause. Thus, News International had managed to close down yet another possible source of information about what they were really doing. Once again they had paid for silence by handing over vastly more money than any possible award of damages for breach of privacy in the courts.

The *New York Times* published its major article in September 2010, but the police just stuck to their line that there was no new evidence. Despite having all Mulcaire's notes to hand, and the certainty that something very serious had been going on growing by the day, the Metropolitan Police continued stubbornly to refuse to look at the evidence in their possession.

It was not possible to pursue the matter properly and effectively from Monaco, so I decided to return temporarily to the UK. On 17 September 2010 I moved into a property in London. Having learned just how widespread voicemail interception had become, I used regularly to leave a message on my own voicemail saying: 'I hope you realise you will go to prison for hacking my phone.' I thought if they don't hack me, they won't hear the message, so it doesn't matter – but if they do, it will startle them somewhat. Childish fun but it amused me.

On 22 September 2010, in the week following my return to the UK, there was another Gray's Inn privacy event, this time at Tate Modern. I was impressed to find myself on a panel with Lord Hoffmann, another contemporary from the 1960s, who had recently retired from the Supreme Court. His speech made me realise how big the gap between him and me was when it came to talking about the law. It was a bit like following Jochen Rindt in a Formula Two car all those years before. He discussed the problems of maintaining privacy in the modern world, but explained that we had to if we wanted to live in a civilised society. When it came to my turn, I outlined the absurdity of the way the law currently dealt with privacy and the absolute need for prior notification. There was a very good attendance of lawyers and judges, and I sensed widespread support among the legal profession for what we were trying to do.

A week later, I was invited to speak at a sports law conference at Stamford Bridge, home of Chelsea FC. I was told that Farrers, the *News of the World*'s solicitors, were present. It was obvious that there was a massive cover-up going on, so I went out of my way to tell the audience that News International were running a criminal enterprise over in Wapping. There was a distinct frisson in the room. The audience consisted almost entirely of lawyers, and they all knew that what I had just said was extremely defamatory. They also knew I was talking about the largest and most aggressive media group in the country.

I went on to explain that, despite the presence of the *News of the World*'s lawyers, I was in no danger of being sued. The lawyers knew that disclosure in an action for defamation would be fatal to their client. It would reveal that the one-rogue-reporter story, which was still being vigorously peddled, was a lie. Some of the lawyers present were quite taken aback, but I knew I was on firm ground. There would be no writ.

A few days later, on 7 October 2010, I again went out of my way, this time on the BBC's *Question Time*, to suggest that Andy Coulson, who had been editor of the *News of the World* at the time of Mulcaire's arrest and was now at the heart of government as the prime minister's press spokesman, should not be in Downing Street and why. It was pleasing that the BBC lawyers let it go.

I had already told Quest I was very anxious to get hold of Mulcaire's notes about his work for the *News of the World*. I was also concerned that someone in the Met might decide to destroy the contents of the Mulcaire bin bags. A senior ex-policeman at Quest assured me this would be very difficult for any individual or even for a group within the police to pull off, but it was nevertheless a worry.

Within weeks there was a breakthrough. Later in October, with the help of Quest, I acquired details of what was in Mulcaire's notes, including the names of three senior employees of the *News of the World* who had been using him to hack the phones of a great variety of people. Two of the three had even featured in my case, although only one of them (Thurlbeck) had given evidence in person. Clive Goodman, the 'single rogue reporter', was not one of the three. I also learned that, on each sheet of his notes, Mulcaire had written the name of the target and also, crucially, in the top left-hand corner, the name of the commissioning journalist. His notes included the names of all the *News of the World* journalists who had used him directly and this information was already in the hands of the police.

From this it emerged that one particular senior journalist had given the overwhelming majority of the phone-hacking commissions in the period before Mulcaire's arrest. We now knew his name and, again, it was not Goodman. Unlike Goodman, he had not been charged in the 2006 prosecution. If this information became public, it would expose and fatally undermine the one-rogue-reporter lie that News International had paid out the huge Taylor and Clifford settlements to maintain. It was very reminiscent of the moment I learned of the McLaren emails after they had told the World Council that only one rogue engineer had seen the IP stolen from Ferrari. I felt I had been here before.

We now knew that Mulcaire's notes contained not only clear evidence that the newspaper's defence was a lie, but also evidence of extensive criminality by named journalists other than the convicted Goodman. And all the proof was already in the possession of the police, who by now had been sitting on it for four years. All we had to do was somehow force the police to disclose the contents of the Mulcaire bin bags and the entire *News of the World* cover-up would start to unravel.

It didn't take the lawyers long to come up with a way of doing this. There were already civil actions against News Group Newspapers, publishers of the *News of the World*, for damages for breach of privacy arising out of phone hacking. There were several cases where the newspaper had published information that could only have come from listening to voicemails. There was also an action for judicial review of the Metropolitan Police's conduct in connection with phone hacking brought by Chris Bryant, the former government minister, and Brian (now Lord) Paddick, a former commander in the Met. They were joined later by Lord Prescott, the former deputy prime minister. All three had very good reason to believe their phones had been hacked and they were now challenging the complete failure of the Metropolitan Police to investigate properly.

Given the information that Mulcaire's notes, already in the hands of the Met, included the evidence they needed for their clients, lawyers acting for phone-hacking victims began applying for court orders (so-called Norwich Pharmacal orders) to force the police to disclose Mulcaire's notes relating to their clients. The Met resisted strongly but, in contrast to his control of parliament and the police, Murdoch had no influence over the judiciary. The orders were made and the evidence started to emerge. In December 2010, News Group Newspapers were forced to suspend Ian Edmondson, the news editor at the *News of the World*, who was later sent to prison.

Although lawyers acting for the victims who had brought civil actions against News International were now making successful applications to the High Court for orders forcing the police to disclose the evidence, it emerged that some of the victims were being deterred from litigation for fear of adverse costs orders should they lose, unlikely though that might be. In some cases, this was going to force them to abandon litigation; in others, there was a danger of settlements with draconian confidentiality clauses. Either way, the truth would not come out. Through my solicitors I agreed to stand behind some of them and meet the costs if the worst happened. I also met Chris Bryant with his lawyer and offered to stand behind him and Brian Paddick in their action for judicial review against the Metropolitan Police. This was made public by Lord Prescott, when he joined their action.

In November 2010, I happened to mention all this to Bernie. He was astonished. 'Does Rupert know?' he asked. I said I wasn't sure but assumed he did. Bernie, who's friendly with Murdoch, said he would find out. He called David Hill, a long-standing associate of Rupert Murdoch, who got back to Bernie and said no, Rupert didn't know and would want to hear all the details. Bernie told me: 'Rupert's going to call you.' The call never came.

It has always been my view that Murdoch must have been fully aware of what was going on. He was known to follow his newspapers closely and the *News of the World* was then the world's biggest English-language newspaper. He was also known to call his editors before they went to print on the Saturday evening. It seemed to me inconceivable he didn't know about phone hacking, one of the *News of the World*'s principal sources of information. It was, after all, being carried out on an industrial scale and significant sums were being spent.

I believe Bernie had envisaged the three of us having a quiet dinner in London or New York, during which I would reveal the Wapping criminality to Murdoch. I think he pictured an outraged Murdoch heading straight to Wapping to rid News International of its criminal infestation. In reality, of course, such revelations would have been the last thing he or his lawyers wanted. At that time the newspaper's management, including James Murdoch, was still working hard, and spending a great deal of money, trying to maintain the cover-up. Evidence that he had been told about the hacking in the autumn of 2010 could have been very damaging.

Meanwhile, my lawyers were acting against various websites to try to remove the illegal images originally put on the internet by the *News of the World*. At one time, they were active in 23 different countries. In Germany alone, they secured the removal of images from over 400 sites. Of course, the story was of great interest in Germany because of the Nazi lie, which was enhanced because Formula One had become very big in Germany following the success of Michael Schumacher.

We arranged a meeting with Google and asked them to stop their search engine producing images that had already been ruled illegal for the *News of the World* to publish by the English High Court. That would have solved the problem. It did not matter if the images were on some obscure website – they would only be seen by a very small number of people. What did the harm was the search engine. Its robots would find the images even on the most obscure site and then display the thumbnails (small versions of the actual pictures) on Google's own page of search results whenever someone Googled my name.

Unless it was stopped, for the rest of my life and beyond, anyone looking for me on the web would find the pictures. As the High Court had ruled it illegal to publish the images, it seemed reasonable to ask Google to respect this ruling and uphold the law. We knew that if they agreed, the other search engines would follow suit.

Google said they would take them down each time we complained and indeed did so. Not always very quickly, but at least they took them down. But they refused to stop them altogether. Initially, they claimed they didn't have the necessary technology They have admitted (for example, in a post by Google director J. Fuller on 15 June 2013) that they have been using 'hashing' technology to identify illegal images anywhere on the internet since 2008. However, they refused to use this technology to block my images despite the English High Court ruling that they should never have been published.

Unable to convince them that it was much more rational to do the right thing voluntarily and respect the High Court decision even if it was not directed at them, I brought actions against them in France and Germany thinking that, in the end, Google's general conduct would be a matter for the EU, so it was important to secure decisions in two major European countries and not just in the UK, where I am also suing them. Those actions have now been won in France and Germany (although Google have appealed), and there is also a recent decision in the European Court of Justice making it clear that Google is itself responsible for whatever it puts on the internet.

In January 2011, the dam finally burst around News International. The court orders meant the police could no longer suppress the evidence in Mulcaire's notes and a proper investigation began. Coulson finally left his position as director of communications for the British prime minister, having been with David Cameron since shortly after resigning as editor of the *News of the World* in 2007. My initial suspicion of the police soon gave way to confidence. It became clear that the senior police officer in charge, Deputy Assistant Commissioner Sue Akers, was not going to construct yet another cover-up but, on the contrary, was going to do a thorough job.*

Soon afterwards, the arrests started and one morning in April I received a text message that Neville Thurlbeck had been detained. Other arrests followed. There were more actions by

---

* As of October 2014, eight of the ten *News of the World* journalists charged with phone hacking have either been convicted or pleaded guilty.

victims of phone hacking and I undertook more underwriting of costs. As the year passed, the hacking cases began to be settled and the scale of my financial risk diminished. The Metropolitan Police settled the Bryant/Paddick/Prescott judicial review after quite disgracefully resisting for more than a year at the taxpayer's expense.

In June 2011, the *Guardian* held a dinner for Nick Davies. Whether by then they had an inkling that they were shortly to break a huge story in the phone-hacking saga, I don't know, but the dinner was like a sort of *Who's Who* of hacking victims, lawyers and outstanding *Guardian* journalists. I found myself sitting next to Alan Rusbridger and came away more than impressed. He's one of those full-on intellectuals who make me feel inadequate. Apart from editing the *Guardian*, not exactly a part-time job, it emerged he is an expert on Chopin and writing about him. On top of this, he has other intellectual interests and is a very accomplished pianist. How do such people manage it?

On 4 July 2011, I received a text from Nick Davies telling me to look at the *Guardian* website. They had just published Nick's story about the hacking of Milly Dowler's voicemails. Like everyone else, I was horrified when I read it. Here was a blatant example of the immorality of the *News of the World* and the sort of people who worked for it. As everyone now knows, the *Guardian* story explained that voicemail messages left for the 13-year-old after she disappeared had been hacked by the *News of the World*, as had the messages of her parents.

Instead of just a few long-suffering celebrity victims, most of them well known or connected to someone who was, the general public finally understood what the *News of the World* represented and how it operated. It was clear the senior editorial staff of the newspaper had no concern for its victims. Even a missing child was fair game. The whole country now understood that the *News of the World* thought it quite normal to hack into the private voicemails of a murdered teenager in search of a story. The reaction was extraordinary to witness. It had taken these revelations, but the public could now see what a group of us had known for some time.

There followed an unprecedented wave of national revulsion. The next day, the Media Standards Trust founded Hacked Off, a pressure group for media reform. Brian Cathcart, professor of journalism at Kingston University, joined them, as did Hugh Tomlinson QC, one of the UK's top privacy and defamation lawyers and the person behind the well-known legal blog, Inforrm.com. Dr Evan Harris, a former Lib Dem MP, was a key member and Hugh Grant emerged as their principal spokesman. Hugh turned out to be really good at putting the case and I think he may have surprised himself. When stopped by a TV crew and asked what he would ask Rupert Murdoch, he replied without hesitation: 'What have you done to my country?' He was well able to take on the politicians and professional TV pundits, and did so frequently and with success.

Inexplicably, Murdoch insisted there was no need for Rebekah Brooks, News International's CEO, to resign, even though she had been editor of the paper when Milly Dowler's voicemails were hacked. It seems Murdoch thought he could head off the critics by closing the paper and making a public apology. If he hoped things would calm down, he had completely underestimated the strength of public anger. Stopped in the street by television crews, he was asked what his priority was now. 'This one,' he replied, indicating Rebekah Brooks at his side. The following week she resigned. Three days later she was arrested.

Two days after James Murdoch announced the paper's closure, the staff of the *News of the World* prepared the final edition. They then appeared as a group outside Murdoch's Wapping head-quarters, led by the wretched Colin Myler holding an early example of the last edition. Happily, the story on its front page reporting the end was not a 'spoof'. The staff appeared shocked and some were in tears. For the large number of people whose lives or families had been gratuitously damaged or even ruined, for no better reason than titillation of the worst elements of the public, it was a great moment. Squalid employees of Murdoch who had caused so much misery without a thought for their vic-tims were leaving their offices for the last time – some innocent people lost their jobs, too, but they had nothing or no one to blame but the culture they had been part of and the colleagues they had never spoken out against. In the end, they must have been only too aware that it was the British public who had decided their fate.

While all this was going on, the government was in the final stages of nodding through a takeover of Britain's largest subscrip-tion television company, BSkyB. Murdoch's News Corporation already owned 39 per cent of it and now wanted to buy the rest of this profitable company. This former Australian and natu-ralised American, who does not even pay tax in the UK, would then have had a massive presence in UK television as well as controlling nearly 40 per cent of the British press.

The week after the newspaper's closure, the takeover was the subject of a full-scale debate in the House of Commons. MP after MP got up to denounce Murdoch. It was no longer just a coura-geous few, it was everyone. Even former Murdoch supporters joined in, making it seem as if the spell he had cast over the Commons until that moment had suddenly been broken. Seeing them all turn on him like that was almost sinister, so profound was the change. The vehemence of the attack may have been partly due to some guilt at their previously supine attitude. After all, despite being manifestly wrong, the BSkyB bid would have been nodded through had Nick Davies and the *Guardian* not broken the Milly Dowler story. Now, Murdoch had to withdraw the bid knowing it would be rejected by parliament no matter how hard his allies in government tried to push it through.

Through Alan Donnelly, I had met the Labour MP Tom Watson and we had an immediate rapport. Tom completely understood about Murdoch; in fact, he was way ahead of me. He was also a member of the Culture, Media and Sport Select Committee, so he was in the thick of it when, shortly after the denunciation of Murdoch in the House of Commons, the committee decided to invite the two Murdochs to appear before it. At first they declined with characteristic arrogance, so the committee, very unusually, formally summoned both of them. When I heard about the refusal I rather hoped an official, appropriately dressed in some 18th-century costume, would ride down to Wapping on a horse to deliver the summons. Somewhat disappointingly, he travelled by underground.

The day before the select committee hearing, Tom and I had a meeting with Dominic Crossley in his office to prepare some points. Dominic, who is probably the UK's top privacy and defamation solicitor and has represented me throughout, including against the *News of the World*, was a bit dubious about some of the proposed questions to James Murdoch. Strictly speaking, he was probably right, but Tom and I have a similar approach and we both wanted to take a hard line. The hearing received worldwide coverage and one of the sound bites (that James 'must be the only Mafia boss in history who didn't know he was running a criminal enterprise') attracted the sort of exposure that Murdoch likes to give his enemies. Tom's tactic of keeping James quiet while he questioned Rupert worked very well. However, much of the effect of the session was lost when someone threw a cream pie at Rupert. I was always very suspicious about that – it was so very helpful to Murdoch just when things were getting difficult for him.

We opened up another front when I went to America with Alan Donnelly in September 2012. Murdoch has immense power in the US, and not just because of Fox News and the fact that his News Corporation is a multibillion dollar company. His influence in the media and entertainment business is such that anyone who crosses him is likely to have trouble. It's a different sort of power from the one he exercised in the UK. He does not control the American government, the police or the FBI. But his tentacles reach into almost every corner of the media and entertainment industries.

We had a meeting with the *New York Times* and various people who were interested in Murdoch, following which we got the train down to Washington for more meetings. These included the staff of the Senate Commerce Committee. I had never been in the Senate building before and, like everyone from the UK, I was impressed. Everywhere we went there seemed to be an appreciation of the danger Murdoch presents to society. He may not be particularly political but his influence and power are so enormous and corrupting that he distorts the democratic process. However, what happened next will make it more difficult for him to wield such influence again, at least in Britain.

37

LEVESON AND AFTER

Following the *Guardian*'s Milly Dowler story, the pressure on Cameron was considerable. He had hired former *News of the World* editor, Andy Coulson, as Conservative Party director of communications in 2007. After winning the 2010 election he took Coulson into the heart of government as Downing Street director of communications. Coulson had resigned in January 2011 when the full phone-hacking story started to emerge, and on 11 July 2011 was arrested by the Metropolitan Police. Two days later, Cameron did what politicians do when in difficulty – he announced a public inquiry.

When the Leveson Inquiry was announced, it felt somehow unreal. So much had happened in such a short time after years of trying to get movement. I quickly set up a meeting with Dominic Crossley and David Sherborne. As we discussed the options, we concluded it was vital that victims of press abuse were properly represented at the inquiry. But a major problem was that only a small minority could afford to retain lawyers, and most might not want to get involved or even know how to go about it. There was also the risk that, if those who could afford their own lawyers all turned up with different representatives, the victims might appear diffuse and all over the place. They would be up against a phalanx of top Queen's Counsel representing the press, all co-ordinated and highly organised. We decided the only way to make sure the victims' voices were heard properly was to establish a legal team for them. I agreed to pay. Hugh Grant insisted on contributing and the inquiry itself eventually met a proportion of the costs.

Dominic set about contacting and organising the victims and getting in touch with the solicitors of those who had been in prominent recent cases. Eventually, he and David were appointed the official representatives of the victims of press abuse at the inquiry. The victims were all given 'core participant' status, along with other concerned individuals. This meant they would have advance information and better access to documents than the general public.

By co-ordinating the victims, Dominic and David were able to agree an order of appearance with the inquiry legal team. It is now clear that the fortnight or so of victims' evidence exposed for the first time to the general public the full iniquity of tabloid conduct and the utter inadequacy of the Press Complaints Commission. I think the extent and seriousness of the misconduct that emerged as the victims appeared one after another took even the tabloids by surprise. We all feel strongly when something outrageous happens, such as the monstering of Christopher Jefferies or the treatment of the McCanns, but it's largely forgotten by the time the next one comes along. Being presented with a succession of such incidents one after the other made a real impression. It showed just how bad the conduct of the tabloids had been.

The inquiry started with a 'seminar'. A number of experienced journalists and media pundits were invited to explain to Lord Justice Leveson how they saw things and how the press worked. Some newspapermen, particularly former *Sun* editor Kelvin MacKenzie and *Daily Mail* editor Paul Dacre, put in very self-satisfied and smug performances. The press generally seemed to be taking the inquiry lightly. This was understandable: they had successfully seen off six or seven similar initiatives since the Second World War. I hoped that this time, they might be making a mistake. And, indeed, the condescending and complacent tone they had adopted for their lectures at the opening seminar changed as the victims' evidence started to emerge. Dacre's arrogant and patronising attitude later changed to one of sweaty resentment when he was recalled to the inquiry to explain why his publications had branded Hugh Grant's evidence a 'mendacious smear'.

When the inquiry proper began, our legal team's excellent work assembling the victims' evidence paid dividends. They managed to bring them on in the right order for maximum effect and were able to help the inquiry team counter the arguments the newspapers offered in response. The result was devastating and the tabloids began to realise they had a real problem.

Lord Justice Leveson himself was impressive. Nothing seemed to get past him – he was completely impartial and went to great lengths to be fair to everyone, but always seemed to make the key point at the right moment. With all the proceedings broadcast live on the internet and much of the time on national television, the general public could watch. It was important that the public should see what was going on and come to their own views upon the evidence, rather than relying on newspapers whose spin on the proceedings turned out to be every bit as self-serving as expected. I learned later that the hearings also had a big audience outside the UK, particularly in Washington, where a lot of people were keenly interested in Rupert Murdoch's conduct.

When the time came for me to give evidence on 24 November 2011, I had a short talk with Robert Jay QC (as he then was) beforehand. He had a slightly unusual job for a lawyer: he was assisting the inquiry, helping it get to the truth, but he had to be neutral, unlike counsel for one side or the other in litigation. So sometimes he was perhaps more gentle with witnesses who were being less than honest than would normally have been the case, but he had various subtle techniques for highlighting the moments when witnesses were not being straightforward.

He gave me plenty of opportunities to say what needed to be said. It was great to have the chance to make points I really cared about, particularly about access to justice. When I suggested that only 1 per cent of the population could afford to bring an action for defamation or breach of privacy, Leveson looked at me and said: 'I think you'll find it's less than that.' He was right, of course, and in the inquiry's report he set out a means of rectifying this very major problem.

As he already had with other witnesses, Leveson asked what I thought he should do. I volunteered to send in some ideas. He thanked me but made it clear he might well ignore them – it was up to me if I wanted to do the work. I worked on my proposals over Christmas 2011 and, when a first draft was ready, I sought views from lawyers and journalism experts like Professor Steve Barnett. The responses were all very helpful and positive and I sent in the final version. Some weeks later I was invited to elaborate and resubmit, which I did. I don't know whether the ideas I sent in had any real effect, but on reading the inquiry report I could see they had at least been taken seriously. I gave evidence again in July 2012, this time quite briefly.

When evidence of widespread phone hacking by *News of the World* journalists had emerged towards the end of 2010, the Murdoch organisation had been forced to abandon its elaborate cover-up of the phone-hacking scandal because the 'single rogue reporter' story was now obvious nonsense. Their response was to come up with a new line. They now claimed there was 'zero tolerance of wrongdoing' within the News Corporation organisation and its subsidiaries. Murdoch himself repeatedly claimed that this was now the rule.

Having heard about the new zero-tolerance line, I wrote to Rupert Murdoch at his New York headquarters on 10 March 2011:

Dear Mr Murdoch

   By email and by post

   Your companies have a policy of zero tolerance towards wrongdoing by employees. This has been reiterated by you and by those speaking on your behalf, particularly in the context of recent allegations of phone hacking at the News of the World.

   You may know that in 2008, I sued the News of the World *over a story about my private life. However, you are probably not aware that during the trial it emerged that the chief reporter of the newspaper, a Mr Neville Thurlbeck, had set out to blackmail two of the women involved.*

   The News of the World *published its story about me on 30 March 2008. It wanted a follow up. To this end Mr Thurlbeck sent emails to two of the women seeking their stories. He threatened to publish their pictures in the next edition of the* News of the World *if they refused to give him what he wanted.*

Mr Thurlbeck's conduct is described in detail in Mr Justice Eady's judgment (Ref. [2008] EWHC 1777 (QB), starting at paragraph 79. The blackmailing emails are quoted by the judge at paragraphs 81 and 83. As Mr Justice Eady points out: 'It is elementary that blackmail can be committed by the threat to do something which would not, in itself, be unlawful' (paragraph 87).

The editor of the News of the World, *Mr Myler, was questioned about this during the trial. The relevant exchange is at paragraph 85. Mr Myler was then asked if he had raised the matter with Mr Thurlbeck (paragraph 86). Mr Myler said he had not because he had not been aware of the emails at the time and, when he did become aware, did not raise it because it was 'considerably after the event'. The trial was at the beginning of July 2008, the emails were sent just three months earlier.*

The judge (again at paragraph 86) said this was 'effectively a non-answer from which it would appear that Mr Myler did not consider there was anything at all objectionable about Mr Thurlbeck's approach to the two women, as he did not query it at any stage. **This disclosed a remarkable state of affairs'** *(emphasis added).*

Since then, despite strong evidence that Mr Thurlbeck had committed a serious criminal offence in the course of his employment, he is still the chief reporter of the News *of the World. No disciplinary proceedings of any kind appear to have been taken. As your lawyers will confirm, blackmail carries a maximum sentence in the UK of 14 years' imprisonment.*

In the light of your zero-tolerance policy towards wrongdoing, would you please give instructions that this matter be investigated without further delay and appropriate action taken?

Yours sincerely

When Murdoch didn't bother to reply, I had given the letter to the inquiry. It duly came back to haunt him when he gave evidence on 26 April 2012. He was questioned about it by both Robert Jay and Lord Justice Leveson:

ROBERT JAY: Can I ask you, please, about the letter Max Mosley wrote you, 10 March 2011? It's MODI this time, 00031562. *[A reference to where the letter was in the inquiry's documents.]* I think you remember this letter, don't you, Mr Murdoch? It's going to come up on the screen in a few moments, I hope. We can find it for you.

RUPERT MURDOCH: No. I have looked into the question of correspondence with Mr Mosley, and I did not read – I was out of town or something and my assistant sent them to whoever was the chief executive of News International to handle and I received an email, a coded email only yesterday about it from him, passed again to Mr Mockridge, the chief executive, to handle.

Q: The point Mr Mosley was making accurately was that Mr Justice Eady, in a judgment given out of this building, referred to blackmail being committed by journalists employed by the *News of the World*. You were aware of Mr Justice Eady's comments, weren't you?

A: **I am aware now, and with great respect to Mr Justice Eady I think he suggested that one of the ladies in the picture of this Nazi orgy had been offered to have her face pixelated out of *[sic]* they would co-operate with the story. Again, with great respect to Mr Justice Eady, I'm not as shocked as he is by that. I'm much more shocked by the behaviour of Mr Brett in not telling him the truth of a lot of things.**

Q: Don't worry about Mr Brett, Mr Murdoch. Have you read Mr Justice Eady's judgment?

A: **No.**

Q: Because he, in a very careful and considered judgment, having analysed all the evidence, oral and written, came to the clear conclusion, some may say it was the only conclusion he could possibly have reached, that your journalists, or at least one of them, had perpetrated blackmail of these two women. Is it really your—

A: **Two women or one?**

Q: Yes. Is it really your position: we don't have to worry about what he says?

A: **No, it's not my position at all. I respect him and I accept what he says. I'm just simply saying that a journalist doing a favour for someone in returning [sic] for a favour back is pretty much everyday practice.**

Q: Well—

LORD JUSTICE LEVESON: I'd just like to go into that for just a moment, please, Mr Murdoch. First of all, I think it ought to be made very, very clear that Mr Justice Eady rejected the allegation there were Nazi overtones to this incident, but I merely identify that fact. It's not what I want to ask you about.

Do you say, from all your experience of journalists and journalism, that it's appropriate to say to a member of the public, 'We have this photograph of you, we can do this two ways: we can embarrass you by unpixelating your photograph, even though there may not be a public interest in identifying who you are, and that's what we will do, or alternatively, we'll give you some money and you tell us the inside story'? Is that an appropriate way for a journalist to behave?

A: **I don't know that she was offered money, but it happens.**

LORD JUSTICE LEVESON: She certainly was offered money.

A: **Well I accept that, sir, if you say so, and I apologise—**

LORD JUSTICE LEVESON: Look, Mr Murdoch, I wasn't there, I've only read the judgment.

A: **Yes.**

LORD JUSTICE LEVESON: And I've heard the evidence about it. But I ought to make it clear to you, and I would be very grateful for your help on the topic, that I find that approach somewhat disturbing, because I don't think Mr Justice Eady is using too strong a word if he describes it as a form of 'blackmail'. And therefore, if it is the culture and the practice of the press that this is acceptable or justifiable, then I would like to know that. I really would.

A: **Look, I apologise, sir. I have not read Mr Justice Eady's thing.**

LORD JUSTICE LEVESON: Yes.

A: **And I may well agree with every word if I read it. But it's a common thing in life, way beyond journalism, for people to say, 'I'll scratch your back if you scratch my back.'**

LORD JUSTICE LEVESON: Yes—

A: **To seek to go beyond that, I disagree.**

LORD JUSTICE LEVESON: That's the point.

A: **And I accept your words. Or Mr Justice Eady's words, but I have not read it, I'm sorry.**

LORD JUSTICE LEVESON: No, but you can see why this is at the very core of part of what I am doing?

A: **Yes.**

LORD JUSTICE LEVESON: And therefore, without asking you to return, I think I would ask you, if you don't mind, to look at that judgment and let me know whether you think what Mr Eady there describes, if it be right – and I don't ask you to reach a judgment on right or wrong, the newspaper could have appealed the judgment, they didn't – reveals a culture and practice that you think is (a) accurate in the sense that it's more widespread and therefore everything everybody does, or (b) inappropriate. Do you understand the question?

A: **I understand it, sir, and I will be very happy to read it and to write to you and submit a document.**

LORD JUSTICE LEVESON: That's perfect, that's fine. But I would like your considered view on that question.

A: **Yes. I'm sorry that I haven't got one.**

LORD JUSTICE LEVESON: No, no, that's quite – you've had more than enough to cope with, although one might ask whether the fact that a High Court judge in England had reached this conclusion about one of your papers would itself be brought to your attention, but I gather it wasn't.

A: **No.**

LORD JUSTICE LEVESON: Yes, Mr Jay.

MR JAY: Well, you said it was a common thing in life, 'I'll scratch your back if you scratch my back', and that's true, that's human nature, but it's interesting that you say that's no part of the implied deal in your relations with politicians over 30 years, Mr Murdoch. Is that right?

A: **Uh – yes. I don't ask any politician to scratch my back.**

After trying to pretend that Thurlbeck had done nothing wrong, something that Lord Justice Leveson plainly would not buy, Murdoch was forced to put in a second witness statement to try to extricate himself from his untenable position. In this he explained that his New York office had sent my letter of 10 March 2011 to Rebekah Brooks who, however, was 'consumed with the emerging facts about phone hacking'. I suspect that in reality she saw no point in investigating. Blackmail was such a well-established technique at the *News of the World* that she would have known there was nothing to investigate.

Murdoch's second witness statement also explained that when Brooks's successor, Tom Mockridge, realised I had not had a reply he wrote to me on 17 April 2012 apologising for the delay of more than a year. Mockridge's letter was written 13 months after News Corporation received my letter and just nine days before Murdoch was due to give evidence to the inquiry. This was obviously not a coincidence. They probably suspected (rightly as it happens) that I had evidence of delivery from the US Postal Service.

In his letter, Mockridge promised he would write to me with a full response as soon as he was able to. Needless to say, more than three years later the promised full response has still not arrived. Perhaps if there is a further inquiry I will get it – once again, just before Murdoch has to give evidence. I believe that the way Murdoch and his people dealt with my letter was a perfect illustration of their attitude of utter contempt for the law, the judiciary and the courts.

As the inquiry continued, the press, police and many of the politicians were left looking compromised. We were confident that some useful proposals were likely to emerge but, if this happened, the press would strongly object. Accordingly, the ultimate battle would be political. In an attempt to cover this, I hired political strategists BBM as experts to help in what I knew would be a difficult phase. But we were by no means alone – Hacked Off plus several of the victims' lawyers were on the same side.

Hacked Off were doing an excellent job. Hugh Grant proved a very effective spokesman and Professor Brian Cathcart wrote one article after another demolishing Leveson's critics. But an almost united press was by now doing its utmost to discredit the inquiry, sometimes in an extraordinarily dishonest way. They were desperate to get back to business as usual, as they had succeeded in doing after each previous government inquiry into the press. They had the megaphone and used it relentlessly to drown out all attempts at balanced debate.

Finally, in November 2012, the Leveson Report was published. At first sight, I was disappointed because it did not recommend prior notification. Yet on closer reading it had almost everything that was really needed, particularly access to justice for those who suffer defamation or a breach of privacy but cannot risk hundreds of thousands of pounds in costs. It had some of the things I had tried to suggest, but was far more extensive and subtle than anything I had come up with.

Although it did not recommend a legal obligation to notify of the kind I had sought in Strasbourg (indeed, it specifically said its proposed regulator should not be able to prevent publication of a story), its recommendations, if implemented in full, would strongly encourage prior notification because of the financial risk to a newspaper that failed to behave properly. It also contained proposals for a vitally important arbitral system to give access to justice at minimal cost. Leveson had fully understood that there was no point in introducing new libel laws if fewer than 1 per cent of the population could afford to use them. Legal aid has never been available for libel; therefore, an inexpensive arbitral system was essential in order to provide access to justice for those whose rights have been infringed.

The arbitral system was equally necessary to deal with breach of privacy. Here, redress after the event does not right the wrong because the issue is not whether the private information was true, but whether the newspaper had sufficient reason for publishing it. Unlike libel, where an award is vindication and shows the story was untrue, damages for invasion of privacy can do nothing to protect the victim's reputation or family life.

Leveson's proposed system of arbitration suggested a way of dealing with both sets of problems. It offered protection against libel by giving access to justice for individuals with limited resources, while newspapers would also see their legal costs plummet if they joined the scheme. And it offered protection for privacy by setting up incentives for newspapers to think very carefully before publishing a story that was a breach of privacy. This mechanism would be entirely voluntary; a newspaper could insist on going to court, but would then be at risk of paying the costs of both sides as well, perhaps as exemplary damages in a really bad case.

Publication of the Leveson Report brought a deafening chorus of tabloid disapproval. Most of the press did their utmost to misrepresent his proposals. Nonsensically, they claimed that 300 years of press freedom was under threat. It's quite difficult to understand how anyone can describe the UK print media as 'free' when 70 per cent is controlled by four individuals. But apart from that, there was nothing in Leveson's proposals that would interfere with genuine press freedom; quite the reverse – they would also prevent wealth being used to inhibit investigative journalism. He had managed to reconcile complete and continuing press freedom with just (but only just) enough statute to prevent the worst elements of the press simply going back to their old ways after a year or two. The claim that his ideas amounted to state control of the press was plainly absurd – there was no mechanism for this – but even some serious journalists objected to his proposals. Theirs was a thin-end-of-the-wedge argument, but in the end most would admit their objections were theological rather than rational.

The level of tendentiousness, even dishonesty, of the newspapers' criticisms was breathtaking. For me, the only moment of light relief came when the *Daily Mail* suggested I was 'the brains behind Leveson'. If only! Sadly, this example of dishonesty was over the top even by the *Mail*'s extreme standards. Everyone knew it was nonsense. A pity – I should have liked people to think I was clever enough for it to be true.

Yet, interestingly, opinion polls conducted by YouGov showed the public were standing firm. Poll after poll reported an overwhelming majority in favour of Leveson's plan for an independent press regulator that would be stabilised by a very light-touch law. It seemed that, despite owning the megaphone, the tabloids were not as influential as they imagined. The public was on to them. I often wondered what the owners thought: did the Rothermeres approve of Dacre fighting to defend the *News of the World*? Would they and their friends not object to Murdoch's so-called journalists filming them having sex in their bedrooms? Or, when the criminal trials started, did they see anything strange in the spectacle of expensive lawyers at the Old Bailey fighting hard for Brooks's and Coulson's Article 8 (privacy) rights to stop too many details of their six-year affair emerging?

In contrast, perhaps, to Rothermere, the public know exactly what Brooks and Coulson would have done if they had heard of two film stars conducting a doubly adulterous relationship like that. The megaphone was beginning to fall on deaf ears.

As is well known, one of Leveson's recommendations was a form of statutory underpinning for the independent body tasked with checking that the independent regulator was doing its job. Previous experience had shown that, without this, the press would agree to all sorts of things then, when the dust had settled, they would be back to their old ways. This cycle had been repeated at least six times since the Second World War. Cameron, much too hastily, stood up in parliament and dismissed any form of statutory backing for a regulator – he did this within 24 hours of the inquiry's report appearing. He said that to introduce a statute, however distant from the regulator, would be 'crossing the Rubicon'. It was a very basic mistake. He could easily have taken his time, saying the government would study the inquiry's report. It was, after all, 2000 pages long. The press had got at him, and this was obvious not just to us but also, crucially, to the public.

With the public backing Leveson, and Labour and the Lib Dems tending to support his conclusions, the press became desperate. Above all, they wanted no statute. A statute could not be quietly forgotten after a decent interval. They did not want any risk that a Leveson-style regulator would become permanent; their aim was to get back as quickly as possible to business as usual, with no tiresome impediments. Having managed to do this several times in the past 60 years, they did not intend to fail this time. The political battle lines began to be drawn.

The tabloids were in full cry, but there was also much activity on our side. The newspapers were lobbying furiously and secretly. Editors were seen coming and going from Downing Street. They seemed to have the prime minister on their side. They certainly had his ear. Cameron's appointee, Oliver Letwin, suggested a royal charter. This was intended as a fudge but fooled no one: he and the press were saying that because a royal charter needed no statute, the politicians could be kept away from press regulation.

The reality, of course, was exactly the opposite. A royal charter could be quietly changed by a handful of ministers acting as the Privy Council. They could do this secretly, without reference to parliament. Far from removing the press from political control, it would put a regulator under direct ministerial authority. The tabloids were happy with that because they knew it would put them back in charge. They would soon be able to pressure a future government into allowing them to get back to their old tricks. It would just be a matter of waiting for the right moment.

Labour and the Lib Dems started to understand this. Hacked Off did an excellent job keeping up a steady stream of information to counteract the tendentious nonsense coming from the *Daily Mail* camp. Increasingly, the politicians, including some Tory rebels, were onside. At one point, encouraged by Tom Watson, Ed Miliband came out for Leveson and openly criticised Murdoch. He was the first political leader to do so, and it was a bold move because conventional wisdom was very much against. Yet his support in the opinion polls immediately leapt. This was another indication that, despite all the efforts of the tabloids, the public knew what was going on. Many of them may still read the *Sun*, but they now know what's behind it and that it cannot be trusted.

BBM were active behind the scenes and very effective in parallel with Hacked Off. It was quickly apparent that the government would not allow time for a parliamentary bill to implement Leveson, but there was a plan B. This was to try to amend the Defamation Bill at its report stage in the House of Lords. If this succeeded, it would put the government in a difficult position. If they did not move, they would risk losing the Defamation Bill the press and others desperately wanted. Some suggested amendments were produced. These were put into proper form and redrafted.

The amendments placed great emphasis on access to justice. Despite all the confusion that was being created by the tabloids and their supporters, everyone could see there was something wrong if 99 per cent of the population had no means of redress if their privacy were invaded or they were libelled, particularly so now that Leveson had offered a complete solution to the problem. A formidable alliance then emerged in the House of Lords, headed by Lord Puttnam. Hacked Off were briefly unhappy because the amendments did not seek to implement the whole of Leveson. To begin with they perhaps missed the point that these amendments were never intended to become law; they were meant to send a message about access to justice to Downing Street and to the country beyond.

There was a huge majority (131) in the House of Lords for the Puttnam amendments – the message had been sent and could not have been clearer. The government and the press realised they had a problem and, consequently, press attacks on the Leveson proposals became even more irrational, verging on hysteria. Even the serious papers began to misrepresent the inquiry's proposals. As already mentioned, even for the better editors, it had become theological. They absolutely did not want outsiders interfering with what they did.

I personally understood this somewhat. I had felt much the same when we had a succession of serious accidents in Formula One in 1994. Outsiders were talking about banning it, or getting governments and health and safety legislation involved. The thought of a bunch of well-meaning non-experts trying to fix the problem was anathema to me. But I knew back then that, if we did not genuinely and seriously set out to put things right, we would get what we didn't want. Unlike the press, we hadn't been through this several times before and each time failed to act properly. Whatever sympathy I had was removed by the knowledge that, if the theologians got their way, we would be back to the old tabloid habits in no time at all.

To maintain the pressure, more Leveson amendments appeared in the House of Lords. This time it was the Enterprise Bill. These were much more complete, having been prepared by Hacked Off and drafted by parliamentary counsel. Robert Skidelsky, who is a cross-bench peer, tabled them and immediately came under intense pressure from Downing Street to withdraw. He refused. Then the *Daily Mail* discovered he was an old friend of mine from Oxford days and mounted a full-page attack. Again, he took no notice and stood firm. Next, the Leveson supporters indicated they would also seek to amend the Crime and Courts Bill as it went through the Commons.

The government finally got the message. Unless the Leveson Report was implemented properly, which meant a degree of statutory support, there would be constant disruption to the government's parliamentary business. Every piece of legislation with a suitable bill would be met with amendments to give effect to the Leveson proposals. On Thursday 14 March 2013 Cameron abruptly terminated the cross-party talks on Leveson that had dragged on for months. This crystallised the debate at exactly the right moment – pro-Leveson politicians had even been contemplating ending the talks themselves. Over that weekend, Cameron learned that some courageous Tories would vote with Labour and the Lib Dems on the amendments to the Crime and Courts Bill, despite enormous pressure from Downing Street not to do so. It was increasingly clear that, if it came to a vote in the Commons, the government was likely to lose.

During the same weekend, Hacked Off had a late-night meeting with Ed Miliband and Nick Clegg in Miliband's office and explained that the victims wanted cross-party agreement. Apparently, Oliver Letwin joined the meeting a bit later. The press represented this as a meeting in which the royal charter was thrown together over pizzas. The Hacked Off people saw no pizzas and the accusation of secret meetings and deals was strange coming from the press, who had had endless meetings with the government over the preceding months. All the meeting really did was give the victims an opportunity to comment on the proposals that were already in the draft royal charter which had been negotiated by the government with the press over a number of months.

But we had all long since grown used to the press dissembling at every opportunity. Although I was in touch with them, I was not part of Hacked Off and was not at the meeting. I did not know what had happened so was slightly wrong-footed doing a live radio interview in a van outside my London base the following morning. Fortunately, Harriet Harman was on just ahead of me and before I had to say anything it emerged that agreement had been reached.

The key question remained statute or no statute. In particular, whether there should be a statutory provision to prevent ministerial amendment of the royal charter. This was the fundamental difference between the position of the government and what had become an alliance of Labour, Lib Dems and other parties in the Commons backed by cross-benchers in the Lords. It was a vital issue because stopping ministers amending the charter without parliamentary scrutiny was essential if the press were to be prevented from going back to their old ways once things had calmed down. No one understood this better than the press themselves – hence their virulent opposition to any sort of statute. Above all, they did not want to be made to keep to their agreement.

Until his hand was forced, Cameron backed the press, no doubt with an eye to his own career and their support during the 2015 election. But over that weekend he heard from some of his backbenchers and eventually conceded the point. On the Monday, we at last had cross-party agreement that the royal charter could not be amended without a vote in parliament. There would be no quiet deals with ministers letting the press off the hook. A debate was scheduled for that afternoon and Tom Watson arranged a seat in the gallery for me. With everything that had happened over the past five years, it was a strange sensation listening to the speeches of the three party leaders congratulating each other on the agreement they had reached.

Next day I appeared once again before the Culture, Media and Sport Select Committee, this time with Brian Cathcart and Hugh Tomlinson QC. Three of the press-supporting Tories on the committee were clearly furious about the cross-party agreement. They seemed to be almost biting the carpet in their rage and repeatedly attacked, although rather ineffectually. Each time, they came off second best, particularly in exchanges with Hugh Tomlinson, who was much more than a match for them. The rest of the committee were objective and understood the issues. It was an entertaining morning, but with more to come.

Two days later I took part in a Joint Criminal Bar Association and Law Reform Committee debate on 'Protecting free speech: A Public Interest Defence for the Media?', with Gavin Millar QC and Gill Phillips, the *Guardian*'s lawyer, on the other side and Richard Drabble QC on the same side as me. Sir Anthony Hooper, a recently retired Appeal Court judge, was in the chair.

Afterwards, Lady Hooper told me she'd once interviewed my mother and that I said 'do' in exactly the same way as her. That was a bit disconcerting, as even my father used to make fun of my mother's posh voice. On his retirement, Sir Anthony had given a brilliant lecture to the Inner Temple (22 June 2012) that anyone who is interested in the rule of law and individual liberty, as well as the problem of drugs in modern society, should read.

No sooner had a draft royal charter been prepared than the press put forward a different charter and submitted it to the Privy Council. This was calculated to delay the entire process. It succeeded but by October 2013 the charter prepared by some of the press had been rejected and the Queen signed the government's version. Elements of the press even commenced legal proceedings to stop the royal charter by judicial review, but predictably this failed. Meanwhile, a bigger danger was that the three main press groups were setting up their own wholly inadequate regulator with many essential Leveson elements missing, not least the vitally important arbitral arm giving general access to justice. It was to be under the financial control of the three press barons and their newspaper groups: Associated Newspapers, Telegraph Media Group and, of course, Murdoch's News International, now renamed News UK.

Having repeatedly said there must be no political influence, the press barons initially appointed two Conservative peers (Lords Black and Hunt) to be in charge. It was remarkable that they were prepared to ignore Lord Justice Leveson's recommendations plus an almost unanimous House of Commons and, according to innumerable opinion polls, a steady 70 per cent or so of the general public. It was two fingers to democracy and the rule of law. Their arrogance is astonishing.

Their hope, quite clearly, was that if they set up their own regulator it would become a fait accompli, despite falling way short of Leveson and having no statutory underpinning to stop the press backsliding. Then, in the absence of a Leveson-compliant regulator, the provisions of the Crime and Courts Act would not come into operation and the royal charter would be a dead letter.

The structure they have created consists of a supposedly independent regulator known as IPSO (Independent Press Standards Organisation). They have appointed Sir Alan Moses, an independent-minded former Appeal Court judge, as chairman. Coincidentally, it was he who chaired the first Gray's Inn event in January 2010 mentioned in the previous chapter. That appointment was promising but the difficulty was, and remains, that IPSO is not only constitutionally far short of Leveson, but it also sits under another body, the Regulatory Funding Company (RFC), which is controlled by the usual coterie of Murdoch, Rothermere and the Barclay twins. The RFC has veto rights over IPSO covering the so-called Editors' Code, the IPSO regulations, any arbitral system, investigations, the voting regulations, financial sanctions guidance and so on. In other words, total industry control. It will be interesting to see if Sir Alan can rebalance things.

Meanwhile, an alternative body to IPSO has been set up by Jonathan Heawood.* Called IMPRESS, it will be fully Leveson compliant and has attracted a number of local newspapers and other publishers. It is supported by public money. Importantly, it includes an arbitral system that can give members of the public and less wealthy newspapers access to justice in disputes about

---

* Jonathan Heawood is a former director of programmes at the Sigrid Rausing Trust, Europe's largest private human rights foundation, director of the English Centre of International PEN, deputy literary editor of the *Observer* and editor of the *Fabian Review*.

libel, breach of privacy, harassment and so on. This will prevent financial bullying of individuals by rich newspapers. It will also stop financial intimidation of freelance journalists and small local newspapers by wealthy individuals. Quite clearly, press regulation is in a state of flux but, for the first time since the Second World War, it seems possible that the tabloids will not be able to go back to their old ways, as they always have in the past.

Apart from my interest in press regulation and privacy in the human rights sense, I am following closely what is happening about Rupert Murdoch and his companies in both the UK and the USA. There are also further trials involving Murdoch's journalists in the UK, and questions about how involved James was in everything that happened while he was in charge of his family's UK operation. I am also pursuing litigation against Google in the hope that they will eventually understand that a free and open internet (which I fully support) does not require them to ignore court decisions of democratic countries. On the contrary, responsible adults accept the rule of law as being, among other things, the guarantor of our most basic freedoms.

In a very real sense, I am still living the last chapters of this book, but it will be some time before the open questions on privacy are resolved. All are works in progress and the lawyers say they cannot yet be written about in any detail. I therefore have no choice but to leave them open for the time being if I want this book to come out while the last years of my involvement in Formula One are still of interest. My work on road safety, in particular crash-testing with Global NCAP, also continues and this, too, is far from finished. So, nearly 50 years after abandoning the law for a more exciting life there's no chance of retirement just yet.

APPENDIX

HOW THE FIA WORKS

In 1979, immediately after Jean-Marie Balestre was first elected president of the FIA's sporting division, the Commission Sportive Internationale or CSI, the FIA was divided into five international commissions:

- Touring
- Traffic
- Customs
- Sporting
- Technical

These were all under a Committee and an Executive Committee elected by the FIA's General Assembly. Except for sport, the original purpose of these commissions was to co-ordinate internationally the attempts of the national motoring organisations to encourage and facilitate motoring on the roads. For example, the FIA Customs Commission issued the *carnet de passage en douane*, which enabled a motorist to drive into another country without paying duty on the car. The FIA Traffic Commission lobbied successfully for international conventions on traffic signs and the Technical Commission persuaded the car industry to agree that the accelerator and brake pedals should be in the same place on all cars. In some early models the accelerator was in the middle, the brake on the right – not ideal in an emergency if you were used to driving a car with the other layout.

Thus the FIA's sporting division, the CSI, was technically just one of the FIA's five commissions. However, despite the importance of the FIA's general motoring commissions in the first half of the 20th century, by 1979 the Commission Sportive Internationale, or CSI, was by far the most important part of the FIA. The commissions dealing with everyday motoring still existed but had become more or less moribund. Even the Customs Commission had lost a lot of its *carnet* business to a rival organisation, the Alliance Internationale de Tourisme, to which all the major clubs also belonged. Several big clubs with no involvement in motor sport, like the British AA and the Dutch ANWB, were AIT only.

Under the CSI, there were a number of sporting sub-commissions. These dealt with different forms of racing, rallies, circuits, the scheduling of international events, karting, historic racing cars and so on. As noted in chapter 12, soon after his election Balestre persuaded the FIA to change the name of the CSI to Fédération Internationale du Sport Automobile, or FISA. This, as he intended, gave the illusion that FISA was an international sports federation like any other, but in reality it was still just a commission of the FIA. When Balestre became president of the FIA itself in 1985, he retained his presidency of FISA. This caused him problems later, as described in chapter 17.

This remained the structure until 1993 when I was elected president of the FIA (after two years as president of FISA). I then proposed a new constitution to the FIA General Assembly, giving sport and the non-sporting side equal status.

The new structure looked like this:

FEDERATION INTERNATIONALE de L'AUTOMOBILE

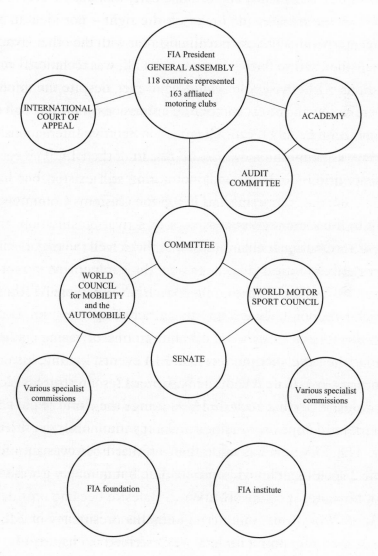

Having made these changes, we began the revival of the non-sporting side, as explained in chapters 31 and 32.

The evolution of international motor sport

The FIA was founded in 1904 by the national motoring clubs in 13 countries. Apart from the need for internationally co-ordinated lobbying on behalf of their motorist members, the clubs realised that, with significant and growing motor sport activity, there had to be internationally agreed technical rules – engine size, weight, dimensions and so forth – if there were to be international competitions. Otherwise you would have cars built to completely different specifications competing against one another, making competition largely meaningless.

How a competition was to be run in each country was left almost entirely to its national motor sport authority but, at least after 1904, the competing cars in a given category would now be built to the same regulations.

For international championships, there were similar but not necessarily identical rules as to how the competition would be run in different countries, but generally the national authority decided the non-technical questions, including schedules, race or rally distances, categories of car allowed to compete and so on.

Early on, the members of the FIA agreed an International Sporting Code to deal with the basic rules for international competitions, including such things as procedures for rule changes, protests and appeals. Modified and expanded, it survives to this day. The FIA now has more than 135 member countries with some 230 clubs, although some are purely motoring organisations with no motor sport involvement.

Apart from this minimal international supervision, each national motor sport authority was sovereign in its territory. As the FIA's official motor sport rule book rather quaintly put it back in 1969:

The sporting power entrusted to the FIA as regards motoring sport originated in the uniting of the powers detained in their respective countries by the ACNs. This power is therefore a common property.

(The official language of the FIA has always been French, hence this rather strange English translation.)

By the time I became involved in motor sport 62 years after the FIA was founded, it had become universally recognised as the regulatory body for all international motor sport. Its position was reinforced by the fact that, in many countries, its member organisation was recognised by law as the sole national motor sport authority.

In each country, the ACN or 'Automobile Club Nationale' was the body that had overall charge of motor sport and issued competition licences, including licences to compete internationally. In some countries, the ACN would delegate its sporting authority to a specialised body, the so-called 'Association Sportive Nationale' or ASN. Although there is often more than one FIA member organisation in a country, only one FIA member is recognised in each country as the national sporting authority.

The FIA was therefore effectively a forum in which the different countries, represented by ACNs and ASNs, agreed the international motor sport rules. Formula One, for example, started off as a set of technical regulations for single-seat racing cars internationally agreed in 1948 by the ACNs and ASNs within the FIA. The same was later true for Formula Two and Formula Three.

Technical regulations for an international competition might also be devised by a commercial entity – for example, Formula Renault by the eponymous car company – and then submitted to the FIA for approval via the ACN or ASN of the organising company's country. Technical regulations for purely national competitions were not the concern of the FIA and could be different in each country.

All international races were subject to the above-mentioned International Sporting Code and still are to this day. Disputes were settled by stewards appointed by the country where the competition took place (and in some cases by the FIA) with a right of appeal to the FIA's International Court of Appeal if more than one nationality was involved in the dispute.

In this way, international events were organised and managed by the ACN or ASN, the national sporting authority in each country under the ultimate authority of the FIA. However, the commercial rights to events on the FIA calendar belonged in each case to the promoter of the event. The rights to commercial series like Formula Renault are governed by contracts between the organising company and the race promoters. The company would often pay the promoter to include the race in its programme. These commercial arrangements were not the concern of the FIA. Its role was entirely supervisory – its function was to ensure the rules were observed in international events and settle disputes of a sporting nature.

Licences to compete internationally were issued to both drivers and teams by their national sporting authority. Surprisingly, there were no international standards and the experience necessary to gain the right to compete in an international event anywhere in the world varied widely. When I was racing in the 1960s, the RAC, the UK's national motor sport authority, would give you an international licence once you had raced in 12 club events without incident. You could then race in Formula One if you could get hold of a car.

It wasn't until the 1980s that the FIA, under pressure from FOCA and the drivers, required a certain minimum level of experience for Formula One drivers and began to issue the so-called super licence. In other forms of racing, international licences issued by an ACN (or ASN) continued to suffice. The licensing and rules for purely local or national competitions are still entirely under the control of the ACN in each country.

As recently as 1969, the FIA's International Sporting Code was a small publication intended to fit in a pocket. It was even padded out with pictures of cars and drivers, advertisements, lists of circuits, addresses of racing car manufacturers and all the ACNs. The rules set out in the code were minimal. Almost everything was left to the ACNs, who would lay down detailed regulations for each international event in accordance with the code and send them to the FIA for approval three months in advance.

For major events like Formula One, the promoter was very often the ACN or ASN itself. Motoring clubs, too, sometimes own international races. For example, the Le Mans 24-hour race is owned by the Automobile Club de l'Ouest, an important French regional club. As the promoter, the ACO owns the television rights, the circuit advertising, all the ancillary rights (such as allowing a sponsor to have people in promotional livery on the starting grid, and so on) as well as the right to accept or reject an entry and charge a competitor an entry fee.

A promoter wishing to run an international event – meaning one open to competition licence-holders from another country – would ask its ACN or ASN (if the promoter was not itself the relevant national sporting authority) to apply to put it on the FIA's international calendar drawn up by the FIA's Calendar Commission. Inclusion on the calendar publicised the event for the benefit of potential competitors but, more importantly, the commission would ensure that there were not two international events for the same kind of car on the same day. There were also rules to stop big events falling on the same weekend and conventions for determining priority if two promoters asked for the same date.

As the FIA was a federation of national motor sport authorities (ACNs and ASNs), it was they who provided the membership of the Calendar Commission and decided the calendar of international events. The FIA charged a modest calendar fee for each of these and that was the extent of its commercial involvement.

In time, championships began to emerge. For example the Formula One World Championship for drivers began in 1950 (the Constructors' Championship started in 1958 as a 'cup'). Any promoter could decide to run a Formula One race at any time and the FIA would put it on the international calendar provided certain basic requirements were met. But the event would not necessarily be part of the Formula One World Championship. In 1969, for example, in addition to the 11 events making up the Formula One World Championship, there were three non-championship Formula One events in the UK – the Race of Champions at Brands Hatch, the International Trophy at Silverstone and the Gold Cup at Oulton Park – plus a non-championship race, the Madrid Grand Prix, at Jarama in Spain.

The agreement between the ACN/ASNs and race promoters within the FIA was that no country should have more than one event counting for the Formula One World Championship each year, although an exception was later made for the USA because of its size. Then Italy got an extra event in 1981 as the San Marino Grand Prix. This was a FOCA tribute to Ferrari (the Imola circuit was named after his deceased son Dino); then the

UK was given an extra event in 1983 as the European Grand Prix at Brands Hatch. As a result, a second race in a single country for FOCA's commercial reasons became quite usual. The FIA's only financial interest in its championships (including Formula One) was its calendar fee for each event. All the commercial rights belonged to the promoter in each case, as they still do at Le Mans.

The FIA's role in motor sport was to provide the forum in which rules were agreed, then to supervise and referee the resulting events. It was never a commercial body. Balestre's efforts, and to a lesser extent mine, to involve the FIA in the sport commercially came to an end in 2002 when we made the deal with the European Commission. In effect, that deal returned things to the *status quo ante* and made sure they would stay there. Probably best for everyone in the end.

INDEX

2i's Coffee Bar, Soho 9

Acropolis Rally 239
advertising rights 168, 169
Agnelli, Gianni 275–6
Ahrens, Kurt 38
air restrictors 334–6
Akers, Sue 444
Al-Fayed, Mohamed 247
Alessi, Rosario 217
Alfa Romeo 64, 135, 137, 145, 146, 149,
    156, 158
Alliance Internationale de Tourisme
    (AIT) 198, 356, 357, 474
Alonso, Fernando 306, 342, 351, 352
American Automobile Association
    (AAA) 299, 356
American racing scene 228–30
Amon, Chris 51–2, 55, 56, 57, 59, 61–2,
    238
Andretti, Mario 56, 57, 79, 87, 100, 305
Anstey, Gordon 28
anti-lock braking system (ABS) 373
antitrust violation 378
Argentine Grand Prix 98–9
    1974 73
    1977 86–9
    1979 135–6
    1981 158

Armco barriers 252
Ashley, Ian 49
Ashman, Jonathan 199
Association Sportive Nationale (ASN)
    477, 478, 479, 480
ATS team 91
Audetto, Daniele 79, 110
Austin, Ronnie 159
Australian Grand Prix
    1994 271
    2009 307, 349
Austrian Grand Prix 1975 75–6
Auto Union 73
Automobilclub von Deutschland (AvD)
    132
Automobile Association (AA) 356
Automobile Club de France (ACF)
    118–19
Automobile Club de l'Ouest (ACO) 479
Automobile Club di Milano 124
Automobile Club Nationale (ACN) 477,
    478, 479, 480
Automobile Competitions Committee
    for the United States (ACCUS)
    228, 328
Autosport 27, 30, 84, 169, 292
Axel Springer Verlag 424

Bahrain Grand Prix 404–5

Balestre, Jean-Marie 97, 103–4, 119, 120, 132–3, 134, 135, 136–7, 140–2, 143–4, 145–7, 148, 150–1, 152, 157, 159, 160, 167, 168, 176–7, 178, 179, 187–9, 190, 191, 192, 193, 194, 195, 196, 198, 209–10, 214, 227, 241, 242, 271, 276, 290, 375, 474, 481

Bangemann, Martin 359, 367

Banks, Tony 201

Barclay brothers 471

'barge boards' 274–5

Barnett, Professor Steve 453

Barrichello, Rubens 248

Bayer AG 51

BBM 461, 465

Belgian Grand Prix 113
    1970 59, 61
    1980 143
    1998 377–8

Beltoise, Jean-Pierre 69

Benetton 263, 264, 269, 270

Benson, David 121–2

Berger, Gerhard 226, 257, 358, 359

Berger, Jacques 336

Berkeley, Humphry 181, 182

Berlusconi, Silvio 256, 257–8

Bermondsey by-election (1983) 184–5

Bertarelli, Ernesto 247

Betjeman, John 5

Beuttler, Mike 67

Bild 424

Black and Tans 6

blackmail 399–400, 401, 403, 423, 454, 455, 458, 460

Blair, Cherie 199–200

Blair, Tony 199, 200, 202, 203, 242, 387, 431

Blatter, Sepp 389

Bloor, Rodney 21

BMW 68, 69–70, 73, 123, 181, 266, 291, 318, 409

Boeri, Michel 100, 101, 108, 112, 119, 121, 124, 150, 153, 195, 217, 406–7

Bolt, Robert 9

Bordeo, Eduardo 114, 115, 119, 127

Bossom, Sir Clive 110, 111, 121, 142

Bower, Tom 347

Brabham, Jack 39, 64, 243

Brabham BT23C 32, 33, 44, 47

Brabham team 49, 81, 82, 90, 91, 128–9, 163, 177, 178, 180

Brambilla, Vittorio 73, 74, 75–6, 78, 81–2, 238

Brands Hatch 30, 33, 64, 163, 480, 481

Brawn, Ross 275

Brawn team 306

Brazilian Grand Prix 98

breakaway proposals 287–91, 294, 323, 325, 326

breakaway series 1980–81 152–4, 157–8

Briatore, Flavio 247, 290, 293, 301, 302, 311, 321, 324, 342, 351, 352, 353, 354, 408

Bridgestone 260, 301, 303

Briggs, Pete 54

British American Tobacco 272–3, 339

British Grand Prix
    1968 165
    1973 70
    1977 139
    1994 270
    1999 274
    2003 207
    2009 323

British Union of Fascists 1

BRM 55, 59, 63, 65

Brooks, Rebekah 425–6, 431, 446, 460, 463–4

Brundle, Martin 238

Bryant, Chris 431, 441–2

BSkyB 447, 448

Buenos Aires 86

Buzzi, Aleardo 149–50, 156–7

Cadwell Park 48

Caesars Palace Grand Prix 1981 174–6

Caldwell, Alastair 80

Callaghan, Jim 16

Cameron, David 431, 444, 450, 464, 467, 469

Canadian Grand Prix 1975 104–5

CanAm 41, 50, 51, 61, 238

Cantarella, Paolo 217, 218, 219

carbon sequestration project 364–5

Carey, Lord 421–2

Carman, George 270

Carmen, César 126–7
CARS 21 High Level Group 363
catalysers 364
Cathcart, Brian 446, 461, 469
Cercle National des Armées 159
Cevert, François 252
Chambelland, François 119
Chandler, Morrie 192–3
Channon, Paul 194
Chapman, Colin 54, 63, 64, 76, 94, 130,
    131, 155–6, 165, 252, 260
cheating 333–54
Chinese motor sport 230–1
Churchill, Winston 1, 2, 110
Clarendon Laboratory, Oxford 16
Clark, Jim 17, 35, 36, 169, 260
Clarke, Kenneth 272
Clegg, Nick 468
Clifford, Max 436, 437
Clonfert 6, 8
Clubmans Sports Cars 27, 28, 358
Coaker, Graham 43, 48, 50, 61
Commission Sportive Internationale
    (CSI) 97, 103–27, 133, 136, 137, 474
    name change to FISA 136–7
competition law, European 106, 152,
    161, 167, 212–13, 233, 378, 383
Concorde Agreement 159–61, 162, 167,
    177, 188, 208–9, 210, 281, 312–17,
    322, 326, 327, 328, 329, 330–1, 412
Concorde airliner 41
Coninck, Pierre de 190
Constantin Medien 326, 328–9
Constructors' Championship 52, 61, 64,
    345, 480
copper brake discs 63–4
Corbari, Pier Luigi 145
cornering speeds 139–40, 148–9, 151,
    230, 252–3, 259, 260
Corsmit, Jan 191
Cosworth 41, 49, 53, 137, 139, 287
    DFV engine 53, 138, 177
    Ford Cosworth 53
    FVA engine 35
    V8 engine 149, 151, 180
Coughlan, Mike 341, 343, 345, 348
Coulson, Andy 425–6, 439, 444, 450,
    463–4

Courage, Piers 37–8, 41, 59
Crabbe, Colin 58
crash tests 254, 358–9, 360–3, 366, 368–9
Cresto, Sergio 188
Crime and Courts Act 467, 471
criminal law in sport 235–6, 258–9, 386
Crombac, Gérard 145
Crone, Tom 397, 404, 414
Crossley, Dominic 394, 425, 432, 448,
    450, 451
Crowood 2–3, 4, 5, 14
Crux Easton 2, 5
Crystal Palace 30
Cubas, Marqués de 144, 145
Currie, Mal 123
Curzon, Cynthia 3
CVC 222, 223, 303, 325–6, 328, 329, 331,
    408–10

Dacre, Paul 407, 421, 429, 431, 436, 452,
    463
Daily Express 412
Daily Mail 184, 394, 401, 403, 407, 417,
    421, 434, 463, 465, 467
Daily Telegraph 201
Daly, Ken 276, 330, 375, 381–2, 385
Dance, Bob 77
dangerous sports
    common law approaches to 259
    manslaughter charges 235–6
    prosecution for negligence 258–9
Darbelnet, Bob 299
Davies, Nick 436, 437, 445, 448
Dawson, John 370
Daytona 24 hours 163
de Adamich, Andrea 64
de la Rosa, Pedro 342
deaths in motor racing
    drivers 36, 38, 59, 65, 74, 75, 90, 129,
        188, 248–50, 252
    marshals 75, 90
    spectators 74
Defamation Bill 465–6
Delamont, Dean 110, 111, 121, 123, 126
Dennis, Ron 195, 227, 238, 302, 339,
    342, 346–7
Denton Wilde Sapte 288
Depailler, Patrick 73, 151

Devonshire, Duke and Duchess of 183
diffusers 306–7
Domingo, Placido 273
Donington Park 70
Donnelly, Alan 357, 358, 359, 361, 367,
      370, 375, 406, 411, 448, 449
Donohue, Mark 75
Dowler, Milly 436, 445, 446, 448
Drabble, Richard 469
Drake, Sir Maurice 25, 259, 386
drugs 80–1
Duckworth, Keith 53, 310
Duffeler, Pat 106, 107, 109, 115, 117,
      119, 121, 122, 123, 124, 125, 127
Dutch Grand Prix
   1973 70
   1976 77
'Dying Agreement' 211

Eady, Sir David 402, 417, 420, 421, 422,
      455, 456, 457, 458, 459
Eason, Kevin 359
Ecclestone, Bernie 49–50, 61–2, 74, 82,
      89, 97, 98–9, 100, 101, 111–13, 195,
      279, 302, 303, 343, 346, 385, 395,
      406, 442
   and cost caps 311
   Concorde Agreement 159–61, 162,
      167, 177, 188, 208–9, 210, 281,
      312–17, 322, 326, 327, 328, 329,
      330–1, 412
   confrontations with CSI–WCR
      103–27
   contract with FIA 210, 211, 212–14,
      216, 217–23, 224, 290, 327, 328,
      384
   control of Formula One 132, 161,
      165, 166, 167–8, 169–71, 172–3,
      174–6, 208, 209, 211, 219–20,
      287–8, 289, 290, 312–17, 326,
      386
   dispute with Competition Directorate
      216–17
   'Dying Agreement' 211
   FIA vice president 189–90
   floats Formula One assets 172,
      213–15, 216
   and GPWC plan 287–90
   Labour Party donation 200–1, 202,
      203–4, 273, 376
   media and commercial rights 161,
      165, 166, 167, 168, 209, 211, 214,
      220, 221
   and Mosley scandal 395, 408, 410,
      411, 412
   negotiating style 95, 104–5, 120–1,
      218
   opportunism 96
   and other types of motorsport 232–3,
      234
   pranks 95, 99, 119, 180, 385
   sets up World Federation of Motor
      Sport 152
   strategic limitations 96
   takes over Brabham 91, 94, 128–9,
      163
   wealth 172, 214, 216, 225
   World Council member 188
   see also Formula One Constructors'
      Association (FOCA)
Ecclestone, Slavica 247
Editors' Code 471
Edmondson, Ian 441
electronic driver assistance 249–50,
      261–4, 265
electronic stability control 265, 373
Elf 73, 119, 267
Elford, Vic 58
EM.TV 218–19, 222
energy efficiency 292–5, 300
energy recovery and reuse system
      (KERS) 294, 295
engines
   cost-reduction measures 282–7
   limit on numbers used per season 285
   naturally aspirated 139
   new engine rules 293–4
   standard engine proposal 286
   supercharged 138
   turbocharged 138–9, 180, 181, 336–7
   see also Cosworth
Enterprise Bill 467
ERTICO Intelligent Transport Systems
      Europe 370, 372
eSafety Aware Communications
      Platform 372

eSafety Forum 371
Essex Overseas Petroleum Corporation 174
Eton 3
European arrest warrant (EAW) 235–6
European Automobile Manufacturers' Association (ACEA) 217, 311
European Commission 161, 201, 202, 215, 288, 290, 313, 357, 359, 361, 371, 375–89
    CARS 21 High Level Group 363
    Competition Directorate 216–17, 375–89
    'European Model of Sport' 387
    Nice Declaration on Sport 388
European Convention on Human Rights 428–9, 432
European Court of Human Rights 428, 432–4
European Grand Prix 481
    1997 203, 273
European New Car Assessment Programme (Euro NCAP) 254, 360–3, 368
European Parliament Automobile Users' Intergroup 357
European Touring Car Championship 64
Eurovision 166

Fangio, Juan Manuel 87, 98, 114, 115, 119, 381
Faure, Patrick 290
Federación Española de Automovilismo (FEA) 144, 145
Fédération Internationale de Football Association (FIFA) 389
Fédération Internationale de l'Automobile (FIA) 86, 100, 111, 118, 473–81
    Balestre presidency see Balestre, Jean-Marie
    Calendar Commission 479
    championships 480–1
    close relationship with the car industry 134–5, 137–8
    and commercial rights 161, 164, 166–7, 208–23, 383, 386, 481
    commissions 473–4

Concorde Agreement 159–61, 162, 167, 177, 188, 208–9, 210, 281, 322, 326, 328
control of technical regulations 135
European Commission investigation 375–89
FIA Foundation 223–5, 369, 370
Formula One Working Group 117, 123, 136, 150
formula restricting number of starters 101–2
General Assembly 145, 198, 212, 223, 268, 379, 381, 410, 413
Governance in Sport working group 388
GT Commission 55
Hundred Year Agreement 222, 223, 224, 327, 329
Institute for Motor Sport Safety 34
International Court of Appeal 178, 191, 268, 276–7, 307, 339, 343–4, 345, 353, 384
member organisations 477
Mosley presidency see under Mosley, Max
non-profit-making body 123, 194–5
origins of 476
receipts from Formula One 209–10, 386, 481
regulator of international motor sport 96, 161, 375, 383–4, 386, 476–8
road car division 198, 355–63
safety work 55, 223, 224–5, 251–7, 273, 299, 355–63, 366
Senate 198, 360, 404
sport categories 234–5
structure and operation of 473–81
technical department 268–9, 293, 307
Todt presidency see Todt, Jean
World Motor Sport Council 141, 160, 187, 188, 190, 197–8, 243, 255, 270, 273, 313–17, 330, 412
see also Commission Sportive Internationale (CSI); Fédération Internationale du Sport Automobile (FISA)
Fédération Internationale de Motocyclisme (FIM) 234, 255, 259

Fédération Internationale du Sport
    Automobile (FISA)
  FOCA–FISA war 134–62, 166, 213,
    290, 326
  Manufacturers' Commission 187, 188,
    189, 190, 336–7
Feisal Al Hussein, HRH Prince 406
Ferguson, Andrew 100, 165
Ferrari, Dino 480
Ferrari, Enzo 99, 110, 111–13, 115, 130,
    136, 138, 146, 147, 156, 159, 176,
    178–9
Ferrari, Piero 113, 195
Ferrari team 35, 52, 64, 77, 79, 81, 85,
    88, 100, 110, 114, 117, 135, 136,
    137, 138, 143, 145, 149, 150, 157,
    158, 160, 176, 178, 252, 257, 274–5,
    278, 289, 307, 311, 312, 321, 322,
    323, 339–45, 347, 348, 411
Fiat 138, 319
Firestone 56–7
Fittipaldi, Emerson 115, 238
Flimm, Otto 217
flywheel technology 295–6
Foot, Paul 15
Ford 53, 283, 309
Ford, Anna 436
Ford Mexico 64
Forghieri, Mauro 89, 114, 115
Formula 5000 40
Formula E 225
Formula Ford 50, 51
Formula Libre 39
Formula One
  cheating 338–54
  commercial rights 125, 161, 165–8,
    173, 208–15, 220–1
  cost caps 310–11, 318–24, 328
  deaths see deaths in motor racing
  event rationalisation 161–2
  expenditure 50, 280–1, 282, 309–10
  licences 51, 176, 478–9
  power struggle for control of 132, 133,
    134–62, 166, 213, 290, 326
  prize fund 103, 104–5, 107, 124–5, 131,
    147, 164, 165, 169–70, 170, 172
  R&D expenditure 282, 292, 310, 311,
    320

race contracts 169
team size 69
Formula One Constructors' and
    Entrants' Association 94, 165
  see also Formula One Constructors'
    Association (FOCA)
Formula One Constructors' Association
    (FOCA) 85, 94–127, 108, 130,
    130–3, 167, 179, 183, 327, 481
  FOCA–FISA war 134–62, 166, 213,
    290, 326
Formula One Teams' Association
    (FOTA) 286, 320–4
Formula One Technical Working Group
    255
Formula One World Championship
  1969 53
  1971 64
  1976 78
  1977 88
  1983 180
  1994 271
  1995 274
  2007 343
Formula Three 46, 48–9, 50, 51, 68, 76
Formula Two 30–1, 32–9, 45–6, 50, 51,
    65, 68, 69, 70, 91
France, Bill 229
French Grand Prix
  1968 38
  1980 151
Frère, Paul 252, 260
Frost, Ron 149, 192
fuel 265–7, 292
fuel-flow formula 142

Ganley, Howden 73, 86
Gardner, Colin 28, 29
Gardner, Derek 89, 90
Gendebien, Olivier 252
general elections
  1959 13
  1966 23, 26
  1983 185–6
  1992 431
  2010 450
George, Tony 302
German Grand Prix 132

1975 104–5
1978 132, 170, 171
1994 269
Ghosn, Carlos 311–12
Giggs, Ryan 433
Glasgow, Edwin 276
global financial crisis 309, 318–19, 326–7
Global NCAP 368–9, 373
Gold Cup 480
Goldman Sachs 288
Goodman, Clive 397, 440
Goodwin, Fred 406
Goodyear 154, 157
Google 443–4, 472
Göschel, Professor Burkhard 291–2, 294
Goutard, Guy 230, 240
GP2 288, 320
Grabiner, Anthony 272
Granatelli, Andy 56
Grand Prix see entries for individual countries
Grand Prix Drivers' Association 253
Grand Prix World Championship (GPWC) 287–91
grandi costruttori 145, 149
Grant, Hugh 446, 451, 452, 461
Great Train Robbery 73
Green, Ron 184, 185
green technology 364–5
grooved tyres 260
ground-effect car design 77, 149
Guardian 436, 445, 448, 469
Guild of Motoring Writers 121–2
Guinness, Bryan (2nd Baron Moyne) 3
Guinness, Desmond (MM's half-brother) 2, 3
Guinness, Henrietta 32
Guinness, Ingrid 8
Guinness, Jonathan (MM's half-brother, later, 3rd Baron Moyne) 2, 3, 8, 66
Guiter, François 119, 120, 125

Hacked Off 446, 461, 465, 466, 467, 468
Hahne, Hubert 59–60
Hahnenkamm downhill ski race 155
Hailsham, Lord 26
Häkkinen, Mika 238, 274

Hamilton, Lewis 245, 342, 343, 346, 349–50
Hanstein, Huschke von 106, 107, 116, 119, 123
Harman, Harriet 468
Harris, Dr Evan 446
Harrod, Roy 10
Harvey, Ian 185
Haug, Norbert 282, 347
Hawthorn 351
Hayes, Walter 53, 59
Head, Patrick 236, 258
Heawood, Jonathan 471
helicopter refuelling times 206–7
helmets 243, 244
Henderson, Dr Michael 34
Herbert Smith 220, 221, 388
Herd, Robin 41, 42, 43, 44, 48, 49, 50, 51, 54, 56–7, 58, 59, 61, 63, 64, 65, 66, 67, 68, 73, 74, 75, 77–8, 81, 83, 84, 86, 90–1, 92–3, 163, 259
Hersant, Robert 103
Hesketh, Lord 68–9, 72, 73
Hesketh, Walter 19–20
high-octane fuel 266
Hill, Damon 200, 257, 271
Hill, David 442
Hill, Graham 17, 31, 35–6, 37, 45, 46
hill climbs 235
historic cars 238–9, 243–4
Hitler, Adolf 1, 3, 4, 7
Hobbs, Professor Adrian 360–1
Hockenheim 35–6, 37, 132, 171
Hoffmann, Lord 438
Honda 282–3, 318, 319, 338–9
Hooper, Sir Anthony 469, 470
Hornegold, Bob 28, 29
Howett, John 318, 321, 324
Huddleston, Father Trevor 14
Hulme, Denny 41, 75
Hundred Year Agreement 222, 223, 224, 327, 329
Hunt, James 33, 49, 68–9, 72–3, 78, 79, 80–1, 85, 109
hurling 6

Ickx, Jacky 31, 74
Imola 170, 179, 180, 183

IMPRESS 471–2
Inch Kenneth 3, 4
Independent Press Standards
    Organisation (IPSO) 471
Indianapolis 36, 92, 229–30, 278, 301–5
IndyCar 228, 328
Institut du Cerveau et de la Moelle
    Épinière 299
International Olympic Committee
    386–7, 389
International Road Assessment
    Programme (IRAP) 369–70
International Sporting Code 152, 208,
    290, 321, 322, 383, 476, 478, 479
International Trophy 480
    1961 17
internet technology 173, 234
Iraq, invasion of 206
Irion, Tanja 424
Irish War of Independence 6
Irvine, Eddie 274
Italian Grand Prix 165
    1971 61–2
    1976 77, 78
    1978 129
    1994 255–7
Italian Olympic Committee 258, 386

Jackson, Derek 10–11
Jackson, Pamela (MM's aunt) 2, 10
Jägermeister 73
Jaguar 311
James, Roy 73–4
Japanese Grand Prix
    1976 78
    1989 191
    1990 191
    1991 226
Japanese manufacturers 190–1
Jarier, Jean-Pierre 69, 70
Jaussaud, Jean-Pierre 38
Jay, Peter 15
Jay, Robert 453, 456–7, 459
Jefferies, Christopher 451
Johnson, Lyndon B. 278
Johnson, Melanie 221
Jones, Alan 146
Jordan, Eddie 277

Jordan team 277
Jowell, Tessa 201–2

Kahn-Harris, Dr Keith 403
karting 244–6
Keown, Tim 238
Kerr, Pete 54, 71
Kincraft 39–40
Kingston, Mike 221
Kinnock, Neil 376
Kinsella, Stephen 375, 376, 377, 385,
    388
Kirch, Leo 218, 219, 221, 222
Kiryanov, General 373
Kohl, Helmut 387
Kyalami 57

Labour Party
    1000 Club 199
    Ecclestone's donation to 200–1, 202,
        203–4, 273, 376
Lambton, Lord 194
Lamplough, Robs 169
Large, John 217, 233
Las Vegas 174–5
Lauda, Niki 65–6, 67, 78, 79, 85, 87–8,
    89–90, 109, 129, 176
launch control 263–4
Lausanne Agreement 150, 156, 157, 192
L'Auto-Journal 104, 187
Le Guezec, Claude 105–6, 118, 124
Le Mans 38, 51, 163, 245–6, 247, 252,
    360, 479, 481
Lehman Brothers 309, 318
Letta, Gianni 256
Letwin, Oliver 464–5, 468
Leveson, Sir Brian 452, 453, 457–9
Leveson Inquiry 399, 403, 423, 450–4,
    456–60, 461
Leveson Report 461, 462–3, 464, 466,
    467
Levy, Lord 200
Liedekerke, Count de 113, 114, 122
Ligier, Guy 37, 178
Liikanen, Erkki 371
Lisbon Treaty 389
Lloyd, R.G. 26
Loitron, Maître 276–7

Lombardi, Lella 74
Long Beach 152, 158–9
long-distance races 52–3, 163, 234,
    245–6, 247
Longines 389
Lotus 35, 44–6, 49, 55, 67, 76–7, 79, 87,
    155
  Lotus 25 54
  Lotus 59 46–7
  Lotus 72 63
  Lotus Elite 21, 27
Lowe, Paddy 348

Maastricht Treaty 357
McCann, Gerry and Kate 451
Macdonald, Sir Ken 435
McDonnell, John 18, 19
McGuinness, Martin 242–3
Macintosh, Peter 165, 171
Mackenzie, Donald 317, 326, 329
MacKenzie, Kelvin 452
McLaren, Bruce 17, 30, 41, 42, 43, 59
McLaren team 79, 80, 90, 135–6, 150,
    275, 278, 281, 340, 341–50
Macmillan, Harold 183–4
McNally, Paddy 168–9, 172
McRae, Colin 238, 239
Madrid Grand Prix 480
Maffezzoli, Ottorino 124
Maher, Patrick 311
Major, John 431
Make Roads Safe campaign 374
Malaysian Grand Prix 1999 275–6
Malek, Ali 353
Mallock, Major Arthur 28, 29
Mallock U2 27, 28–30
Mallory Park 32, 69
Mandelson, Peter 203
March 43, 46–7, 48–61, 63–8, 69–70, 72,
    73–4, 75–6, 77–9, 81–2, 83–6, 90–3,
    163, 334
  March 701 55–6, 58
  March 751 75
Marchionne, Sergio 319, 342
Marlboro 106, 136, 150, 169
Marsaglia, Stefano 142
Martinez, Ricardo 367
Mass, Jochen 68

Massa, Felipe 346
Mateschitz, Dietrich 318, 411
Matra 35, 53, 61, 63, 100–1
Mayer, Sally 155
Mayer, Teddy 80, 85, 89, 155, 156, 179
Meadspeed Racing 28, 29
Media Standards Trust 446
medical cars 249
Mercedes 141, 244, 282, 409
Metropolitan Police 436, 438, 441, 445,
    450
Metternich, Klemens von 97
Metternich-Winneburg, Prince Paul
    Alfons von 97, 104, 119, 120
Mexican Grand Prix 1970 60–1
MI5 400
Michelin 154, 157, 278, 301, 302, 303,
    304
Michelin, Édouard 305
Miliband, Ed 465, 468
Mill, Ian 339, 341, 343
Mill, John Stuart 14
Millar, Gavin 469
Millfield 8–9
minimum weight limit 142, 177
Mitford, Bertram (MM's great-
    grandfather) 190–1
Mitford, Nancy (MM's aunt) 24
Mitford, Unity (MM's aunt) 1, 3–4
Mittal, Lakshmi 247
Mitterrand, François 103, 178
Mockridge, Tom 460
Modena Agreement 156–7, 159
Monaco Grand Prix 165, 247, 376
  1961 165
  1970 39, 58
  1971 64, 100–2
  1973 72
  1994 199, 250
monocoque construction 54
Montezemolo, Luca di 99, 307–8, 317,
    319, 324, 328, 330, 342, 411
Monti, Mario 380–1, 382, 385, 388
Montjuïc 74
Monza 34, 38–9, 50, 102–3, 129, 139,
    238, 255
Moore, Jim 39–40
Moseley, Alf 28, 182

Moses, Sir Alan 435, 471
Mosley, Alexander (MM's brother) 2, 4, 5, 6, 7, 8–9, 13, 14
Mosley, Alexander (MM's son) 279, 321, 424–5
Mosley, Diana, Lady (MM's mother) 1–2, 3, 7, 13, 24, 66, 470
Mosley, Jean (MM's wife) 7, 10, 12–13, 15–16, 18–19, 24, 26, 31, 36, 46, 185, 230, 255, 308, 391, 422
Mosley, Katherine Maud (MM's grandmother) 5
Mosley, Max
  childhood 2–7
  co-founds March 43, 163
  Concorde Agreement 159–61, 162, 167, 177, 188, 208–9, 210, 281, 312–17, 322, 326, 327, 328, 329, 330–1, 412
  confrontation with CSI–WCR 103–27
  court action against Google 443–4, 472
  court action against the *News of the World* 393, 394–7, 400–4, 414–23
  education 4, 7–9, 10–11, 12, 15–16, 18, 19
  Euro NCAP crash-test programme 254, 361–3, 368
  family name, problem of 18, 28, 182, 199
  FIA presidency 162, 198, 209, 279, 297–9, 300, 324–5, 329–30, 331–2, 355, 474–5
  first encounter with motor racing 17
  FISA presidency 160, 193–8, 208, 226
  FISA's Manufacturers' Commission 187, 188, 189, 190, 336–7
  helicopter pilot 185
  honorary president of European Parliament Automobile Users' Intergroup 357
  Labour Party member 206
  legal career 18, 22, 23, 25–7, 31, 40–1, 43, 50
  Légion d'honneur 363
  and the Leveson Inquiry and Report 450–4, 456–60, 461, 462–3, 464, 466, 467
  marries Jean Taylor 15–16
  Moseley v United Kingdom (against UK privacy laws) 428–9, 432–4
  moves to Monaco 236
  'Nazi' slur 391–2, 398–9, 401, 402, 403, 407, 408, 409, 415–16, 417, 418, 420, 421, 443, 457
  at Oxford University 10–11, 12, 15–16, 18, 19
  and the phone-hacking scandal 397–8, 436–42, 444–6, 450, 454
  political interests and activities 13–14, 19–21, 183, 184–6, 199–200, 202, 206
  race driving career 17–18, 27–40, 44–6, 64–5
  relationship with Bernie Ecclestone 95, 96, 211–12, 412
  safety interests and work 26, 34, 36, 59, 71, 223, 224–5, 241–2, 243–4, 251–7, 259–60, 265, 273, 355–74
  scientific interests 9, 10–11, 15, 16
  sets up World Federation of Motor Sport 152
  sex scandal 390–7, 398–424
  and son's death 424–5
  and 'spygate' 275, 339–49
  Territorial Army service 21–3
  World Council member 188, 190
  see also Formula One Constructors' Association (FOCA)
Mosley, Michael (MM's half-brother) 3
Mosley, Nicholas (MM's half-brother) 3, 8, 14–15
Mosley, Sir Oswald (MM's father) 1–3, 5, 6, 7, 8, 9, 10, 13–14, 20, 47, 182, 184
  death of 195
  internment 1–2, 14
  postwar political activity 13, 14, 19, 22, 23
  war service 2, 9, 65
Moss, Stirling 17, 165, 243, 351
Mulcaire, Glenn 397, 436, 437, 439–40, 441, 444
Muller, John 54
Murdoch, James 397, 398, 423, 442, 447, 448–9, 472

Murdoch, Rupert 393, 395, 399–400, 412, 426, 431, 433, 437, 442, 446, 447–8, 449, 454–60, 465, 471, 472
Murray, Gordon 89, 128
Myler, Colin 392, 396, 404, 417, 421, 447, 455

National Association for Stock Car Auto Racing (NASCAR) 228, 229
National Hot Rod Association (NHRA) 228–9
Neerspasch, Jochen 67–8, 73
negligence, law of 258–9
Nehru, Jawaharlal 16
Neill, Sir Patrick 204
New Zealand Federation 192
News Corporation 399, 447, 449
News International 325, 412, 418, 435, 437, 438–9, 440–1, 444
News of the World 194, 313, 318, 341, 390–424, 425–6, 431–2, 435, 436–7, 438, 439–41, 442, 443, 444, 445–7, 454, 455, 460
News UK 470
Nilsson, Gunnar 76
Nissan 311
Noon, David 311
North One Television 233
Northern League 256
Nürburgring 31, 45–6, 68, 78, 105, 109
Nürburgring 1000 km 163

Observatory Affair 178
octane rules 181
Oulton Park 480
oval racing 92, 228, 229–30
Oxford University 10–11, 12, 15–16, 18, 19

Pace, Carlos 80
Paddick, Brian 441, 442
Paddock Club 169, 172
Paisley, Ian 242, 243
Palacio, Loyola de 371
Paletti, Riccardo 249
Pannick, David 272, 304, 339, 432, 433
parc fermé 281
Parr, Adam 408

passes 102–3
pay TV 173
Penske, Roger 75
Peterson, Ronnie 46–7, 48, 49, 51, 56, 58, 60, 63, 64, 66, 67, 76, 77, 78, 80, 81, 82, 107–8, 129
Peugeot 188–9, 247
Philip Morris 119, 150, 154, 169
Phillips, Gill 469
phone-hacking scandal 397–8, 418, 425–6, 436–42, 444–6, 450, 454
   see also Leveson Inquiry
Piccinini, Marco 99–100, 142, 143, 145, 146–7, 150, 156, 159–60, 176, 178, 179, 193, 406–7
Piquet, Nelson 131, 175, 180, 228–9, 230, 351
Piquet, Nelson, Jr 306, 351, 352
Piromi, Didier 176
Pook, Chris 126, 158
Porsche 52
Portuguese Grand Prix 1958 351
Powell, Jonathan 200, 201, 387
Prescott, John 441, 442
Press Complaints Commission 424, 425, 429, 436, 451
press regulation 462–72
Price, James 415, 417, 419
privacy laws 184, 392, 394–5, 404, 426, 428–34, 435, 438, 462
   see also phone-hacking scandal
prize fund 103, 104–5, 107, 124–5, 131, 147, 164, 165, 169–70, 170, 172
promoters 163–4, 167, 168, 170, 172, 212
Prost, Alain 191, 226, 249
Prudom, Alan 263
Pryce, Tom 90
pump fuels 266–7, 292
Purley, David 70
Purnell, Tony 293, 311, 322
Puttnam, Lord 466

qualifying cars 280–2, 297, 347
Quest 351, 400, 401, 424, 425, 439

Race of Champions 480
radio communications between cars and pits 264–5

Räikkönen, Kimi 343
Ratzenberger, Roland 248, 250
Real Automóvil Club de España
    (RACE) 144, 145
Red Arrows 165, 171–2
Red Brigades 129
Red Bull 318, 411
Rede Globo 97–8
Redesdale, Sydney, Lady 3
Redgrave, Jon 33, 36, 38, 46, 54
Reding, Viviane 372
Rees, Alan 37, 43, 46, 49, 50, 54, 61, 65,
    66
Reeves, David 28, 44, 45, 54, 69
Regazzoni, Clay 77, 79
Regulatory Funding Company (RFC)
    471
regulatory harmonisation 366–7
Renault 135, 137, 138–9, 145, 156, 158,
    159, 178, 180, 191, 276, 283, 306,
    311, 349, 351–3, 362
Reul, Jürgen 291, 292
Reutemann, Carlos 87, 88, 89, 98, 158,
    175
Reynolds Metals 41–3
Ribeiro, Alex 82, 90
Richards, David 233
right of appeal 177, 268, 339
Rindt, Jochen 37, 38, 39, 43, 45, 46, 49,
    50, 59, 63, 255
Ritvay, Dr Alexander 221
Riverside 74
road cars
    accident statistics and social costs 370,
        372
    crash tests 254, 358–9, 360–3, 366,
        368–9
    electronic stability control 265, 373
    hybrid cars 294, 295
    International Road Assessment
        Programme (IRAP) 369–70
    Make Roads Safe campaign 374
    safety 355–63
    traffic management 370, 371, 372
    'Vision Zero' road safety concept 368,
        369
Rodriguez, Pedro 59, 60
Rogge, Jacques 258, 388, 389

Rosche, Paul 68, 69–70, 181
Rose, Jeffrey 198
Rothermere, Viscount 426, 463, 471
Rothmans 82, 84
Rover 362
Royal Automobile Club (RAC) 25, 96,
    110, 111, 199, 203, 238, 478
'The Rules of the Game' (conference)
    388
running under weight 338–9
Rupert, Johann 257–8
Rusbridger, Alan 435, 445
Ryan, Dave 350

S&M 390–1, 407, 415, 416–17
safety cars 237–8, 349
safety issues
    cornering speeds 139–40, 148–9, 151,
        230, 252–3, 259, 260
    Formula Two cars 32–3, 34
    historic car racing 243–4
    rallying 241–2
    regulatory harmonisation 366–7
    seatbelts 34
    spectators 241–2
    tyre grip 259–60
    'Vision Zero' road safety concept 368,
        369
    see also road cars
Sage, Jean 145
Saillant, Professor Gérard 299
Sainz, Carlos 239
Salman bin Hamad bin Isa Al Khalifa,
    HRH Prince 404–5
Salvadó, Sebastià 299–300
Samaranch, Juan Antonio 386, 387, 389
San Marino Grand Prix 480
    1982 179, 183
    1994 248–9, 264
Scheckter, Ian 82, 87, 90
Scheckter, Jody 82, 89, 136, 274
Schlesser, Jo 37, 38
Schumacher, Michael 203, 270–1, 273–4,
    277, 443
Schweitzer, Louis 362
Scrivener, Anthony 276, 407, 411
Sears, Jack 110
seatbelts 34

Sebring 12 hours 163, 246
Second World War 1–2, 3–4
self-regulatory function of sports governing bodies 387–9
Senna, Ayrton 191, 200, 226–7, 248–9, 250, 258, 261–2
September 11, 2001 terrorist attacks 277, 372
Servoz-Gavin, Johnny 56
Shadow 66, 90
Shamuyarira, Dr Nathan 182
Sherborne, David 394, 432, 450, 451
side pods 54–5, 77
Siffert, Jo 52, 56, 58, 63, 65, 165
Silverstone 17, 40, 45, 55–6, 60, 480
Simpson, O.J. 257
Singapore Grand Prix 2008 306, 351
six-wheelers 84–5, 86, 108
ski racing 155
Skidelsky, Robert 15, 19, 467
skirts, ban on 140, 141, 142, 148–9, 151
slick tyres 237
Smith, Chris 387
Smith, John 199, 357
Snetterton 27–8, 29, 33, 46
South African Grand Prix 181–2
    1970 56–7
    1971 100
    1977 90
    1980 140–1
    1981 157–8
    1982 176
Spanish Grand Prix 58–9
    1969 45
    1970 57, 58–9
    1975 74
    1980 143–6, 148
Specialised Mouldings 55
Spence, Mike 36
Sports Car Commission 246
sports car racing 52–3, 163, 246
Sports Prototypes 225
'spygate' 275, 339–49
Stallone, Sylvester 257
start money 163–4, 165
Stepney, Nigel 344, 345, 348–9
Stevens, Lord 351
Stewart, Jackie 47, 49, 53, 55, 56, 57, 70

Stommelen, Rolf 74
Stone, Bill 48, 54
Stoppard, Tom 436
STP 56, 57, 69
Street, Len 27
stress analysis 42
strikes 176
Stuck, Hans 73
Stuck, Hans-Joachim 73, 79
Sumption, Jonathan 272
Sun 431, 434, 465
super licences 479
Surtees, John 17, 45, 64, 81, 82
Swedish Grand Prix 1978 128, 129
Symonds, Pat 353

Tasman Series 41
Tauranac, Rob 32–3
Taylor, Gordon 397, 398, 414, 436
Taylor, Simon 30
technological devices, new, legality of 268–9, 307
Territorial Army Parachute Regiment 21–3
Thatcher, Margaret 194
Thieme, David 174
Thompson, John 54
Thruxton 36
Thurlbeck, Neville 396, 399, 400, 401, 403, 404, 417–18, 420, 439–40, 444, 454–5
Tingvall, Claes 368
tobacco sponsorship 82, 201–6
Todt, Jean 189, 195, 225, 247, 274, 295, 299, 300, 310, 318, 324–5, 330, 331, 332, 339, 354, 409, 435
Toivonen, Henri 188
Tomlinson, Hugh 446, 469
Torres, César 240
Toyota 295, 306, 318, 324, 335–6, 340
traffic management 370, 371, 372
Treaty of Rome 106, 109, 167, 168
Treu, Henri 105
Troodos Mountains 22
truck racing 234
Trulli, Jarno 277, 349–50
tyre controversies 278, 301–5
tyre grip 259–60

Tyrrell, Ken 31, 53, 60, 180, 212
Tyrrell team 56, 82, 84, 108, 179

Ugeux, Pierre 113, 117, 119, 120, 121,
    123, 126, 132
United Nations 366, 367, 374
United States Grand Prix
   1973 72
   2001 277
   2005 300–5

Van Miert, Karel 216, 375–6, 377–8,
    380–1, 382, 385
Van Rappard, Rolly 329
Vatanen, Ari 331–2
Verstappen, Jos 269
vertical wings 44–5, 86
Villeneuve, Jacques 203, 273
'Vision Zero' road safety concept 368, 369

Wagner, Winifred 7
Walker, Rob 165
Walters, Martin 83, 84
Warby, Mark 414, 415–17, 418–20
Ward, David 199, 200, 201, 202, 204,
    223, 276, 356, 357, 358, 362, 367,
    368, 370, 373, 374, 376, 387
Wardell, Ray 54
Warr, Peter 102
water tank appeal 177–9
water-cooled brakes 177, 179
Watkins, Professor Sid 249, 251, 254,
    255, 299
Watkins Glen 169–70
Watson, John 135–6
Watson, Tom 448, 449, 465
Weinberger, Billy 174–5
Wendlinger, Karl 250
Werring, Luc 361
Wheatcroft, Tom 70
Wheeler, Sir John 184
Whitehead, Phillip 15, 16
Whiting, Charlie 255, 268, 269, 303, 352

Whitmarsh, Martin 348, 350
Williams, Frank 32, 37, 41–2, 64, 195,
    236, 258, 282, 318
Williams, Jonathan 38
Williams team 41, 116, 146, 177, 178,
    257, 281, 296, 306, 322, 408, 411
Williamson, Roger 59, 70–1, 260
Wilson, Colin 239
Windsor, Duke and Duchess of 24
Wirth, Nick 197, 206
Wolf, Walter 116
Wolf team 89
Woods, Richard 390
Woodward-Hill, Sasha 221
World Championship Racing (WCR) 85,
    106, 107, 108–9, 110–11, 112, 113,
    114–15, 116, 117–18, 119, 120, 121,
    122, 123, 124, 126
World Endurance Championship 247
World Federation of Motor Sport 133,
    152–3
World Forum for Motor Vehicle
    Harmonisation 367
World Motor Sport Council (WMSC)
    141, 187, 188, 190, 197–8, 313–17
World Professional Drivers'
    Championship 152, 153–4
World Rally Championship (WRC) 188,
    192, 209, 225, 231–4, 239–42, 335,
    336–7, 406
Wright, Peter 55, 77, 293

Yasukawa, Hiroshi 260
Young, John 29
Young, Mike 29

Zandevoort 34, 70
Zanon, Count 74, 76, 77, 85, 107–8
Zelkowitz, David 119
Zerbi, Francesco 258–9
Zhuhai 230
Zimbabwe 181–2
Zolder 39, 77, 113, 114